AF606044

THE HISTORY OF AL-ṬABARĪ

AN ANNOTATED TRANSLATION

VOLUME XXX

The ʿAbbāsid Caliphate in Equilibrium

THE CALIPHATES OF MŪSĀ AL-HĀDĪ AND HĀRŪN AL-RASHĪD

A.D. 785–809/A.H. 169–193

The History of al-Ṭabarī

SUNY

SERIES IN NEAR EASTERN STUDIES

Said Amir Arjomand, Editor

The general editor acknowledges with gratitude the support received for the execution of this project from the Division of Research Programs, Translations Division of the National Endowment for the Humanities, an independent federal agency.

Bibliotheca Persica
Edited by Ehsan Yar-Shater

The History of al-Ṭabarī
(*Ta'rīkh al-rusul wa'l-mulūk*)

VOLUME XXX

The ʿAbbāsid Caliphate in Equilibrium

translated and annotated
by

C. E. Bosworth

The University of Manchester

State University of New York Press

The preparation of this volume was made possible in part by a grant from the Division of Research Programs of the National Endowment for the Humanities, an independent federal agency.

Published by
State University of New York Press, Albany

Printed in the United States of America

For information, address State University of New York Press, State University Plaza, Albany, N.Y. 12246

Library of Congress Cataloging-in-Publication Data

Ṭabarī, 838?-923.
The ʿAbbāsid Caliphate in equilibrium.
(The history of al-Tabarī = Ta'rikh al-rusul wa'l-mulūk; v.30)
(SUNY series in Near Eastern studies)
(Bibliotheca Persica)
Translation of extracts from: Ta'rikh al-rusul wa-al-mulūk.
Bibliography: p.
Includes index.
1. Islamic Empire—History—750-1258. I. Bosworth, Clifford Edmund. II. Title. III. Series: Ṭabarī, 838?-923. Ta'rīkh al-rusul wa-al-mulūk. English; v.30.
IV. Series: SUNY series in Near Eastern studies.
V. Series: Biblioteca Persica (Albany, N.Y.)
DS38.2.T313 1985 vol. 30 909'.1 s [909'.09767101]87-7124
[DS38.6]
ISBN 0-88706-564-3
ISBN 0-88706-566-X (pbk.)

10 9 8 7 6 5 4 3 2 1

Preface

THE HISTORY OF PROPHETS AND KINGS [*Ta'rīkh al-rusul wa'l-mulūk*] by Abū Ja'far Muḥammad b. Jarīr al-Ṭabarī (839–923), here rendered as the *History of al-Ṭabarī,* is by common consent the most important universal history produced in the world of Islam. It has been translated here in its entirety for the first time for the benefit of non-Arabists, with historical and philological notes for those interested in the particulars of the text.

Ṭabarī's monumental work explores the history of the ancient nations, with special emphasis on biblical peoples and prophets, the legendary and factual history of ancient Iran, and, in great detail, the rise of Islam, the life of the Prophet Muḥammad, and the history of the Islamic world down to the year 915. The first volume of this translation will contain a biography of al-Ṭabarī and a discussion of the method, scope, and value of his work. It will also provide information on some of the technical considerations that have guided the work of the translators.

The *History* has been divided here into 38 volumes, each of which covers about two hundred pages of the original Arabic text in the Leiden edition. An attempt has been made to draw the dividing lines between the individual volumes in such a way that each is to some degree independent and can be read as such. The page numbers of the original in the Leiden edition appear on the margins of the translated volumes.

Each volume has an index of proper names. A general index volume will follow the publication of the translation volumes.

Al-Ṭabarī very often quotes his sources verbatim and traces the chain of transmission (*isnād*) to an original source. The chains of transmitters are, for the sake of brevity, rendered by only a dash (—) between the individual links in the chain. Thus, according to Ibn Ḥumayd—Salamah—Ibn Isḥāq means that al-Ṭabarī received the report from Ibn Ḥumayd who said that he was told by Salamah, who said that he was told by Ibn Isḥāq, and so on. The numerous subtle and important differences in the original Arabic wording have been disregarded.

The table of contents at the beginning of each volume gives a brief survey of the topics dealt with in that particular volume. It also includes the headings and subheadings as they appear in al-Ṭabarī's text, as well as those occasionally introduced by the translators.

Well-known place names, such as, for instance, Mecca, Baghdad, Jerusalem, Damascus, and the Yemen, are given in their English spellings. Less common place names, which are the vast majority, are transliterated. Biblical figures appear in the accepted English spelling. Iranian names are usually transcribed according to their Arabic forms, and the presumed Iranian forms are often discussed in the footnotes.

Technical terms have been translated wherever possible, but some, such as dirham and imām, have been retained in Arabic forms. Others that cannot be translated with sufficient precision have been retained and italicized as well as footnoted.

The annotation aims chiefly at clarifying difficult passages, identifying individuals and place names, and discussing textual difficulties. Much leeway has been left to the translators to include in the footnotes whatever they consider necessary and helpful.

The bibliographies list all the sources mentioned in the annotation.

The index in each volume contains all the names of persons and places referred to in the text, as well as those mentioned in the notes as far as they refer to the medieval period. It does not include the names of modern scholars. A general index, it is hoped, will appear after all the volumes have been published.

For further details concerning the series and acknowledgments, see Preface to Volume I.

Ehsan Yar-Shater

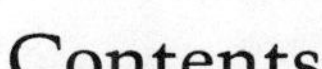

Contents

Abbreviations

AKAk. Berlin: Abhandlungen der Königlich Preussische Akademie zu Berlin
BGA: Bibliotheca geographorum arabicorum
EHR: *English Historical Review*
EI[1]: *Encyclopaedia of Islām*, first edition
EI[2]: *Encyclopaedia of Islam*, new edition
EIr: *Encyclopaedia Iranica*
GAL: C. Brockelmann, *Geschichte der arabischen Literatur*
GAS: F. Sezgin, *Geschichte des arabischen Schrifttums*
GMS: Gibb Memorial Series
IC: *Islamic Culture*
IJMES: *International Journal of Middle East Studies*
Isl.: *Der Islam*
JA: *Journal Asiatique*
JESHO: *Journal of the Economic and Social History of the Orient*
JNES: *Journal of Near Eastern Studies*
JRAS: *Journal of the Royal Asiatic Society*
JRASB: *Journal of the Royal Asiatic Society, Bengal*
JSAI: *Jerusalem Studies in Arabic and Islam*
R.Afr.: *Revue Africaine*
RCAL: *Rendiconti della Reale Accademia dei Lincei*
REI: *Revue des Etudes Islamiques*
RSO: *Rivista degli Studi Orientali*
SI: *Studia Islamica*
WbKAS: *Wörterbuch der klassischen arabischen Sprache*
WZKM: *Wiener Zeitschrift für die Kunde des Morgenlandes*
ZDMG: *Zeitschrift der Deutschen Morgenländischen Gesellschaft*

In citations from the Qur'ān, where two different numbers are given from a verse, the first is that of Flügel's text and the second that of the official Egyptian edition.

Translator's Foreword

The section of Ṭabarī's history devoted to the reigns of Mūsā al-Hādī and his brother Hārūn al-Rashīd spans twenty-four years, al-Hādī's caliphate lasting for only fifteen months of these, at the most. The historical events dealt with by the chronicler are located in a wide expanse of territory embracing most of the still largely united caliphate (although Muslim Spain had of course never acknowledged the ʿAbbāsids from the outset, and Ṭabarī takes no cognizance of happenings there), from Morocco in the west to Transoxania in the east.

The ʿAlids and their Shīʿī supporters, despite having been the beneficiaries of a comparatively conciliatory policy toward them by the previous Caliph al-Mahdī, remained basically unreconciled to ʿAbbāsid rule and the deflection of the caliphate-imamate, as they saw it, from the Prophet's direct descendants, the offspring of ʿAlī and Fāṭimah, to those of the mere paternal uncle of Muḥammad, al-ʿAbbās. Something of the polemical battles of the early ʿAbbāsid period, fought on the literary plane by the poets who lent their support to the ʿAbbāsids and ʿAlids, respectively, emerges in our section of Ṭabarī's history from the verse of the ʿAbbāsid court poet Marwān b. Abī Ḥafṣah cited at III, 743 (below, 308).

The struggles of these opposing parties were, however, by no means literary only. The episode which dominates Ṭabarī's account of al-Hādī's reign is that of the ʿAlid rising in Medina and then Mecca of the Ḥasanid al-Ḥusayn b. ʿAlī b. Ḥasan, which ended with the latter's death in battle at Fakhkh in 169 (786); one result of the scattering of the ʿAlids after this débâcle was the eventual foundation of the Idrīsid state in Morocco by the fugitive Idrīs b. ʿAbdallāh b. Ḥasan, involving the first subtraction of a province, albeit a very distant one, from the ʿAbbāsids' orbit. In al-Rashīd's reign, the rising of the Ḥasanid Yaḥyā b. ʿAbdallāh b. Ḥasan in Daylam and northwestern Persia in 176 (792), brought to an end through the military and diplomatic skills of the Barmakī al-Faḍl b. Yaḥyā, is treated only briefly by Ṭabarī; but the chronicler adds much anecdotal material on Yaḥyā's subsequent tribulations and death at the Caliph's hands.

Thereafter, al-Rashīd's uncompromising maintenance of Sunnī orthodoxy seems to have dampened further Shīʿī efforts. Yet Iraq and al-Jazīrah continued all through his reign to be troubled by the sectarian activities of the Khārijites among the Arabs there, apparently affecting the countryside rather than the towns but requiring punitive expeditions to be sent out from the capital. Syria, with its endemic tribal factionalism going back to Umayyad times, remained a potential focus for disaffection against the Iraq-centered ʿAbbāsids. Fears of the possible use of Syria as a power base by the ʿAbbāsid prince ʿAbd al-Malik b. Ṣāliḥ, himself with maternal connections with the Umayyads and governor in Syria for several years like his brother and father before him, may have lain behind al-Rashīd's arrest and imprisonment of his great-uncle in 187 (803); and the Caliph's virtual abandonment of Baghdad as the effective capital and his move in 180 (796) to al-Raqqah may have been motivated not only by a desire to be near the military front with Byzantium, as Kennedy has suggested,[1] but also by a need to keep an eye on Syria. Egypt was in these years not so much chafing under ʿAbbāsid domination specifically as it was disaffected through the fiscal policies of the ʿAbbāsid governors, which provoked unrest among both the Copts and the Bedouins of the Nile delta, whilst similar oppression by a caliphal governor in the Yemen resulted in a prolonged revolt of the Yemenis.

On the northern frontier of the caliphate, a state of rough equilibrium with the Byzantines seems to have been reached by al-Rashīd's time. The period of transition from rule by the Isaurian dynasty in the Empire to that of the Amorian dynasty was a

1. H. Kennedy, *The early Abbasid caliphate,* 120.

troubled one, with upheavals in the state caused by the Empress Irene's seizure of sole power in 797 and her deposition five years later by Nicephorus I; and this should have enabled al-Rashīd—highly conscious of his image as the great Ghāzī-Caliph—to intensify military pressure in the region of the *thughūr*; in fact, the annual Arab raids and the Greek counterattacks resulted in no extensive or permanent transfers of territory at this time. Potentially very serious, but stemmed by the energetic measures of the general Yazīd b. Mazyad (whose family was later to establish a power base in the region as the Yazīdī line of Sharwān-Shāhs), was the invasion of Armenia and Arrān through the Caucasus in 183 (799–800) by the Khazar Turks.

Affairs in the eastern parts of the caliphate were in the early years of al-Rashīd's caliphate the responsibility of al-Faḍl b. Yaḥyā al-Barmakī, who from 178 (794) onward continued the earlier Arab policy of expansion into the pagan steppes of Central Asia, himself raiding as far as the Syr Darya valley and despatching one of his commanders into what is now eastern Afghanistan; he also recruited fresh contingents of local Iranian troops from Khurāsān and Transoxania in order to stiffen and to supplement the ʿAbbāsids' original backing of Khurāsānian guards, the *Abnāʾ al-Dawlah.* But with the recall of al-Faḍl to Baghdad and then the fall of the Barmakīs, Khurāsān came under the governorship of ʿAlī b. ʿĪsā b. Māhān, whose financial exactions there rendered the province discontented and ready to support the revolt raised at Samarqand in 190 (806), with Turkish support from the steppes, by Rāfiʿ b. Layth b. Naṣr b. Sayyār. Only the belated decision of the Caliph to dismiss his very profitable servant (from the viewpoint of revenue-raising) ʿAlī b. ʿĪsā led Rāfiʿ to submit to al-Maʾmūn "because of his just conduct" in 193 (809), when al-Rashīd himself was actually dead.

Al-Rashīd's dealings with ʿAlī b. ʿĪsā and his despatch of his mawlā Harthamah b. Aʿyan as replacement governor in Khurāsān and as restorer of order there are narrated in considerable detail by Ṭabarī; but the most extensive treatment accorded by him to a single episode is of course with regard to the fall of the Barmakī family of secretaries and viziers in 187 (803). These dramatic events excited the shocked wonder and the pity of contemporaries, and continued thereafter to intrigue mediaeval Muslims, who came to weave around them imaginative, even semilegendary embroideries. Living as they did in a society where abrupt changes of fortune were far from uncommon, these Muslims came to view the Barmakīs' fate as the supreme *ʿibrah* or warning example of pride and riches brought low at one stroke. Yet such embroideries, designed to amplify and to explain for contemporaries what was not easily explicable, should not surprise; for it is not completely clear today precisely what tangled motives lay behind al-Rashīd's actions, beyond the obvious one of humbling subjects who had grown overmighty.[2]

The reign of al-Hādī is really too short for us to arrive at a completely balanced estimate of his character as ruler, and we do not have enough material for us to follow Von Kremer in stigmatizing al-Hādī as "the Arabic Nero."[3] But he does emerge as a capricious, unreliable person whom it was dangerous to oppose or thwart, with a distinct streak of violence and cruelty, as his indiscriminate striking of passersby when once at ʿĪsābādh and his killing of the two lesbian slave girls indicate.[4]

For al-Rashīd, we have a much ampler documentation in both the historical and the *adab* sources. The popular image of the despotic but bluff and genial monarch, patron of poetry and the arts, under whom Baghdad became a city of luxury and *douceur de vie* unparalleled in the previous history of the Islamic world, was fostered in the West from the eighteenth century onward under the seductive but delusory depiction of life there in the *Thousand and One Nights.* The materials for the art of biography as we know it in the West today are generally meager in the premodern Islamic sources, and the real mainsprings of al-Rashīd's character will probably remain as obscure to us as those of most leading figures in early Islam. Yet this image of "good old Hārūn al-Rashīd" has been potent enough to have spawned several popular books on the

---

2. See the discussions of the causes of the fall of the Barmakīs, so far as they are discernible, in D. Sourdel, *Le vizirat ʿabbāside,* I, 156–8, and Kennedy, 127–9; and for further secondary sources, below, 201, n. 697.

3. See F.-C. Muth, *Die Annalen von aṭ-Ṭabarī im Spiegel der europäischen Bearbeitungen,* 99, and also S. Moscati, *Le califat d'al-Hādī,* 24–8, for an estimate of the Caliph's personality.

4. Ṭabarī, III, 586, 590 (below, 67, 72–73).

Caliph and his age, such as E. H. Palmer's *Haroun Alraschid, Caliph of Baghdad* (London and Belfast, 1881), H. St. J. B. Philby's *Harun al Rashid* (London, 1933), and Sir John Glubb's *Haroun al Rasheed and the great Abbasids* (London, 1976). At least the first two of these writers were too familiar with the realities of mediaeval Islamic life and with some of the mediaeval Islamic sources to accept unquestioningly the picture of al-Rashīd's age as a golden one.[5] Palmer noted that "hitherto we have found him very unlike the Merry Monarch of the Arabian Nights," and his final verdict was that "as a man, he showed many indications of a loyal and affectionate disposition, but the preposterous position (i.e., as God's vicegerent on earth, with the servility thereby engendered) in which he was placed almost necessarily crushed all really human feelings in him. . . . That such a man should not be spoilt, that such absolute despotism should not lead to acts of arbitrary injustice, that such unlimited power and absence of all feelings of responsibility could be possessed without unlimited indulgence, was not in the nature of human events."[6] Philby asserted that "the reigns of Harun and his son Mamun stand out conspicuously against the dark background of the world's ignorance as beacons welcoming the rebirth of the arts and sciences after their long eclipse," but he readily conceded that "in surveying the circumstances of Harun's Califate we seem to be assisting at the spectacle of a heart beating fast and furiously in a paroxysm of fever which was reducing the body of an empire to the extremes of sickness and misery. The shadows of future decay were thrown forward on to the screen of history by the brilliant kaleidoscope of a puppet-show, which dazzled its beholders at the time and has blinded posterity—thanks to the unholy alliance of the historian and the

5. The only primary sources which Palmer mentions specifically in his book are Abū al-Faraj al-Iṣfahānī's *Kitāb al-Aghānī* and "El Amraniy" (99, 154) (this last author being presumably Muḥammad b. ʿAlī, Ibn al-ʿImrānī, whose history *al-Inbāʾ fī taʾrīkh al-khulafāʾ* has recently been edited and published by Qasim al-Samarrai, Leiden, 1973, an author whom Palmer could have cited from Ibn al-Ṭiqṭaqā's *Kitāb al-Fakhrī*); but, of course, the printed texts of Ibn al-Athīr and of the Persian abridgment of Ṭabarī by Balʿamī would have been available to him at that time. I have not seen Glubb's book, but the semipopular book of ʿAbd al-Jabbār al-Jūmard, *Hārūn al-Rashīd, dirāsah taʾrīkhiyyah ijtimāʿiyyah siyāsiyyah,* 2 parts (Beirut, 1956), adds nothing to what is already known.

6. *Haroun Alraschid,* 138, 222–3.

storyteller—to the emptiness of a limelit scene of splendour surrounded by the murky night of wailing and gnashing of teeth."[7]

Certainly, al-Rashīd does not stand out in either personal character or executive competence above others of the early ʿAbbāsid Caliphs. His extravagant gifts to poets, singers, popular preachers, ascetics, and so forth, were merely what was expected of a ruler, and one should always recall that somewhere in the caliphal lands someone—whether a fellah in the Nile valley, a merchant in Baghdad, or an artisan in Nishapur—was paying for all such manifestations of royal conspicuous consumption. Ṭabarī notes that al-Rashīd's intellectual horizons were narrow and that he had no taste for disputation and argumentation such as his son al-Maʾmūn was to encourage at his court.[8] In the early years of his caliphate he was content to leave much of the burden of administration to the Barmakīs, and then subsequently to mawlās like al-Faḍl b. al-Rabīʿ and Ismāʿīl b. Ṣubayḥ al-Ḥarrānī. The decision, embodied in the "Meccan documents" of 186–7 (802–3), to arrange in his own lifetime a division of the empire between his sons al-Amīn and al-Maʾmūn (with belated provision for a third son, al-Qāsim al-Muʾtaman) undeniably seems, with the hindsight of our knowledge of the Civil War which ensued after al-Rashīd's death, to have been an unwise one, as some contemporaries averred at the time.[9] But Kennedy may be right in seeing the Caliph's move as an attempt, unfortunately unsuccessful but worth trying, to resolve some of the tensions and ambitions rife within the ruling groups of the state by providing for these groups defined sectors of power in the caliphate.[10] Finally, one may note that al-Rashīd's mode of executing the captured brother of Rāfiʿ b. Layth, Bashīr,[11] shows a refinement of cruelty, even of sadism, which the fact of the Caliph's being racked with incessant pain from his incurable internal malady at that time cannot wholly excuse.

For his historical information and for his anecdotes on the Caliphs' lifestyles, Ṭabarī relied on reports going back to leading

---

7. *Harun al Rashid*, 60, 75–6.
8. III, 741 (below, 306).
9. Ṭabarī, III, 653–4 (below, 181–82).
10. Kennedy, 124–6.
11. Ṭabarī, III, 734–5 (below, 298).

historians such as Hishām Ibn al-Kalbī and Wāqidī, and on reports from noted *adībs* and philologists like Isḥāq al-Mawṣilī and al-Mufaḍḍal al-Ḍabbī, as well as on information from *rāwīs* who are quite obscure to us. The interval of only a century or less between the events in question and Ṭabarī's writing his history meant that he was able to draw on a great fund of family tradition preserved by the direct descendants of the protagonists in these events, such as al-Hādī's own great-grandson Hārūn b. Muḥammad b. Ismāʿīl.[12] Ṭabarī also gives in this section the texts *in extenso* of numerous official documents, including among others the encomia on the accession of al-Rashīd by the secretary Yūsuf b. al-Qāsim (III, 600–1; below, 93–94) and by Jaʿfar b. Yaḥyā al-Barmakī in gratitude for his appointment as governor of Syria in 180 (796–7) (III, 642–4; below, 159–62); al-Rashīd's letter of dismissal in 191 (806–7) to ʿAlī b. ʿĪsā and the letter of appointment of ʿAlī's successor in Khurāsān, Harthamah b. Aʿyan (III, 716–18; below, 273–75); but above all, that of the "Meccan documents," the stipulations by which the two princes al-Amīn and al-Ma'mūn bound themselves to their father's arrangements, and the letter to the provincial governors announcing these measures (III, 654–66; below, 183–99). These documents are not yet couched in so florid a style, made up of balanced, assonantal [*musajjaʿ*] phrases as was to become standard in Islamic chanceries after circa 900; but their at times tortuous syntax poses problems for the translator, especially where the reconstructed Arabic text is by no means certain; an Arabist of the caliber of F. Gabrieli has confessed, on the occasion of his essaying the task of translating the "Meccan documents" and other similar documents of the period, that the precious style of such texts makes absolute certainty in translation impossible.[13]

For a considerable part of Ṭabarī's account of al-Ma'mūn's caliphate, we have extant Ṭabarī's verbatim source, Aḥmad b. Abī Ṭāhir Ṭayfūr's *Kitāb Baghdād*; but for the reigns of al-Hādī and al-Rashīd, we possess no such controlling parallel text. The editor of this section of the text of Ṭabarī's history, Stanislas Guyard, could only have recourse to later, epitomizing historians—like the anonymous author of the *Kitāb al-ʿUyūn wa-al-ḥadāʾiq*, Ibn al-Jawzī

12. Ṭabarī, III, 581 (see below, 60), 1148.
13. See below, 191, n. 686.

in his *Muntaẓam* and Ibn al-Athīr in his *Kāmil*—for supplementing the two manuscripts of Ṭabarī on which he had to rely for this section; namely, the Istanbul one, Köprülü 1041 (ms. C) copied in 651 (1253), which covers the whole of this particular section; and the Algiers one, 594 (ms. A) copied in the Maghrib, which contains, however, four lacunae in our section, two of substantial length, and which ends abruptly at III, 755 of the printed text, after which point the text depends on the unicum C. A Berlin fragment, Petermann II, 635 (ms. Pet) served as a third manuscript for a mere four and a half pages of the printed text.[14] Thus, Guyard's task was far from easy, and he had perforce to leave certain cryptic passages unresolved; unless fresh manuscripts or hitherto unknown parallel sources turn up, it does not seem possible for the state of the text to be improved.

The pleasant task of thanking those who have given advice and help over the translation is the sole remaining one. I am particularly grateful to the late Dr. Martin Hinds (Cambridge), Dr. Patricia Crone (Oxford), and Professor Yūsuf ʿIzz al-Dīn (al-ʿAyn, U.A.E.) for help with the text; and to Professors Ch. Pellat (Sorbonne) and R. Sellheim (Frankfort) for their efforts at identifying some of the more obscure poets cited in this section. But since all human endeavors are susceptible to the onslaughts of the *ʿayn al-kamāl*, for the imperfections of this translation I alone am responsible.

C. E. Bosworth

---

14. See *Introductio*, p. LXV.

Genealogical Tables and Maps

Genealogical Table of the ʿAbbāsids
(Special reference to those members of the family mentioned in this section of al-Ṭabarī's *History*)

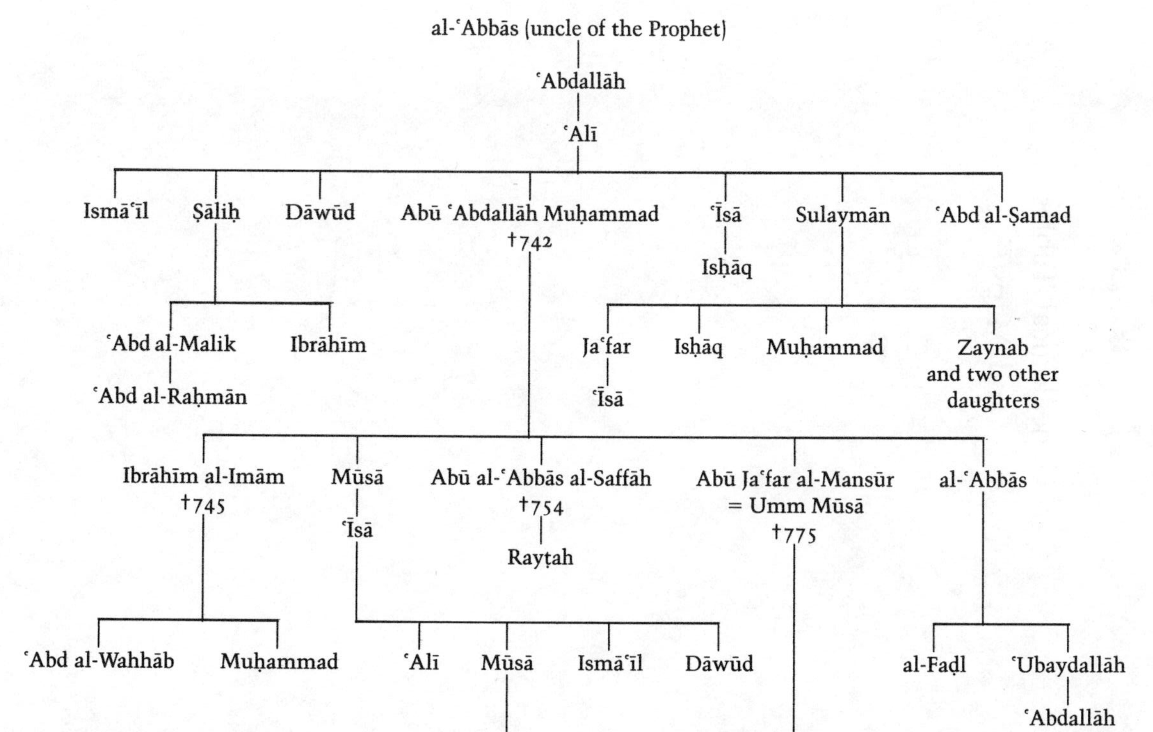

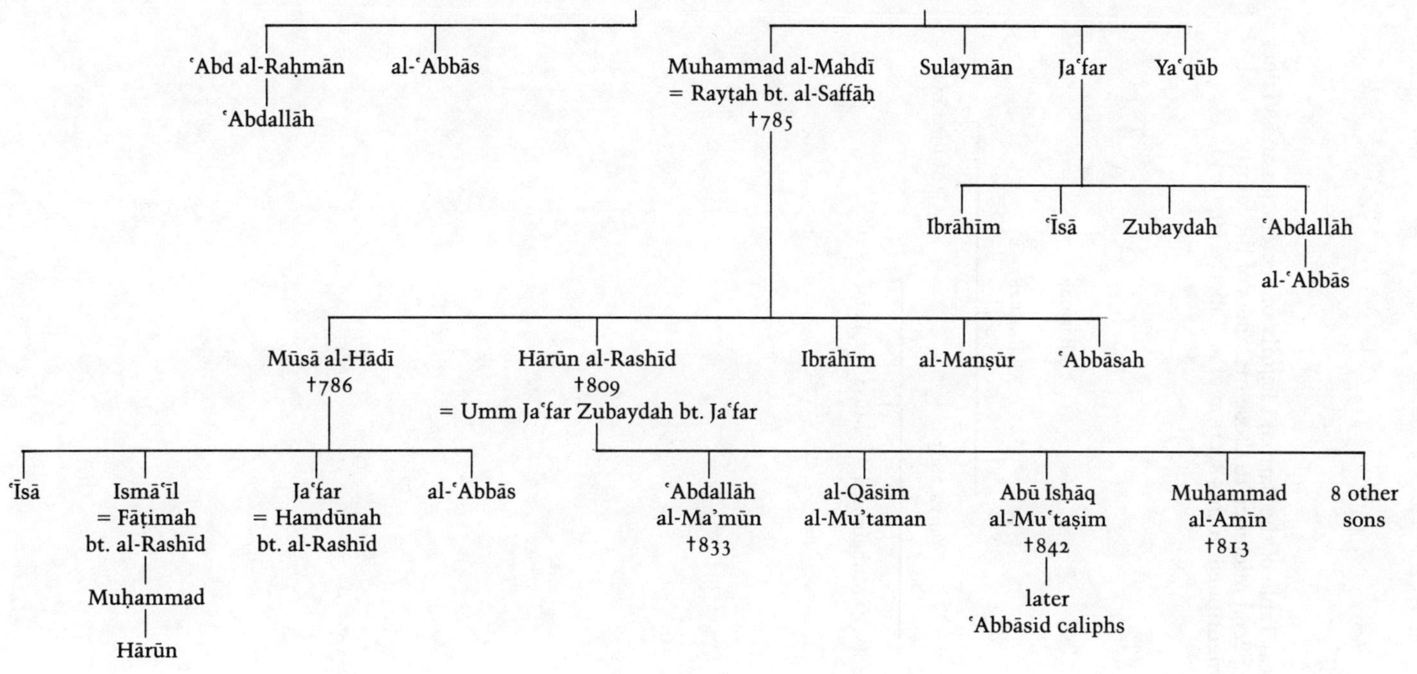

ʿAbd al-Raḥmān
al-ʿAbbās
ʿAbdallāh
Muhammad al-Mahdī
= Rayṭah bt. al-Saffāḥ
†785
Sulaymān
Jaʿfar
Yaʿqūb
Ibrāhīm
ʿĪsā
Zubaydah
ʿAbdallāh
al-ʿAbbās
Mūsā al-Hādī
†786
Hārūn al-Rashīd
†809
= Umm Jaʿfar Zubaydah bt. Jaʿfar
Ibrāhīm
al-Manṣūr
ʿAbbāsah
ʿĪsā
Ismāʿīl
= Fāṭimah
bt. al-Rashīd
Muḥammad
Hārūn
Jaʿfar
= Hamdūnah
bt. al-Rashīd
al-ʿAbbās
ʿAbdallāh
al-Maʾmūn
†833
al-Qāsim
al-Muʾtaman
Abū Isḥāq
al-Muʿtaṣim
†842
later
ʿAbbāsid caliphs
Muḥammad
al-Amīn
†813
8 other
sons

Genealogical Table of the Barmakī Family of Secretaries and Viziers
(Special reference to those members of the family
mentioned in this section of al-Ṭabarī's *History*)

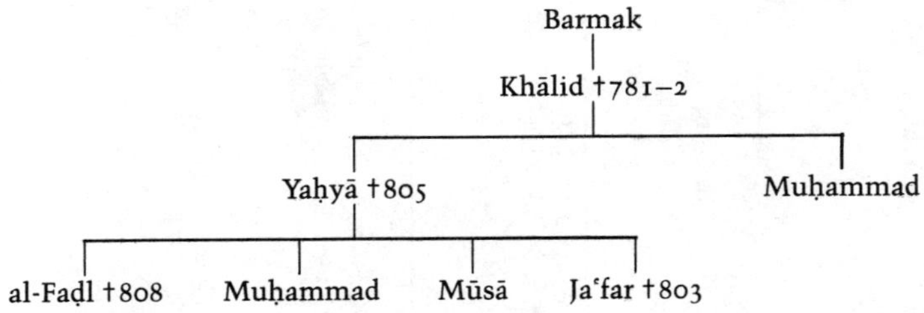

Map 1

Egypt, Syria, Iraq, and the Eastern Provinces during the Reigns of al-Hadī and al-Rashid.

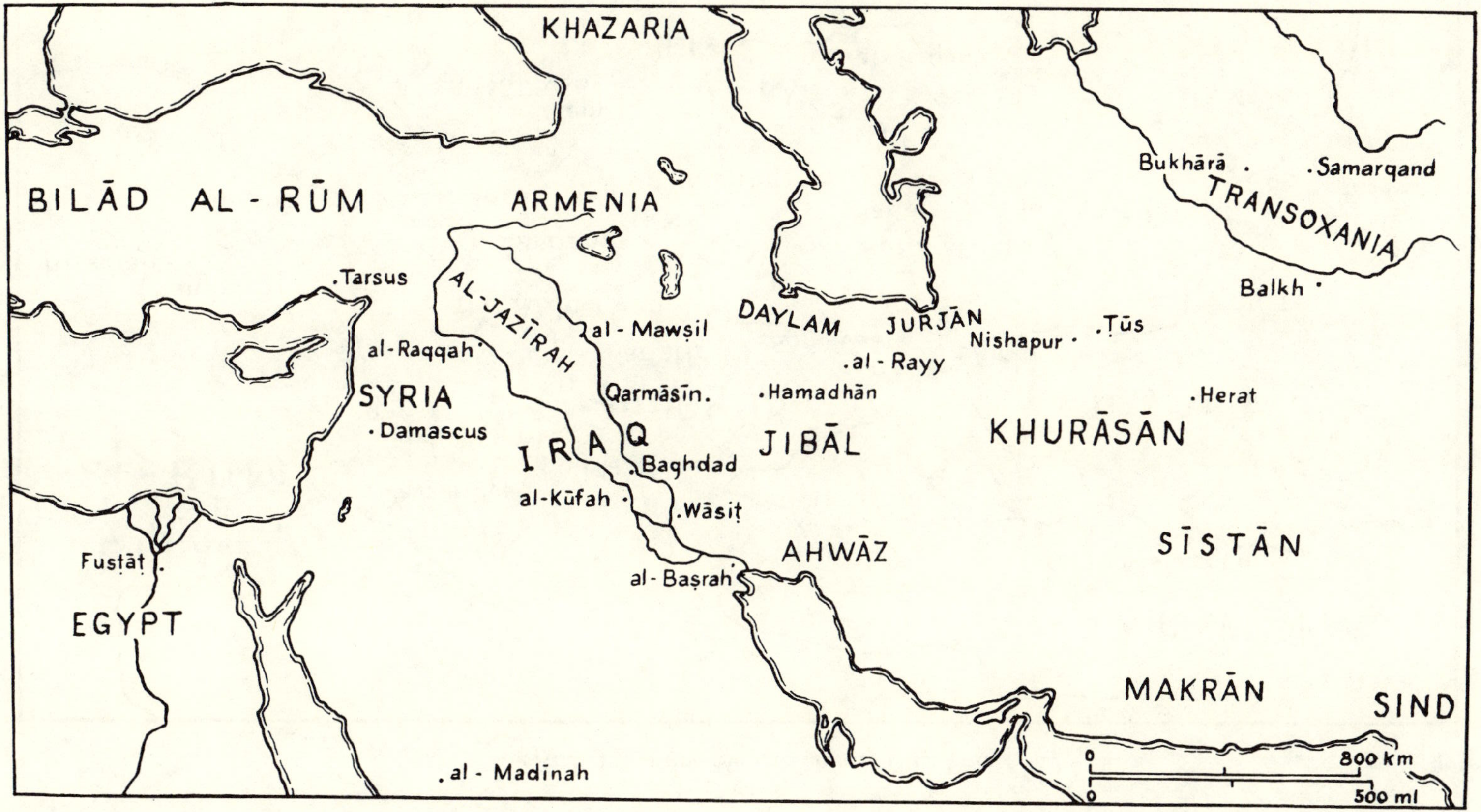

Map 2
The Arab–Byzantine Marches during This Period.

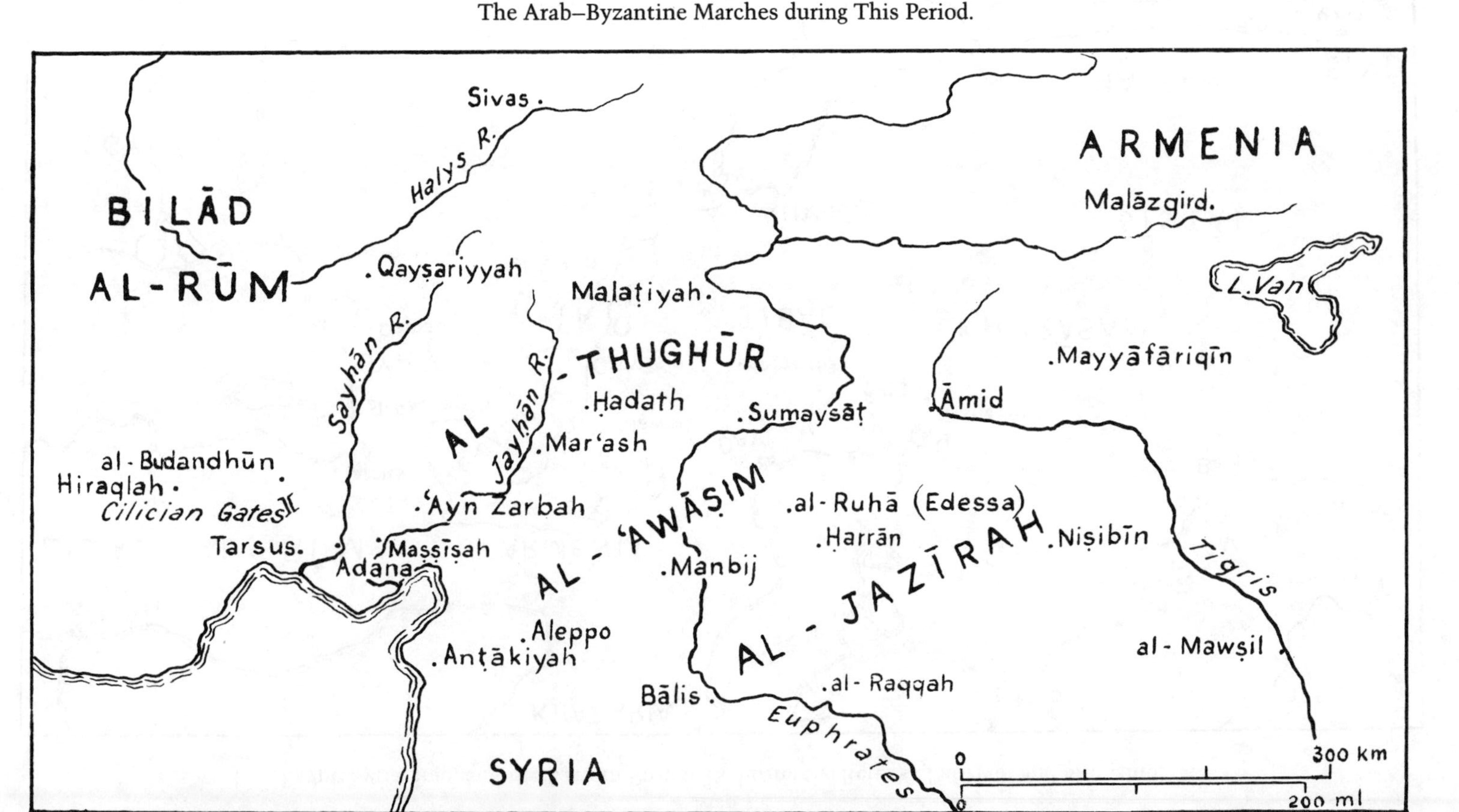

The Caliphate of Mūsā al-Hādī

The Events of the Year 169 (cont'd)

(July 14, 785–July 2, 786)

The Succession of Mūsā al-Hādī as Caliph on His Father al-Mahdī's Death and His New Administrative Appointments [544]

In this year (169 [July 14, 785–July 2, 786]), allegiance was given to Mūsā b. Muḥammad b. ʿAbdallāh b. Muḥammad b. ʿAlī b. ʿAbdallāh b. al-ʿAbbās as Caliph on the day of al-Mahdī's death[1] and
when he was actually established in Jurjān making war on the [545]
people of Ṭabaristān. Al-Mahdī died at Māsabadhān,[2] having present with him his son Hārūn and having left his mawlā al-Rabīʿ[3] behind in Baghdad as his deputy there.

---

1. I.e., on Thursday, the twenty-second of Muḥarram (August 4, 785). See S. Moscati, "Nuovi studi storici sul califatto di al-Mahdī," *Orientalia,* N.S. XV (1946), 171–2; *EI*² s.v. al-Mahdī (H. Kennedy). On al-Mahdī's arrangements for al-Hādī as his successor, see Moscati, op. cit., 158–61.

2. A district in the Zagros mountains on the borders of Luristān and Iraq. See Yāqūt, *Muʿjam al-buldān,* V, 41; G. Le Strange, *The lands of the Eastern Caliphate,* 202; P. Schwarz, *Iran im Mittelalter,* 464–70; *EI*² s.v. Luristān (V. Minorsky).

3. Al-Rabīʿ b. Yūnus b. Muḥammad, mawlā of al-Manṣūr and *ḥājib* or chamberlain under that Caliph and his two successors al-Mahdī and al-Hādī. See on him al-Khaṭīb al-Baghdādī, *Taʾrīkh Baghdād,* VIII, 414, no. 4521; Ibn Khallikān, *Wafayāt al-aʿyān,* II, 294–9, tr. M. G. de Slane, I, 521–6; Moscati, *Le califat d'al-Hādī,* 17–18; D. Sourdel, *Le vizirat ʿabbāside,* I, 85–90, 118–21; P. Crone, *Slaves on horses. The evolution of the Islamic polity,* 193–4; *EI*¹ s.v. (A. S. Atiya).

It has been mentioned that, when al-Mahdī died, the mawlās[4] and army commanders rallied round his son Hārūn and told him, "If the army (at large) gets to know about al-Mahdī's death, we cannot guarantee[5] that a tumult will not occur. The wisest thing to do would be for his corpse to be borne away and for the return homewards to be proclaimed among the army, so that you may eventually bury him secretly in Baghdad." Hārūn replied, "Summon my father[6] Yaḥyā b. Khālid al-Barmakī to me." (Al-Mahdī had made Hārūn [nominal] governor of all the Western lands between al-Anbār and Ifrīqiyah and had ordered Yaḥyā b. Khālid to assume actual control over them. Hence all these administrative regions [*aʿmāl*] were under him, and he was in charge of all their government offices and was acting as Hārūn's deputy over the administrative duties in his charge until al-Mahdī's death.)[7]

He related: Yaḥyā b. Khālid went to Hārūn, and the latter said to Yaḥyā, "O my father, what is your opinion about what ʿUmar b. Bazīʿ,[8] Nuṣayr[9] and al-Mufaḍḍal[10] say?" He replied, "What in fact

---

4. The rise of the *mawālī*, a social group which included men of many races, is a feature of the early ʿAbbāsid period, above all, of al-Manṣūr's reign, when we find a numerous and cohesive body of *mawālī* grouped around the Caliph's person, at the side of other groups such as the slaves [*ghilmān, mamālīk, wuṣafāʾ*], the eunuchs [*khadam*, etc.] and the *Abnāʾ al-Dawla*, i.e., the Arabs and Iranians of Khurāsān now largely settled in the capital Baghdad. Al-Manṣūr boasted to his son al-Mahdī at the end of his reign that he had gathered together round his person such a body of *mawālī* as had never been known before (Ṭabarī, III, 448). On this social and military role of the mawlās, see D. Ayalon, *The military reforms of Caliph al-Muʿtaṣim: their background and consequences*, 1–3, 39–42; P. Forand, "The relation of the slave and the client to the master or patron in medieval Islam," *IJMES*, II (1971), 59–66; Ayalon, "Preliminary remarks on the *Mamlūk* military institution in Islam," *War, technology and society in the Middle East*, 48–50; Farouk Omar, "The composition of ʿAbbāsid support in the early ʿAbbāsid period 132/749–169/785," in *ʿAbbāsiyyāt. Studies in the history of the early ʿAbbasids*, 46–50; Crone, 66–8, 78; D. Pipes, *Slave soldiers and Islam. The genesis of a military system*, 107–9, 131 ff.

5. Following the preferred reading of n. *b*, *lā naʾmanu*.

6. The sources note that Hārūn was wont to call Yaḥyā his "father"; see, e.g., Jahshiyārī, *K. al-Wuzarāʾ wa-al-kuttāb*, 134; Abū al-Faḍl Bayhaqī, *Taʾrīkh-i Masʿūdī*, 414; anon., *K. al-ʿUyūn wa-al-ḥadāʾiq*, 282, 285; Ibn al-Athīr, *al-Kāmil*, VI, 88. As Yaʿqūbī, *Taʾrīkh*, II, 490, and Ibn Khallikān, VI, 221, tr. IV, 104–5, explain, al-Mahdī had entrusted his son Hārūn to the suckling of Yaḥyā's womenfolk, so that the young prince and al-Faḍl b. Yaḥyā were foster-brothers.

7. *K. al-ʿUyūn*, 282; Ibn al-Athīr, VI, 96.

8. Secretary and boon-companion of al-Mahdī, in charge of the office of account-

have they said?" So Hārūn told him. Yaḥyā said, "I don't agree with that view." Hārūn replied, "Why?" Yaḥyā said, "Because this is an affair which cannot be concealed, and I do not feel confident that the army, when they get to know, will accompany his funeral bier and that they will not say, 'We won't let it go forward freely until we are given pay allotments for three years or more,' or that they will not make arbitrary claims [*yataḥakkamū*] and act wrongfully. My judgement is that his corpse—may God have mercy on him!—should be buried secretly here and that you should send Nuṣayr to the Commander of the Faithful al-Hādī[11] with the seal ring and the sceptre,[12] with congratulatory greetings (on his accession) and condolences (on his father's death). For Nuṣayr is in charge of the postal service [*barīd*]; hence no one will regard his departure with any suspicion, since he is head of the *barīd* for this district. I also consider that you should order the members of the army at present with you to be paid two hundred (dirhams) each and that you should proclaim among them the imminent return, because once they have got their hands on the money, their only thought will be of their families and their homeland, and nothing will deflect them from getting back to Baghdad."

He related: So Hārūn did this, and when the troops received their money, they all shouted, "To Baghdad, to Baghdad!" They [546]
pressed forward in their haste to depart for Baghdad, urging the relinquishment of Māsabadhān. But when they reached Baghdad, and heard the news about the Caliph (i.e., of al-Mahdī's death and the succession of a new ruler), they went along to al-Rabīʿ's gate and set it on fire, demanding more pay allotments and raising a

---

ing control [*dīwān al-azimmah*] for that Caliph and subsequently head of the chancery for al-Hādī. See Ṭabarī, III, 598; Sourdel, *Vizirat*, I, 112–3, 121–3.

9. Eunuch slave [*khādim, waṣīf*] of al-Mahdī's. See Ṭabarī, III, 461, 536, 547.

10. Mawlā of al-Mahdī (Ṭabarī, III, 514, 558) and a eunuch (ibid., 562).

11. Bernard Lewis has noted that the honorific *al-Hādī* seems to mark the transition from titles with distinctly messianic connotations (*al-Manṣūr, al-Mahdī*) to purely regnal ones. See "The regnal titles of the first Abbasid caliphs," *Dr. Zakir Husain presentation volume*, 22 n. 30.

12. On the insignia of royalty, which included the Prophet's cloak [*burdah*], the sword [*sayf*], and the parasol [*miẓallah*], as well as the seal ring [*khātam*] and sceptre [*qaḍīb*], see Sourdel, "Questions de cérémoniale ʿabbaside," *REI*, XXVIII (1960), 135; M. M. Ahsan, *Social life under the Abbasids 170–289 AH, 786–902 AD*, 52; *EI*[2] s.v. Marāsīm. 1. Under the Caliphate and the Fāṭimids (P. Sanders).

great clamor. Hārūn reached Baghdad. Al-Khayzurān then sent to al-Rabīʿ and Yaḥyā b. Khālid seeking their advice over this matter. Al-Rabīʿ did in fact go to her, but Yaḥyā would not go, knowing the intensity of Mūsā's resentment. He related: Money was gathered together until the army was paid two years' pay allotments, so that they then quietened down.[13] The news reached al-Hādī, and he then wrote a letter to al-Rabīʿ in which he threatened him with execution, but another one to Yaḥyā b. Khālid rewarding him with acts of beneficence and ordaining that he should retain his position as tutor and adviser of Hārūn just as he had always been and should retain charge of his affairs and administrative responsibilities exactly as previously.[14]

He related: Al-Rabīʿ, who used to have a great affection for Yaḥyā, used to trust him and used to rely on his judgement, then sent word to Yaḥyā b. Khālid, "O Abū ʿAlī, What do you think I should do, for I can't endure dragging iron fetters around (i.e., the prospect of prison)?" He replied, "I think that you should not move from where you are, but that you should send your son al-Faḍl[15] forward formally to meet his approaching party, bearing with him the most impressive amount of presents and precious objects that you can get together. I am very hopeful that he will not then come back without your being reassured against what you fear, if God so wills." He related: The mother of al-Faḍl, al-Rabīʿ's son, happened to be in a position to overhear their intimate conversation (i.e., of al-Rabīʿ and Yaḥyā), and she said to al-Rabīʿ, "By God, he has given you sound advice!" He said, "I would like to make my last testament to you (i.e., to Yaḥyā), for I don't know what might happen."

---

13. It is not explicit whether this payment (or eighteen months' pay, according to the next account, that from al-Faḍl b. Sulaymān) was in settlement of pay arrears or whether it was an extraordinary payment intended to secure a smooth succession for al-Hādī. If the latter, it became a dangerous precedent, for similar payments became common in the later third (ninth) and fourth (tenth) centuries. See *EI*[2] s.v. Māl al-bayʿa (Kennedy).

14. Dīnawarī, *al-Akhbār al-ṭiwāl*, 386; Masʿūdī, *Murūj al-dhahab*, VI, 261–2 = ed. Pellat, § 2469; Ṭabarī, Persian tr. Balʿamī, tr. H. Zotenberg, IV, 446–7; *K. al-ʿUyūn*, 282–3; Ibn al-Athīr, VI, 87–8; L. Bouvat, *Les Barmécides d'après les historiens arabes et persans*, 44–5; Nabia Abbott, *Two queens of Baghdad*, 72–9; Moscati, *Le califat d'al-Hādī*, 5–6.

15. Subsequently chief minister, if not actually with the title of vizier, to Hārūn and then al-Amīn, of whom he was a leading supporter. See Sourdel, *Vizirat*, I, 183–94; A. J. Chejne, "Al-Faḍl b. al-Rabīʿ—a politician of the early ʿAbbāsid period," *IC*, XXXVI (1962), 167–81; Crone, 194; *EI*[2] s.v. (Sourdel).

He[16] said, "I don't want to stand aside from you in anything, and I don't want to neglect anything which seems necessary, as long as you desire me to play some role in this or in any other matter; but associate with me in this design your son al-Faḍl and this woman, for she is indeed of sound judgment and worthy of being brought [547] into this affair by you." Al-Rabīʿ accordingly did that and made his testament to (all three of) them.[17]

Al-Faḍl b. Sulaymān[18] has related: When the army rose up against al-Rabīʿ in Baghdad, released the prisoners in his custody, and set on fire the gates of the houses belonging to him in the main square, al-ʿAbbās b. Muḥammad,[19] ʿAbd al-Malik b. Ṣāliḥ[20] and Muḥriz b. Ibrāhīm[21] witnessed all these events. Al-ʿAbbās realized that the troops would (only) be satisfied, their minds set at rest, and the dispersal of their tumultuous gathering brought about, if they were given their pay allotments. So he offered these to them, but they were still not satisfied and did not feel assured about the pay allotments which had been guaranteed to them, until Muḥriz b. Ibrāhīm (personally) guaranteed them, and they were then content with his bond and dispersed. Muḥriz then fulfilled his promise to them over that, and they were given pay allotments for eighteen months, this being before Hārūn's arrival.[22]

---

16. I.e., Yaḥyā, following the reading *fa-qāla* envisaged in n. *h* and adopted in the Cairo text, VIII, 188, for the text's *fa-qultu.*

17. Ibn al-Athīr, VI, 89.

18. Presumably the al-Faḍl b. Sulaymān b. Isḥāq al-Hāshimī also cited as a *rāwī* in Ṭabarī, III, 598 (below, 86).

19. I.e., the senior ʿAbbāsid prince al-ʿAbbās b. Muḥammad b. ʿAlī (d. 186 [802]), younger brother of al-Saffāḥ and al-Manṣūr, and owner of an extensive property to the west of the Round City in the island between the Greater and Lesser Ṣarāt Canals, named after him al-ʿAbbāsiyyah. See Ibn Qutaybah, *Maʿārif,* 377, 381; Le Strange, *Baghdad under the Abbasid Caliphate,* 142, 148; J. Lassner, *The topography of Baghdad in the early Middle Ages,* 75, 80, 188; idem, *The shaping of ʿAbbāsid rule,* 240–1.

20. Also a grandson of ʿAlī b. ʿAbdallāh b. al-ʿAbbās, brother of Ibrāhīm b. Ṣāliḥ and first cousin of al-Saffāḥ and al-Manṣūr, and holder of many governorships until his death in 196 (811–12). See Ibn Qutaybah, 375, 384.

21. Abū al-Qāsim Muḥriz b. Ibrāhīm al-Jūbānī, participant in the ʿAbbāsid Revolution as a lieutenant of Qaḥṭabah b. Shabīb, a *rāwī* for Ṭabarī of events concerning Abū Muslim and an official with the functions of a quartermaster under al-Mahdī. See Ṭabarī, III, 1, 9, 46, 99, 461.

22. Moscati, *Le califat d'al-Hādī,* 6 n. 2, regards this variant account from al-Faḍl b. Sulaymān as less plausible than the first one emphasizing the roles of Yaḥyā and al-Rabīʿ in quelling the mutinous troops' outbreak in Baghdad.

When Hārūn in fact arrived, acting as the deputy for Mūsā al-Hādī and accompanied by al-Rabīʿ as a helper [*wazīr*] of his, he despatched delegations to the provincial main cities [*amṣār*], he announced to them the death of al-Mahdī, he required their oath of allegiance to Mūsā al-Hādī (in the first place) and then to himself as the next designated heir [*walī al-ʿahd*] after him, and he got a firm grip of affairs in Baghdad (i.e., he took in hand its pacification).

(Previously to this), Nuṣayr the slave [*al-waṣīf*][23] had immediately set off from Māsabadhān to Jurjān with the news of the death of al-Mahdī and the giving of allegiance to al-Hādī. When Nuṣayr had reached al-Hādī, the latter had given the signal for departure and had forthwith set off by means of the *barīd* service,[24] as if he were a noble, swift horse, accompanied by Ibrāhīm (i.e., his brother) and Jaʿfar (i.e., his son) from his own family and by ʿUbaydallāh b. Ziyād al-Kātib, the head of his chancery, and Muḥammad b. Jamīl,[25] his secretary for military affairs, from among his administrative staff [*al-wuzarā*ʾ].[26] Now, when he drew within sight of the City of Peace, a group of people from his own family and others came out to meet him. Al-Hādī had meanwhile been showing resentment towards al-Rabīʿ for what he had been doing, including his sending out delegations and his giving pay allotments to the army before al-Hādī's arrival. For his part, al-Rabīʿ had despatched his son al-Faḍl. He went to meet al-Hādī with all the presents prepared for him and came face-to-face with him at Hamadhān. Al-Hādī summoned him into his presence and
[548] brought him close, and said to him, "How was my master (i.e., al-Rabīʿ) when you left him?" Al-Faḍl then wrote back these words to his father. Al-Rabīʿ thereupon went forth to meet al-Hādī. The

---

23. This seems to be the correct rendering here of this—i.e., as a common noun; but it can also be a personal name of slaves, as with the Turkish military slave, the *ḥājib* Waṣīf, prominent in the events of the reigns of al-Mutawakkil and his successors.

24. In Jahshiyārī, 125, and Thaʿālibī, *Laṭāʾif al-maʿārif,* 131, tr. C. E. Bosworth, 104–5, it is recorded as noteworthy that al-Hādī was the first and only Caliph personally to use the *barīd* system.

25. Caliphal mawlā, subsequently governor of al-Baṣrah and Egypt for al-Rashīd. See Crone, 191.

26. See Sourdel, *Vizirat,* I, 117; and for ʿUbaydallāh b. Ziyād b. Abī Laylā, who died shortly after this (Jahshiyārī, 127), ibid., I, 119–20.

latter reproached him gently, but al-Rabīʿ made his excuses and informed him of the reasons which had impelled him to behave thus. Al-Hādī accepted this apology, and appointed him vizier in place of ʿUbaydallāh b. Ziyād b. Abī Laylā, and added to his responsibilities the office of control of expenditure [*al-zimām*], which ʿUmar b. Bazīʿ had until then exercised.[27] He appointed Muḥammad b. Jamīl over the financial department [*dīwān al-kharāj*] concerned with the two Iraqs (i.e., Mesopotamia and western Persia, ʿIrāq ʿAjamī). He appointed ʿUbaydallāh b. Ziyād over the financial administration of Syria and adjoining lands. He confirmed ʿAlī b. ʿĪsā b. Māhān[28] as commander of his personal guard [*ḥaras*], adding to his responsibilities the department of the army [*dīwān al-jund*]. He appointed ʿAbdallāh b. Mālik (al-Khuzāʿī)[29] as commander of the security police [*shuraṭ*] (in Baghdad) in place of ʿAbdallāh b. Khāzim.[30] Finally, he entrusted the seal ring to the hands of ʿAlī b. Yaqṭīn.[31]

Mūsā al-Hādī's arrival at Baghdad, at the time of his journey from Jurjān, was on the nineteenth of Ṣafar (August 31, 785) in this year.[32] It has been mentioned in this connection that he travelled from Jurjān to Baghdad in twenty days.[33] When he actually arrived in Baghdad, he established himself in the palace known as al-

27. On these administrative arrangements, see Jahshiyārī, 125; al-Khalīfah b. Khayyāṭ, *Ta'rīkh*, II, 709; *K. al-ʿUyūn*, 283; Ibn al-Athīr, VI, 89; Sourdel, *Vizirat*, I, 119.

28. Son of a deputy *naqīb* and *dāʿī* in Marw during the ʿAbbāsid Revolution, who founded a leading Abnā' family in Baghdad; during al-Amīn's caliphate, he was one of the Caliph's most strenuous supporters, and died in battle against al-Ma'mūn's general Ṭāhir. See Crone, 178–9.

29. Son of one of the twelve *naqībs*, Mālik b. Haytham al-Khuzāʿī, from Khurāsān who participated in Abū Muslim's rising; ʿAbdallāh eventually recovered favor under Hārūn, despite his support at this juncture for al-Hādī. See Crone, 181–2; Kennedy, *The early Abbasid Caliphate. A political history*, 80–1.

30. Read thus for the text's Ḥāzim. ʿAbdallāh's father Khāzim b. Khuzaymah al-Tamīmī had been one of the deputy *naqībs* from Marw al-Rūdh in the ʿAbbāsid Revolution, hence he stemmed from a prominent family of the Abnā'. See Crone, 180–1; Kennedy, 81–2.

31. On him, already earlier in life suspected of Shīʿī sympathies, see Sourdel, *Vizirat*, I, 112, 120; Masʿūdī, *Murūj*, ed. Pellat, *Index*, VII, 520. For all these administrative arrangements, see Abbott, 78–80; Moscati, *Le califat d'al-Hādī*, 17–18; Sourdel, *Vizirat*, II, 119–20.

32. Ṭabarī-Balʿamī, tr. IV, 447, has the date of the tenth of Ṣafar.

33. Cf. Thaʿālibī, loc. cit.

Khuld and stayed there for a month; then he moved to the Garden of Abū Jaʿfar and thence to ʿĪsābādh.[34]

In this year, al-Rabīʿ (b. Yūnus), the mawlā of Abū Jaʿfar al-Manṣūr, perished.[35]

ʿAlī b. Muḥammad al-Nawfalī[36] has mentioned that his father transmitted the information to him that Mūsā al-Hādī had a slave girl whom he prized greatly and who used to love him, this being at the time when he was in Jurjān on the occasion when al-Mahdī sent him thither. She composed some verses and wrote to him (with them) whilst he was staying in Jurjān, including the verse

O far-away one in a distant place,
who has encamped in Jurjān!

He related: When Mūsā al-Hādī received the homage and he returned to Baghdad, his only thought was of her. He went into her presence, at a moment when she was singing her verses, and stayed with her all that day and night, before he showed himself to any of the people.[37]

Mūsā al-Hādī's Repression of the Dualist Infidels

In this year, Mūsā sought out with severity the dualist infidels
[549] [*zanādiqah*], and during it killed a considerable number of them.[38]

---

34. The palace built by al-Mahdī for his son ʿĪsā as a pleasure resort, in the eastern part of Baghdad (cf. Ṭabarī, III, 517). See Yāqūt, *Muʿjam,* IV, 172–3; Le Strange, *Baghdad,* 194; Abbott, 85–6; Lassner, *Topography,* 194.

35. Al-Rabīʿ had not remained long in al-Hādī's favor, having lost all his offices except control of the *zimām* (Tabari, III, 598); certain sources, e.g., Ṭabarī, III, 597–8 (below, 85–86), and Masʿūdī, *Murūj,* VI, 265–6 = ed. Pellat, § 2473, state that the Caliph plotted to kill his minister. See Abbott, 86–7; Moscati, *Le califat d'al-Hādī,* 17–18.

36. *Rāwī* much cited by Ṭabarī for the period from al-Manṣūr to Hārūn, by Masʿūdī (*Murūj,* ed. Pellat, Index, VII, 517) and also by Iṣfahānī, *Aghānī,* Būlāq, XVII, 29 = Cairo, XVIII, 209. For his full *nasab,* see Ṭabarī, III, 563 (below, 32).

37. Cf. Abbott, 85.

38. For a general study of this persecution of the *zindīq*s, comprising mainly Manichaean dualists but probably also Mazdakites and other remnants of the many once-flourishing faiths and sects of Mesopotamia, see G. Vajda, "Les zindîqs en pays d'Islam au début de la période abbaside," *RSO,* XVII (1938), 173–229; F. Gabrieli, "La «zandaqa» au Ier siècle abbasside," *L'élaboration de l'Islam,* Paris 1961, 23–38; F. Omar, "Some observations on the reign of the ʿAbbāsid caliph al-Mahdī 775–785 A.D.," in *ʿAbbāsiyyāt,* 89–93; S. N. C. Lieu, *Manichaeism in the*

Among those who were executed was Yazdān b. Bādhān, the secretary of Yaqṭīn (b. Mūsā)[39] and of the latter's son ʿAlī b. Yaqṭīn, who was a native of al-Nahrawān.[40] It has been mentioned concerning him that he made the Pilgrimage. He looked at the people tripping round performing the circumambulation of the Kaʿbah, and said, "I can only compare them with oxen trampling round a threshing-floor!" Al-ʿAlāʾ b. al-Ḥaddād al-Aʿmā addressed to him (i.e., to al-Hādī) the verse,

O one whom God has made His trustee over His creation,
and heir of the Kaʿbah and the (Prophet's) pulpit!
What do you think about an unbeliever
who compares the Kaʿbah with a threshing-floor,
And who makes the people, when they perform the running [*saʿy*],
into asses trampling wheat and corn?[41]

Thereupon, Mūsā killed and then gibbeted him. Subsequently, the wooden scaffolding on which he was gibbeted fell down on top of a pilgrim and killed both him and his ass.[42] Also executed was Yaʿqūb b. al-Faḍl from among the Hāshimites.

It has been mentioned from ʿAlī b. Muḥammad (b. Sulaymān b. ʿAbdallāh) al-Hāshimī,[43] who said: There were brought before al-Mahdī, as dualist infidels and in two separate court sessions, a son of Dāwūd b. ʿAlī[44] and Yaʿqūb b. al-Faḍl b. ʿAbd al-Raḥmān b.

---

later Roman empire and medieval China. A historical survey, Manchester 1985, 83–4; *EI*[1] s.v. Zindīḳ (L. Massignon). For al-Hādī's measures in particular, see Vajda, 186–7; Moscati, *Le califat d'al-Hādī,* 7–8.

39. Yaqṭīn b. Mūsā is mentioned at several points in the narratives of Yaʿqūbī and Ṭabarī, from the beginning of al-Manṣūr's reign onwards, as a trusted servant and commander for the Caliphs, and was presumably one of the Abnāʾ. He held a land grant [*qaṭīʿah*] along the Ṣarāt Canal to the south of the Round City; see Yaʿqūbī, *Buldān,* 243, tr. G. Wiet, 21. His son ʿUbayd is also mentioned as fighting in the government forces at Fakhkh; Ṭabarī, III, 562 (below, 30–31).

40. The name of the canal, town and district to the east of Baghdad. See Yāqūt, *Muʿjam,* V, 324–7; Le Strange, *Lands,* 59–61.

41. *Dawsar,* according to R. P. A. Dozy, *Supplément,* I, 442a, *Aegylops ovata,* or in the form *dawshar,* ibid., I, 475b, corn, Canary grain.

42. Cf. al-Muṭahhar al-Maqdisī, *K. al-Badʾ wa-al-taʾrīkh,* VI, 100; Vajda, 186.

43. Described more specifically in Ṭabarī, III, 360, as "al-ʿAbbāsī," possibly the grandson of the Sulaymān b. ʿAbdallāh who was governor of Mecca in 214/829.

44. Paternal uncle of al-Saffāḥ and al-Manṣūr, most respected of the ʿ*umūmah* in the early decades of ʿAbbāsid rule and governor of al-Kūfah for al-Saffāḥ. See Ibn Qutaybah, 216, 372, 374; Lassner, *The shaping of ʿAbbāsid rule,* 146 and Appendix E.

ʿAbbās b. Rabīʿah b. al-Ḥārith b. ʿAbd al-Muṭṭalib.[45] Al-Mahdī said the same words to each of them after both of them had affirmed to him their infidel beliefs. As for Yaʿqūb b. al-Faḍl, he said to the Caliph, "I affirm my beliefs privately between the two of us, but I refuse to proclaim them publicly, even though you were to cut me into little pieces with shears." Al-Mahdī said to him, "Woe upon you! Even though the heavens were to be laid open for you and the affair were as you say, you would still have had ineluctably to show family solidarity [*taʿaṣṣaba*] with Muḥammad![46] If it were not for Muḥammad, who would you be? Would you be anyone but an ordinary person? By God, if it were not for the fact that I have laid upon myself, before God, a charge when He invested me with this office (i.e., with the caliphate) that I would never kill a Hāshimite,
[550] I would not have argued with you like this but would have killed you outright!" Then he turned to Mūsā al-Hādī and said, "O Mūsā, I solemnly adjure you, by my own right (to this office), that if you succeed to this position of authority after me, you do not engage in disputation with these two for a single moment!"

The son of Dāwūd b. ʿAlī died in prison before al-Mahdī's own death. As for Yaʿqūb, he remained (in prison) until al-Mahdī died and Mūsā arrived from Jurjān. Immediately he entered (Baghdad), he remembered al-Mahdī's injunction, and he despatched to Yaʿqūb someone who threw a mattress over him; several persons were then set down on top of him till he suffocated to death.[47] Al-Hādī's attention was then diverted from Yaʿqūb by the ceremony of homage to himself as ruler and by the need to make firm his caliphal power. All this happened on an extremely hot day. Yaʿqūb's corpse stayed there until the early part of the night had elapsed, but then people reported to Mūsā, "O Commander of the Faithful, Yaʿqūb's body has begun to swell up and stink." The Caliph said, "Send it along to his brother Isḥāq b. al-Faḍl and tell him that Yaʿqūb has

---

45. Hence, a direct descendant of a paternal uncle of the Prophet.

46. I.e., as a Hāshimite you cannot gainsay your genealogical connection with the Prophet. The Cairo edition, VIII, 190, has for *taʿaṣṣaba* [= *tataʿaṣṣaba*], *taghḍaba* (*li-Muḥammad*) "you would still have to show anger towards Muḥammad."

47. Obviously to avoid the impiety and scandal of openly shedding Hāshimite blood.

died in prison." Yaʿqūb's corpse was put in a skiff [*zawraq*][48] and brought to Isḥāq. The latter took a look, and it was clear that there was no way of washing the corpse, so he buried Yaʿqūb immediately in a garden of his. He then went off in the morning and sent a message to the Hāshimites informing them about Yaʿqūb's death and summoning them to his obsequies. He gave orders for a wooden beam to be procured, and this was then carved into the rough shape of a man. It was then swathed in cotton bands and Isḥāq had it enshrouded. Then he had it mounted on a funeral bier, and none of those present at the ceremony had any idea that the corpse was in fact an artificial substitute. Yaʿqūb left behind various issue of his loins, comprising ʿAbd al-Raḥmān, al-Faḍl, Arwā and Fāṭimah. In regard to Fāṭimah, she was found to be pregnant by her father, and she herself confessed this.[49]

ʿAlī b. Muḥammad continued to relate: My father related: Fāṭimah and Yaʿqūb b. al-Faḍl's wife, who was not herself a Hāshimite and who was called Khadījah, were brought into al-Hādī's presence, or into al-Mahdī's presence at an early date. They both affirmed their adherence to dualist beliefs, and Fāṭimah acknowledged that she was pregnant by her father. He sent the two of them to Rayṭah bt. Abī al-ʿAbbās.[50] She saw that they both had their eyelids darkened with kohl and their hands and hair dyed with henna, and she reproached them strongly, being particularly voluble against the daughter (i.e., Fāṭimah). The latter protested, "He compelled me (to submit to him)." Rayṭah, however, replied, "What is the meaning, then, of this dyestuff, this kohl and this air of gaiety, if you were compelled?" and she cursed them both. [551]

He related: I was informed that they were both reduced to an extremity of fear, and so died of this fear; they were beaten on the head with a thing called the *ruʿbūb*,[51] were stricken with terror by

48. See A. Mez, *The renaissance of Islam*, tr. Khuda Bakhsh and D. S. Margoliouth, 487; H. Kindermann, *"Schiff" im Arabischen*, 37–8; Darwīsh al-Nukhaylī, *al-Sufun al-islāmiyya*, 59–62: a small river craft used in Iraq.

49. Cf. Abbott, 40. Accusations of incest, like those of unnatural vice, are clichés of heresy trials as much in the Islamic world as in other cultures.

50. Daughter of al-Saffāḥ and the wife of her own first cousin al-Mahdī. See Abbott, 25, 39–40; Kaḥḥālah, *Aʿlam al-nisāʾ*, I, 479.

51. Literally, "that which instills terror, *raʿb*," clearly some kind of club; cf. *Glossarium*, p. CCLXV.

it and thus died. As for Arwā, she survived; her paternal cousin al-Faḍl b. Ismāʿīl b. al-Faḍl, a man of unimpeachably orthodox religion, married her.[52]

In this year, Windā(d)hurmuz, the ruler of Ṭabaristān, came to Mūsā under a guarantee of safety; the Caliph rewarded him munificently and sent him back to Ṭabaristān.[53]

The Remainder of the Events of This Year

These included the revolt of al-Ḥusayn b. ʿAlī b. al-Ḥasan b. al-Ḥasan[54] b. al-Ḥasan b. ʿAlī b. Abī Ṭālib, the one killed at Fakhkh.[55]

The Revolt and Killing of al-Ḥusayn b. ʿAlī

It has been mentioned from Muḥammad b. Mūsā al-Khwārazmī[56] that he related: Between al-Mahdī's death and al-Hādī's assump-

---

52. Ibn al-Athīr, VI, 89; Vajda, 186–7; Moscati, *Le califat d'al-Hādī*, 7–8; Omar, in *ʿAbbāsiyyāt*, 91. Ṭabarī-Balʿamī, tr. IV, 447–53, devotes a lengthy, special section to *zandaqah* under al-Hādī, with many novel details.

53. See on Windādhurmuz and his reign in Ṭabaristān, Ibn Isfandiyār, *Ta'rīkh-i Ṭabaristān*, tr. E. G. Browne, 125–32; Moscati, "Studi storici sul califatto di al-Mahdī," 347–50; idem, "Le califat d'al-Hādī," 8–9; W. Madelung, in *Cambridge history of Iran*, IV, 202. For the name Wi/andād Hurmuz, see Justi, *Iranisches Namenbuch*, 369–70.

54. Hence, grandson of the Ḥasanid known as al-Ḥasan al-Muthallath and great-grandson of al-Ḥasan al-Muthannā. See K. Öhrnberg, *The offspring of Fāṭima. Dispersal and ramification*, Table 16.

55. The primary sources for this episode of yet another futile ʿAlid rebellion are: Khalīfah, *Ta'rīkh*, II, 704; Yaʿqūbī, *Ta'rīkh*, II, 488; Masʿūdī, *Murūj*, VI, 266–8 = ed. Pellat, §§ 2474–5; Iṣfahānī, *Maqātil al-Ṭālibiyyīn*, 285–6, 289–307; Azdī, *Ta'rīkh al-Mawṣil*, 258–9; *K. al-ʿUyūn*, 284–5; Ibn al-Athīr, VI, 90–4; Ibn al-Ṭiqṭaqā, *K. al-Fakhrī*, 172–3, tr. C. E J. Whitting, 187; Fāsī, in *Die Chroniken der Stadt Mekka*, ed. and tr. F. Wustenfeld, II, 184–5; Nahrawālī, in ibid., III, 212–13. The main secondary sources are: F. Wüstenfeld, *Chroniken . . . IV. Geschichte der Stadt Mekka nach den arabischen Chroniken bearbeitet*, 178–9; Moscati, *Le califat d'al-Hādī*, 9–14; C. Van Arendonck, *Les débuts de l'Imāmat Zaidite au Yemen*, 62–5; L. Veccia Vaglieri, "Divagazioni su due rivolte alidi," *A Francesco Gabrieli. Studi orientalistici offerti nel sessantesimo compleanno . . .*, 315–6, 320–2, 335–9, 341–50; Y. Marquet, "Le Šīʿisme au IXe siècle à travers l'histoire de Yaʿqūbī," *Arabica*, XIX (1972), 109; Kennedy, 109–10; *EI*[2] s.v. al-Ḥusayn b. ʿAlī, Ṣāḥib Fakhkh (Veccia Vaglieri).

On the place Fakhkh, one of the wadis running down into Mecca from the direction of the Juddah and Tanʿīm roads, see Yāqūt, *Muʿjam*, IV, 237–8; Bakrī, *Muʿjam māʾstaʿjam*, III, 1014–15; Azraqī, *Akhbar Makkah*, 282, 298.

56. Celebrated mathematician and astronomer, who worked in al-Ma'mūn's

tion of the caliphate, there were eight days. He related: The news (i.e., of al-Mahdī's death) reached him when he was in Jurjān, and up to the point when he entered the City of Peace, up to al-Ḥusayn b. ʿAlī b. al-Ḥasan's revolt, and (finally) up to the killing of al-Ḥusayn, was a period of nine months and eighteen days.

Muḥammad b. Ṣāliḥ[57] has mentioned that Abū Ḥafṣ al-Sulamī transmitted the information to him as follows. He related: Isḥāq b. ʿĪsā b. ʿAlī[58] was governor of Medina. When al-Mahdī died and Mūsā was appointed Caliph, Isḥāq set off on a mission to Mūsā in Iraq, leaving behind as his deputy in Medina ʿUmar b. ʿAbd al-ʿAzīz b. ʿAbdallāh b. ʿAbdallāh b. ʿUmar b. al-Khaṭṭāb.[59] Al-Faḍl [552]
b. Isḥāq (b. Sulaymān) al-Hāshimī[60] has mentioned that Isḥāq b. ʿĪsā b. ʿAlī, when he was in charge of Medina, asked al-Hādī to release him from his duties and to permit him to come to Baghdad. Al-Hādī duly relieved him of his duties and appointed as governor in his stead ʿUmar b. ʿAbd al-ʿAzīz. He has likewise mentioned that the reason behind al-Ḥusayn b. ʿAlī b. al-Ḥasan's revolt was that ʿUmar b. ʿAbd al-ʿAzīz, when he took over the governorship of Medina—as al-Ḥusayn b. Muḥammad has mentioned on the authority of Abū Ḥafṣ al-Sulamī—arrested Abū al-Zift al-Ḥasan b. Muḥammad b. ʿAbdallāh b. al-Ḥasan,[61] Muslim b. Jundub the poet of Hudhayl,[62] and ʿUmar b. Sallām, a mawlā of the house of ʿUmar,

---

reign and died ca. 232 (846–7). See Brockelmann, *GAL*, I², 239–40, S I, 381–2; Sezgin, *GAS*, V, 228–41, VI, 140–3; *EI²* s.v. (J. Vernet).

57. Unidentified, but not the Muḥammad b. Ṣāliḥ b. Dīnār al-Madanī, narrator of historical traditions, who had died in 168/784; see *GAS*, I, 284.

58. First cousin of al-Saffāḥ and al-Manṣūr; hence, a scion of the ʿ*umūmah*, and governor of Medina 167–9 (784–6); see Ibn Qutaybah, 374.

59. Descendant of the Caliph ʿUmar I and brother of the noted ascetic ʿAbdallāh b. ʿAbd al-ʿAzīz feared and respected by Hārūn al-Rashīd; see Ṭabarī, III, 750–1 (below, 316–18).

60. Probably the son of the ʿAbbāsid prince Isḥāq b. Sulaymān who held various governorships under Hārūn.

61. I.e., the son of the Ḥasanid rebel against al-Manṣūr killed at Medina in 145 (762), al-Nafs al-Zakiyyah. See Öhrnberg, Table 7; *EI¹* s.v. Muḥammad b. ʿAbd Allāh (F. Buhl).

62. The reference to this person is rather enigmatic. Abū ʿAbdallāh Muslim b. Jundub (or Jundab) al-Hudhalī is mentioned by Jāḥiẓ as a judge [*qāḍī*] and popular preacher [*qāṣṣ*] of the Prophet's Mosque at Medina (*al-Bayān wa-al-tabyīn*, I, 367–8), who had been tutor to the Caliph ʿUmar II b. ʿAbd al-ʿAzīz and who had himself died in 106 (724–5). This death date rules out our poet of the same unusual name; one wonders whether Ṭabarī's *rāwī* confused a possibly similar name with that of the earlier figure.

when they were engaged in a wine-drinking session which they had organized. He gave orders, and they were beaten en masse; and he gave further commands regarding them, and ropes were placed round their necks and they were paraded around Medina. Protests were raised regarding them, and al-Ḥusayn b. ʿAlī went along to ʿUmar b. ʿAbd al-ʿAzīz. He spoke with him, and said, "They should not be subjected to this; you have had them beaten when you had no right to have them beaten, since the scholars of Iraq don't see any harm in wine-drinking;[63] so why are you having them paraded publicly?"[64] ʿUmar b. ʿAbd al-ʿAzīz accordingly sent a messenger after them—they having at this point reached the paved open place round the Prophet's Mosque [*al-balāṭ*][65]—and brought them back, ordering that they should be imprisoned instead. They were in jail for a day and a night, and then some people spoke up on their behalf and he released them all. They were required to report for inspection, but al-Ḥasan b. Muḥammad was found to be missing, al-Ḥusayn b. ʿAlī being surety for his appearance.

Muḥammad b. Ṣāliḥ related: Also, ʿAbdallāh b. Muḥammad al-Anṣārī transmitted the information to me that al-ʿUmarī (sc. the governor ʿUmar b. ʿAbd al-ʿAzīz) had required various people to act as sureties for other people in the community, and al-Ḥusayn b. ʿAlī b. al-Ḥasan and Yaḥyā b. ʿAbdallāh b. al-Ḥasan[66] both stood as guarantors for al-Ḥasan b. Muḥammad b. ʿAbdallāh b. al-Ḥasan; the latter had married a freedwoman [*mawlāt*] of theirs called

---

63. Alluding to the Ḥanafīs' allowing the drinking of *nabīdh* or date wine in moderation and for medicinal purposes. See *EI*² s.v. Khamr. 1. Juridical aspects (A. J. Wensinck).

64. According to Iṣfahānī, *Maqātil*, 295, the Hāshimites objected to the ignominious treatment of members of their clan.

65. See Bakrī, I, 271, and Samhūdī, *Wafā' al-wafā'*, II, 734–40, where it emerges that this *balāṭ* (here, from Greek *plateia* "street" rather than in the sense of "court [in a palace]" from *palation*, see S. Fraenkel, *Die aramäischen Fremdwörter im Arabischen*, 28–9, 281), was originally the walkway to the mosque, paved with stones by the governor Marwān b. al-Ḥakam on the Caliph Muʿāwiya's orders, but then extended by him to the whole area stretching to the market. See also Ṭabarī, III, 555 (below, 20) for another *balāṭ* in Medina.

66. Yaḥyā was a half-brother on his father's side to al-Nafs al-Zakiyyah. Like his brother Idrīs, he escaped from the field of Fakhkh and, allegedly with the connivance of the Barmakī al-Faḍl b. Yaḥyā, escaped and eventually reached Daylam, where he subsequently rebelled in 176 (792) against Hārūn al-Rashīd. See Ṭabarī, III, 612–24, 669–72, and the sources detailed below, 115–16, n. 440.

Sawdāʾ, daughter of Abū Layth, the mawlā of ʿAbdallāh b. al-Ḥasan, and he used to visit her and stay with her. He failed to turn up for inspection on the Wednesday, Thursday, and Friday. Al-ʿUmarī's deputy[67] carried out the inspection on the Friday evening, and then he got hold of al-Ḥusayn b. ʿAlī and Yaḥyā b. ʿAbdallāh and interrogated them about al-Ḥasan b. Muḥammad; he upbraided them somewhat harshly for a while, and then went back to al-ʿUmarī and informed him of what had happened concerning them, saying, "May God guide you uprightly! Al-Ḥasan b. Muḥammad has been missing for three (nights)!" Al-ʿUmarī replied, "Bring me al-Ḥusayn and Yaḥyā." He went away and summoned them. When they came into al-ʿUmarī's presence, he said to them, "Where's al-Ḥasan b. Muḥammad?" They replied, "By God, we don't know; he was absent from us on Wednesday, then Thursday came along and we received news that he was ill; and then we were under the impression that there was no inspection required today."[68] But ʿUmar b. ʿAbd al-ʿAzīz spoke to them very harshly; hence, Yaḥyā b. ʿAbdallāh gave his oath that he would not sleep until either he came back to him with the missing man or he would knock on the door of ʿUmar b. ʿAbd al-ʿAzīz's house with the news that he had indeed brought al-Ḥasan b. Muḥammad back to him. [553]

When they went out together, al-Ḥusayn said to Yaḥyā, "God is above all imperfection! Whatever impelled you to promise this? Where are you going to find Ḥasan?[69] You have given your oath to him for something which is impossible for you to perform!" Yaḥyā replied, "I have only sworn an oath in regard to Ḥasan." Al-Ḥusayn said, "God is above all imperfection! What thing, then, have you sworn an oath about?" Yaḥyā replied, "By God, may I not sleep until I beat on the door of his house (i.e., al-ʿUmarī's) with the sword!" He related: Ḥusayn said, "(If we do that,) we shall ruin the arrangements which we made with our supporters (i.e., by antici-

---

67. According to Iṣfahānī, *Maqātil*, 295, the man thus deputed was both a mawlā and a weaver, both socially despised statuses.

68. I.e., because it was Friday, the day of congregational worship and holiday.

69. There does not seem to be any rationale behind the fact that, whilst the names al-Ḥasan and al-Ḥusayn normally appear with the definite article, on occasion this is absent.

pating the planned revolt)." Yaḥyā replied, "What has happened has happened, and there is no going back on it."

According to what they have mentioned, they had indeed made a mutual agreement to raise the standard of revolt at Minā or in Mecca itself during the season of the Pilgrimage. A group of the people of al-Kūfah, who were among their partisans and who had given their oath of allegiance to Ḥusayn, had been lying in wait inside a certain house.[70] They now went off, and made their plans for action during the evening and night, until, when it was the latter part of the night, they sallied forth in revolt. Yaḥyā b. ʿAbdallāh went along until he beat on the gate of the residential complex [*dār*] of Marwān (b. al-Ḥakam)[71] in order to get at al-ʿUmarī, but did not find him there. Then he went along to al-ʿUmarī's house in
[554] the residential complex of ʿAbdallāh b. ʿUmar,[72] but did not find him there either; he had hidden from them.

The rebels went along, and then they surged into the mosque, until when the call for the morning worship was given to the people,[73] al-Ḥusayn took his seat in the pulpit, wearing a white turban.[74] The people began to come into the mosque, but when

---

70. As now emerges, the revolt had been previously planned in concert with Shīʿī sympathizers in al-Kūfah, if not in a very detailed fashion, and cannot have been caused by the governor ʿUmar b. ʿAbd al-ʿAzīz's rigor against the wine drinkers (a detail which, understandably, the Shīʿī sources do not dwell upon). Moscati states, *Le califat d'al-Hādī*, 9–10, that discontent had been exacerbated among the Shīʿah by al-Hādī's abandonment of al-Mahdī's policy of conciliating the ʿAlids and of allotting to them subsidies, mentioned by Yaʿqūbī, *Taʾrīkh*, II, 488, and Ṭabarī, III, 563, so that various of the Shīʿah rallied round al-Ḥusayn b. ʿAlī as their natural leader and planned the revolt. In fact, there cannot have been sufficient interval of time for the implications of al-Hādī's change of policy to have sunk into the minds of Shīʿī sympathizers, and Veccia Vaglieri notes (*EI*² s.v. al-Ḥusayn b. ʿAlī) that there were signs that al-Mahdī himself was latterly abandoning his earlier pro-Shīʿī attitudes, and al-Hādī was simply continuing these recent trends. It is very probable that both Caliphs had become exasperated by al-Ḥusayn's irresponsibility in financial matters and his fecklessness; see Van Arendonck, *Les débuts de l'Imāmat Zaidite*, 62–3, and Ṭabarī, III, 563 (below, 33, and n. 137).

71. See for this, Ibn al-Ḥusayn al-Marāghī, *Taḥqīq al-nuṣrah*, 80; Samhūdī, II, 720–1. It adjoined the Prophet's Mosque, and on the authority of ʿUmar b. Shabbah, was purchased by the state and used as a gubernatorial residence.

72. Marāghi, 73. According to Samhūdī, II, 718–19, this was the first house built adjoining the Prophet's Mosque when Muḥammad allotted plots of land there for houses, and was connected to the Mosque by a private passage [*khūkhah*].

73. According to Iṣfahānī, *Maqātil*, 297, the rebels compelled the muezzin at swordpoint to make the *adhān* in the Shīʿī wording.

74. In the early ʿAbbāsid period, as a contrast to ʿAbbāsid black, white seems to

they saw the rebels, they turned back without performing the worship. But when al-Ḥusayn had performed the morning worship, people began to come to him and to give him their allegiance on the basis of the Book of God and the *Sunnah* of His Prophet, for "the one pleasing (to God) [*al-murtaḍā*] from the house of Muḥammad."[75]

(At this point,) there appeared Khālid al-Barbarī,[76] who was at this time in charge of the state domains [*al-ṣawāfī*] at Medina and was the commander of a force of two hundred soldiers from the regular forces stationed at Medina. He advanced with his troops, and al-ʿUmarī came along, together with Wazīr b. Isḥāq al-Azraq and Muḥammad b. Wāqid al-Sharawī, and with a considerable number of persons, including al-Ḥusayn b. Jaʿfar b. al-Ḥusayn b. al-Ḥusayn[77] who was mounted upon an ass. Khālid al-Barbarī rushed into the courtyard of the mosque [*al-raḥbah*], having put on two coats of mail, with the sword in his hand and a club slung round his waist, his sword being unsheathed, and he was shouting at Ḥusayn, "I am a stout warrior [*kaskās*]![78] May God strike me dead if I do not succeed in killing you!" He charged them until he drew near to their ranks. The two sons of ʿAbdallāh b. Ḥasan, Yaḥyā and Idrīs,[79] blocked his path. Yaḥyā struck him on the nasal of his helmet, and then cut through the helmet and cut off his nose. His eyes were filled with blood and he was unable to see. He was driven down to his knees and began to beat about with his sword to protect himself, being all this time unable to see. Idrīs

---

have become the favored color of a wide spectrum of opposition movements, from pro-Umayyad Syrian ones to ʿAlid ones, as here, and to heterodox Persian groups like the *Mubayyiḍah* or *Ispīdh-jamāgān* of Muqannaʿ in Transoxania. See Farouk Omar, "The significance of the colours of banners in the early ʿAbbāsid period," in *ʿAbbāsiyyāt*, 149–50.

75. It thus seems that al-Ḥusayn was formally claiming the caliphate and imāmate, an impression strengthened by the apparent adoption of *al-Murtaḍā* as a *laqab* or honorific.

76. As Moscati notes, *Le califat d'al-Hādī*, 11 n. 1, the sources give numerous variant forms of this name.

77. Presumably a descendant of the Third Imām al-Ḥusayn b. ʿAlī b. Abī Ṭālib.

78. According to *WbKAS*, I, 168b, this means "a stocky but tough person," as in Ibn Manẓūr, *Lisān al-ʿArab*[1], VIII, 80: *al-qaṣīr al-ghalīẓ*.

79. Brother of al-Nafs al-Zakiyyah, hence, uncle to al-Ḥusayn b. ʿAlī, and after his escape from the débâcle of Fakhkh—presumably having mingled with the pilgrims in Mecca to escape detection—founder of the Idrīsid dynasty of Sharīfs in Morocco (172–314 [789–926]). See Ibn Qutaybah, 213; Ṭabarī, III, 561, 562 (below, 28–30, 31); Öhrnberg, Table 30; *EI*[2] s.v. Idrīs I (al-Akbar) (D. Eustache).

came up round him from the rear and struck him, knocking him to the ground, and Yaḥyā and Idrīs hacked at him with their swords from above until they finally killed him. Their companions fell upon Khālid's two mailed coats; they pulled them off his corpse and seized his sword and club. They brought along his body, and then orders were given that it should be dragged into the paved
[555] open space [*al-balāṭ*]. They launched an attack on Khālid's forces, and the latter took to flight. ʿAbdallāh b. Muḥammad related: All this I report as an eyewitness.

ʿAbdallāh b. Muḥammad has mentioned that Khālid struck Yaḥyā b. ʿAbdallāh and cut through his headdress. The blow reached[80] as far as Yaḥyā's hand and left its mark there. Yaḥyā struck Khālid in the face, and a one-eyed man from the people of al-Jazīrah came round and fell upon him from behind; he struck him on his legs, and they hit Khālid by turns with their swords and thus killed him. ʿAbdallāh b. Muḥammad has related: The wearers of black [*al-musawwidah,* sc. the partisans of the ʿAbbāsids] went into the mosque to hold it against the ʿAlid forces, when al-Ḥusayn b. Jaʿfar appeared mounted on his ass, but the wearers of white [*al-mubayyiḍah,* sc. the partisans of the ʿAlids] launched an attack and drove them out. Al-Ḥusayn (b. ʿAlī) shouted to them, "Treat the shaykh gently!" meaning al-Ḥusayn b. Jaʿfar. The public treasury was plundered, and around ten thousand dīnārs, which remained from the soldiers' salaries [*ʿaṭāʾ*],[81] seized from it. It has been said that the latter amounted (originally) to seventy thousand dīnārs which ʿAbdallāh b. Mālik had sent along to be distributed as subsidies for the Khuzāʿah.[82]

He related: The combatants [*al-nās*] dispersed, and the people of Medina locked their doors against them. The next morning, the ʿAlid partisans gathered together, and the supporters of the ʿAbbāsids came together and fought with them in the paved open space [*balāṭ*] which lies between the courtyard before al-Faḍl's house and al-Zawrāʾ.[83] The wearers of black began to attack the

80. Following n. *a, balaghat,* and the Cairo text, VIII, 194, *waṣalat,* for the text's *khalaʿat.*

81. Fāsī, *Shifāʾ al-gharām,* in *Die Chroniken der Stadt Mekka,* II, 184.

82. The powerful Ḥijāzī tribe of the region around Mecca, once themselves masters of the city and, subsequently, close allies of Quraysh; see *EI*² s.v. (M. J. Kister).

83. A section of the market quarter of the city; see Samhūdī, IV, 1228–9.

wearers of white until they drove them into the courtyard before al-Faḍl's house, and then the wearers of white counterattacked until they drove them back[84] to al-Zawrā'. Both sides suffered many casualties through wounds. They fought until midday and then dispersed. When it was towards the end of daylight on the second day, that being Sunday, the news arrived that Mubārak al-Turkī was encamping at the Well of al-Muṭṭalib.[85] The supporters of the ʿAbbāsids were roused into activity again. They went out to him and persuaded him to come (into the town). So he came the next morning until he reached al-Thaniyyah.[86] The ʿAbbāsid partisans and those who were eager to fight rallied round him. The two sides fought together extremely fiercely in the paved open space until midday, and then dispersed. The partisans of the ʿAlids withdrew to the mosque, and those of the ʿAbbāsids to Mubārak al-Turkī, to the house of ʿUmar b. ʿAbd al-ʿAzīz at al-Thaniyyah in [556]
order to shelter there from the noonday heat. He made an undertaking with his supporters to return later, towards evening (i.e., to fight). But when they showed no interest in him, he mounted his riding beasts and rode away. The ʿAbbāsid partisans did in fact come back later, towards evening, but did not find him. So (they returned to the fray and) fought their opponents in a somewhat desultory fashion till sunset, and then they dispersed.

Ḥusayn and his partisans remained for several days, equipping themselves with travelling supplies. Their stay in Medina amounted to eleven days. He then departed on the twenty-fourth of Dhū al-Qaʿdah, six days from its end (May 28, 786).[87] When

84. Following the preferred reading of n. c, *yablaghū*; the Cairo text, VIII, 195, has *yublagha bihim* "they were driven back."

85. See Samhūdī, IV, 1141–2. It is said to have lain seven or five miles from Medina and to have been named after al-Muṭṭalib b. ʿAbdallāh al-Makhzūmī.

86. A frequent toponym in the area of Medina (*thaniyyah* "mountain road, track, which climbs over a height," see Mubarrad, *Kāmil*, I, 384), one of the best-known being the Thaniyyat al-Wadāʿ on the left of the road from Syria coming into the city. See Marāghī, 144, and Samhūdī, IV, 1166–72, who mentions, however, other *thanāyā*, such as that of al-Sharīd, IV, 1066–7.

87. The rebels had obviously failed to secure any appreciable part of the city and had been compelled to "hole up" in the mosque. As Iṣfahānī concedes, *Maqātil*, 297–8, two of the Ṭālibids of Medina refused to join the rising, al-Ḥasan b. Jaʿfar b. al-Ḥasan b. al-Ḥasan and Mūsā al-Kāẓim b. Jaʿfar al-Ṣādiq, the Seventh Imām of the Shīʿah (cf. *EI*[1] s.v. [R. Strothmann]), who told al-Ḥusayn b. ʿAlī that his revolt was doomed to failure. Iṣfahānī also adds, ibid., 299, that al-Ḥusayn's force numbered about 300 men, apparently including some local Bedouin; see Van Arendonck, 64.

they left Medina, the muezzins came back; they made the call to worship, and the people went back into the mosque. They found there discarded bones which the ʿAlids had been eating and other traces of their stay, and they began to bring down God's curses upon them, "May God deal with them as He thinks fit!"

Muḥammad b. Ṣāliḥ related: Nuṣayr b. ʿAbdallāh b. Ibrāhīm al-Jumaḥī transmitted the information to me that when Ḥusayn reached the marketplace, on his way to Mecca, he turned towards the people of Medina and said, "May God not replace your losses with anything good!" But the people and the market traders retorted, "On the contrary, may God not replace your losses with anything good, and may He never bring you back (here)!" For Ḥusayn's followers had been defecating in the mosque and had filled it with filth and urine; hence, when they left, the people washed down the mosque.[88]

He related: The son of ʿAbdallāh b. Ibrāhīm transmitted the information to me, saying: Al-Ḥusayn's partisans took the coverings of the mosque and used them as robes for themselves. He related: Al-Ḥusayn's partisans proclaimed in Mecca, "Every slave who comes to us is free!" The slaves came to him, and one slave belonging to my father came to him and then joined his side. When al-Ḥusayn resolved on departure, my father went to him and spoke with him. He said to al-Ḥusayn, "You have made approaches to slaves whom you did not yourself own, and then you have freed them; on what grounds do you consider this lawful?" Ḥusayn therefore said to his companions, "Take him along with you, and whichever slave he recognizes, hand that slave back to him (i.e., to the narrator's father)." So they went off in company with him, and he recovered his slave boy [*ghulām*] and two (other) slave boys belonging to neighbors of ours.[89]

---

88. Ibn al-Athīr, VI, 92. Here as elsewhere, Ṭabarī is careful to note the swinish habits of the Shīʿī followers, doubtless to emphasize their plebeian nature.

89. Ibn al-Athīr, loc. cit.; Fāsī, 184–5; Pipes, 134. Veccia Vaglieri, *EI*[2] s.v. al-Ḥusayn b. ʿAlī, regards this attempted emancipation of the slaves at Mecca, plus the sharing-out of the money found in the state treasury at Medina, as manifestations of the Zaydī policy of greater social justice as being incumbent upon the Imām in return for the people's *bayʿah.* Cf. also the appeal during the ʿAlid revolt in Mecca in 200 (816) in the name of the Ḥusaynid Muḥammad b. Jaʿfar al-Ṣādiq to the black slaves and similar elements there, mentioned by Ṭabarī, III, 992. See further, below, 34, n. 140.

The news of al-Ḥusayn's revolt reached al-Hādī. Several male members of his family had gone on the Pilgrimage that year, [557] including Muḥammad b. Sulaymān b. ʿAlī,[90] al-ʿAbbās b. Muḥammad and Mūsā b. ʿĪsā,[91] as well as the younger members. Sulaymān b. Abī Jaʿfar[92] acted as leader of the Pilgrimage. Al-Hādī now ordered the investiture patent appointing Muḥammad b. Sulaymān as military commander to be written out. People said to him, however, "What about your paternal uncle al-ʿAbbās b. Muḥammad?" He replied, "Don't interfere with me! No, by God, I won't be deprived of my royal authority!" The patent investing Muḥammad b. Sulaymān b. ʿAlī with the military command was therefore put into effect, but the document only reached them when they were on the way back from the Pilgrimage.

Muḥammad b. Sulaymān had gone forth with a full panoply of weapons and men, because the road was fearful and dangerous on account of the Bedouins. Ḥusayn did not get his forces ready to confront them. The news about them (i.e., about Muḥammad b. Sulaymān's approaching forces) came to him when they were already in his direction, so he set out with his slaves and his brothers. Mūsā b. ʿAlī b. Mūsā had meanwhile proceeded to Baṭn Nakhl[93] thirty (farsakhs) from Medina. The news reached him, he having his brothers and his slave girls with him. The news further reached al-ʿAbbās b. Muḥammad b. Sulaymān, and he entered into correspondence with them (i.e., with Muḥammad b. Sulaymān's approaching forces). They came to Mecca and entered it. Muḥammad b. Sulaymān came forward, his followers having donned the ritually pure garments (i.e., the *iḥrām*) for performing the ʿUmrah. They then proceeded to Dhū Ṭuwā[94] and encamped there.

---

90. First cousin of al-Saffāḥ and al-Manṣūr, hence a noted scion of the ʿ*umūmah*, and first husband of al-Rashīd's sister al-ʿAbbāsah; see Ibn Qutaybah, 375–6, 380–1.

91. Grandson of Mūsā b. Muḥammad b. ʿAlī, brother of al-Saffāḥ and al-Manṣūr, and third cousin of al-Hādī.

92. I.e., the son of al-Manṣūr; see Ibn Qutaybah, 379.

93. See Abdullah Al-Wohaibi, *The Northern Hijaz in the writings of the Arab geographers 800–1150*, 377. According to Yāqūt, *Muʿjam*, I, 449–50, it lay on the Baṣrah road.

94. This wadi marked the edge of the central hollow of Mecca and the boundary of the *ḥaram* or sacred area. See Azraqī, II, 297–301; Hamdānī, *Ṣifat Jazīrat al-ʿArab*, 436; Bakrī, III, 896–7. The name is still known in contemporary Mecca for part of the Jarwal quarter there.

Amongst their number was Sulaymān b. Abī Jaʿfar. All those supporters of the ʿAbbāsids, their mawlās and their military commanders who had arrived in Mecca that year, joined up with them.[95] The people had come in successive groups that year for the Pilgrimage, and had grown to a great number.

Muḥammad b. Sulaymān then sent ahead of himself ninety mounted men, some mounted on horses and some on mules, whilst he himself was riding a powerful thoroughbred horse. Behind him were forty men also mounted on noble horses, bearing the travelling baggage, and behind them men riding on donkeys,[96] all in addition to the infantrymen and others who were with them.
[558] These appeared to the people as a very numerous force, and they filled (the streets/the mosque[97]); they imagined that they were several times their (real) numbers. They circumambulated the (Holy) House, made the running [*saʿy*] between al-Ṣafā' and al-Marwah, and completed their performance of the ʿUmrah. They then moved on, and came to Dhū Ṭuwā and encamped there, this being Thursday. Muḥammad b. Sulaymān sent forward Abū Kāmil, a mawlā of Ismāʿīl b. ʿAlī,[98] with a force of twenty-odd cavalrymen, this being on the Friday, and he met up with them. There was at this time in the ranks of his troops a man called Zayd who had attached himself to al-ʿAbbās, hence, al-ʿAbbās had brought him with him as a fellow-pilgrim. Now when he saw the enemy, he threw down on the ground his shield and sword, and went over to join their side; this was at Baṭn Marr.[99] Subsequently, they got hold of his body, which had been battered with clubs.

During the night of Friday-Saturday, they sent forward fifty cavalrymen. The first person whom they invited (i.e., to act as their leader) was Abū al-Dhayyāl Ṣabbāḥ, then another and another and another. Abū Khalwah the eunuch [*al-khādim*],[100] Muḥammad's

95. The high proportion of mawlās, slaves, and eunuchs in the ʿAbbāsid forces confronting al-Ḥusayn b. ʿAlī is notable; cf. Pipes, 137.

96. The Cairo text, VIII, 196, specifies "200 men mounted on donkeys."

97. To be thus added to complete the sense, according to n. *a*; the Cairo text has "and they filled their breasts (i.e., with reassurance)."

98. I.e., of Ismāʿīl, brother of Muḥammad b. ʿAlī, father of al-Saffāḥ and al-Manṣūr, and holder of various provincial governorships; see Ibn Qutaybah, 374.

99. District of Mecca where the two streams forming the Wādī al-Nakhlatayn joined together; see *Yāqūt*, Muʿjam, I, 449.

100. That this general term "servant" was by this time very frequently used as

mawlā, was the fifth. Then they went to al-Mufaḍḍal, the mawlā of al-Mahdī, and sought to make him commander over them. He refused, however, and exclaimed, "No, appoint someone else over them, and I will be one of the rank and file." So they appointed as commander over them ʿAbdallāh b. Ḥamīd b. Razīn al-Samarqandī, who was at that time a comparatively young man of thirty years. They went off, being a force of fifty cavalrymen, on the night of Friday-Saturday.

The enemy drew near, and the cavalry drew back[101] and the troops prepared for battle. Al-ʿAbbās b. Muḥammad and Mūsā b. ʿĪsā were on the left wing; Muḥammad b. Sulaymān on the right wing; and Muʿādh b. Muslim[102] was (in the centre) between Muḥammad b. Sulaymān and al-ʿAbbās b. Muḥammad.[103] Just before sunrise began to gleam, Ḥusayn and his followers advanced. Three of Sulaymān b. ʿAlī's mawlās[104] launched an attack, one of these being Zanjawayh, Ḥassān's slave, and then came back with a (severed) head and threw it down in front of Muḥammad b. Sulaymān; they had previously promised five hundred (dirhams) to the [559] (first) person who came back with a head. Muḥammad's troops came along and hamstrung the (enemy's) camels so that their litters and saddles fell down. Then they slaughtered them (i.e., the ʿAlid forces) and put them to flight.

Before this, they (i.e., the ʿAlid forces) had gone forth from those mountain tracks [*thanāyā*] with only the smaller part of them marching against Muḥammad b. Sulaymān's wing; their main force marched towards the wing of Mūsā b. ʿĪsā and his troops (i.e., against the ʿAbbāsids troops' left wing). Hence, the ʿAlid forces' main assault was against the latter. When Muḥammad b. Sulay-

---

one of several euphemisms for "eunuch," rather than the stark terms *khaṣī* and *majbūb*, has been emphasized by Ayalon. See his *The military reforms of Caliph al-Muʿtaṣim*, 3–4, 42–3; idem, "Preliminary remarks on the *Mamlūk* military institution in Islam," 50–1; idem, "On the eunuchs in Islam," *JSAI*, I (1979), 74–89.

101. *Rajaʿat*; the Cairo text, VIII, 197, has *zaḥafat* "moved forward slowly."

102. Muʿādh b. Muslim b. Muʿādh al-Dhuhlī was a Khurasanian mawlā and one of the Abnāʾ al-Dawlah settled in Baghdad in the Caliphs' service; see Crone, 183–4.

103. A slight variation in the pattern of command is given by Iṣfahānī in *Maqātil*, 300; cf. Moscati, *Le califat d'al-Hādī*, 12 n. 2; but all the sources agree essentially on the actual course of the battle.

104. I.e., the freedmen of the ʿAbbāsid prince Sulaymān b. ʿAlī b. ʿAbdallāh, uncle of al-Saffāḥ; see Ibn Qutaybah, 374–6.

mān had dealt with the troops assailing his wing, and his troops were conscious of the first gleams of dawn, they turned their attention to the ʿAlid troops attacking Mūsā b. ʿĪsā's wing—and behold, they were massed together as if they were a compact ball of spun thread. The center and right wing of the ʿAbbāsid forces penetrated into their ranks and became locked with them in fighting, (and they put to flight al-Ḥusayn's forces).[105] They (i.e., the ʿAbbāsid forces) returned toward Mecca, not knowing what had become of al-Ḥusayn himself. They were still without information, having by then reached Dhū Ṭuwā or somewhere near it, until a soldier from the Khurāsānian troops shouted out, "Great news, great news! This is Ḥusayn's head!" He produced it, and there were marks of a blow right along the forehead and another blow on the back of the head. The ʿAbbāsid troops were shouting promises of quarter [*amān*] when they had finished the assault;[106] hence, Abū al-Zift al-Ḥasan b. Muḥammad stumbled forward, with one of his eyes closed by a wound received in the fighting, and stood behind Muḥammad (b. Sulaymān) and al-ʿAbbās (b. Muḥammad b. Sulaymān). Mūsā b. ʿĪsā and ʿAbdallāh b. al-ʿAbbās came up round him and gave orders for him to be killed. Muḥammad b. Sulaymān became extremely angry at that.

Muḥammad b. Sulaymān entered Mecca by one road and al-ʿAbbās b. Muḥammad by another. The heads (of those slain in battle) were cut off, and there turned out to be over a hundred of them, including the head of Sulaymān b. ʿAbdallāh b. Ḥasan.[107] This battle took place on the *Yawm al-Tarwiyah* (i.e., the "Day of Refreshment," the eighth of Dhū al-Ḥijjah [June 11, 786]). Al-Ḥusayn's sister, who had been with him, was taken prisoner; she was sent to the custody of Zaynab bt. Sulaymān.[108] The fugitives from the ʿAlid forces mingled with the pilgrims and then slipped away. Sulaymān b. Abī Jaʿfar was ill at this time; hence, he was not
[560] present at the battle. ʿĪsā b. Jaʿfar[109] led the ceremonies of the

105. This phrase supplied from other, parallel sources, according to n. *b*.

106. Al-Ḥusayn b. ʿAlī himself expressly refused this offer of *amān*, preferring the martyr's crown, according to Iṣfahānī, *Maqātil*, loc. cit.

107. I.e., the brother of Idrīs, who managed to escape to the Maghrib, see below.

108. The daughter of the ʿAbbāsid prince Sulaymān b. ʿAlī (for whom see above, 25, n. 104); see Ibn Qutaybah, 385.

109. Grandson of Abū Jaʿfar al-Manṣūr, and later governor of al-Baṣrah under al-

Pilgrimage in that year. There was among Ḥusayn's followers a blind man who used to exhort them by his edifying stories and narratives [*yaquṣṣu ʿalayhim*], and he was killed (i.e., in the battle). None of them, however, was executed afterwards in cold blood.

Al-Ḥusayn b. Muḥammad b. ʿAbdallāh related: Mūsā b. ʿĪsā took captive four Kūfans, a mawlā of the Banū ʿIjl[110] and another person.

Muḥammad b. Ṣāliḥ related: Muḥammad b. Dāwūd b. ʿAlī transmitted the information to me, from Mūsā b. ʿĪsā, who related: I arrived, bringing with me six captives. Al-Hādī said, "Begone with you! Would you kill my prisoner?" I replied, "O Commander of the Faithful, I reflected at length about him, and said to myself, 'ʿĀʾishah and Zaynab[111] will go to the Commander of the Faithful's mother and weep profusely in her presence, and will speak with her. Then she will speak to the Commander of the Faithful on his behalf, and he will let him go free.' " Then al-Hādī said, "Bring in the captives." I said, "I have made solemn promises and covenants to them that they should be set free and given their liberty." He nevertheless said, "Bring them before me!" He ordered two of them to be killed. The third one was an obscure person, and I said, "O Commander of the Faithful, this man is extremely knowledgeable about (the genealogies of) the house of Abū Ṭālib, and if you spare his life, he will provide you with everything you require." The man himself added, "By God, yes indeed, O Commander of the Faithful, I very much hope that your action in sparing my life will render me of service to you." Al-Hādī bowed his head in thought for a while, and then said, "By God, your emerging safe from my hands, after

---

Rashīd on four separate occasions from 173 (789) onwards, died in 192 (808); see Ibn Qutaybah, 385.

110. An Arab tribe, considered as part of Bakr b. Wāʾil, which had been long established on the desert fringes of Iraq and considerably Christianized. In early Islamic times, ʿIjlīs seem to have been especially inclined to Shīʿī and various heretical tendencies. See the verse quoted in Ch. Pellat, *Le milieu baṣrien et la formation de Ǧāḥiẓ*, 199; M. G. Morony, *Iraq after the Muslim conquest*, 443, 499; *EI*[2] s.v. ʿIdjl (W. Montgomery Watt).

111. Abbott, 88, takes this as specifically referring to the senior ʿAbbāsid princess Zaynab bt. Sulaymān b. ʿAlī b. ʿAbdallāh (hence, the first cousin of al-Saffāḥ and al-Manṣūr; see on her ibid., 43–5), but it may be a reference to female busybodies in general, ʿĀʾishah and Zaynab being in grammatical parlance the female equivalents of ʿAmr and Zayd, N. and M.

falling into them, is certainly a serious matter," but he kept on talking with him until in the end al-Hādī ordered that he should be kept back (i.e., from those sent forward for execution) and that the required guarantee of his safety should be written out for him. As for the other, he forgave him (also). He ordered the execution and gibbeting of ʿUdhāfir al-Ṣayrafī and ʿAlī b. al-Sābiq al-Fallās[112] al-Kūfī, and they accordingly gibbeted them at the Bāb al-Jisr;[113] they had both been captured at Fakhkh. The Caliph vented his rage also on Mubārak al-Turkī, and ordered the confiscation of his goods and property and his demotion to service in the ranks of the grooms of the riding beasts.[114] He further vented his ire on Mūsā b. ʿĪsā because the latter had executed al-Ḥasan b. Muḥammad, and ordered the confiscation of his goods and property.

Idrīs b. ʿAbdallāh b. Ḥasan's Escape to the Maghrib and His Foundation of the Idrīsid Dynasty in Morocco

ʿAbdallāh b. ʿAmr al-Thaljī related, transmitting the information from Muḥammad b. Yūsuf b. Yaʿqūb al-Hāshimī, who had it from
[561] ʿAbdallāh b. ʿAbd al-Raḥmān b. ʿĪsā (b. Mūsā),[115] who said: Idrīs b. ʿAbdallāh b. Ḥasan b. Ḥasan b. ʿAlī b. Abī Ṭālib escaped from the battle of Fakhkh during al-Hādī's caliphate. He reached Egypt, the official in charge of the *barīd* systems of Egypt at that time being Wāḍiḥ, a mawlā of the Commander of the Faithful al-Manṣūr's son Ṣāliḥ, and Wāḍiḥ was a vile partisan of the Shīʿah [*rāfiḍī khabīth*].[116] Wāḍiḥ therefore gave Idrīs the facilities of the *barīd* service mounts to convey him to the Western lands.[117] He ended up

112. The Cairo text, VIII, 198, has al-Qallās.

113. The gate at the western end of the Upper Bridge (*jisr*) over the Tigris connecting the Western Bank with the Shammāsiyyah quarter. See Le Strange, *Baghdad*, 178, 198; M. Canard, *Histoire de la dynastie des H'amdânides de Jazîra et de Syrie*, I, 168; Lassner, *Topography*, 79.

114. Ibn al-Athīr, VI, 93.

115. Grandson of the ʿAbbāsid prince ʿĪsā b. Mūsā b. Muḥammad b. ʿAlī.

116. The mawlā Wāḍiḥ was an ancestor of the historian Yaʿqūbī, called Ibn Wāḍiḥ and certainly a Shīʿī sympathiser; see Crone, 196.

117. Kindī, *K. Wulāt Miṣr*, 131–2, states that al-Hādī's governor in Egypt, the ʿAbbāsid prince ʿAlī b. Sulaymān, sheltered and encouraged the fugitive Idrīs.

in the region of Tangier, at a town called Walīlah,[118] and the Berbers of that place and of the neighboring tracts[119] rallied to his call. Al-Hādī had Wāḍiḥ beheaded and gibbeted. (Alternatively,) it is said that it was al-Rashīd who executed him and who sent, secretly, to plot against Idrīs, al-Shammākh al-Yamāmī, the mawlā of al-Mahdī, at the same time writing for him a letter of recommendation to Ibrāhīm b. al-Aghlab, his governor over Ifrīqiyah.[120] Al-Shammākh proceeded till he reached Walīlah, where he gave out that he was a physician and that he was one of their partisans. He went into Idrīs's presence, so that the latter came to regard him familiarly and to feel at ease with him. Al-Shammākh began ostensibly to show him great respect, support for his cause, and honor to him. Hence he was able to stay by his side at every stage where he halted (sc. on his journeyings). Then at one point, Idrīs complained to al-Shammākh of a toothache, so al-Shammākh gave him a deadly poisonous (supposed) medicament for rubbing on the teeth, and instructed him to rub it on them at daybreak, after he had passed the night. So when it was dawn, Idrīs took the dentifrice and began to rub it back and forth in his mouth repeatedly and energetically, so that it killed him.[121] A search was instituted for al-Shammākh, but he could not be caught. Al-Shammākh reached Ibrāhīm b. al-Aghlab and told him about what he had done. The news of Idrīs's death arrived after al-Shammākh's actual arrival. Ibn al-Aghlab now wrote to al-Rashīd about all this, and the latter appointed al-Shammākh over the *barīd* and intelligence services of Egypt.[122]

---

118. Probably (though the identification is not 100% certain) on the site of the Roman Volubilis, in what was the province of Mauritania Tingitana; see H. Terrasse, *Histoire du Maroc des origines à l'établissement du Protectorat français*, I, 58–9, 65–8, 112–15.

119. Actually, the Berbers of the Awrabah tribe of the Lawātah group.

120. Ibrāhīm was the founder of the Aghlabid line of autonomous governors of Ifrīqiyah (184–296 [800–909]), but was not yet at this time governor of the whole province, which was not formally conferred on him till 184/800. See *EI*[2] s.v. Aghlabids (G. Marçais, etc.).

121. Idrīs actually died in al-Muḥarram 175 (May–June, 791).

122. Yaʿqūbī, *Taʾrīkh*, II, 488–9; Masʿūdī, *Murūj*, VI, 193–4 = ed. Pellat, § 2405; Azdī, 259; *K. al-ʿUyūn*, 285; Ibn al-Athīr, VI, 93–4; E. H. Palmer, *Haroun Alraschid, Caliph of Baghdad*, 73–4; G. Marçais, "La Berbérie au IXe siècle d'après El-Yaʿqoûbî," *R.Afr.*, LXXXV (1941), 60–1; idem, *La Berbérie musulmane et l'Orient au moyen âge*, 116–22; Terrasse, I, 115. An alternative historical tradition makes

A certain poet—I think it was al-H.nāzī[123]—recited concerning these events,

Do you imagine, O Idrīs, that you can escape
the Caliph's wiles or that flight is of any avail?
For they (i.e., the Caliph's wiles) will certainly catch up with you, unless you alight in a land
where (even) a young bustard cannot guide people towards you!
Indeed, when his anger unsheathes the swords,
they are long ones, and lives prove to be short in face of them.
(He is) a monarch, and it is as if death inexorably follows his command,
to the point that people say, "Even destiny obeys him!"

More Accounts of the Battle of Fakhkh and Its Aftermath

[562] Al-Faḍl b. Isḥāq al-Hāshimī has mentioned that when al-Ḥusayn b. ʿAlī raised his revolt at Medina, al-ʿUmarī being governor there, the latter remained in concealment during al-Ḥusayn's stay at Medina until al-Ḥusayn left for Mecca. Al-Hādī had meanwhile despatched Sulaymān b. Abī Jaʿfar to lead the Pilgrimage, and there went forth with Sulaymān, from among those members of the ʿAbbāsid family who intended to make the Pilgrimage, al-ʿAbbās b. Muḥammad, Mūsā b. ʿĪsā and Ismāʿīl b. ʿĪsā b. Mūsā,[124] traveling via the Kūfah Road; Muḥammad b. Sulaymān and a number of the progeny of Jaʿfar b. Sulaymān, traveling, via the Baṣrah Road; and from among the mawlās, Mubārak al-Turkī, the slave[125] al-Mufaḍḍal, and Ṣāʿid the mawlā of al-Hādī. Sulaymān was in charge of all the arrangements, and among the well-known, prominent figures involved were Yaqṭīn b. Musa, ʿUbayd b. Yaqṭīn, and Abū al-

Idrīs's assassin Yaḥyā b. Khālid al-Barmakī's agent Sulaymān b. Jarīr (see Van Arendonck, 65 n. 5).

123. Unidentified; the name is apparently corruptly written in the manuscript.

124. Holder of various provincial governorships; see Ibn Qutaybah, 376.

125. Again, as above, Ṭabarī, III, 547, this seems to be the correct rendering here for *waṣīf*, for it emerges just below that al-Mufaḍḍal was a eunuch.

Wazīr[126] ʿUmar b. Muṭarrif. They gathered together at the point when they received the news that al-Ḥusayn and his companions were making for Mecca, and they appointed as their (military) chief Sulaymān b. Abī Jaʿfar because of his existing office as leader of the Pilgrimage. Abū Kāmil, the mawlā of Ismāʿīl, had previously been placed in command of the vanguard troops, and they met up with him at Fakhkh. They left ʿUbaydallāh b. Qutham[127] behind at Mecca to look after the town and its people. Al-ʿAbbās b. Muḥammad had furthermore promised them (sc. al-Husayn's partisans) a guarantee of safe-conduct for what they had perpetrated, and had undertaken to treat them kindly and to bring about conciliation on the basis of kinship bonds, his envoy to them in this matter being the eunuch [*al-khādim*] al-Mufaḍḍal; but they had refused to accept these terms.

The battle then took place; considerable slaughter occurred; the survivors took to flight; a promise of quarter was proclaimed among them; and no fugitive was hunted down. Among those who fled were Yaḥyā and Idrīs, the two sons of ʿAbdallāh b. Ḥasan. In regard to Idrīs, he managed to reach Tāhart in the Western lands and sought refuge with its people;[128] they treated him with honor, and he remained with them until the secret mission and stratagem against him, with his resultant death. His son Idrīs b. Idrīs followed him as his successor,[129] and he (and his descendants) have remained to this day rulers over that region; all diplomatic connections with them have been severed.

Al-Mufaḍḍal b. Sulaymān[130] has related: When the news of

126. Thus, the reading preferred in *Addenda et emendanda,* p. DCCCLIX, and in the Cairo text, VIII, 199, in the light of mentions of this man in Ṭabarī, III, 491, 516, instead of the text's Abū al-Ward.

127. Hāshimite and great-grandson of ʿUbaydallāh, one of the sons of al-ʿAbbās b. ʿAbd al-Muṭṭalib.

128. A town of what is now eastern Algeria, which was from 144 (761–2) the center of an Ibāḍī Khārijite principality under the Rustamids; see *EI*[1] s.v. Tāhert (Marçais). These anti-ʿAbbāsid Khārijites would naturally have provided a sympathetic haven for the fugitive Idrīs.

129. On Idrīs II al-Aṣghar, the real creator of the city of Fez, see Marçais, *La Berbérie musulmane,* 122–4; *EI*[2] s.v. (Eustache).

130. Presumably the al-Mufaḍḍal b. Jaʿfar b. Sulaymān mentioned by Ṭabarī, III, 43, as a *rāwī* for the accounts of the death of the ʿAbbāsid Ibrāhīm al-Imām b. Muḥammad in 132 (749–50).

[563] al-Ḥusayn's being killed at Fakhkh reached al-ʿUmarī, he being in Medina, he pounced upon al-Ḥusayn's house, and the houses of a group of the members of his family and of others who had joined al-Ḥusayn's rebellion, and had them pulled down. He burnt down their palm groves and appropriated what he did not burn, adding it to the state domains and the confiscated property.[131]

He related: Al-Hādī showed his anger against Mubārak al-Turkī because of what he had heard about Mubārak's shrinking from encountering al-Ḥusayn in battle after he had come within sight of Medina. He ordered Mubārak's goods and property to be confiscated and his demotion to service in the ranks of the grooms of his riding beasts; Mubārak remained in this position till al-Hādī's death. He further showed his ire against Mūsā b. ʿĪsā because he had killed Abū al-Zift al-Ḥasan b. Muḥammad b. ʿAbdallāh and because he had not followed the plan of sending him on as a captive so that he himself (i.e., al-Hādī) might be the arbiter of his fate. He likewise ordered Mūsā's goods and property to be confiscated, and they remained thus sequestrated until Mūsā (al-Hādī) died. The group from among those taken prisoner at Fakhkh was sent forward to Mūsā (al-Hādī), among them being ʿUdhāfir al-Ṣayrafī and ʿAlī b. Sābiq al-Fallās[132] al-Kūfī. He ordered them both to be decapitated and their bodies gibbeted at the Bāb al-Jisr in Baghdad, and this was done.

He related: He (i.e., al-Hādī) sent his mawlā Mahrūyah (or Mahrawayh)[133] (al-Rāzī) to al-Kūfah with orders to treat the people there harshly because some of them had joined the rebellion of al-Ḥusayn.[134]

ʿAlī b. Muḥammad b. Sulaymān b. ʿAbdallāh b. Nawfal b. al-Ḥārith b. ʿAbd al-Muṭṭalib has mentioned that Yūsuf al-Barm,[135] a

---

131. Iṣfahānī, *Maqātil*, 303.

132. Again, in the Cairo text, VIII, 198, we have al-Qallās.

133. Later governor of Ṭabaristān for al-Rashīd, see Ṭabarī, III, 649 (below, 174).

134. The revolt of Medina had in fact been planned in concert with Shīʿī sympathizers in al-Kūfah; see above, 18, n. 70.

135. Presumably, the Yūsuf b. Ibrāhīm al-Barm, also described as a mawlā of Thaqīf, who rebelled in Khurāsān or at Bukhārā in 160 (777) and was subsequently executed. See Yaʿqūbī, *Taʾrīkh*, II, 478–9; Ṭabarī, III, 470–1; W. Barthold, *Turkestan down to the Mongol invasion*, 198; Moscati, "Studi storici sul califatto di al-Mahdī," 331–2; E. Daniel, *The political and social history of Khurasan under Abbasid rule 747–820*, 166–7. His contact with al-Ḥusayn b. ʿAlī must obviously have fallen within the first two years of al-Mahdī's caliphate.

mawlā of the family of al-Ḥasan, whose mother was a freedwoman of Fāṭimah bt. Ḥasan, transmitted the information to him, saying: I was with Ḥusayn at the time when he came to al-Mahdī's court, and the Caliph gave him forty thousand dīnārs. He straightaway divided it up among the people in Baghdad and al-Kūfah, and by God, he left al-Kūfah not possessing a thing to wear except a fur garment without even a shirt beneath it and a loincloth for sleeping in.[136] When he was traveling along the road to Medina and he halted for the night, he had to borrow from his own mawlās sufficient for their subsistence expenses during the coming day.[137]

ʿAlī continued to relate: Abū Bishr al-Sarī,[138] a confederate [*ḥalīf*] of the Banū Zuhrah,[139] transmitted the information to me, saying: I performed the morning worship (or: the morning worship was performed) on the day when al-Ḥusayn b. ʿAlī b. al-Ḥasan, the [564]
protagonist at Fakhkh, began his revolt. Ḥusayn led us in the worship and ascended the pulpit, the Messenger of God's pulpit. He sat down there, wearing a shirt and a white turban which he had unwound and let trail in front and behind himself. His sword was unsheathed, and he had placed it between his legs, when behold, Khālid al-Barbarī and his band of followers approached. When he attempted to enter the mosque, Yaḥyā b. ʿAbdallāh hastened forward to block his way. Al-Barbarī attacked him, whilst I myself was at this very moment watching him, but then Yaḥyā b. ʿAbdallāh rushed forward against him and struck him a blow on the face. He hit his eyes and nose, and cut through his helmet and

136. *Izār al-firāsh.* The phrase "without a loincloth/waist-wrapper" in Ṭabarī, III, 601 (below, 94) would seem to imply that it was the norm to sleep in an *izār*; see also Ṭabarī, III, 668 (below, 202).

137. The Shīʿī sources regard this lavishness and then contentment with penury as signs of al-Ḥusayn's nobility of character and his asceticism, acts of a person for whom "gold, silver and a handful of earth are exactly the same" (Iṣfahānī, *Maqātil,* 294; cf. also Fāsī, 185, and Nahrawālī, 212). In fact, al-Mahdī had given his cousin al-Ḥusayn the money for settling his pressing debts, but because of his lavishness in scattering his new-found wealth, his creditors only received a certain proportion of their due; see Van Arendonck, 62–3. Such actions on al-Ḥusayn's part could well have strained the patience of al-Mahdī and al-Hādī with him to breaking point.

138. This vocalization seems more probable than the text's al-Surrī.

139. Zuhrah b. Kilāb, a clan of the Quraysh al-Biṭāḥ; see Muḥammad b. Ḥabīb, *K. al-Muḥabbar,* 167. Zuhrah was the brother of Quṣayy and father of ʿAbd Manāf. From this clan stemmed the Prophet's mother Āminah bt. Wahb. See al-Muṣʿab al-Zubayrī, *K. Nasab Quraysh,* 257–74; Watt, *Muhammad at Mecca,* 5–8; idem, *EI*[2] s.v. Ḳuraysh.

cap, until I saw the bone of his skull flying in splinters from its place. Yaḥyā likewise attacked Khālid's companions, and they fled in disarray. Then he returned to Ḥusayn, and stood before him with his sword drawn and dripping with blood. Ḥusayn spoke, praising God and eulogizing Him, and he preached to the congregation, saying at the end of his speech, "O people! I am the Messenger of God's offspring, in the Messenger of God's sacred enclosure [*ḥaram*], in the Messenger of God's mosque and seated in the Prophet of God's pulpit! I summon you to the Book of God and the *Sunnah* of His prophet, and if I do not fulfill that for you, then I have no claim upon you for obedience."[140]

He continued to relate: The pilgrims that year were very numerous, and hence had filled the mosque. Suddenly, a man with a handsome face, tall of stature and with a red-dyed cloak,[141] rose up. He took the hand of one of his sons, a handsome, robustly built boy, and then strode through the ranks of assembled people until he reached the pulpit. He went right up to Ḥusayn and said, "O descendant of the Messenger of God, I set out on my journey from a distant land, accompanied by this son of mine, seeking to make the Pilgrimage of God's House and to visit the tomb of His prophet, without it ever occurring to my mind that these events involving you would happen. I have heard what you have said; do you really mean to fulfill what you have taken upon yourself to do?" Al-Ḥusayn replied, "Yes." The man said, "Stretch forth your hand, that I may clasp it in homage to you." He related: He accordingly did homage to al-Ḥusayn, and then he instructed his son, "Draw near and do homage." He related: By God, (later) I saw the
[565] heads of the two of them among all the heads of people at Minā, because it happened that I myself made the Pilgrimage in that year.

140. There is a fuller version of al-Ḥusayn's oration in Iṣfahānī, *Maqātil*, 298–9. The mention to the people of the Imām's obligation to fulfill to the people his side of the *bayʿah* by spreading justice is again characteristic of Zaydī Shīʿī attitudes. See Van Arendonck, 50–1; 135–6, 141, who notes the correspondences here with Muʿtazilī views regarding justice and the state, and Veccia Vaglieri, "Divagazioni su due rivolte Alidi," 332–6, who cites the similarity in themes of al-Ḥusayn's speech to that of Zayd b. ʿAlī b. al-Ḥusayn, Zayn al-ʿĀbidīn, when giving his invitation to the *bayʿah* to himself during his revolt of ca. 122 (740) (cf. Van Arendonck, 30).

141. *Mumashshaq*, "dyed with red ochre or clay," cf. *Glossarium*, p. CDLXXXVI. In earliest Islam, this was used for *iḥrām* garments; see Majd al-Dīn Ibn al-Athīr, *al-Nihāyah fī gharīb al-ḥadīth wa-al-athar*, IV, 334.

He related: A group of the people of al-Madīnah related to me that Mubārak al-Turkī sent a message to Ḥusayn b. ʿAlī, "By God, it would be easier for me to fall from the heavens and then for the birds to snatch me up, or for the wind to carry me along to a remote place, than that I should assault you with military forces or cut off a single hair of your head, but I have to exert myself to the utmost in deeds which must be excused (or: I have to be excused). Hence, fall upon me by night, and I will flee before you." He thereupon gave al-Ḥusayn a covenant and agreement sworn upon God that he would do this. He related: So al-Ḥusayn sent to him, or else al-Ḥusayn went out to him personally with a small force. When they drew near to Mubārak's army, they cried out and uttered *takbīrs,* and Mubārak and his partisans took to flight, until Mubārak himself joined up with Mūsā b. ʿĪsā.

Abū al-Miḍraḥī al-Kilābī has mentioned the following: Al-Mufaḍḍal b. Muḥammad b. al-Mufaḍḍal b. Ḥusayn b. ʿUbaydallāh b. al-ʿAbbās b. ʿAlī b. Abī Ṭālib[142] has related that al-Ḥusayn b. ʿAlī b. Ḥasan b. Ḥasan recited on that day, with reference to a group of people who did not go out with him to battle, although they had promised him previously that they would join him, but who then remained behind, expressing himself in gnomic form,

He who has recourse to the sword will encounter a remarkable opportunity,
(that is), a speedy death, or else he will live to a reasonably mature age.
Do not embark upon an easy affair, for such an affair will only bring about your degradation;
you will never attain glory until you plunge violently into a tough and difficult affair.

Al-Faḍl b. al-ʿAbbās al-Hāshimī has mentioned that ʿAbdallāh b. Muḥammad al-Minqarī[143] transmitted to him the information from his father, who said: ʿĪsā b. Daʾb[144] went into Mūsā b. ʿĪsā's

142. I.e., a descendant of the ʿUbaydallāh b. al-ʿAbbās who had governed Yemen and Azerbaijan for his cousin the Caliph ʿAlī b. Abī Ṭālib.

143. Following *Addenda et emendanda,* p. DCCLX, for this vocalization.

144. I.e., ʿĪsā b. Yazīd b. Daʾb al-Kinānī al-Laythī, resident of Medina and cherished boon-companion of al-Hādī, as appears from the anecdotes concerning him

presence at the time of the latter's return from Fakhkh, and found him in a fearful state, casting around for excuses for the killing of those whom he had slaughtered. ʿĪsā greeted him, "May God guide the Amīr uprightly! May I recite to you some verses which Yazīd b. Muʿāwiyah wrote to the people of Medina, in which he ex-
[566] cused himself for the killing of al-Ḥusayn b. ʿAlī, may God be pleased with him?"[145] He replied, "Go ahead," so he recited to him thus,

O you who ride off early in the morning on your intended journey,
upon a stout she-camel which faces perils in its travelling,
Announce to Quraysh, despite the great distance involved in visiting them,
that between me and al-Ḥusayn lie God and the ties of relationship.
At how many halting-places in the courtyard of the (Holy) House did I adjure him[146]
by the covenant of God, but the conditions of the agreements were not being observed by him!
You have treated harshly your own people, out of excessive pride in your mother (i.e., Fāṭimah, the daughter of the Prophet),
by my life, a virtuous woman,[147] one characterized by family piety, a noble one.
She is a person whose merit no one approaches,
the daughter of the Prophet and of the best of mankind, as they have recognized.
Her merit is accounted a merit for you, and others from yourselves of your people have shares in her merit also.
Indeed, I know, and I hold an opinion like one who knows it firmly
—for an opinion may sometimes express the truth and then become precise and orderly—

---

and the Caliph given by Ṭabarī, III, 589–90, 592–3 (below, 71–72, 76–77); see also Ibn Qutaybah, 537–8.

145. Referring to the killing of the rebel Third Imām of the Shīʿah at Karbalāʾ in 61 (680) by Yazīd's commander ʿUbaydallāh b. Ziyād; see *EI*² s.v. al-Ḥusayn b. ʿAlī b. Abī Ṭālib (Veccia Vaglieri).

146. Following the Cairo text, VIII, 202, *unshuduhu.*

147. Following the Cairo text, loc. cit., *umm*^{un} *ḥaṣān*^{un}.

That the policies which you are at present pursuing will leave you
as corpses, with the eagles and vultures swaggering over you.
O people of ours, do not rekindle the flames of war when they have
died down,
but hold fast to the cords of peace and find security for yourselves!
Do not commit iniquity, for indeed iniquity means a striking-down,
and indeed, the one who drinks from the cup of iniquity becomes sickly and ill.
Those generations who have gone before you have experienced war, [567]
and whole peoples have perished because of it.
So act fairly with your people, and do not go to your destruction
out of haughty pride,
for often a proud person's foot causes him to stumble.[148]

He related: Some of the disquietude which Mūsā b. ʿĪsā felt was thereby dispelled.

ʿAbdallāh b. ʿAbd al-Raḥmān b. ʿĪsā b. Mūsā[149] has mentioned that al-ʿAlāʾ transmitted the information to him that when (the news of) the renunciation of allegiance by the rebels of Fakhkh reached the Commander of the Faithful al-Hādī, he spent that night alone and occupied in writing a letter in his own hand. His mawlās and close companions became perturbed at his shutting himself away, so they got hold of one of his slaves secretly and said, "Go and see what point this matter has reached." He related: The slave went up to Mūsā, and the latter saw him, he asked, "What do you want?" The slave adduced an excuse for his intrusion. He related: Mūsā lowered his glance to the ground and was silent, and then he raised his head towards him and recited,

Those who are not accustomed to travelling by night have gone to
sleep,

148. On Yazīd as a poet—the authenticity of his verses being not, however, altogether certain—see *GAL*, S I, 96, and *GAS*, II, 316–17.

149. As already noted (above, 28, n. 115), a descendant of the ʿAbbāsid prince Mūsā b. ʿIsā present at Fakhkh.

and the one who has not been able to sleep has relieved them of the necessity of setting out at nightfall.

Aḥmad b. Muʿāwiyah b. Bakr al-Bāhilī[150] has mentioned that al-Aṣmaʿī[151] transmitted the information to us and narrated: Muḥammad b. Sulaymān said to ʿAmr b. Abī ʿAmr al-Madanī, on the night preceding the battle of Fakhkh, after he had been shooting arrows in the other's presence at two targets, "Shoot away!" (i.e., at the enemy). He replied, "By God, I won't shoot at the Messenger of God's own offspring; I only came with you to shoot in your presence at the two targets, and not to shoot at the Muslims." He related: Al-Makhzūmī said, "Shoot!" so he let fly. He was eventually to die of leprosy.

He related: When al-Ḥusayn b. ʿAlī was killed and Yaqṭīn b. Mūsā brought in his head, and it was laid before al-Hādī, the latter exclaimed, "By God, it is just as if you had brought me the head of some or other contumacious rebel! (i.e., the head was being hurled down unceremoniously and without any respect for its previous owner). The least way in which I can requite you for this is to deprive you of your (normally due) rewards!" He related: So he deprived Yaqṭīn and his followers in this fashion, and did not give them anything.[152] Mūsā al-Hādī also recited the proverbial verses, when al-Ḥusayn was killed, as follows,

[568] The person who shoots at the (Banū) al-Qārah has only given them their just deserts.
Whenever we encounter a (hostile) group,
We drive back their leading warriors upon the rear ranks.[153]

150. Also mentioned by Ṭabarī, III, 383–4, as a *rāwī* for events in al-Manṣūr's reign.

151. The celebrated philologist and authority on lexicography and ancient poetry. See *GAL*, I², 104, S I, 163–5; *GAS*, VIII, 71–6, IX, 66–7; *EI²* s.v. (B. Lewin).

152. See also Masʿūdī, *Murūj*, VI, 267–8 = ed. Pellat, § 2475; Ibn al-Ṭiqṭaqā, 172–3, tr. 187; Fāsī, 185. Moscati, *Le califat d'al-Hādī*, 13, doubts the authenticity of such stories as this concerning al-Hādī's hesitation and regret over the killing of the ʿAlid rebels, for the accounts elsewhere in Ṭabarī, III, 560, and in other sources about the Caliph's killing in cold blood, among others, captives who had been promised *amān* at Fakhkh, indicate rather a calculated vindictiveness and desire for vengeance.

153. See *Lisān al-ʿArab*¹, VI, 436, and Maydānī, *Majmaʿ amthāl al-ʿArab*, tr.

Various Items of Information

In this year, Maʿyūf b. Yaḥyā (al-Ḥajūrī)[154] led the summer raid (against the Byzantines) by way of the "Monk's Road" [*darb al-rāhib*]. The Byzantines had approached, led by the Patricius,[155] as far as al-Ḥadath.[156] The governor, the garrison troops, and the market traders all fled, and the enemy entered the town. Maʿyūf b. Yaḥyā penetrated into the enemy's territory and reached the town of Ushnah.[157] They then seized captives and prisoners and took plunder.[158]

In this year, Sulaymān b. Abī Jaʿfar al-Manṣūr led the Pilgrimage.[159] ʿUmar b. ʿAbd al-ʿAzīz al-ʿUmarī was governor of Medina; ʿUbaydallāh b. Qutham was over Mecca and Ṭāʾif; Ibrāhīm b. Salm b. Qutaybah[160] was over Yemen; Suwayd b. Abī Suwayd, the Khurāsānian commander, was over al-Yamāmah and al-Baḥrayn; and al-Ḥasan b. Nasīm (?)[161] al-Ḥawārī was over ʿUmān. Mūsā b.

G. W. Freytag, II, 257, for these proverbial verses and the occasion when they were allegedly uttered. The Qārah are said here to have been a group of archers or a component clan of the Banū Kinānah in the Jāhiliyyah, but established in Yemen under Islam and attached to the Banū Asad.

154. This commander had led summer raids into Anatolia in 153 (770) and 158 (775), and was to lead a punitive expedition against the rebellious people of Cyprus in 191 (806); see Ṭabarī, III, 371, 385, 711 (below, 265).

155. *Baṭrīq, biṭrīq,* the Arabized form of the Byzantine title Patricius. See Fraenkel, 279; Ahmed Hebbo, *Die Fremdwörter in der arabischen Prophetenbiographie des Ibn Hischam (gest. 218/834)*, 47–8.

156. The town and fortress, now disappeared, of the Greek Adata, on the Taurus frontier between Marʿash and Malaṭya, where an important pass, the Darb al-Ḥadath, led into the Byzantine lands. See Yāqūt, *Muʿjam,* II, 227–9; Le Strange, *Palestine under the Moslems,* 443–4; idem, *Lands,* E. Honigmann, *Die Ostgrenze des Byzantinischen Reiches von 363 bis 1071,* index s.v.; Canard, 269–70; *EI*[2] s.v. (S. Ory).

157. Honigmann, 141: ? Ūshīn, Ōshēn.

158. Khalīfah, *Taʾrīkh,* II, 704; Balādhurī, *Futūḥ al-buldān,* 190–1; Ibn al-Athīr, VI, 94; E. W. Brooks, "Byzantines and Arabs in the time of the early Abbasids," *EHR,* XV (1900), 740; Moscati, *Le califat d'al-Hādī,* 14–15.

159. Khalīfah, *Taʾrīkh,* II, 704; Muḥammad b. Ḥabīb, 37; Yaʿqūbī, *Taʾrīkh,* II, 491; Azdī, 259.

160. Grandson of the great Umayyad governor of the East Qutaybah b. Muslim al-Bāhilī, both he and his brother Saʿīd being in high favor with al-Hādī (see Ṭabarī, III, 580–1, 587, and below, 59, 68); the family thus successfully made the transition from being servants of the Umayyads to intimates of the ʿAbbāsids. See Crone, 136–8; Kennedy, 83.

161. Thus, in Ibn al-Athīr, VI, 94; the text has ". . . b. Tasnīm."

ʿĪsā was in charge of the leading of the worship at al-Kūfah and over the local security forces [*aḥdāth*][162] and the poor-tax, as well as of Bihqubādh al-Asfal.[163] At al-Baṣrah, Muḥammad b. Sulaymān was in charge of the leading of the worship and the *aḥdāth* there, whilst ʿUmar b. ʿUthmān functioned as judge. Al-Hādī's mawlā al-Ḥajjāj[164] was governor of Jurjān; Ziyād b. Ḥassān was over Qūmis; Ṣāliḥ b. Shaykh b. ʿUmayrah al-Asadī was over Ṭabaristān and al-Rūyān; and al-Hādī's mawlā Ṭayfūr[165] was over Iṣfahān.[166]

---

162. The context would seem to require a sense like that of "local militia, police corps" for this much-discussed, but still mysterious, term. See F. Løkkegaard, *Islamic taxation in the classic period*, 187–8 (the *EI*² art. s.v. by Cl. Cahen deals only with the *aḥdāth* of a later period).

163. "Lower" Bihqubādh comprised the district around al-Kūfah, where the Euphrates enters the Baṭā'iḥ or Great Swamp. See Yāqūt, *Muʿjam*, I, 516; Le Strange, Lands, 81; A. Musil, *The middle Euphrates*, 274–5; Morony, 147–51.

164. See Crone, 191.

165. See ibid., 195.

166. Khalīfah, *Ta'rīkh*, II, 706–7; Ibn al-Athīr, VI, 94–5.

The Events of the Year 170

(July 3, 786–June 21, 787)

The events taking place during this year included the death of Yazīd b. Ḥātim (al-Muhallabī) in Ifrīqiyah; after him, Rawḥ b. Ḥātim became governor over it.[167] [569]

In this year, ʿAbdallāh b. Marwān b. Muḥammad[168] died in the Maṭbaq (or Muṭbaq) prison.[169]

In this year, Mūsā al-Hādī died at ʿĪsābādh. There are varying reports concerning the reason for his death. Some say that he died of an abdominal ulcer.[170] Others say that his death was at the hands of some slave girls belonging to his mother al-Khayzurān,

---

167. The governorship of North Africa was a Muhallabid fief at this time; see Crone, 134–5, and Kennedy, 83. But according to Yaʿqūbī, *Taʾrīkh*, II, 496, and Ibn al-Athīr, VI, 108, 113–14, Yazīd was briefly succeeded by his son Dāwūd, whose misrule, however, provoked a rebellion of the local Ibāḍiyyah, so that Hārūn al-Rashīd replaced him after nine months by his uncle Rawḥ.

168. One of the few surviving Umayyad princes, son of the last Umayyad Caliph Marwān II b. Muḥammad, imprisoned by al-Mahdī (Ṭabarī, III, 485).

169. The prison in the Round City of al-Manṣūr. See Yaʿqūbī, *Buldān*, 240, tr. 15–16; Le Strange, *Baghdad*, 27; Lassner, *Topography*, 55, 243.

170. Ibn al-Athīr, VI, 99.

whom she had ordered to kill al-Hādī for various reasons, some of which we shall now mention.[171]

The Reason Why al-Khayzurān Had Ordered the Slave Girls to Kill al-Hādī

Yaḥyā b. al-Ḥasan[172] has mentioned that when al-Hādī became Caliph, he became openly hostile towards and quarreled with his mother. Khāliṣah (i.e., al-Khayzurān's slave girl) came to him one day and told him, "Your mother seeks a gift of clothing from you," so he ordered a storehouse full of clothing to be given to her. He related: There were found in al-Khayzurān's house (after her death) among her possessions eighteen thousand sleeveless robes [*qarāqir*[173]] of figured silk. He related: At the opening of Mūsā's caliphate, al-Khayzurān used to exercise her authority over him in all his affairs without consulting him at all, and she used to behave in regard to him, by assuming sole control over matters of ordaining and forbidding, just as she had done previously with his father (i.e., al-Mahdī). Hence, al-Hādī sent a message to her, "Do not step beyond the boundaries of a woman's traditional modest position into demeaning yourself by being careless with your honor. It is not dignified for women that they should involve themselves in affairs of state. Instead, stick to your performance of the worship, to recounting God's praises, and to devoting yourself to pious works for God. Then after that, be conformable to the female role which is incumbent upon you." He related: During Mūsā's caliphate, al-Khayzurān used frequently to bombard him with requests for favors, and he used to grant whatever she asked. This went on for

---

171. See Abbott, 111–12; Moscati, *Le califat d'al-Hādī*, 23. It is possible that both the illness and the murder were involved here. Thus, the *K. al-ʿUyūn*, 288–9, states that al-Khayzurān's slave girls suffocated al-Hādī in the harem because al-Khayzurān feared that he was going to recover from his sickness. Certainly, his death appears as too opportune for so many people concerned that it should have been a natural one. Also, the touching story in Masʿūdī, *Murūj*, VI, 282–3 = ed. Pellat, § 2486, of al-Hādī's sickbed death holding his mother's hand to his heart and commending Hārūn as his successor seems highly improbable, perhaps the invention of a later tradition favorable to al-Hādī.

172. I.e., Yaḥyā b. al-Ḥasan b. ʿAbd al-Khāliq, frequently cited as a *rāwī* and described in Ṭabarī, III, 322, as the maternal uncle of al-Faḍl b. al-Rabīʿ.

173. Sing. *qarqar.* See *Glossarium*, p. CDXXII (< Latin *caracalla*); R. B. Serjeant, *Islamic textiles. Material for a history up to the Mongol conquest*, 93–4.

four months of his caliphate, and people thronged round her, seeking her aid, and processions of people used to resort to her door. [570]

He related: One day, al-Khayzurān spoke to him about a matter concerning which he saw no way to satisfy her. He made an appropriate excuse, but she exclaimed, "You must satisfy my request without fail!" He replied, "I won't do it!" She expostulated, "But I've already promised this unreservedly to ʿAbdallāh b. Mālik." He related: Mūsā became enraged and said, "Woe upon the son of a whore! I have already realized that he is the person behind this request, but by God, I won't grant you it!" She retorted, "In that case, by God, I'll never ask anything of you again!" He said, "By God, in that case, I don't care a bit!" and he grew hot and enraged. Al-Khayzurān got up to go, equally angry, but he ordered her, "Stay where you are, and take good note of my words! (I swear) by God, on pain of forfeiting my status as a kinsman of the Messenger of God if I do not fulfill this oath, that if ever I hear about any of my commanders or any of my close courtiers or servants standing at your door, I shall certainly have their heads chopped off and their possessions confiscated. Let whoever will, follow that course! What are all these processions of suppliants which come each day, by morning and evening, to your door? Have you no spindle to keep you busy, or copy of the Qurʾān to remind you (of God) or house to keep you safe (from the public gaze)? Beware, and again beware, lest you open your door, whether to any Muslim or to any Dhimmī!" So she went off, hardly conscious where she was stepping; and after this, she never again uttered in his presence a single word (literally, either a sweet or a bitter word).[174]

Yaḥyā b. al-Ḥasan related that his father transmitted the information to him, saying: I heard Khāliṣah telling al-ʿAbbās b. al-Faḍl b. al-Rabīʿ[175] that Mūsā sent to his mother al-Khayzurān a dish of rice, saying, "I found this tasty and accordingly ate some of it; so you have some too!" Khāliṣah related: But I said to her, "Don't

---

174. Ibrāhīm b. Muḥammad al-Bayhaqī, *K. al-Maḥāsin wa-al-masāwī,* ed. Schwally, 591 = ed. Ibrāhīm, II, 365–6; Masʿūdī, *Murūj,* VI, 269–70 = ed. Pellat, § 2477; Ṭabarī-Balʿamī, tr. IV, 453–4; *K. al-ʿUyūn,* 283–4; Ibn al-Athīr, VI, 99–100; Ibn al-Ṭiqṭaqā, 173, tr. 187–8; Abbott, 89–92.

175. Son of the subsequent vizier, who seems to have acted as an assistant to his father when the latter was chamberlain (Sourdel, *Vizirat,* I, 154, 190–1) and who is cited as a *rāwī* by Ṭabarī on three or four occasions, e.g., III, 682 (below, 222).

touch it until you investigate further, for I am afraid that it might contain something to your detriment." So they brought in a dog; it ate some and fell down dead. Mūsā sent to al-Khayzurān afterwards and said, "How did you like the dish of rice?" She replied, "I enjoyed it very much." He said, "You can't have eaten it, because if you had, I would have been rid of you. When was any Caliph ever
[571] happy who had a mother (still alive)?"

He related: A certain man of the Hāshimites transmitted the information to me that the cause of al-Hādī's death was that when the latter directed his efforts at depriving Hārūn (of his succession rights as next heir) and at having allegiance done to his own son Ja'far[177] (as heir instead of Hārūn), and when al-Khayzurān became fearful for Hārūn's safety at al-Hādī's hands, she secretly despatched at the time of al-Hādī's illness some of her slave girls to kill him by covering over (his mouth and nose) and sitting on his face (i.e., thus suffocating him). She sent to Yaḥyā b. Khālid the message that "The man has died, so act decisively in what you have to do and don't fall short in the appropriate measures!"[178]

Muḥammad b. 'Abd al-Raḥmān b. Bashshār has mentioned that al-Faḍl b. Sa'īd[179] transmitted the information to him from his father, saying: Mūsā kept receiving information about his commanders' resorting to his mother al-Khayzurān, these persons hoping by speaking with her thereby to have their various requests fulfilled by the Caliph. He related: She, for her part, was aiming at securing an ascendancy over his affairs just as she had enjoyed over al-Mahdī's affairs. Al-Hādī kept barring her from achieving this and would say, "What have women to do with the discussing of men's affairs?" When he began to find excessive the number of his commanders who were resorting to his mother, he gathered the commanders together one day and said to them, "Who is better, I

---

176. Bayhaqī, *Maḥāsin*, ed. Schwally, 591–2 = ed. Ibrāhīm, II, 366; Ṭabarī-Bal'amī, tr. IV, 454–5; *K. al-'Uyūn*, 289; Ibn al-Athīr, VI, 100; Ibn al-Ṭiqṭaqā, 173, tr. 188; Abbott, 104.

177. Apparently al-Hādī's son by a slave concubine called Raḥīm. As noted by Ṭabarī, III, 577–8 (below, 55), Hārūn subsequently married his daughter Ḥamdūnah to Ja'far; see Abbott, 66, 157.

178. Jahshiyārī, 132–3; Ṭabarī-Bal'amī, tr. IV, 455; Ibn al-Athīr, loc. cit.; Abbott, 109.

179. Possibly a son of Sa'īd b. Salm b. Qutaybah, on whom see Ṭabarī, III, 580–1 (below, 59).

or you?" They replied, "Certainly, you are, O Commander of the Faithful!" He said, "Who then is better, my mother or your mothers?" They replied, "Assuredly, your mother, O Commander of the Faithful!" He continued, "Which then of you would like to have men talking about his mother's affairs, saying 'So-and so's mother did this, and so-and-so's mother acted in this way, and so-and-so's mother said this'?" They replied, "None of us would like that." He said, "So what do you think about the men who keep coming to my mother and who subsequently make her affairs the subject of their conversations?" When they heard this, they ceased their visits to her completely. Al-Khayzurān was deeply mortified by that; she kept away from him and swore that she would never speak to him again. Thereafter, she never entered his presence until death came upon him.[180]

The reason why Mūsā al-Hādī wished to deprive his brother Hārūn of the succession, to the point that he brought force to bear on the latter and exerted himself strongly (in applying this pressure), according to what Ṣāliḥ b. Sulaymān has mentioned, was that al-Hādī, when the caliphate passed to him, confirmed Yaḥyā b. Khālid (b. Barmak) in the administration of the Western lands which Hārūn was governing (nominally). Al-Hādī then had the idea of depriving Hārūn al-Rashīd of the succession and of securing homage as successor for his own son Jaʿfar b. Mūsā al-Hādī, and [572]
the commanders, including Yazīd b. Mazyad (al-Shaybānī),[181] ʿAbdallāh b. Mālik, ʿAlī b. ʿĪsā (b. Māhān) and their likes, followed his lead (or: assisted him) in that.[182] Hence they removed Hārūn from

180. Ṭabarī-Balʿamī, tr. IV, 454; Ibn al-Athīr, loc. cit.; Abbott, 91–2.

181. Nephew of the famous late Umayyad and early ʿAbbāsid general Maʿn b. Zāʾidah, al-Hādī and al-Rashīd employed him as governor of Armenia and Azerbaijan till his death in 183 (799). With this power base in the eastern Caucasus region, Yazīd's sons established the local dynasty in Shirwān of the Shirwān-Shāhs, who endured until the early Seljuq period. See Minorsky, *A history of Sharvān and Darband in the 10th–11th centuries*, passim; Madelung, in *Cambridge history of Iran*, IV, 243–9; Crone, 169–70; Kennedy, 84–5.

182. See Abbott, 96; Kennedy, 110–11. Yaʿqūbī, *Taʾrīkh*, II, 489–90, states that the commander of the Azd, Abū Hurayrah Muḥammad b. Farrūkh al-Azdī (who was governor of al-Jazīrah but was executed by Hārūn in 171 [787–8], see Ṭabarī, III, 606, below, 102), was active in denigrating Hārūn (hence, doubtless, his speedy fate when Hārūn secured the throne) and was sent by al-Hādī to al-Jazīrah, Syria, Egypt, and the West with an army to terrorize people into assenting to Hārūn's removal

the succession and did homage to Jaʿfar b. Mūsā. They spoke surreptitiously to the "party" [*al-shīʿah*] (sc. of the ʿAbbāsid dynasty's supporters),[183] so that these last talked about Hārūn's position and spoke slightingly of him in the public sessions at court, saying, "We won't accept him!" Their whole plan became complicated and difficult, until it became clear, and al-Hādī ordered that no escort should go before Hārūn with a spear.[184] As a result, the people (at court) avoided him and left him by himself, to the point that no one would dare even to greet him or to approach his presence. Yaḥyā b. Khālid used to take charge of arrangements for al-Rāshid's lodging and subsistence expenses, and he and his sons used never to leave him, according to what has been mentioned.[185]

Ṣāliḥ (b. Sulaymān) related: Ismāʿīl b. Ṣubayḥ (al-Ḥarrānī)[186] was Yaḥyā b. Khālid's secretary, and Yaḥyā wanted very much to get him installed in a position from which he could pass back to Yaḥyā information about what was going on. Ibrāhīm (b. Dhakwān) al-Ḥarrānī[187] held the position of vizier to Mūsā, and he now took Ismāʿīl into his service as secretary. This appointment was reported to al-Hādī, but news of this fact reached Yaḥyā b. Khālid, so he ordered Ismāʿīl to set off for Ḥarrān;[188] Ismāʿīl accordingly

---

from the succession; cf. Jahshiyārī, 132, and Moscati, *Le califat d'al-Hādī,* 19. However, according to an account from al-Hādī's personal physician, ʿAbdallāh al-Ṭayfūrī, Harthamah b. Aʿyan, alone among the great commanders, condemned al-Hādī's plan to deprive Hārūn of the succession and dissuaded him. See Ibn Abī Uṣaybiʿah, *ʿUyūn al-anbāʾ*, I, 154–5; Abbott, 105–6.

183. *Al-Shīʿah,* or phrases like *Abnāʾ al-Shīʿah,* occurs frequently in Ṭabarī and other sources as a designation for the Abnāʾ al-Dawlah, originally the Arabs of Khurāsān plus some Iranians who had spearheaded the ʿAbbāsid Revolution and were now largely resident in Baghdad. See Ayalon, *The military reforms of Caliph al-Muʿtaṣim,* 4 ff.; Crone, 66.

184. On ceremonial occasions, it was the custom for the ruler (or here, his designated heir) to be preceded by the commander of the police guard [*ṣāḥib al-shurṭah*] with his lance or spear held erect as a symbol of authority. See Sourdel, "Questions de cérémoniale ʿabbaside," 144–5.

185. *K. al-ʿUyūn,* 285.

186. Secretary, originally from the community of Sabians at Ḥarrān, who later served Hārūn and al-Amīn as a leading chancery official; see Sourdel, *Vizirat,* I, 122, 190.

187. Also from Ḥarrān, originally a mawlā of al-Manṣūr, and treasurer for al-Hādī, but not apparently acting as vizier in the full sense of the word. See Khalīfah, *Taʾrīkh,* II, 709; Masʿūdī, *Tanbīh,* 344, tr. Carra de Vaux, 442–3; Moscati, *Le califat d'al Hādī,* 17–18; Abbott, 86, 92–4; Sourdel, *Vizirat,* I, 121–4.

188. A town of northern Syria, classical Carrhae. See Yāqūt, *Muʿjam,* II, 235–6; Le Strange, *Lands,* 103; Canard, 93–4; *EI*[2] s.v. (G. Fehérvári).

departed thither. Some months later, al-Hādī asked Ibrāhīm al-Ḥarrānī, "Who is acting as your secretary?" He replied, "So-and-so is acting as secretary," giving his name. Al-Hādī commented, "Didn't I receive a report that Ismāʿīl b. Ṣubayḥ was acting as your secretary?" Ibrāhīm replied, "(That must have been) a false report, O Commander of the Faithful; Ismāʿīl is in Ḥarrān!"[189]

He related: Slanderous reports were passed on to al-Hādī about Yaḥyā b. Khālid, and al-Hādī was told, "There are no real grounds of difference between you and Hārūn, it is merely that Yaḥyā b. Khālid is exercising a bad influence on him; so send for Yaḥyā, threaten him with death and accuse him of ingratitude." All that accordingly stirred up Mūsā al-Hādī's anger against Yaḥyā b. Khālid.

Abū Ḥafṣ al-Kirmānī[190] has mentioned that Muḥammad b. Yaḥyā b. Khālid (al-Barmakī) transmitted the information to him, saying: Al-Hādī sent to Yaḥyā by night. Yaḥyā despaired therefore of his life; he said farewell to his family, he anointed himself with the aromatic substances used in preparing corpses for burial, he put on new clothes, and he did not doubt that al-Hādī was going to put him to death. When Yaḥyā was brought into the Caliph's presence, the latter said, "O Yaḥyā, what is the relationship between us?" Yaḥyā replied, "I am your slave, O Commander of the Faithful, and the only possible relationship which there can be between the slave and his master is one of obedience towards him." The Caliph said, "Why, then, are you coming between me and my brother, and [573]
are influencing him unfavorably against me?" He replied, "O Commander of the Faithful, who am I that I should presume to come between the two of you? It is merely that al-Mahdī appointed me to accompany him, and ordered me to look after him and his needs, so I undertook this in accordance with his command. Then you yourself ordered me to do that, and I fulfilled your command." The Caliph said, "What exactly has Hārūn been up to?" Yaḥyā replied, "He hasn't been up to anything, and it is not in his character or capability to do anything untoward." He related: al-Hādī's wrath thereupon subsided.[191]

---

189. Jahshiyārī, 126–7; Abbott, 96; Sourdel, *Vizirat*, I, 122.

190. Presumably, the al-Kirmānī mentioned by Jahshiyārī, 208, as one of his *rāwīs*.

191. *K. al-ʿUyūn*, 285–6; Ibn al-Athīr, VI, 96.

Hārūn personally had reconciled himself to being deprived of his succession rights, but Yaḥyā said to him, "Don't behave thus!" Hārūn replied, "Won't it leave me in a contented state of mind and a healthy physical state? These two things will be sufficient for me, and I shall live (peacefully) with my paternal uncle's daughter (i.e., with Zubaydah)—Hārūn was passionately enamored of Umm Jaʿfar—but Yaḥyā said to him, "What is that in comparison with the dignity of the caliphate? It may well be that this (happiness of life) will not be left open for you, to the point that it will elude you altogether!" and he stopped him from responding (to al-Hādī's pressures).[192]

Al-Kirmānī related that Ṣāliḥ b. Sulaymān transmitted the information to him, saying: "Al-Hādī sent to Yaḥyā b. Khālid by night when he was at ʿĪsābādh. This summons filled Yaḥyā with fear. He went into the private presence of the Caliph, and was then instructed to search out a man whom the Caliph had rendered fearful (or: whom the Caliph had become suspicious about), so that he had disappeared from the Caliph's sight; al-Hādī was now wanting to take him as a boon-companion and prevent him from continuing in his friendly relationship with Hārūn. The Caliph now treated Yaḥyā as a favored companion, and Yaḥyā spoke with the Caliph about the man. Al-Hādī then gave the man a guarantee of personal security and gave Yaḥyā a red, ruby ring which was on his own hand, saying, "This is (a token of) the guarantee of security for the man."[193] Yaḥyā went away; he sought out the man, and brought him to al-Hādī. At this, the Caliph rejoiced greatly. He related: Several people have transmitted to me the information that the person whom the Caliph was seeking was Ibrāhīm al-Mawṣilī.[194]

Ṣāliḥ b. Sulaymān related: Al-Hādī said to al-Rabīʿ one day, "Don't let Yaḥyā b. Khālid enter except at the end of everybody else." He related: So al-Rabīʿ sent to Yaḥyā, and he devoted his

192. Jahshiyārī, 128; *K. al-ʿUyūn*, 286; Ibn al-Athīr, VI, 96–7.

193. Following *Addenda et emendanda*, p. DCCLX, *hādhā amānuhu*.

194. I.e., Ibrāhīm b. Māhān or Maymūn, father of Isḥāq al-Mawṣilī and famous musician and composer, in great demand at the courts of al-Mahdī, al-Hādī and al-Rashīd, died in 188 (804). See Iṣfahānī, *Aghānī*, ed. Būlāq, V, 2–48 = ed. Cairo, V, 154–258; H. G. Farmer, *A history of Arabian music to the XIIIth century*, 116–17; *GAS*, I, 370; *EI*[2] s.v. (J. W. Fück).

undivided attention to him.[195] He related: When al-Hādī held court the next morning, he gave permission (for suppliants and others to come forward), until the point arrived when there were none of these remaining. Yaḥyā came into his presence, the Caliph having around him (from among his permanent entourage of courtiers) ʿAbd al-Ṣamad b. ʿAlī,[196] al-ʿAbbās b. Muḥammad, and the senior members of his own family, together with his commanders. Al-Hādī kept summoning Yaḥyā to draw near to him until he made him sit directly before him, and he said to Yaḥyā, "I have been wronging you and branding you as one who has denied God's favors, but please absolve me now from this." Those present were astonished at the Caliph's show of honor towards him and his [574] words. Yaḥyā kissed his hand and gave thanks to him,[197] and al-Hādī then said to him, "Who is it who says concerning you, O Yaḥyā,

If a miser were to touch Yaḥyā's palm,
his mind would glow with a feeling of generosity for the lavishing of gifts?"

Yaḥyā replied, "That is your generous palm, O Commander of the Faithful, not that of your slave."

He related: When al-Hādī spoke to Yaḥyā about depriving Hārūn of the succession, Yaḥyā said to him, "O Commander of the Faithful, if you urge the people to break their oaths, they will come to regard their oaths lightly; but if you leave them to retain their oath of allegiance to your brother, and then make Jaʿfar the designated heir after Hārūn, that will make Jaʿfar's position as designated heir all the firmer." The Caliph replied, "You have spoken truly and

---

195. Following the text here and that of Cairo, VIII, 209, *tafarragha lahu*; but the Leiden editor also suggests, n. *d*, the possible reading *tafazzaʿa lahu* "he pretended to seek his aid"; cf. for this meaning, Ṭabarī, III, 333, and *Glossarium*, p. CDII.

196. The youngest paternal uncle of al-Saffāḥ and al-Manṣūr, died in 185 (801–2); hence, one of the *ʿumūmah*. Having been involved in the revolt against al-Manṣūr of the latter's discontented uncle ʿAbdallāh b. ʿAlī (ʿAbd al-Ṣamad's elder brother) in 137 (754), he was not allowed thereafter to play any outstanding role in affairs. See Ibn Qutaybah, 374; Kennedy, 53, 59–60.

197. A person summoned to the Caliph's presence normally halted at the edge of the ruler's personal carpet [*bisāṭ, muṣallā*] and then kissed his hands (and possibly feet; see Ṭabarī, III, 509, *jathā bayna yadayhi*); see Sourdel, "Questions de cérémoniale ʿabbaside," 137–8.

have given good advice, and this will be a sound plan of action for me."[198]

Al-Kirmānī related, that Khuzaymah b. ʿAbdallāh also transmitted the information to him, saying: Al-Hādī ordered Yaḥyā b. Khālid to be imprisoned because of the course of action which Yaḥyā had endeavored to make him adopt over al-Rashīd's being deprived of the succession to the caliphate. Yaḥyā, however, sent a message to the Caliph containing these words, "I have some good advice," so the Caliph sent for him. Yaḥyā said, "O Commander of the Faithful, permit me to speak to you alone," so the Caliph took him in privately with himself. Yaḥyā continued, "O Commander of the Faithful, do you think that, if that momentous event (i.e., al-Hādī's own death)—and I pray God that we may never live to see it and that He may bring forward our own demise before that occurs!—takes place, do you really imagine that the leading figures in the state [*al-nās*] will hand over the caliphate to Jaʿfar, when he has not yet reached the age of puberty, and be satisfied with him as leader in their worship, in the Pilgrimage, and in military expeditions?" He replied, "By God, I don't imagine that they would." Yaḥyā continued, "O Commander of the Faithful, are you, moreover, sure that your own family and prominent members of it, like so-and-so and so-and-so, will not aspire to the caliphate, and that others may not have designs on it, with the result that the office might become diverted from the offspring of your father?" Al-Hādī replied to him, "You have made me alert to all that, O Yaḥyā!" He related: Yaḥyā used to say, "I never spoke with any Caliph who was more intelligent than Mūsā." He related: Yaḥyā further told him, "If it had not been for the fact that this affair (i.e., the succession to the caliphate) had already been settled on your brother, would it not have been necessary for you yourself to designate him (sc. Hārūn) as successor in the rule? How then can you contemplate removing him from the succession, when al-Mahdī appointed
[575] him to it? It is my opinion, O Commander of the Faithful, that the best course is to confirm this arrangement as it now stands. Then when Jaʿfar reaches puberty—and may God bring him to this

198. Jahshiyārī, 128; Azdī, 260; Ibn al-Athīr, VI, 96–7; Palmer, 33–4; Abbott, 94; Moscati, *Le califat d'al Hādī*, 19.

stage!—you can bring al-Rashīd into his presence, and al-Rashīd will renounce his succession rights in his favor and be the first to swear allegiance and to clasp his hand." He then related: Al-Hādī accepted his arguments and his judgement, and ordered his release.[199]

Al-Mawṣilī[200] has mentioned, from Muḥammad b. Yaḥyā (b. Khālid al-Barmakī), who said: Al-Hādī (nevertheless) resolved on depriving Hārūn of the succession after my father's words with him. A group of his mawlās and commanders urged him on to this course of action, whether Hārūn agreed to his own deprivation or not. Al-Hādī's anger against Hārūn grew more intense, and he put more and more pressure on him. Yaḥyā said to Hārūn, "Ask the Caliph for permission to go off hunting, and when you go forth, keep yourself far away and put off the days (of your return)." So Hārūn sent in a request, seeking permission to depart, and the Caliph gave his permission. Hārūn journeyed to Qaṣr Muqātil[201] and stayed there for forty days, until al-Hādī began to show disapproval of Hārūn's actions, and his keeping away caused al-Hādī disquiet. He began writing to him and telling him to come back,[202] but Hārūn made excuses (for not returning), until the affair assumed serious proportions. Al-Hādī began to abuse Hārūn, and his

199. Jahshiyārī, 128–9; Masʿūdī, *Murūj*, VI, 280–1 = ed. Pellat, § 2485; Palmer, loc. cit.; Abbott, 94–5; Moscati, *Le califat d'al Hādī*, 19–20. Yaʿqūbī, *Taʾrīkh*, II, 590, and a later author on the history of the Barmakīs, ʿAbd al-Jalīl al-Yazdī, in his *Taʾrīkh-i āl-i Barmak*, state that both Yaḥyā and Hārūn were nevertheless imprisoned (Masʿūdī, *Murūj*, loc. cit.: Yaḥyā only) and only saved from execution by al-Hādī's own death. A later account in Ṭabarī, III, 599–600 (below, 92), places both Yaḥyā and Hārūn in jail and on the point of execution when al-Hādī conveniently died. Finally, an account in the *K. al-ʿUyūn*, 286–8, states that al-Hādī ordered Harthamah b. Aʿyan to kill Yaḥyā secretly during the night, but Harthamah feared that al-Hādī would then kill him in order to conceal all knowledge of the murder; he was saved from his dilemma by al-Hādī's death during the night.

200. I.e., Isḥāq b. Ibrāhīm, the celebrated poet, musician and singer, died in 235 (850). See Farmer, 124–6; *GAS*, I, 371, II, 578; *EI*² s.v. (Fück).

201. According to Yāqūt, *Muʿjam*, IV, 364, a place out in the Samāwah or desert between the Euphrates and Syria, beyond ʿAyn al-Tamr to the south of Hīt, originally built by one Muqātil b. Ḥassān of the Banū Imruʾ al-Qays b. Zayd Manāt (thus in Balādhurī, *Futūḥ*, 282) and restored by the ʿAbbāsid prince ʿĪsā b. ʿAlī b. ʿAbdallāh, Hārūn's great-great-uncle. Ibn al-Athīr, VI, 97 and elsewhere, inserts *Banī* before the name *Muqātil*.

202. *Yaṣrifuhu*, perhaps with the additional nuance, from the idea of "embellishing speech" [*ṣarf al-kalām*], of "cajoling, trying to persuade by fair words."

mawlās and commanders made slanderous talk about him. At this particular moment, al-Faḍl b. Yaḥyā was acting as the representative of his father and al-Rashīd at the caliphal court; he kept sending reports of all this to Hārūn, so that the latter then returned, the whole affair having become prolonged.[203]

Al-Kirmānī related that Yazīd, the mawlā of Yaḥyā b. Khālid, transmitted the information to him, saying: Al-Khayzurān sent ʿĀtikah, who had been a wet nurse for Hārūn, to Yaḥyā. She tore at the neck opening of her gown in his presence, all the while weeping to him and saying, "The lady (i.e., al-Khayzurān) says to you, 'I beseech you by God to have regard for my son's interests! Don't bring about his death, just let him agree to what his brother demands and seeks from him, for his preservation is more dear to me than this present world and everything in it!'" He related: Yaḥyā cried out to her and told her, "What do you know about this? If it is as you say (i.e., that my advice is likely to bring about Hārūn's death), then I, my children and my family will all be killed before Hārūn, and even if I am held in suspicion (by al-Khayzurān) on account of him, I cannot be held in suspicion on account of my own self and my family."[204]

[576] He related: When al-Hādī saw that Yaḥyā b. Khālid was not going to go back on what he had undertaken to do for Hārūn, despite his lavishing on him marks of honor, grants of land, and presents, he sent a messenger to Yaḥyā threatening him with death unless he renounced this course of action. He related: This state of fearfulness and sense of danger continued unremittingly. Yaḥyā's mother died whilst he was in the Khuld Palace[205] at Baghdad, because Hārūn used to live there, accompanied by Yaḥyā, whilst he was heir to the succession, staying in his residence and constantly in contact with him night and day.

Muḥammad b. al-Qāsim b. al-Rabīʿ[206] has mentioned that Mu-

203. Masʿūdī, *Murūj*, VI, 281–2 = ed. Pellat, § 2486; Ibn al-Athīr, VI, 97–8; Bouvat, 46 n. 1; Moscati, *Le califat d'al-Hādī*, 20.

204. Abbott, 104–5.

205. The palace on the west bank of the Tigris and to the northeast of the Round City, built by al-Manṣūr, who took up residence there in 158 (775). See Le Strange, *Baghdad*, 101–5; Lassner, *Topography*, 55, 149.

206. Presumably a grandson of the minister al-Rabīʿ b. Yūnus, on whom see Ṭabarī, III, 545 (above, 3, and n. 3).

ḥammad b. ʿAmr al-Rūmī transmitted the information to him from his father,[207] saying: After he had achieved royal power and in the opening days of his caliphate, Mūsā al-Hādī held a court session of his intimates [*julūs khāṣṣ*].[208] He summoned Ibrāhīm b. Jaʿfar b. Abī Jaʿfar,[209] Ibrāhīm b. Salm b. Qutaybah and (Ibrāhīm b. Dhakwān) al-Ḥarrānī. These last took their places on his left hand, together with one of al-Hādī's black eunuchs who had the name of Aslam and the patronymic of Abū Sulaymān; al-Hādī used to repose great confidence in him and put him forward into a prominent place. Whilst the Caliph was in this situation, behold, the *ṣāḥib al-muṣallā* Ṣāliḥ[210] came in and announced the arrival of Hārūn b. al-Mahdī. Al-Hādī said, "Allow him to come in." So Hārūn entered, greeted the Caliph, kissed his hand, and took his seat on al-Hādī's right, but at some distance and at one side. Mūsā lowered his gaze and was silent, whilst regarding him, and he remained thus for a while. Then he turned to him and said, "O Hārūn, it appears to me that you are dwelling too lengthily on the fulfillment of the dream[211] and are hoping for something which is beyond your reach; but before that can come to pass, you will have to strip the spiny leaves from the tragacanth bush's branches.[212] Do you really hope for the caliphate?"

He related: Hārūn knelt on both knees and answered, "O Mūsā, if you act haughtily, you will be abased; if you show humility, you will be exalted in rank; and if you act oppressively, you will be

207. ʿAmr al-Rūmī was a freedman of al-Hādī, who was in charge of the laying out of a new settlement, called Madīnat Mūsā, which the Caliph laid out opposite Qazwīn when he journeyed to Rayy; see Balādhurī, *Futūḥ*, 323.

208. On the distinction between, and different conventions for, public and intimate court sessions, see Sourdel, "Questions de cérémonial ʿabbaside," 136.

209. I.e., Zubaydah's brother and first cousin of al-Hādī; see Ibn Qutaybah, 379.

210. The *muṣallā* here seems to have been the prayer carpet covering the divan or seat [*sarīr*] on which the Caliph sat, regarded as one of the insignia of royalty; it was an honor to be invited to sit on it. Ṣāliḥ is mentioned by Jahshiyārī, Yaʿqūbī, and Ṭabarī on various occasions as being the official responsible for the placing of the *muṣallā* and admitting of those privileged to sit on it, from the reign of al-Manṣūr to that of al-Amīn, and his son ʿAlī had the office, and then that of chamberlain, under al-Maʾmūn, according to Ibn Abī Ṭāhir Ṭayfūr and Shābushtī. See Sourdel, "Questions de cérémonial ʿabbaside," 131–2, 146 n. 181.

211. Explained below.

212. This was a proverbial expression for anything extremely difficult, the tragacanth bush being very spiny. See Mubarrad, *Kāmil*, I, 329; Maydānī, tr. Freytag, I, 476.

deceived (by God). I certainly hope that the ruling power will come to me in due course, so that I may then mete out justice to those whom you have oppressed and give bounty to those whom you have cut off (from your generosity). I shall place your sons above my own ones and give them my daughters in marriage, and I shall bring to pass the due rights of the Imām al-Mahdī (i.e., in regard to his wishes for his descendants)." He related: Mūsā then said to
[577] him, "That is what I would have expected of you, O Abū Jaʿfar! Draw near to me!" So Hārūn drew near and kissed his hands, and then he withdrew back to his place. Al-Hādī exclaimed to him, "Nay, by the illustrious shaykh and noble monarch—I mean your grandfather al-Manṣūr—you shan't sit anywhere else but here with me!" and he made Hārūn sit with him in the center of the court assembly. Next he said, "O Ḥarrānī, convey a million dīnārs to my brother (immediately), and when the collection of the land tax is in hand [*idhā iftataḥa al-kharāj*],[213] convey to him half of it; throw open for him all our wealth in the treasuries and what was confiscated from the members of the accursed house (i.e., the Umayyads), and let him take everything he desires." He related: He put all that into execution, and when Hārūn rose (to leave), he said to Ṣāliḥ, "Bring his mount near to the (Caliph's) carpet."[214]

ʿAmr al-Rūmī related: Hārūn used to regard me as a close companion, so I stood up before him and said, "O my master, what was the dream which the Commander of the Faithful spoke to you about?" He replied, "Al-Mahdī stated, 'I saw myself in my dream giving a rod each to Mūsā and Hārūn, and Mūsā's rod put forth leaves for a little way at the top only, whereas Hārūn's one sprouted leaves from one end to the other.' Al-Mahdī summoned al-Ḥakam b. Mūsā al-Ḍamrī,[215] who had the patronymic of Abū Sufyān, and said to him, 'Give an interpretation of this dream.' Al-Ḥakam

---

213. *Iftitāḥ al-kharāj* was a technical term of the financial secretaries denoting the beginning of the collection process, and is defined as such by Muḥammad b. Aḥmad al-Khwārazmī; see Bosworth, "Abū ʿAbdallāh al-Khwārazmī on the technical terms of the secretary's art," *JESHO*, XII (1969), 134–5 = *Medieval Arabic culture and administration*, no. XV.

214. I.e., as a sign of honor. Ibn al-Athīr, VI, 98; cf. Bayhaqī, *Maḥāsin*, ed. Schwally, 208–9 = ed. Ibrāhīm, I, 314–5.

215. The "al-Ḥakam b. Isḥāq al-Ṣaymarī" of Masʿūdī, *Murūj*, VI, 285, should, as Pellat notes in his edition, IV, 194 = § 2489 n. 5, and see *Index*, VI, 283, be corrected in the light of Ṭabarī's text here.

replied, 'Both of them will exercise the royal power; but as for Mūsā, his reign will be short, whereas in regard to Hārūn, his reign will extend further than that of any other Caliph who has ever lived; his days will be the finest of days and his age the finest of ages.'" He related: only a few days passed before Mūsā fell ill and died, his illness lasting for three days only. ʿAmr al-Rūmī related: The caliphate passed to Hārūn. He gave (his daughter) Ḥamdūnah in marriage to Jaʿfar b. Mūsā and Fāṭimah to Ismāʿīl b. Mūsā; he [578]
fulfilled everything which he had promised, and his age was the finest of ages.[216]

It has been mentioned that al-Hādī had set out for al-Ḥādithah, that is, Ḥādithat al-Mawṣil;[217] he took ill there and his sickness grew worse, so he turned back homewards.[218] ʿAmr al-Yashkurī, who was one of the body of eunuchs, has mentioned that al-Hādī came back from al-Ḥādithah after he had written to all his governors, those in the East as well as those in the West, ordering them to report to him. When his illness became serious, the gang of persons who had done homage to al-Hādī's son Jaʿfar as successor to the throne came together and said to each other, "If the power in the state passes to Yaḥyā, he will kill us and will not spare us." Hence, they plotted together that one of them should go to Yaḥyā with a (forged) order from al-Hādī and cut off his head. But then they said, "Perhaps the Commander of the Faithful will recover from his illness, and what excuse will we be able to give him?" So they gave up the plan. Then al-Khayzurān sent a message to Yaḥyā[219] informing him that the man (i.e., al-Hādī) was near to his

216. Bayhaqī, *Maḥāsin*, ed. Schwally, 208–9 = ed. Ibrāhīm, I, 315–16; Masʿūdī, *Murūj*, VI, 285 = ed. Pellat, § 2489; Ibn al-Athīr, VI, 98; Abbott, 97–8, who notes that al-Hādī seems to have had a superstitious and irrational streak in his makeup, perhaps inflamed by tales like this and similar prognostications, if these are genuine and not *ex post facto* explanations for his short reign (for al-Hādī's horoscope, see Yaʿqūbī, *Taʾrīkh*, II, 487; according to Masʿūdī, *Murūj*, VI, 281–2 = ed. Pellat, § 2486, it forecast a short reign only).

217. I.e., the Ḥadīthah to the south of al-Mawṣil, at the confluence of the Tigris and the Great Zāb, as opposed to that on the middle Euphrates. See Yāqūt, *Muʿjam*, II, 230; Le Strange, *Lands*, 90–1; Canard, 122–3; *EI*² s.v. Ḥadītha (E. Herzfeld).

218. *K. al-ʿUyūn*, 284, attributing al-Hādī's return to Baghdad to the onset of his illness plus receipt of the news of al-Ḥusayn b. ʿAlī's rebellion in al-Madīnah; Abbott, 106.

219. According to Yaʿqūbī, *Taʾrīkh*, II, 490, al-Khayzurān went personally to deliver Yaḥyā from jail.

return (to God, i.e., near death) and ordering him to be prepared to do what was necessary. Al-Khayzurān was the real directing influence behind al-Rashīd's candidature and the direction of caliphal affairs up to al-Hādī's actual death. Yaḥyā b. Khālid gave orders, and the secretaries were summoned and gathered together in al-Faḍl b. Yaḥyā's house. They spent the whole night writing letters from al-Rashīd to the provincial governors announcing al-Hādī's death and instructing them that al-Rashīd confirmed them in their existing governorships. When al-Hādī was actually dead, they despatched the letters by the mounts of the *barīd* service.[220]

Al-Faḍl b. Saʿīd has mentioned that his father transmitted the information to him that al-Khayzurān had sworn that she would never speak to Mūsā al-Hādī again, and she had removed herself away from his presence. When death came to al-Hādī, and the messenger announcing that news came to her, she exclaimed, "What shall I do concerning him?" Khāliṣah said, "Arise and go to your son, O noble lady, since this is no time for recrimination and displays of anger."[221] She said, "Give me some water, that I may perform the lesser ablutions in preparation for the worship." Then al-Khayzurān added, "Did we not use to say among ourselves that in this one night, one caliph would die, another caliph would succeed to power, and a third caliph would be born?" He related: At that point, Mūsā died, Hārūn came to power and al-Maʾmūn was born.[222] Al-Faḍl related: I handed on this account to ʿAbdallāh
[579] b. ʿUbaydallāh,[223] and he transmitted it on my authority in the same words that my father had told me. I asked him, "How did al-Khayzurān acquire this piece of knowledge [*ʿilm*]?" He replied, "She had heard it from al-Awzāʿī."[224]

---

220. Azdī, 261; Ibn al-Athīr, VI, 99; Abbott, 107, 109–10; Kennedy, 112. According to Jahshiyārī, 133, Yaḥyā's secretary Yūsuf b. al-Qāsim b. Ṣubayḥ did the actual writing of the letters.

221. Ibn al-Athīr, VI, 101; Abbott, 107.

222. I.e., to his Persian concubine Marājil; see Jahshiyārī, 133, and Ṭabarī, III, 758 (below, 327). This became celebrated as the "night of the caliphate," *laylat al-khilāfah. See Thaʿālibī, Thimār al-qulūb,* 510; idem, *Laṭāʾif,* 141, tr. 109–10; Bayhaqī, *Maḥāsin,* ed. Schwally, 160–1 = ed. Ibrāhīm, I, 244; Shābushtī, *K. al-Diyārāt,* 227.

223. Apparently the ʿAbbāsid prince ʿAbdallāh b. ʿUbaydallāh b. al-ʿAbbās b. Muḥammad, second cousin of al-Hādī and subsequently governor of Yemen under al-Muʿtaṣim, also cited by Ṭabarī, III, 450, as a *rāwī* for events in al-Manṣūr's reign.

224. Cf. Abbott, 41. Al-Khayzurān must accordingly have heard this prophecy

Yaḥyā b. al-Ḥasan (b. ʿAbd al-Khāliq) has mentioned that Muḥammad b. Sulaymān b. ʿAlī transmitted the information to him, saying that he got it from his paternal aunt Zaynab the daughter of Sulaymān,[225] who said: When Mūsā died at ʿĪsābādh, al-Khayzurān gave us the news, we being four ladies, myself, my (full) sister, Umm al-Ḥasan and ʿĀʾishah, (we four being) the youthful daughters of Sulaymān, together with Umm ʿAlī Rayṭah.[226] Khāliṣah came along at that point, and al-Khayzurān asked her, "What are the people doing?" She replied, "O my lady, Mūsā is dead and they have buried him." Al-Khayzurān exclaimed, "If Mūsā is dead, then Hārūn has been spared. Bring me some *sawīq*!"[227] Khāliṣah brought in some *sawīq*. She drank some herself, and then gave us some to drink. She said, "Fetch four hundred thousand dīnārs for my masters," and then, "What has my son Hārūn been doing?" Khāliṣah answered, "He has sworn that he will not perform the noon worship anywhere else except in Baghdad." She said, "Fetch the riding saddles and equipment, for there's no point in my sitting here when he has departed!" She subsequently caught up with him at Baghdad.[228]

The Time of al-Hādī's Death, the Term of His Life, the Extent of His Rule and (the Names of) Those Who Led the Worship over Him

Abū Maʿshar related:[229] Mūsā al-Hādī died during the night of Friday (i.e., of Thursday-Friday), in the middle (i.e., the fifteenth or sixteenth) of Rabīʿ I (September 14 or 15, 786). Aḥmad b. Thābit (al-Rāzī)[230] transmitted the information to us about that from

---

(see on it, Thaʿālibī, Laṭāʾif, 141, tr. 109–10) from the famous Syrian jurist before 157 (774), the date of his death, see *EI*[2] s.v. al-Awzāʿī (J. Schacht).

225. See on her, Ṭabarī, III, 559 (above, 26, and n. 108).

226. I.e., al-Saffāḥ's daughter, the widow of al-Mahdī. See for the daughters of Sulaymān, Ibn Qutaybah, 375.

227. In the first place, a dish made from flour, and then a soup made from flour and added ingredients. See Thaʿālibī, *Laṭāʾif*, 10, tr. 41 and n. 20; *EI*[1] s.v. (J. Ruska).

228. Abbott, 109–11.

229. Presumably the historian Abū Maʿshar Najīh b. ʿAbd al-Raḥmān al-Sindī, who himself died in the year 170 (786) and was the author of a history of the Caliphs. See *GAL*, S I, 207; *GAS*, I, 291–2.

230. Often cited by Ṭabarī as a *rāwī* of Abū Maʿshar's historical information; see *GAS*, I, 292.

someone who had mentioned it to him from Isḥāq. Al-Wāqidī[231] related: Mūsā died at ʿĪsābādh in the middle of Rabīʿ I. Hishām b. Muḥammad (Ibn al-Kalbī)[232] related: Mūsā al-Hādī perished on the fourteenth of Rabīʿ I (September 13, 786), this being the night of Friday, in the year 170.[233] A certain authority related: He died during the night of Friday, the sixteenth of that month, and the length of his caliphate was one year and three months. Hishām
[580] related: He reigned for fourteen months and died at the age of twenty-six.[234] Al-Wāqidī related: His period of power was one year, one month, and twenty-two days. Others, however, have related that he died on Saturday, the tenth of Rabīʿ I (September 9, 786) or else on the night of Friday, when he was twenty-three years old, and his caliphate was one year, one month, and twenty-three days. His brother Hārūn al-Rashīd b. Muḥammad led the worship over him. His patronymic was Abū Muḥammad and his mother al-Khayzurān, the former slave concubine [*umm walad*]. He was buried in his garden at ʿĪsābādh the Greater. Al-Faḍl b. Isḥāq (al-Hāshimī) has mentioned that he was tall, full-bodied handsome, whitish in complexion but tinged with red, and with a contracted upper lip.[235] He used to have the nickname of "Mūsā, shut your mouth!" He was born at al-Sīrawān[236] in the region of al-Rayy.[237]

Mention of His Children

He had nine children, seven sons and two daughters. Regarding the sons, one of them was Jaʿfar, whom he was grooming for the role of his successor in the caliphate, and (the others were) al-ʿAbbās, ʿAbdallāh, Isḥāq, Ismāʿīl, Sulaymān, and Mūsā b. Mūsā the blind

---

231. The celebrated historian of the Prophet's *maghāzī* or raids, Muḥammad b. ʿUmar, died in 207 (823). See *GAL*, I², 141–2, S I, 207–8; *GAS*, I, 294–9; *EI*¹ s.v. (J. Horovitz).

232. Noted Kūfan historian and genealogist, died in 204 (819–20) or 206 (821–2). See *GAL*, I², 144–5, S I, 211–12; *GAS*, I, 268–71; *EI*² s.v. al-Kalbī (W. Atallah).

233. This gives the exact correspondence of the day and date, and seems the most likely one.

234. Thus also in Yaʿqūbī, *Taʾrīkh*, II, 491; the *K. al-ʿUyūn*, 289, places his death at the age of 24 or 25; Khalīfah, *Taʾrīkh*, II, 705, and Dīnawarī, 386, state that he died in mid-Rabīʿ I at age 24.

235. Ṭabarī-Balʿamī, tr. IV, 455; Thaʿālibī, *Laṭāʾif*, 44, tr. 62; Abbott, 61.

236. See on this place Yāqūt, *Muʿjam*, II, 297; Schwarz, 799–800.

237. Ibn al-Athīr, VI, 101; Abbott, 106 ff.; Moscati, *Le califat d'al Hādī*, 23.

one, all of them born from originally slave mothers. The blind son, Mūsā, was actually born after his father's death. Of the two daughters, one of them was Umm ʿĪsā, who became the wife of al-Ma'mūn,[238] and the other was Umm al-ʿAbbās bt. Mūsā, who had the nickname of Nūnah.[239]

Some of the Historical Events Involving Him and Some Aspects of His Behavior

Ibrāhīm b. ʿAbd al-Salām,[240] the son of al-Sindī's brother, and called Abū Ṭūṭah,[241] has mentioned that al-Sindī b. Shāhik[242] transmitted the information to him, saying: I was with Mūsā in Jurjān. At that point, there came to him the messenger announcing the death of al-Mahdī and his own succession to the caliphate. So he set off for Baghdad, in company with Saʿīd b. Salm (b. [581]
Qutaybah),[243] using the relays of the *barīd* system, and sent me on to Khurāsān.[244]

Saʿīd b. Salm transmitted the information to me, saying: We travelled along, with the pastoralists' tents of Jurjān on one side, and the gardens and orchards on the other. He related: He then heard a noise from one of those gardens, made by a man who was singing. So al-Hādī said to the commander of his guard, "Fetch me that man immediately!" He related: I said, "O Commander of the Faithful, how similar is the episode of this wretch (literally, "treacherous one") to the episode involving Sulaymān b. ʿAbd al-Malik!" Al-Hādī said, "How is that?" He related: I said to him: Sulaymān b. ʿAbd al-Malik was once in one of his pleasure gardens, with the womenfolk of his household accompanying him, when

238. She was the mother of his two eldest sons, see Ṭabarī, III, 836.

239. Ibn al-Athīr, loc. cit. Ibn Qutaybah, 381, simply says "his progeny was numerous."

240. A *rāwī* of this name is mentioned in Iṣfahānī, *Aghānī*, ed. Būlāq, IV, 82 = ed. Cairo, IV, 219.

241. Literally, "the man affected by satyriasis."

242. Mawlā of al-Manṣūr, who contrived to survive and to serve every Caliph up to al-Amīn and then Ibrāhīm b. al-Mahdī; see Crone, 194–5.

243. Brother of Ibrāhīm (see Ṭabarī, III, 568, above, 39, n. 160) and like him a boon-companion of al-Hādī (Ṭabarī, III, 587, below, 68); later, he became governor for Hārūn of among other places al-Jazīrah and Armenia (Ṭabarī, III, 645, 647). See Crone, 137–8; Kennedy, 83.

244. See Ṭabarī, III, 545, 547 (above, 5, 8).

he heard from another nearby garden the sound of a man singing. He thereupon summoned the commander of his guard and instructed him, "Fetch me the man who is singing!" The man was brought into his presence, and when he appeared before him, the Caliph said to the man, "What impelled you to start singing, when you are in close proximity to me and I have my ladies with me? Have you not realized that when stud-mares hear the sound of a stallion, they feel drawn towards him? O slave, emasculate this man!"[245] So the man was emasculated. The next year, Sulaymān returned to the pleasure garden, and sat down in exactly the same place as on the previous occasion. He thereupon remembered the same man, and what he had done to him, and he said to the commander of his guard, "Fetch me the man whom we caused to be emasculated!" So he brought him into the Caliph's presence. When he appeared before him, Sulaymān said to him, "Either you sold them (i.e., his testes), and we will give you the full price; or else you gave them freely, and we will reward you." He related: By God, the man did not address him as Caliph, but spoke to him thus: "O Sulaymān, I adjure God against you! You have cut off my hopes of progeny, you have taken away all my honor and you have deprived me of all pleasure, and yet now you say, 'Either you gave them freely, and we will reward you, or else you sold them, and we will give you the full price!' Nay, by God, (never,) until I stand before God (i.e., for judgment)!" He related: Mūsā then said, "O slave, bring back the commander of the guard," so he brought him back, and the Caliph instructed him, "Don't place any obstacles in the man's way (i.e., let him go free)."

Abū Mūsā Hārūn b. Muḥammad b. Ismāʿīl b. Mūsā al-Hādī[246] has mentioned that ʿAlī b. Ṣāliḥ transmitted the information to him that one day, when he was still a boy, he was standing close to
[582] al-Hādī at a time when the latter had avoided[247] the duty of hear-

245. Sulaymān had the reputation later in Islamic lore of being a devotee of sex and of being extremely jealous about his harem. See Thaʿālibī, *Laṭāʾif*, 117, tr. 96; Ibn al-Ṭiqṭaqā, 114, tr. 123.

246. I.e., the grandson of al-Hādī's son Ismāʿīl, who married Hārūn's daughter Fāṭimah (Ṭabarī, III, 577–8, above, 55).

247. Following the reading here of *jafā*, preferred by the editor, who notes, however (*Addenda et emendanda*, p. DCCLX) that there seems to be a lacuna here, judging by the parallel passages in Bayhaqī's *Maḥāsin* and Ibn al-Athīr (see below, 62, n. 251).

ing petitions and complaints [*maẓālim*][248] for three entire days. (Ibrāhīm b. Dhakwān) al-Ḥarrānī came into his presence and said to him, "O Commander of the Faithful, the mass of subjects will not remain obedient to your rule if you persist in these habits; it is three days since you last heard petitions and complaints." He thereupon turned to me and said, "O ʿAlī, let the people into my presence *bi-al-jafalā* and not *bi-al-naqarā*." I rushed forth from his presence in a headlong manner, but then I stopped short, and (I realized that) I did not know what he had told me to do. I said to myself, "If I refer back to the Commander of the Faithful for an explanation, he will say to me, 'Do you claim to act as my doorkeeper when you don't understand what I have said?'" Then my native wit returned, and I accordingly sent a message to a Bedouin who had arrived in a visiting delegation and questioned him about the words *jafalā* and *naqarā*. He replied, "*Al-jafalā* means *jufālah* (i.e., "group, body of people") and *al-naqarā* is when he summons only the élite among them."[249] So I then gave orders for the curtains (i.e., those veiling the Caliph from the masses of petitioners) to be drawn aside and for the doors to be opened, and this was done.[250] The people entered en masse, and the Caliph remained busy receiving their petitions and complaints till nightfall. Then when the sessions broke up, I appeared before him and he said, "It looks as if you wish to mention some matter, O ʿAlī!" I replied, "Yes, O Commander of the Faithful, you spoke to me using expressions which I had never heard before this very day, and I was afraid

---

248. Concerning this duty of meting out justice personally to the subjects, see H. F. Amedroz, "The Mazālim jurisdiction in the Ahkam Sultaniyya of Mawardi," *JRAS* (1911), 635–74; R. Levy, *The social structure of Islam,* 348–51; *EI*[2] s.v. Maẓālim (J. S. Neilsen).

249. The lexica give *jafalā, jufālah, ajfalā,* etc., with the sense of "group, body of people, invited en masse and without distinction of person," the root *j.-f.-l* having the general meaning, however, of "to disperse quickly, flee in disorder" (Lane, *Lexicon,* s.v.); perhaps the connection lies in the idea of a mass stampede. The root *n.-q.-r* conveys such ideas as "pecking out, carving out, hollowing out, boring, excavating" (Lane, s.v.). The word *naqarā* used here obviously stems from the eschatological concept of the Angel Isrāfīl blowing [*naqara*] a horn [*nāqūr*] to summon the resurrected bodies for judgement (Qur'ān, LXXIV, 8), summoning them one by one.

250. On the curtains [*astār,* sing. *sitr*] veiling the monarch from the public, see E. Tyan, *Institutions du droit public musulman. I. Le califat,* 498–501; Sourdel, "Questions de cérémonial ʿabbaside," 132.

to refer back to you lest you say, 'Do you claim to act as my doorkeeper when you don't understand what I have said?' Hence, I sent a message to a Bedouin who was here with us, and he elucidated the expressions for me. So reward him suitably on my behalf, O Commander of the Faithful!" He said, "Certainly; one hundred thousand dirhams will be conveyed to him." I protested to him, "O Commander of the Faithful, he is only a rough Bedouin, and ten thousand dirhams would satisfy him and be adequate recompense for him." He replied, "Shame upon you, O ʿAlī, I am being generous and you are behaving like a miser!"[251]

He related: ʿAlī b. Ṣāliḥ also transmitted the information to me, saying: Al-Hādī rode off one day with the intention of visiting his mother al-Khayzurān because of some illness from which she had suffered. But ʿUmar b. Bazīʿ planted himself in his path and said to him, "O Commander of the Faithful, let me point out to you a course of action which will be more advantageous to you (i.e., in the sight of God) than this present one." He enquired, "What is that, O ʿUmar?" ʿUmar replied, "Looking into petitions and complaints—you haven't attended to them since three (nights) ago now." He related: The Caliph thereupon made a sign to his well-trained she-camel that he wished to turn aside to the building where petitions and complaints were heard. Then he sent a mes-
[583] sage to al-Khayzurān by the hand of one of his eunuchs conveying his excuses to her for his neglect in not visiting her, saying (to him), "Tell her that ʿUmar b. Bazīʿ has informed us about duties owed towards God which are more pressing upon us than duty towards you, so we have inclined to his words. We shall, however, visit you tomorrow morning, if God wills."[252]

It has been mentioned from ʿAbdallāh b. Mālik (al-Khuzāʿī) that he related: I used to hold the office of commander of the police guard [*shurṭah*] under al-Mahdī. Al-Mahdī would send for al-Hādī's boon-companions and singers and order me to have them beaten. Al-Hādī, in turn, would beg me to treat them with gentleness and consideration, but I would pay no heed to that and would just go on carrying out al-Mahdī's orders to me. He related: When

251. Bayhaqī, *Maḥāsin*, ed. Schwally, 206–7 = ed. Ibrāhīm, I, 311–13; Ibn al-Athīr, VI, 101–2.

252. Ibn al-Athīr, VI, 102; Abbott, 84.

al-Hādī succeeded to the caliphate, I felt certain that I was going to perish. He sent for me one day. I entered into his presence, with my shroud wrapped around me and having anointed myself with the spices and aromatic substances used to prepare corpses for burial, and behold, he was seated there on a stool [*kursī*][253] with the executioner's sword and leather mat before him. I greeted him with the *taslīm* salutation, but he replied, "May God not grant peace to the one regarded as an outcast! Do you recall the day when I sent to you concerning the matter of al-Ḥarrānī, and the beating and imprisonment which the Commander of the Faithful had ordered for him, yet you would not respond to me; and likewise, the matters of so-and-so and so-and-so"—and he began to enumerate the names of his boon-companions—"yet you paid no attention to my words nor to my orders!"

I responded, "True, O Commander of the Faithful, but will you now allow me to provide a complete justification?" He said, "Yes." I began, "I adjure you by God, O Commander of the Faithful, would you yourself be pleased if you had appointed me to the office to which your father appointed me, and you commanded me to do a certain thing, and then one of your sons sent a message to me ordering me to do something which was completely counter to your original command, and I then carried out his orders but disobeyed yours?" He admitted, "No." I then replied, "That is how I stand in relationship to you at present, and how I stood in relationship to your father in the past." He thereupon made me draw near, and I kissed his hands. He ordered robes of honor (to be brought), and largesse was bestowed on me. Then he said, "I have reappointed you to your old office, so go forth as one established in the right course." I departed from his presence and proceeded to my residence, reflecting about my position and his attitude, and I said to myself, "(He is) a young man who drinks wine, and the group of persons regarding whom I disobeyed him (during the previous reign) are now his boon-companions, viziers, and secretaries. I can visualize myself in regard to them, when the effects of [584]

253. For the *kursī*, originally an Iranian article of furniture, see Sourdel, "Questions de cérémoniale ʿabbaside," 131; J. Sadan, *Le mobilier au Proche Orient médiéval*, 92–4, 123 ff; *EI*[2] s.v. (Huart and Sadan). Here the implication is that it was exceptional for al-Hādī to sit himself thus.

wine take control of them and they will have countermanded his decision about me and will have impelled him to act concerning me in a way which I would hate and fear (i.e., they would bring about his destruction)."

He related: I was sitting there, round about that time, with one of my small daughters before me and with a brazier in front of me and some thin cakes of bread which I was dividing up with some spicy vinegar relish [*kāmakh*][254] and then toasting on the fire and feeding to the child, when suddenly there was a great noise, till I imagined that the whole world had been torn up by its roots and shaken with the beating of hoofs and the immense clamor. I said to myself, "By God, this is what I thought would happen, and what I feared of the Caliph's vengeance (or: of God's decree, *min amrihi*) has now caught up with me." Then the door was thrown open, the eunuch attendants burst in, and there was the Commander of the Faithful, al-Hādī, mounted on an ass in their midst. When I saw him, I jumped up from my seat, hastening (towards him), and kissed his hand, his foot, and the hoof of his ass. Then he said to me, "O ʿAbdallāh, I have been thinking about your affair, and I said to myself, 'It may readily come into your mind that, when I have been drinking wine, surrounded by your enemies, they might controvert the favorable attitude which I now have towards you.' This could have perturbed you and given you cause for alarm. Hence, I have come to your house in order to put you at ease and to let you realize that all rancor towards you has been dispelled from my mind. So come and bring me to eat something of what you yourself were eating, and carry on preparing the food which you were preparing, so that you may know that, through eating your food, I have entered into a relationship which prevents me from harming you and have become completely at home in your house; thus your fear and apprehension will vanish away." I brought before him the thin cakes of bread and the bowl[255] containing the spicy

254. From Persian *kāmah,* older form *kāmak,* "sour and piquant hors d'oeuvres," various types of *kawāmikh* being described by Masʿūdī, *Murūj,* VIII, 392–4 = ed. Pellat, § 3554. Also, the Ayyūbid period cookery book, the *K. al-Wuṣlah ilā al-ḥabīb,* defines *kāmakh baghdādī* as a kind of concoction for seasoning with gourds and yoghourt. See M. Rodinson, "Recherches sur les documents arabes relatifs à la cuisine," *REI* (1949), 142; Ahsan, 106–7.

255. *Sukurrajah,* presumably the *sukrūjah* of Dozy, *Supplément,* I, 668b.

vinegar relish, and he ate some of it. Then he said, "Bring in the gifts which I have bestowed on ʿAbdallāh from my own court session," and four hundred mules loaded with dirhams were brought in to me. He said, "This is a gift for you, so use it for your own personal affairs, and keep these mules for me in your care, for I may need them one day for some journey or other of mine." Then he said, "May God protect you with goodness!" and he went away homewards.[256]

Mūsā b. ʿAbdallāh has mentioned that his father gave him the garden which he had in the midst of his residence, and he then built around it stables for those mules. He used to supervise them personally and look after their welfare as long as al-Hādī remained alive. [585]

Mūsā b. ʿAbdallāh b. Yaʿqūb b. Dāwūd b. Ṭahmān al-Sulamī[257] has mentioned that his father related to him, saying: ʿAlī b. ʿĪsā b. Māhān used to get angry when the Caliph got angry and show himself pleased when the Caliph was pleased. My father (sc. Yaʿqūb b. Dāwūd) used to say: I don't feel towards any Arab or non-Arab the way I feel towards ʿAlī b. ʿĪsā, for he came in one day to me in prison with a whip in his hand and said, "The Commander of the Faithful Mūsā al-Hādī has ordered me to beat you with a hundred lashes." He related: He stepped forward, and laid it on my arms and shoulders, striking me with it until he had counted out a hundred strokes, and then he left. He (i.e., the Caliph) said to him (i.e., ʿAlī b. ʿĪsā b. Māhān), "What did you do with the fellow?" He replied, "I dealt with him according to your command." He said, "And how is he now?" He replied, "He is dead." The Caliph exclaimed, "Indeed we belong to God and to Him we shall return! Woe upon you! By God, you have brought me into disgrace in the eyes of the people! This was a righteous man! The people will say, 'He has killed Yaʿqūb b. Dāwūd!'" He related: When ʿAlī b. ʿĪsā saw how violently the Caliph was grieved, he informed him, "He

---

256. Bayhaqī, *Maḥāsin*, ed. Schwally, 189–90 = ed. Ibrāhīm, I, 286–8; Ibn al-Athīr, VI, 102–3; Ibn al-Ṭiqṭaqā, 171–2, tr. 185–6.

257. *Rāwī* mentioned several times by Ṭabarī for events in al-Mahdī's reign, and despite the similarity in names and *nisbah*, his grandfather is not apparently to be confused with al-Mahdī's chief minister Yaʿqūb b. Dāwūd b. ʿUmar b. ʿUthmān al-Sulamī, on whom see Ṭabarī, III, 688 (below, 230, n. 800), and Masʿūdī, *Murūj*, ed. Pellat, *Index*, VII, 775–6.

is in fact alive, O Commander of the Faithful, he didn't die!" The Caliph exclaimed, "God be praised for that!"[258]

He related: Al-Hādī had appointed as his doorkeeper [*ḥājib*] after al-Rabīʿ[259] the latter's son al-Faḍl. He said to al-Faḍl, "Don't keep back the people from access to me, for that will deprive me of the aura of divine blessing, and don't bring before my attention any matter which, when I have investigated it, turns out to be of no consequence, for that depreciates royal power and is harmful to the subjects."[260]

Mūsā b. ʿAbdallāh (b. Mālik) related: A man was brought before Mūsā (al-Hādī), and the latter began to reproach him for his crimes and to threaten him. The man replied to him, "O Commander of the Faithful, my excusing myself from what you are reproaching me with would be contradicting you, whilst my acknowledging its truth would be imputing to myself a crime. I would rather say to you,

'If you have been hoping to merit divine mercy by inflicting punishment,
then do not hold yourself back from the recompense earned by an act of pardoning.' "

He related: The Caliph ordered the man to be set at liberty.[261]

[586] ʿUmar b. Shabbah[262] has mentioned that Saʿīd b. Salm was once with Mūsā al-Hādī. A delegation from the Byzantines came into his presence, and Saʿīd b. Salm was at that moment wearing a cap [*qalansuwah*]; he had become bald even though he was still only young. Mūsā said to him, "Take off your cap, so that you give an appearance of wisdom and seniority [*tatashāyakhu*] through your bald head!"[263]

---

258. Ibn al-Athīr, VI, 103–4.

259. Who had died around this time, conceivably poisoned by al-Hādī, see Ṭabarī, III, 597–8 (below, 85–86).

260. Cf. Bayhaqī, *Maḥāsin*, ed. Schwally, 173 = ed. Ibrāhīm, I, 262–3.

261. Jahshiyārī, 127–8 (according to whom the man was one of his secretaries); Masʿūdī, *Murūj*, VI, 283 = ed. Pellat, § 2487; Azdī, 260–1; Ibn al-Abbār, *Iʿtāb al-kuttāb*, 75.

262. Baṣran reciter of historical traditions, died in 264 (877), author of several works known only fragmentarily and of a history of al-Madīnah recently edited by Ḥabīb Muḥammad Aḥmad, *Ta'rīkh al-Madīnah al-munawwarah*, Jeddah 1393/1973, 4 vols.; see *GAS*, I, 345–6.

263. Azdī, 269.

Yaḥyā b. al-Ḥasan b. ʿAbd al-Khāliq has mentioned that his father transmitted to him the information, saying: I set off for ʿĪsābādh, intending to visit al-Faḍl b. al-Rabīʿ, and I encountered the Commander of the Faithful, Mūsā, but I did not recognize him. For lo, he was wearing a thin shift,[264] mounted on a horse and with a bamboo spear shaft in his hand. Every person he met, he thrust at with this shaft.[265] He said to me, "O son of a whore!" He related: I perceived a man, with the stature of an idol—I had actually seen him previously in Syria—whose thighs were like the thighs of a camel. I clapped my hand to the hilt of my sword, but a man then said to me, "Woe upon you, (this is) the Commander of the Faithful!" At that, I spurred on my riding beast—which happened to be a horse of Persian breed,[266] which al-Faḍl b. al-Rabīʿ had presented to me, he having purchased it earlier for four thousand dirhams—and went into the residence of Muḥammad b. al-Qāsim, the commander of the Caliph's personal bodyguard. The Caliph halted at the gate, with the bamboo shaft in his hand, and exclaimed, "Get away, you son of a whore!" I nevertheless refused to budge, and he passed by and proceeded on his way. I told al-Faḍl, "I saw the Commander of the Faithful and so-and-so took place." He replied, "In my judgement, your only hope of salvation lies in your making for Baghdad. When I myself go there to perform the Friday worship, meet me then." He related: I never set foot in ʿĪsābādh again until al-Hādī perished.

Al-Haytham b. ʿUrwah al-Anṣārī has mentioned that al-Ḥusayn b. Muʿādh b. Muslim,[267] who was the foster-brother of Mūsā al-Hādī, related: I used to spend a lot of time with Mūsā, with just the two of us present, and I never felt in my mind any feeling of apprehension from his high status when we were alone together because he always used to put me at my ease. On occasion (or: often[268]), he wrestled with me and I would throw him on the

264. *Ghilālah*; see for this garment, Ṭabarī, III, 753 (below, 320, and n. 1070).

265. Cf. Moscati, *Le califat d'al-Hādī*, 26.

266. For *shihrī* (? *shahrī*) "Persian or Kurdish horse," pl. *shahārī*, see BGA, IV, *Indices, glossarium et addenda et emendanda ad Part. I–III*, 277–8: < O Ir. *khshathriya-* "royal"; cf. Jāḥiẓ, *Risālah fī manāqib al-Atrāk wa-ʿāmmat jund al-khilāfah*, in *Majmūʿat rasāʾil*, Cairo 1323 (1905–6), 11: *al-khuyūl al-shihriyyah.*

267. Son of a Khurasanian mawlā and brother of Muʿādh, who later served as deputy governor of Khurasan and governor of Syria. See Ṭabarī, III, 711; Crone, 184.

268. Inserting the word *rubbamā*, as in the Cairo text, VIII, 218.

ground, without any fear of him, and would pound the ground with him. But when he assumed the mantle of the caliphate, and then took his place on the seat from which commands and prohibitions are given out, I stood by his head; and by God, I could hardly contain myself from terror and fear of him!

Yaḥyā b. al-Ḥasan b. ʿAbd al-Khāliq has mentioned that Muḥam-
[587] mad b. Saʿīd b. ʿUmar b. Mihrān[269] transmitted the information to him from his father, who had it from his grandfather, who said: The highest rank at al-Hādī's court was held by Ibrāhīm b. Salm b. Qutaybah. One of Ibrāhīm's sons called Salm died, and Mūsā al-Hādī came to him on a visit of condolence for the son's death mounted on a greyish-white ass—no one coming to visit him (i.e., al-Hādī) was ever prevented and no one giving a greeting was sent back—until he dismounted in his (i.e., Ibrāhīm's portico. Then he said, "O Ibrāhīm, (one's child) brings you joy, even when he is hostile and a source of dissension, and brings you grief, even when he is a source of blessing and mercy!" Ibrāhīm replied, "O Commander of the Faithful, every part of me that formerly contained grief has now become filled with consolation." He related: When Ibrāhīm died, the highest rank (at court) passed to (his brother) Saʿīd b. Salm after him.[270]

ʿUmar b. Shabbah has mentioned that ʿAlī b. al-Ḥusayn b. ʿAlī b. al-Ḥusayn b. ʿAlī b. Abī Ṭālib[271] used to be called al-Jazarī.[272] He married Ruqayyah bt. ʿAmr al-ʿUthmāniyyah, who had previously been the wife of al-Mahdī.[273] The news of this reached Mūsā al-Hādī in the opening days of his caliphate, and he sent a messenger to him, accusing him of acting imprudently. He said (in the message), "Was it impossible for you to find, among all other women, any wife except one who had been the Commander of the Faithful's wife?" He replied, "The only women whom God has declared

---

269. Presumably the grandson of the ʿUmar b. Mihrān, secretary to al-Khayzurān, who restored order in Egypt in 176 (792–3); see Ṭabarī, III, 626–8 (below, 134–37).

270. Azdī, 270; Ibn al-Athīr, VI, 104; Ibn al-Ṭiqṭaqā, 172, tr. 186–7.

271. I.e., the grandson of the Fourth Imām ʿAlī Zayn al-ʿĀbidīn and first cousin of Jaʿfar al-Ṣādiq.

272. This is normally the *nisbah* from al-Jazīrah, i.e., northern Iraq and north-eastern Syria; see Samʿānī, *K. al-Ansāb*, III, 269–71.

273. Al-Mahdī had married her during his Pilgrimage visit to al-Madīnah in 160 (777). See Ṭabarī, III, 483; Abbott, 39.

forbidden for His creatures are the wives of my own forefather (i.e., of the Prophet); as for the rest, there is no prohibition whatsoever." The Caliph thereupon lashed him round the head with a staff which he happened to have in his hand, and ordered him to be given five hundred lashes of the whip; he was accordingly beaten thus. The Caliph wanted him to divorce her, but he refused.[274] He was then borne away from the Caliph's presence in an executioner's leather mat and hurled down away at one side. He had a very choice seal ring on his hand; one of the eunuchs saw it, at the time when ʿAlī had lost consciousness from the flogging, and the eunuch bent over (ʿAlī) to the ring (i.e., in order to steal it from him). But ʿAlī clutched at the eunuch's hand and struck it, so that the eunuch cried out. Mūsā flared up in anger and exclaimed, "He does this to my eunuch, in addition to his slighting my father and his (insolent) words to me!" He sent a message to him, "What [588]
impelled you to do that?" He replied, "Speak with the eunuch, and inquire of him, and order him to place his hand on your head, and he will of certainty tell you the truth." Mūsā did that, and the eunuch told him the true story. He exclaimed, "By God, he acted correctly! I myself testify that he is truly a paternal cousin of mine! If he had not acted thus, I would have disowned him!" Then he ordered him to be set free.[275]

Abū Ibrāhīm al-Mu'adhdhin has mentioned that al-Hādī used to leap up on to his mount wearing two coats of mail, and al-Mahdī used to call him "My dear son!" (literally, "my sweet-smelling herb," *rayḥānatī*[276]).

Muḥammad b. ʿAṭā' b. Muqaddam al-Wāsiṭī has mentioned that his father transmitted the information to him that al-Mahdī said to Mūsā one day—at a time when a dualist infidel [*zindīq*] had just been brought before him, and he had asked the dualist to repent of his error, but the latter had refused, so the Caliph had had him decapitated and had ordered his corpse to be gibbeted—"O my

274. Abbott, 98.

275. Bayhaqī, *Maḥāsin*, ed. Schwally, 515–16 = ed. Ibrāhīm, II, 256–7; Ibn al-Athīr, VI, 104.

276. From the tradition of the Prophet that he called al-Ḥasan and al-Ḥusayn *rayḥānatayya* "my two sweet-smelling herbs"; see Majd al-Dīn Ibn al-Athir, *Nihāyah*, II, 288.

dear son, if this royal authority passes to you, turn your whole attention vigorously to this gang [ʿ*iṣābah*]"—he meant the adherents of Mani—"for they are a sect who summon men to what are superficially fine doctrines, such as the avoidance of immoral deeds, abstinence from the affairs of the material world, and conduct aimed at achieving a place in the hereafter. Then they lead men on to the prohibiting of all meat, the use of purified water only (i.e., for ritual ablutions), and the avoidance of killing any crawling insects or reptiles, as measures for avoiding all sinfulness and criminal behavior. Then from this stage, they lead men on to the worship of two principles, one of them light and the other darkness. After this, they declare lawful sexual relations with sisters and daughters, washing oneself in urine and stealing infants from the streets in order to save them from the erroneous path of darkness for the rightly guided way of light. So erect gibbets for this sect, unsheathe the sword among them, and by dealing with them thus draw yourself near to God, He has no partner! For indeed, I saw in a dream your ancestor al-ʿAbbās investing me with two swords[277] and commanding me to kill the dualists." He related: Mūsā said, ten months of his reign having elapsed, "Ho, by God, if I live, I shall certainly exterminate this sect in its entirety, to the point that I won't leave a single eye whose gaze can range forth!" It is said that he ordered one thousand palm-tree trunks to be erected for him to use (i.e., by gibbeting the dualists). He pronounced these words in such-and-such a month, and died two months later.[278]

Ayyūb b. ʿInābah[279] has mentioned that Mūsā b. Ṣāliḥ b.

277. The two swords in this dream are symbolic, but it was an ancient Arabian practice for warriors to bear two swords, and girding them on was adopted as part of the investiture ceremony for high officials under the ʿAbbāsids, whence the honorific Dhū al-Sayfayn. See I. Goldziher, "Zwei Schwerter," *Isl.* XII (1922), 198–9 = *Gesammelte Schriften,* V, 469–70.

278. Ibn al-Athīr, VI, 104–5; Vajda, "Les zindîqs en pays d'Islam," 190–1, citing valuable parallels to this description of allegedly Manichaean doctrines and practices, but noting that certain accusations, such as those of incest and immorality (cf. Ṭabarī, III, 551–2, above), are commonly launched at religious dissidents who have to pursue a clandestine existence, and that other accusations, such as that of washing in urine, reflect rather Zoroastrian practice; Farouk Omar, in ʿ*Abbāsiyyāt,* 92–3.

279. Mentioned as a *rāwī* in Iṣfahānī, *Aghānī,* ed. Būlāq, VII, 109 = ed. Cairo, VIII, 152.

Shaykh[280] transmitted the information to him that ʿĪsā b. Daʾb [589]
was the most knowledgeable person of the Ḥījāzīs about polite learning [*adab*] and the one with the sweetest speech. He had secured a place in al-Hādī's favor which no one else enjoyed in the Caliph's eyes. The Caliph used to summon for him a cushion or backrest on which he could prop himself,[281] a privilege which he never extended to anyone else in his court circle, and he used to say, "I have never deemed a single day or night with you to be too long, nor have you ever been absent from my sight without my wishing that I might see no one but you." ʿĪsā was amusing company to joke with, a pleasant companion for nocturnal storytelling sessions, full of remarkable stories, excellent at poetry and adept at citing verses appositely.[282]

He related: Hence, on a certain night, the Caliph ordered him to be given thirty thousand dīnārs. When Ibn Daʾb arose next morning, he sent his steward to Mūsā's gate, and he said to the steward, "Make contact with the chamberlain, and tell him to forward this sum of money to us." The steward accordingly made contact with the chamberlain and conveyed to him Ibn Daʾb's message. But the chamberlain smiled and said, "This is not within my sphere of responsibility; go off and find the man who will countersign (the order) [*ṣāḥib al-tawqīʿ*], so that he may issue for Ibn Daʾb a letter of authorization to the *Dīwān* (i.e., the exchequer). You can then make the necessary arrangements for it here, and subsequently proceed concerning it in such-and-such a manner." So he went back to Ibn Daʾb and told him the story. Ibn Daʾb said, "Drop the whole affair; don't devote any more effort to it and don't make any more inquiries about it."

He related: Now whilst Mūsā was up on a belvedere [*mustashraf*] of his in Baghdad, he suddenly noticed that Ibn Daʾb had drawn near, unaccompanied except by a solitary slave boy. So he said to Ibrāhīm al-Ḥarrānī, "Just look at Ibn Daʾb! He hasn't changed a single feature of his usual mode of life, nor has he spruced himself up for us, even though we showed our bountiful-

280. *Rāwī* who is later mentioned by Ṭabarī, III, 1641, as taking part in the events around the abdication of the Caliph al-Mustaʿīn in 251 (866).

281. *Muttakaʾ*, for which see Sadan, 113–14.

282. Bayhaqī, *Maḥāsin*, ed. Schwally, 207 = ed. Ibrāhīm, I, 313; Masʿūdī, *Murūj*, VI, 263–4 = ed. Pellat, § 2471.

ness to him yesterday in order that our marks of favor might be visible upon him." Ibrāhīm said to him, "If the Commander of the Faithful commanded (a similar favor) for me, I would display something of that to him." The Caliph commented, "No, he knows his own business best." Ibn Da'b entered and started to engage in conversation with the Caliph until Mūsā raised with him the topic of some aspects of his present condition, saying to him, "I see that your robe is much washed, and this is winter weather; a new and soft robe is required for it." Ibn Da'b replied, "O Commander of the Faithful, my means are too exiguous for me to satisfy my needs." The Caliph said, "How can this be, when we have just allocated to you as much of our largesse as we thought
[590] would provide fittingly for your status?" He responded, "It hasn't reached me (yet) and I haven't got my hands on it!" So the Caliph sent for the official in charge of the Privy Exchequer [*ṣāḥib bayt māl al-khāṣṣah*] and told him, "Rush thirty thousand dīnārs to him this very instant!" The sum was brought in, and was transported (to his house) in front of his gaze.[283]

ʿAlī b. Muḥammad[284] has mentioned that his father transmitted the information to him from ʿAlī b. Yaqṭīn, saying: One night, I was with Mūsā, in the company of a group of his companions, when suddenly there came to him a eunuch who whispered something in his ear secretly. Thereupon, the Caliph sprang up with alacrity, saying, "Don't disperse," and went off. He was away for a considerable time, but then came back, breathing heavily. He hurled himself down on his couch, still breathing heavily for a while until he became calm again. He had with him a eunuch carrying a dish covered over with a napkin. The eunuch stood before him and then came forward trembling. We were amazed at all this. Then the Caliph sat up and said to the eunuch, "Set down what you are carrying," so he put down the dish. He said to the eunuch, "Take off the napkin," so he did this, and behold, the dish

---

283. Bayhaqī, *Maḥāsin*, ed. Schwally, 207–8 = ed. Ibrāhīm, 313–14; Ibn al-Athīr, VI, 105–6. For further anecdotes of Ibn Da'b and al-Hādī, see Masʿūdī, *Murūj*, VI, 264–5, 270–7 = ed. Pellat, §§ 2472, 2478.

284. I.e., ʿAlī b. Muḥammad b. ʿAbdallāh b. Abī Sayf al-Madā'inī, historian who was among Ṭabarī's most important sources; he probably died in 228 (843). See *GAL*, S I, 214–15; *GAS*, I, 314–15; *EI*[2] s.v. (U. Sezgin).

held the heads of two slave girls, with more beautiful faces and hair, by God, than I had ever seen before; there were jewels on their heads, arranged in the hair, and a sweet perfume was diffused (from them). We found this a horrific sight. The Caliph said, "Do you know what these two were up to?" We replied in the negative. He said, "We received information that they were in love with each other, and had got together for an immoral purpose. So I set this eunuch to watch over them and to report to me what they were doing. In due course, he came to me and informed me that they had got together, so I went along and found them under a single coverlet committing an immoral act. I thereupon killed them." After saying this, he told the slave to take the two heads away. He related: The Caliph then resumed his former conversation as if he had done nothing unusual in the meantime.[285]

Abū al-ʿAbbās b. Abī Mālik al-Yamāmī has mentioned that ʿAbdallāh b. Muḥammad al-Bawwāb related: I used to act as al-Hādī's doorkeeper and chamberlain, deputizing for al-Faḍl b. al-Rabīʿ. He related: One day, the Caliph was holding a court session when I was in his palace. He had just eaten his midday meal, and had called for some date wine [*nabīdh*]. Previous to that, he had gone into his mother al-Khayzurān's presence and she had asked him to appoint his maternal uncle al-Ghiṭrīf[286] as governor of the Yemen; he had replied, "Remind me about it before I get involved in the wine-drinking session." He related: When the Caliph had determined on his drinking session, al-Khayzurān sent to him either Munīrah or Zahrah (i.e., one of her slave attendants) in order [591]
to remind him. The Caliph said, "Go back and tell her, 'Choose for him (i.e., for Ghiṭrīf) either the divorcing (i.e., by myself) of his daughter ʿUbaydah or else the governorship of the Yemen!' " However, the slave girl only understood his words "Choose for him!"

285. See on this episode of lesbianism—which must have been rife in the enclosed life of the harem—Abbott, 98–9. On lesbian sexual activity (*saḥq, siḥāq*) in early ʿAbbāsid society, see Ṣalāḥ al-Dīn al-Munajjid, *al-Ḥayāt al-jinsiyyah ʿind al-ʿArab*², 89–92, and E. Wagner, *Abū Nuwās, eine Studie zur arabischen Literatur der frühen ʿAbbāsidenzeit,* 179–80.

286. See Yaʿqūbī, *Taʾrīkh,* II, 481. Al-Ghiṭrīf b. ʿAṭāʾ was the brother of al-Hādī's mother al-Khayzurān, and also his father-in-law; he rose from slave origins to this governorship and then to that of Khurāsān. See *EI*² Suppl. s.v. (Bosworth), and for this particular episode, Abbott, 88–9, and Moscati, *Le califat d'al-Hādī,* 26.

and she went on her way. Al-Khayzurān said, "I have already chosen for him the governorship of the Yemen." Al-Hādī thereupon divorced al-Ghiṭrīf's daughter ʿUbaydah. The Caliph heard the clamor (i.e., arising from the women's quarters), and said (to al-Khayzurān), "What's the matter with you all?" Al-Khayzurān then told him what had happened. He retorted, "You yourself made the choice for him," but she protested, "The message from you wasn't conveyed to me in those terms." He related: The Caliph ordered Ṣāliḥ, the *ṣāḥib al-muṣallā,* to stand with his sword over his boon-companions, with the instructions that they were to divorce their wives. The eunuchs came out to me with these instructions, and also to inform me that I was not to allow anyone in.[287]

He related: There was standing at the door a man muffled up in his *ṭaylasān,*[288] shifting his weight from one foot to the other. At that point, there occurred to me two verses of poetry, and I recited them, those verses being:

O my two friends of the tribe of Saʿd, halt and greet
Maryam—may God not make Maryam distant!
And say to her, "Have you really resolved on this separation,
and is there any act of favor after this which might be known
[*fa-yuʿlamā*]?

He related: The man muffled up in his *ṭaylasān* then said to me, "(The correct word is) *fa-naʿlamā* ("Which we might know")!" I replied, "What is the difference between *yuʿlamā* and *naʿlamā*?" He said, "Poetry is rendered excellent by its meaning, and it may be spoilt by its meaning; (in this instance), we don't want people in general to know our secret thoughts."[289] I said to him, "I have a better knowledge of this poetry than you." He said, "Who is the author of the poetry?" I replied, "Al-Aswad b. ʿUmārah al-

287. Iṣfahānī, *Aghānī,* ed. Būlāq, XIII, 13 = ed. Cairo, XIV, 171–2.

288. I.e., the hood or scarf-like garment which went over the head and shoulders, often considered to be in origin a Persian garment. See Dozy, *Dictionnaire détaillé des noms de vêtements chez les arabes,* 278–90; D. A. Agius, *Arabic literary works as a source of documentation for technical terms of the material culture,* 218–20.

289. I.e., the specific, more restrictive first person plural active verb gives a better meaning in the context of the two verses than the vague, general third person singular passive verb.

Nawfalī."[290] He then informed me, "I am he." I went up to him closely and related to him the story of Mūsā, and gave my apologies to him for my repeated questioning and arguing with him. He related: He turned away his mount and observed, "The best plan is to quit this residence!"[291]

Muṣʿab (b. ʿAbdallāh) al-Zubayrī[292] related that Abū al-Muʿāfā[293] said: I recited to al-ʿAbbās b. Muḥammad[294] a eulogy on Mūsā and Hārūn,

O Khayzurán, may greeting on greeting be upon you! [592]
Your two sons will surely rule over the people![295]

He related: He told me, "I am giving you sound advice; al-Yamānī has said, 'Don't mention my mother either with good or ill!' "[296]

Aḥmad b. Ṣāliḥ b. Abī Fanan (?)[297] has mentioned that Yūsuf al-Ṣayqal, the poet of Wāsiṭ,[298] transmitted the information to him, saying: We were with al-Hādī in Jurjān before he succeeded to the caliphate and entered Baghdad. He went up on to a fine belvedere which he had, and someone[299] sang this verse of poetry,

---

290. Poet who was at one point of his career head of the state treasury in al-Madīnah. See Iṣfahānī, *Aghānī,* ed. Būlāq, XIII, 12–14 = ed. Cairo, XIV, 169–73.

291. Ibid., ed. Būlāq, XIII, 13–14 = ed. Cairo, XIV, 172.

292. Descendant of the Successor Muṣʿab b. al-Zubayr and author of the genealogical work *al-Jamharah fī nasab Quraysh,* died in 233 (848) or 236 (851). See *GAL,* S I, 212; *GAS,* I, 271–2.

293. I.e., Abū al-Muʿāfā Yaʿqūb b. Ismāʿīl al-Muzanī, poet of Syria and Iraq. See Iṣfahānī, *Aghānī,* ed. Būlāq, IV, 122 = ed. Cairo, IV, 415–16; Marzubānī, *Muʿjam al-shuʿarā',* 496; *GAS,* II, 479.

294. Presumably, the senior ʿAbbāsid prince, see Ṭabarī, III, 547 (above, 7).

295. Masʿūdī, *Murūj,* VI, 269 = ed. Pellat, § 2476; Azdī, 257; Munierah al-Rasheed, *The Abū Ḥafṣah family of poets,* 149, no. 130; Abbott, 53. In Thaʿālibī, *Laṭā'if,* 81, tr. 81, the verse is attributed to Ibn Abī Ḥafṣah, presumably Abū Simṭ Marwān b. Sulaymān (105–82 [723–97]) of the famous poetic family; see *GAL,* I², 73, S I, 112–13, and *GAS,* II, 447–8.

296. I.e., such a reference would be impolite and a personal intrusion. The reference to "al-Yamānī" is obscure; Marzubānī, 515, mentions a poet named Abū al-Humaysiʿ al-Yamānī.

297. Iṣfahānī, *Aghānī,* ed. Būlāq, XX, 93 = ed. Cairo, XXIII, 217, has Aḥmad b. Ṣāliḥ al-Hishāmī for this name.

298. I.e., Yūsuf b. al-Ḥajjāj al-Ṣayqal al-Thaqafī, nicknamed al-Laqwah "having a contorted face," poet and secretary from al-Kūfah of the period of al-Hādī and al-Rashīd, and companion of Abū Nuwās. See Iṣfahānī, *Aghānī,* ed. Būlāq, XX, 93–6 = ed. Cairo, XXIII, 217–23; Ibn al-Abbār, 96–7, with the *nisbah* of "al-Kūfī"; *GAS,* II, 615.

299. In Iṣfahānī, *Aghānī,* loc. cit., the singer is Ibrāhīm al-Mawṣilī.

And their men have hoisted over their shoulders[300]
their Rudaynī spears,[301] getting ready for action.

He said, "How does this poem go?" So they recited (the whole of it) to him. He went on, "I would have preferred this singing to be of a more tender and delicate poem than this; go along to Yūsuf al-Ṣayqal and get him to recite (some much more suitable poetry)." He related: So they came to me and told me the story. I accordingly recited,

Do not blame me for showing grief,
(for) my lord has become distant and inaccessible (to me).
Alas for my sorrow, if the former relations
between us have been severed!
Indeed, Mūsā, through his generosity,
has gathered together within himself all generosity.

He related: He looked up, and behold, there was a camel before him. Al-Hādī said, "Load up this beast with dirhams and dīnārs and convey that load of money to him." He related: They then brought to me the loaded camel.[302]

Muḥammad b. Saʿd[303] has mentioned that Abū Zuhayr transmitted the information to him, saying: Ibn Daʾb was the most highly favored of men in al-Hādī's eyes. One day, al-Faḍl b. al-Rabīʿ sallied forth and announced, "The Commander of the Faithful orders everyone waiting at his gate to go away, but as for you, O Ibn Daʾb, please enter!" Ibn Daʾb related: I went into the Caliph's presence and found him sprawled out on his couch, and his eyes
[593] were bloodshot and red from sleeplessness and from the wine which he had drunk the previous night. He said to me, "Recount to me a story about wine drinking." I replied, "Certainly, O Commander of the Faithful. A group of men from the tribe of Kinā-

300. There are significant variants for this hemistich in Ms. C and in Iṣfahānī, *Aghānī*, ed. Būlāq, XX, 93 = ed. Cairo, XXIII, 217.

301. I.e., with well-straightened shafts, allegedly from a woman called Rudaynah who was expert at straightening these; see *Lisān al-ʿArab*[1], XVII, 37.

302. Iṣfahānī, *Aghānī*, ed. Būlāq, XX, 93–4 = ed. Cairo, XXIII, 217.

303. The great traditionist, historian, and biographer of the generations of early Muslims, died in 230 (845). See *GAL*, I[2], 142–3, S I, 208; *GAS*, I, 300–11, *EI*[2] s.v. Ibn Saʿd (Fück).

nah[304] went forth in search of wine from Syria.[305] The brother of one of them died, so they all sat round his grave, drinking wine, and one of them recited,

Do not be niggardly in giving to the screech-owl[306] its required drink;
give the dead man wine to drink, even though he has been laid in his tomb.
Give to drink limbs, skulls and contents of the skull
in the manner of a wind which dispels the morning clouds and as one setting out in the morning.
He was a noble one, and he came to his death among those who died;
every spring and branch is shattered.[307]

He related: The Caliph sent for an inkstand and wrote the verses down, and then he instructed al-Ḥarrānī (to issue to Ibn Daʾb) forty thousand dirhams, saying that ten thousand were for himself and thirty thousand were for the three verses of poetry. He related: I went to al-Ḥarrānī, and he said, "Come to an arrangement with us over ten thousand dirhams, with the stipulation that you swear to us never to mention it to the Commander of the Faithful." I duly swore that I would never mention it to the Commander of the Faithful until he should predecease me. Then he (i.e., Mūsā al-Hādī) died, and he never mentioned it until the caliphate passed to al-Rashīd.[308]

---

304. Tribe of the Ḥijāz, to whom Quraysh of Mecca were reckoned; see *EI*² s.v. (Watt).

305. Wine had, of course, to be imported into the Arabian peninsula from the wine-growing lands to the north.

306. The owl [*hāmah*], generally regarded as a bird of ill-omen, was believed to hover over the grave of an unavenged person until blood had been exacted in reparation. See Goldziher, "Der Seelenvogel im islamischen Volksglauben," *Globus,* LXXXIII (1902), 302–3 = *Gesammelte Schriften,* IV, 404–5; Sir Charles Lyall, *Translations of ancient Arabian poetry chiefly pre-Islamic,* pp. xxx, 67; T. Fahd, *La divination arabe,* 513; and now the penetrating study by T. E. Homerin, "Echoes of a thirsty owl: death and afterlife in pre-Islamic Arabic poetry," *JNES,* XLIV (1985), 165–84, with an examination at pp. 175–7 of the semantic connections of the terms *hāmah* "owl/skull" and *ṣadā* "owl/brain/contents of the skull" used in the verses cited here.

307. Emending the vowelling of the last words of each line, in accordance with the Cairo text, VIII, 224: *qubir, al-mubtakir, munkasir.*

308. In Jahshiyārī, 130–1, the indignant Ibn Daʾb tears up the promissory note

Abū Duʿāmah[309] has mentioned that Salm b. ʿAmr al-Khāsir[310] eulogized Mūsā al-Hādī and recited,

At ʿĪsābādh is a noble one of Quraysh,
  at whose sides is always to be found abundantly flowing wine.
The Muslims resort to his flanks for protection
  whenever there is anything to be feared or to be hoped for.
In the main square (i.e., of Baghdad) are lofty residences
  which people who claim a relationship have erected.
But how many persons make the claim, "I am of sound lineage,"
  when all created beings and the person of handsome appearance reject it!
Such a person has a pride in lineage, which he is niggardly over, in order that he may achieve a permanent reputation;
  yet no one who is niggardly over this secures immortality!
[594] There is blame[311] upon al-Ḍabbī, which cannot be concealed;
  he conceals it, but the cover is ripped away.
By my life, if Abū Khadīj were to construct
  a house, the structure would never be demolished![312]

He related: Salm al-Khāsir recited, when Mūsā took over the caliphate after al-Mahdī,

Mūsā has obtained the caliphate and the divine guidance,
  and the Commander of the Faithful Muḥammad (i.e., al-Mahdī) has died.
Thus the one whose loss has affected the whole of mankind has died,

---

but is cheated of obtaining justice by the Caliph's death shortly afterwards; cf. Sourdel, *Vizirat*, I, 123 n. 2.

309. I.e., ʿAlī b. Yazīd, a *rāwī* mentioned in Iṣfahānī, *Aghānī*, ed. Būlāq, III, 129 = ed. Cairo, IV, 8, as quoting Yaḥyā b. Khālid al-Barmakī.

310. Eulogist of the early ʿAbbāsids, died in 186 (802). See Pellat, *Le milieu baṣrien*, 165; *GAL, S I, 113; GAS*, II, 511–12.

311. The Cairo text, VIII, 224, has *luʾm* "ignobleness" for the Leiden text's *lawm* "blame."

312. G. E. von Grunebaum, "Three Arabic poets of the early Abbasid age. V. Salm al-Ḫâsir," *Orientalia*, XIX (1950), 62, no. II = *Shuʿarāʾ ʿAbbāsiyyūn*, 92, no. 2. The reference to "Abū Khadīj," literally "father of a prematurely born camel foal, or of a sickly calf," is presumably to Mūsā as the father of a newly born son at that particular moment.

and the one who will satisfactorily take the place for you of
the one whose loss is felt, has arisen (in his place).[313]

He also recited,

(Other) monarchs become hidden on account of Mūsā, on the
occasion of his rise to eminence,
just as the stars (are concealed) because of the shining rays of
the sun, when these last appear.
There is not a single person, out of all creation, who sees a full
moon and its rising into view,
and is not abased or becomes submissive (before it).[314]

He also recited,

Were it not for the Caliph Mūsā (coming) after his father,
there would be no successor for the people after their divinely
appointed leader [*mahdiyyihim*].[315]
Do you not see the community of the gentile prophet [*ummat al-ummī*] going down to get water (i.e., life enhancement, succor),
as if they were scooping up water from the regions adjoining
the sea,
From the two hands of a monarch whose munificent gifts have
become universal,
as if his gifts, because of his generosity, were spendthriftiness?[316]

Idrīs b. Abī Ḥafṣah[317] has mentioned that (Abū Simṭ) Marwān b. Abī Ḥafṣah[318] transmitted the information to him, saying: When

---

313. Von Grunebaum, op. cit., 64, no. IX = *Shuʿarāʾ ʿAbbāsiyyūn*, 96, no. 9. There is a play on words from the same root [*jinās*] in this verse, between *faqd* "loss" and *man yutafaqqadu* "the one who loss is felt."

314. Von Grunebaum, op. cit., 71, no. XXXI = *Shuʿarāʾ ʿAbbāsiyyūn*, 107, no. 31.

315. With a play upon words between the Caliph al-Mahdī's *laqab* or honorific and the concept of the eschatological figure of the awaited charismatic leader, whose appearance on earth will herald the coming end of the world; see *EI*[2] s.v. al-Mahdī (Madelung).

316. Von Grunebaum, op. cit., 71, no. XXXIII.

317. I.e., Abū Sulaymān Idrīs b. Yaḥyā b. Abī Ḥafṣah, brother of Abū Simṭ Marwān, and himself a poet of secondary importance. See Ibn al-Nadīm, *Fihrist*, 182, tr. B. Dodge, I, 354; *GAS*, II, 582.

318. The first poet of major importance from this famed poetic family, and a

Mūsā al-Hādī came to power, I went into his presence and recited to him,

If my soul were granted immortality after the Imām Muḥammad (i.e., al-Mahdī),
it would not rejoice at its prospect of perpetual existence.[319]

He (i.e., Marwān) related: I uttered panegyric poetry, and recited concerning him,

Your father strengthened my personal position with (a gift of) 70,000 (dirhams) and provided me with nourishment and clothing,
and indeed, I saw face-to-face in that a remarkable sight.[320]
Indeed, I am certain, O Commander of the Faithful,
that my share of liberality (literally, "my drink") from your hands will not be seen as one doled out in a niggardly fashion.[321]

When I recited this poetry to him, he said, "Who can reach the extent of al-Mahdī (in generosity)? Nevertheless, we shall render you contented." He related: But death came upon him before anything else, and he never gave me anything; I did not receive a single dirham from anyone until al-Rashīd's accession.

[595] Hārūn b. Mūsā al-Farawī[322] has mentioned that Abū Ghuzayyah (al-Anṣārī)[323] transmitted the information to him from al-Ḍaḥḥāk

---

fierce defender of the legal claims to rule of the ʿAbbāsids against the ʿAlids, died ca. 181 (797). See A. H. Harley, "Abu's-Simṭ Marwān b. Abī Ḥafṣah—a postclassical Arab poet," *JRASB*, Letters, III (1937), 71–90; *GAS*, II, 447–8; *EI*[2] s.v. Marwān al-Akbar b. Abī Ḥafṣa (J. E. Bencheikh).

319. Six other verses of this poem are to be found in the anthology of Muḥammad b. ʿAbd al-Raḥmān al-ʿUbaydī, *al-Tadhkirah al-saʿdiyyah*, see Munierah al-Rasheed, 184; *Shiʿr Marwān b. Abī Ḥafṣah*, ed. Ḥusayn ʿAṭawān, 15 no. 1; Harley, 83.

320. Reading with the Cairo text, VIII, 225, *mashhadā.*

321. Munierah al-Rasheed, 119 no. 58; *Shiʿr Marwān b. Abī Ḥafṣah*, 30 no. 14,

322. Following *Addenda et emendanda*, p. DCCLX, and the Cairo text, VIII, 225, *pace* the text's "al-Qarawī." He is mentioned as a *rāwī* in Iṣfahānī, *Aghānī*, ed. Būlāq, I, 187 = ed. Cairo, II, 55.

323. Judge of Medina and a *rāwī* in *Aghānī*, ed. Būlāq, III, 135, 155, VIII, 104–5 = ed. Cairo, IV, 20, 58, IX, 165–6, for events in connection with the poet Abū al-ʿAtāhiyah at al-Mahdī's court.

b. Maʿn al-Sulamī, who said: I went into Mūsā's presence, and I recited to him the verses,

O you two places of the heart's yearning, speak,
for at you I often used to see (in the past) al-Rabāb and Kulthum (i.e., two beloved ones)!
There are not two places of former encampment, in a condition of ancientness and decay,
which move to tears more strongly what lies beneath the ribs (i.e., the heart) than you two places!
Return a salutation on an old man, whose emotions
the ruined traces of the two encampments have stirred up and who has become deeply moved, and then give a (further) salutation!

He related: I eulogized him in these verses, and then when I reached the verse,

With the agility of his fingertips in activity (i.e., in bestowing largesse) I thought
that he would not leave a single dirham in the treasuries

he turned to the treasurer Aḥmad and said, "Woe upon you, O Aḥmad! It is as if he were looking at us only yesterday!" He related: He had in fact brought out that night a great sum of money and then distributed it.

It has been mentioned from Isḥāq al-Mawṣilī, or from someone else, relating from (Isḥāq's father) Ibrāhīm, who said: One day, we were in Mūsā's presence, and he had with him Ibn Jāmiʿ[324] and Muʿādh b. al-Ṭabīb.[325] It was the first day that Muʿādh had ever come into our circle; he was very expert in singing melodies and very knowledgeable about the more ancient songs. The Caliph said, "Whichever of you moves me the most to emotion, he can choose what he likes." So Ibn Jāmiʿ sang a song for him, but it failed to move the Caliph. I knew what kind of songs made up his

---

324. I.e., Abū al-Qāsim Ismāʿīl b. Jāmiʿ, musician and singer of Mecca and rival of Ibrāhīm al-Mawṣilī, died in 192 (808). See Farmer, 115–16; Ziriklī, *Aʿlām*, I, 306; *EI*² s.v. Ibn Djāmiʿ (A. Shiloah).

325. Cited as a *rāwī* and composer of melodies in Iṣfahānī, *Aghānī*, ed. Būlāq, XIII, 133–4, XIV, 45 = ed. Cairo, XV, 68–71, 253.

object of desire. The Caliph said, "Step forward, O Ibrāhīm," so I sang to him,

Sulaymā has brought us together;
 but where, O where, can we say[326] that she is?

At this, he became transported with emotion, to the point that he rose up from his seat, raised his voice and exclaimed, "Sing it again!" So I sang it again. He said, "This is the kind of song which is to my taste, so decide now what you want!" I said, "O Commander of the Faithful, the walled garden of ʿAbd al-Malik and its murmuring spring." At that, his eyes rolled round in his head until they became like two gleaming red-hot coals. Then he burst out, "O son of a stinking, uncircumcised whore! You wanted to let the people at large know that you were able to stir up my emotions and that I gave you your free choice and accordingly granted to you an estate! By God, were it not for the hasty error caused by your stupidity,
[596] which has clouded your sound judgment, I would strike off that which contains your eyes (i.e., your head)!" Then he bowed his head in silence for a brief while, and I had a vision of the angel of death standing between me and him awaiting his word of command. Then he summoned Ibrāhīm al-Ḥarrānī and told him, "Take the hand of this stupid fellow, and lead him into the treasury; and then let him take from there whatever he likes." So al-Ḥarrānī brought me into the treasury and said, "How much are you going to take?" I replied, "A hundred purses."[327] He said, "Let me consult him (i.e., the Caliph)." He related: I said, "Eighty, then." He replied, "(Wait) until I consult him." I thereupon realized what he wanted, so I said, "Seventy purses for me and thirty for you!" He said, "Now you have put forward the correct solution! Please go ahead!" So I went away with seven hundred thousand dirhams, and the angel of death vanished from before my face.[328]

---

326. Reading, in accordance with *Glossarium*, P. DXXVIII, *naqūluhā*, for the text's *nuqūluhā*.

327. A *badrah* contained 10,000 dirhams, so this meant a total of one million dirhams.

328. In Jahshiyārī, 133–4, the singer is Isḥāq b. Ibrāhīm al-Mawṣilī, who arouses the Caliph's ire by asking for the property of Marwān (b. al-Ḥakam) in al-Madīnah, but is able to take his full reward without Ibrāhīm b. Dhakwān exacting his usual commission (cf. Ṭabarī, III, 593, above, 77). In Iṣfahānī, *Aghānī*, ed. Būlāq, V, 16 =

ʿAlī b. Muḥammad (al-Nawfalī) has mentioned that Ṣāliḥ b. ʿAlī b. ʿAṭiyyah al-Aḍjam[329] transmitted the information to him from Ḥakam al-Wādī,[330] who said: Al-Hādī used to be fond of a moderate, measured emotional pitch of singing [*al-ghināʾ al-wasaṭ*], the kind which has few often-repeated refrains [*tarjīʿ*],[331] but it did not have much appreciable effect of lightening his spirits. He related: One night, we were at one of his sessions, at which Ibn Jāmiʿ, al-Mawṣilī, al-Zubayr b. Daḥmān[332] and al-Ghanawī were also present, when the Caliph suddenly called for three purses of money. He ordered them to be brought in, and they were set down in the midst of the circle of the Caliph and his companions. Then he put them altogether in one heap and said, "Whoever can sing to me a melody which is consonant with the emotional state which I am at present feeling, shall have the whole lot." He related: Al-Hādī had a laudable trait of character in that, if he disliked a thing, he would never linger over it but would turn away from it. Ibn Jāmiʿ now sang to him, but he showed his aversion from it. All the other members of the assembled company then sang, but he started displaying a similar aversion until I myself sang. I adapted my singing to his emotional state, so that he cried out "Bravo! Bravo! Give me some wine to drink!" He then drank and became stirred with feeling. I got up and then sat down by the purses of money, and I knew that I had won possession of them. Ibn Jāmiʿ came forward in an approving, congratulatory manner and said, "O Commander of the Faithful, he (has sung), by God, just as you said, whereas all the rest of us, apart from him, have not sung in harmony with your present feelings." He related: The Caliph said,

---

ed. Cairo, VI, 184–5, the singer is Ibrāhīm, with the essential points in the story being those of Jahshiyārī.

329. Literary figure of Abnāʾ origin and resident in Wāsiṭ. It was allegedly (but improbably) he who strangled the poet Marwān b. Abī Ḥafṣah when the latter was ill in 181 (797) or 182 (798); see *Aghānī*, ed. Būlāq, IX, 48, XVIII, 37, 46 = ed. Cairo, X, 95, XX, 138, 147.

330. I.e., al-Ḥakam (b. Yaḥyā) b. Maymūn, a mawlā of Persian origin but a cameleer engaged in trade along the Wādī al-Qurā (hence his *nisbah*) in early life, and a famous singer under the last Umayyads and the early ʿAbbāsids up to Hārūn's time; see *Aghānī*, ed. Būlāq, VI, 64–8 = ed. Cairo, VI, 2808 *et passim*.

331. I.e., music which neither excited the emotions nor unduly depressed them.

332. Musician of Mecca of mawlā origin, and partisan of Ibrāhīm b. al-Mahdī at Hārūn's court; see Farmer, 123–4.

"The purses are yours," and he went on drinking until his desire
[597] for melodies was satisfied, and he got up. Then he said, "Instruct three of the attendants to bear the purses with him," and then he entered (his private apartments). We departed, walking across the courtyard, heading homewards. Ibn Jāmiʿ caught me up, and I said, "May I be made your ransom, O Abū al-Qāsim! You behaved as a person of your pedigree could be expected to do; so look in the money bags for what takes your fancy." Ibn Jāmiʿ replied, "May God vouchsafe to you His approval! We desired to increase your share of favour!" Al-Mawṣilī also caught up with us and said, "Present us with a gift (i.e., from the money bags)!" But I retorted, "Why should I? You didn't behave in a suitable manner at the court session! No, by God, you shan't have a single dirham!"[333]

Muḥammad b. ʿAbdallāh has mentioned that Saʿīd al-Qāriʾ al-ʿAllāf, the companion[334] of Abān al-Qāriʾ,[335] told him that Mūsā's boon-companions were with him in his court session, including al-Ḥarrānī, Saʿīd b. Salm and others. Mūsā had a slave girl who used to pour out wine for them. She had a bantering, provocative manner, and she used to address one of the company as "O boorish one [*jilfī*]!"[336] and joke with others of them. Yazīd b. Mazyad came in, and he heard what she was saying to them. He therefore told her, "By the Great God! If you speak to me like you speak to them, I will certainly strike you a blow with my sword!" Mūsā said to her, "Woe upon you! He will indeed, by God, do what he says, so take care!" He related: She accordingly held back from him, and never exchanged any pleasantries with him. He related: Saʿīd al-ʿAllāf and Abān al-Qāriʾ were Ibāḍīs.[337]

---

333. Iṣfahānī, *Aghānī*, ed. Būlāq, VI, 67 = ed. Cairo, VI, 286–7, giving the actual words of Ḥakam al-Wādī's winning song.

334. *Ṣāḥib.* perhaps also "famulus, colleague, master," given the vagueness of this term.

335. Both these Qurʾān readers are mentioned by Ibn Qutaybah, 533. Saʿīd is described as being especially high in al-Rashīd's favor, being known as "the Qurʾān reader of the Commander of the Faithful." He is further cited by Ṭabarī, III, 1134, as an authority for an account of al-Maʾmūn's last illness and death.

336. *Jilf* has many meanings, according to the *Lisān al-ʿArab*[1], X, 375; the one followed here is that of "gross, coarse [*al-jilf: al-aʿrābī al-jāfī*], but another possibility might be "corpulent, with a sack-like figure" [*al-ẓarf mithl al-khurj wa-al-juwāliq*].

337. I.e., of the Ibāḍiyyah subsect of the Khārijites. See *EI*[2] s.v. (T. Lewicki). These

Aḥmad b. Ibrāhīm b. Ismāʿīl b. Dāwūd al-Kātib[338] has mentioned that Ibn al-Qaddāḥ transmitted the information to him, saying: Al-Rabīʿ (b. Yūnus) had a slave girl called Amat al-ʿAzīz, of superlative beauty, a splendidly rounded bosom and shapely body. He presented her to al-Mahdī. When the latter perceived her beauty and fine appearance, he said, "This girl will be more suitable for Mūsā!"; hence he gave her to him. She became the most beloved of all creation to Mūsā, and gave birth to his elder sons.[339] Then a certain enemy of al-Rabīʿ's told Mūsā that he had heard al-Rabīʿ say, "I have never placed between myself and the earth anyone like Amat al-ʿAzīz." Mūsā became violently enraged with [598] jealousy at these words, and swore that he would kill al-Rabīʿ. So when he was appointed Caliph, he summoned al-Rabīʿ one day, and had his midday meal with him, showed him honor and handed to him a cup of wine mingled with honey. He related: Al-Rabīʿ said, "I realized that my life was contained in that cup (i.e., that it was poisoned), and that if I were to hand it back he would cut off my head, since I had for some time back been aware of his animus against me because of my going to his mother (i.e., to al-Khayzurān)[340] and because of (slanderous) reports he had received concerning me, without his having listened to any excuses from me. So I drank the cup." Al-Rabīʿ returned homewards. He gathered together his children and told them, "I am going to die, either on this very day or by next morning." His son al-Faḍl said to him, "Why do you say this, may I be made your ransom?" He said, "Mūsā gave me to drink, with his own hand, a poisoned drink, and I can feel it working in my body now." Then he made his last testament, setting forth his wishes, and died on that day or the fol-

---

two Ibāḍī scholars may well have stemmed from the well-known group of Ibāḍīs in al-Baṣrah; see Pellat, *Le milieu baṣrien*, 212–14.

338. In Ṭabarī, III, 439, given the full *nasab* of . . . b. Muʿāwiyah b. Bakr, this last person described as one of the Prophet's companions. It is therefore possible that this Aḥmad b. Ibrāhīm b. Ismāʿīl is identical with the *rāwī* Aḥmad b. Muʿāwiyah b. Bakr al-Bāhilī mentioned by Ṭabarī, III, 567 (above, 38, and n. 150).

339. According to Abbott, 66, his two eldest sons; see further on her, ibid., 86, 97, 99.

340. I.e., when he had gone to her in Baghdad, at the time of al-Hādī's accession to the throne, see Ṭabarī, III, 546 (above, 6).

lowing morning.[341] After Mūsā al-Hādī's death, al-Rashīd married Amat al-ʿAzīz,[342] and he gave her the child ʿAlī b. al-Rashīd.[343]

Al-Faḍl b. Sulaymān b. Isḥāq al-Hāshimī has asserted that when al-Hādī transferred to ʿĪsābādh in the opening months of the year in which he took over the caliphate, he dismissed al-Rabīʿ from the offices of vizier and head of the correspondence department which he had held up till then, and appointed in his stead ʿUmar b. Bazīʿ. He appointed al-Rabīʿ to be head of the department of accounting control [*al-zimām*], and al-Rabīʿ retained this latter office until he died.[344] His decease came a few months after al-Hādī's accession to power, and his death was publicly proclaimed. Al-Hādī did not attend the funeral; Hārūn al-Rashīd read the prayers over him, being at that time heir to the throne. Mūsā appointed in al-Rabīʿ's place Ibrāhīm b. Dhakwān al-Ḥarrānī, and he appointed as his deputy in the offices which he held Ismāʿīl b. Ṣubayḥ. Then he dismissed Ismāʿīl and appointed as deputy Yaḥyā b. Sulaym, appointing Ismāʿīl to the post of accounting control of the *Dīwān* of Syria and its dependencies.[345]

Yaḥyā b. al-Ḥasan b. ʿAbd al-Khāliq, the maternal uncle of al-Faḍl b. al-Rabīʿ, has mentioned that his father transmitted to him
[599] the information that Mūsā al-Hādī said, "I want to bring about al-Rabīʿ's death but I don't know how to encompass it." So Saʿīd b. Salm told him, "Designate a man to take a poisoned dagger and order him to slay al-Rabīʿ, and then order that assassin himself to be killed." He replied, "That is a good solution." He therefore gave orders to a man, who then crouched down in wait for him by the roadside, and commanded him to do that (i.e., to assassinate al-Rabīʿ). However, a certain subordinate official of al-Rabīʿ's went along to him and told him, "He (i.e., the Caliph) has given orders

341. Abbott, 86–7; Moscati, *Le califat d'al-Hādī,* 17–8, 26.

342. She having attained, after giving sons to al-Hādī, the free status of an *umm walad.*

343. See Ṭabarī, III, 758 (below, 327); Ibn Abī Ṭāhir Ṭayfūr, *Kitāb Baghdād,* 25–6; Ibn al-Athīr, VI, 216.

344. Jahshiyārī, 125–6; Sourdel, *Vizirat,* I, 121.

345. Jahshiyārī, 125–7; cf. Abbott, 96, and Sourdel, *Vizirat,* I, 122 and n. 4. There may be a confusion here between Yaḥyā b. Sulaym and Yaḥyā b. Sulaymān, whom Jahshiyārī names here as Ibrāhīm al-Ḥarrānī's deputy.

regarding you for such-and-such action to be taken." Hence, al-Rabīʿ took a different route from that. He went into his house and feigned illness. Then he became (really) ill after that for eight days, and died a natural death. His death was in the year 169 (785–6). He was al-Rabīʿ b. Yūnus.

The Caliphate of Hārūn al-Rashīd

The Events of the Year 170 (cont'd)

(July 3, 786–June 21, 787)

Hārūn's Assumption of the Caliphate on Mūsā al-Hādī's Death

Allegiance was given to al-Rashīd Hārūn b. Muḥammad b. ʿAbdallāh b. al-ʿAbbās as Caliph on the night of the Friday during which his brother Mūsā al-Hādī died. On that day when he assumed power he was twenty-two years old.[346] It is also said that on the day when allegiance was given to him as Caliph he was twenty-one years old. His mother was a slave wife from Jurash in the Yemen called Khayzurān,[347] and he himself was born at al-Rayy on the twenty-sixth of Dhū al-Ḥijjah 145 (March 17, 763) during al-Manṣūr's caliphate.[348] In regard to the Barmakīs, according to what has been mentioned, they assert that al-Rashīd was born on

346. Thus in *K. al-ʿUyūn*, 290, and Ibn al-Athīr, VI, 106.

347. According to Masʿūdī, *Murūj*, VI, 261 = ed. Pellat, § 2469, and *K. al-ʿUyūn*, 282, she was the daughter of ʿAṭāʾ, a mawlā of al-Mahdī's; see also Ibn al-Athīr, loc. cit., and Abbott, 22–6, 29.

348. Abbott, 24, notes that the dates given for Hārūn's birth vary between 145 (762–3) and 150 (767).

the first of al-Muḥarram 149 (February 16, 766) and that al-Faḍl b. Yaḥyā was born seven days before him, al-Faḍl's day of birth being the twenty-second of Dhū al-Ḥijjah 148 (February 8, 766).[349] Al-Faḍl's mother, Zaynab bt. Munīr, was appointed a wet nurse to al-Rashīd. Thus, she gave milk to al-Rashīd from the suckling of al-Faḍl, and al-Khayzurān gave milk to al-Faḍl from the suckling of al-Rashīd.[350]

Sulaymān b. Abī Shaykh[351] has mentioned that when it was the night in which Mūsā al-Hādī died, Harthamah b. Aʿyan (al-Ḍabbī)[352] brought forth Hārūn al-Rashīd during the hours of dark-
[600] ness and then set him down on the Caliph's official seat.[353] Hārūn thereupon summoned Yaḥyā b. Khālid b. Barmak, who was at that moment in jail; Mūsā had in fact resolved upon killing both Yaḥyā and Hārūn al-Rashīd that very night. He related: Yaḥyā now became present and assumed the office of the vizierate.[354] He sent (a messenger) to Yūsuf b. al-Qāsim b. Ṣubayḥ al-Kātib.[355] He had him appear, and commanded him to compose letters (announcing Hārūn's succession to the throne). When the morning after that night dawned, and the military leaders were all present, Yūsuf b. al-Qāsim stood up. He offered praises to God, eulogizing Him, and gave blessings upon Muḥammad. Then he began to speak in an eloquent fashion, and recounted the death of Mūsā and Hārūn's assumption of control in succession to him, and what Hārūn had commanded by way of pay allotments for the troops.

---

349. Hence, eight days before!

350. Shābushtī, 227, 229; Ibn al-Athīr, loc. cit.; Ibn al-Ṭiqṭaqā, 183, tr. 198–9; cf. Bouvat, 41, and Kennedy, 117. According to Ṭabarī, II, 840, Khālid b. Barmak's wife Umm Khālid bt. Yazīd suckled al-Saffāḥ's daughter Rayṭah, whilst al-Saffāḥ's wife Umm Salamah suckled Khālid's daughter Umm Yaḥyā. As Abbott, 24, implies, Ṭabarī seems to show a certain scepticism about the Barmakī claims to foster-relationship between Hārūn and al-Faḍl.

351. Cited elsewhere by Ṭabarī as a *rāwī* for events in al-Mahdī's reign.

352. Member of the Abnā' who was one of the chief commanders of al-Rashīd and al-Ma'mūn, filling many governorships until his execution through the intrigues of al-Faḍl b. Sahl in 200/816. See Crone, 177, and *EI*² s.v. (Pellat).

353. Azdī, 261; *K. al-ʿUyūn*, 290; Ibn al-Athīr, loc. cit.

354. Ibn al-Athīr, VI, 106–7.

355. Secretary, of mawlā origin, like most of those employed by the Barmakīs; see Sourdel, *Vizirat*, I, 134, 141, 179, 226. He was the founder of a line of secretaries who served subsequent Caliphs and who included in their ranks several poets; see J. Bencheikh, "Les sécretaires poètes et animateurs de cénacles aux IIᵉ et IIIᵉ siècles de l'Hégire," *JA*, CCLXIII (1975), 269 ff.

Aḥmad b. al-Qāsim has mentioned, transmitting information from his paternal uncle ʿAlī b. Yūsuf b. al-Qāsim (b. Ṣubayḥ), as follows: He related: Our mawlā Yazīd al-Ṭabarī transmitted the information to me that he was present at that time, carrying the inkstand for my father Yūsuf b. al-Qāsim, and he remembered the complete text of his words. He related: Yūsuf b. al-Qāsim said, after praising God, He is exalted and magnified, and after offering blessings on the Prophet, as follows:

God, with His favor and His grace, has vouchsafed to you of His goodness, O people of the house of the Prophet, the house of the caliphate and the original stock of the apostleship. He has, moreover, brought to you,[356] O obedient ones from among the supporters of the dynasty and helpers of the mission [*al-daʿwah,* i.e., of the ʿAbbāsids], manifestations of His favor which are innumerable and which will not pass away through the whole extent of eternity, and His all-embracing acts of beneficence, in that He has brought firmly together the bond of your fellowship, has exalted your position, has strengthened your arm, has humbled your enemy, and has shown forth the word of divine truth, for you have become worthy of it and fitting people for it. Hence, God has made you mighty—for God is a powerful and mighty one—and thus you have become supporters of the religion of God, the One who is well-pleased (with you), and have become defenders, by means of His drawn sword, of the members of the house of His Prophet. Through you, He rescued them from the hands of the oppressors, the imāms of tyranny, of those who broke God's covenant, of those who shed innocent blood and of those who consumed and appropriated for themselves the income from the captured lands [*fay*ʾ]. So bear in mind all this favor which God has accorded you, and take care not to change your attitude, or He will change His attitude towards you.

God, He is exalted and magnified, has taken to Himself His Caliph, Mūsā al-Hādī the Imām, and has drawn him to Him- [601]
self. He has appointed as Mūsā's successor a rightly guided, well-pleasing one as Commander of the Faithful for you, one who is

356. Following the Cairo text, VIII, 231, *wa-atākum* instead of the Leiden text's *wa-iyyākum.*

compassionate and merciful towards you, one who will receive cordially those of you who act righteously and who will show himself tender-hearted by pardoning those of you who act evilly. The Caliph—may God grant him the permanent enjoyment of divine favor, preserve for him what He has entrusted to his care of the affairs of the Muslim community, and bestow upon him what He has bestowed on those who are His supporters and the people showing Him obedience—promises for you, from his heart, compassion and mercy towards you and the sharing-out among you of your stipends when you justly deserve them. He will bestow upon you presents from what God has bestowed on His Caliphs, stored up in the state treasury, which will be of such a magnitude that you will not require your regular pay allotments for so-and-so number of months, not however subtracting a corresponding sum to this from any advance pay allotments which you may receive in the future, but making over the remainder of that for the protection of your families and also what monies may accrue to the state treasuries in the provinces and distant areas from rebellious heretics, to the point that the accumulated treasure becomes ample and great in size and is restored to the level which it originally was.

So give praise to God and renew your thanks, and this will inevitably bring you an increase in His beneficence towards you through what He has renewed for you by means of the Commander of the Faithful's lofty judgement and through what He has bestowed upon you by means of it—may God strengthen him through his obedience (to Him)! Make petition to God for the Caliph's long life and for yourselves, that through him you may enjoy long-lasting favor; perhaps you will receive God's mercy! Give (the Caliph) your right hands in the clasp of homage and adhere to your professions of allegiance—may God protect you and defend you, bring about righteousness through you and at your hands, and take you as His helpers just as He takes His righteous devotees!

Yaḥyā b. al-Ḥasan b. ʿAbd al-Khāliq has mentioned, saying that Muḥammad b. Hishām al-Makhzūmī transmitted the information to me, saying: When Mūsā died, Yaḥyā b. Khālid came to al-Rashīd whilst the latter was asleep, wrapped up in a coverlet and without any waist-wrapper. Yaḥyā said, "Arise, O Commander of the Faithful!" At that, al-Rashīd said to him, "How much you

frighten me by your enthusiasm in describing me as Caliph, when you know my position vis-à-vis this man (i.e., al-Hādī)! If news of this reaches him, what will my position be then?" Yaḥyā thereupon told him, "This is (Ibrāhīm) al-Ḥarrānī, Mūsā's vizier, and this is his seal ring." He related: Hārūn sat down on his mattress and said, "Give me guidance on what to do!" He related: Whilst he [602]
was speaking with him, another messenger suddenly appeared and announced, "You have just become the father of a boy!" He replied, "I hereby name him ʿAbdallāh."[357] Then he said to Yaḥyā, "Give me advice on what to do!" Yaḥyā said, "I advise you to take your seat immediately on Mūsā's Armenian carpet." He replied, "I have as good as done that; and by God, I shan't perform the worship at ʿĪsābādh except on that carpet, and I shan't perform the noon worship except in Baghdad and with the head of Abū ʿIṣmah before me!" He related: He then put on his robes and went forth. He performed the worship on it (i.e., the Armenian carpet) and had Abū ʿIṣmah brought forward, and then he had him decapitated and his scalp fastened to the tip of a spear shaft, and with this entered Baghdad.

All this was because he and Jaʿfar b. Mūsā al-Hādī had once been out riding together. They had come to one of the bridges of ʿĪsābādh. At that point, Abū ʿIṣmah had turned to Hārūn and said, "Stay where you are until the heir to the throne crosses over!" Hārūn had replied, "I hear and obey the Amīr!" So he had halted until Jaʿfar had crossed over. This was accordingly the reason for Abū ʿIṣmah's being killed.[358] He related: When al-Rashīd came to the crown of the bridge,[359] he summoned divers and then said, "Al-Mahdī gave me a seal ring which had cost one hundred thousand dīnārs and which was called 'the mountain' [*al-jabal*]. Subsequently, I went into the presence of my brother (i.e., of al-Hādī) with this seal ring on my finger. When I returned homewards, Sulaym al-Aswad caught up with me at the crown of the bridge,

357. Azdī, 261–2; Palmer, 35.

358. *K. al-ʿUyūn*, 290; Ibn al-Athīr, VI, 107.

359. *Kursī al-jisr*, i.e., of one of the main bridges across the Tigris. For *kursī* in this sense, *Glossarium*, p. CDL, has *caput pontis* "crown of the bridge," and *WbKAS*, I, 127a–b, "pillar (of a bridge)." One would expect *kursī* to mean something like "supporting structure," clearly the actual span over the water in this context.

and then said, 'The Commander of the Faithful commands you to give me the seal ring!' At that, I hurled it away in this very spot." They then dived down and fished out the ring. Hārūn rejoiced exceedingly at its recovery.[360]

Muḥammad b. Isḥāq al-Hāshimī has related that several of his companions transmitted the information to him, including Ṣabbāḥ b. Khāqān al-Tamīmī,[361] saying: Mūsā al-Hādī had deprived al-Rashīd of the succession and had secured allegiance to his own son Jaʿfar, this being at the time when ʿAbdallāh b. Mālik was commander of the police. But when al-Hādī died, Khuzaymah b. Khāzim (al-Tamīmī)[362] burst in during that same night, being accompanied by five thousand of his mawlās, bearing arms,[363] pulled Jaʿfar out of his bed and told him, "Unless you renounce your succession rights to the caliphate, I'll chop off your head!" Hence, the next morning the people rode forth to Jaʿfar's gate. Khuzaymah brought him forward and set him up on an elevated place by the
[603] gate of the palace, all the gates being locked. Jaʿfar stepped forward and announced, "O Muslims, I have released from their undertakings all those who gave their allegiance to me as heir; the caliphate belongs to my paternal uncle Hārūn, and I have no claim to it."[364] This was the reason for ʿAbdallāh b. Mālik al-Khuzāʿī's going all the way to Mecca on foot in felt slippers [*lubūd*], because he had sought the opinion of the religious lawyers regarding the oaths he had sworn in recognition of Jaʿfar's succession, and they had told him, "The breaking of any oath you have sworn can only be expiated by your going on foot to the House of God; there is no other way out." So he made the Pilgrimage on foot. Khuzaymah secured favor in al-Rashīd's sight by that action of his.[365]

---

360. Bayhaqī, *Maḥāsin*, ed. Schwally, 502–4 = ed. Ibrāhīm, II, 236–8; Ṭabarī-Balʿamī, tr. IV, 456; Qāḍī Ibn al-Zubayr, *K. al-Tuḥaf wa-al-dhakhāʾir*, 180–3, §§ 232–5; Ibn al-Athīr, loc. cit.; Palmer, 35–6. In Jahshiyārī, 131–2, Yaḥyā b. Khālid is charged by al-Hādī, on pain of death for failure, to get the seal ring from Hārūn, but forgiven when Hārūn himself flings it into the river.

361. Cited previously by Ṭabarī for events in al-Manṣūr's caliphate.

362. Brother of ʿAbdallāh b. Khāzim, see Ṭabarī, III, 548 (above, 9, n. 30).

363. The size of the force seems excessively large for the purpose intended, unless Khuzaymah expected strenuous opposition from the supporters of the child Jaʿfar's succession claim.

364. Nothing further seems to be recorded of Jaʿfar's life after this.

365. Ṭabarī-Balʿamī, tr. IV, 457; Azdī, 262; *K. al-ʿUyūn*, 291; Ibn al-Athīr, VI, 107;

Hārūn's Official Appointments and Dismissals

It has been mentioned that al-Rashīd was angry with Ibrāhīm al-Ḥarrānī and Sallām al-Abrash[366] on the day of Mūsā's death, so he ordered them to be sent to prison and their wealth confiscated. Ibrāhīm was imprisoned under Yaḥyā b. Khālid's charge in the latter's house. Then Muḥammad b. Sulaymān interceded with Hārūn for him, and asked the Caliph to show his favor to Ibrāhīm, to release him and to allow him to accompany Muḥammad on the journey down to al-Baṣrah; the Caliph then gave Muḥammad his consent to this.[367]

In this year, al-Rashīd dismissed ʿUmar b. ʿAbd al-ʿAzīz al-ʿUmarī from the governorship of the City of the Messenger of God (i.e., of Medina) and its administrative dependencies, and he appointed Isḥāq b. Sulaymān b. ʿAlī[368] as governor of all that.

In this year, Muḥammad b. Hārūn al-Rashīd (i.e., the future al-Amīn) was born. According to what Abū Ḥafṣ al-Kirmānī has mentioned, from Muḥammad b. Yaḥyā b. Khālid, he was born on

---

Palmer, 34; Kennedy, 112–13. Khuzaymah's role here secured him a position of influence for the whole of al-Rashīd's reign, whereas ʿAbdallāh b. Mālik was for long under a cloud, according to an anecdote in Bayhaqī, *Maḥāsin*, ed. Schwally, 542–3 = ed. Ibrāhīm, II, 297–8, being for a while boycotted and cut off from contact with the court; no doubt the hatred between Yaḥyā b. Khālid and ʿAbdallāh (ibid., ed. Schwally, 415 = ed. Ibrāhīm, II, 102) was a factor here. Kennedy, 116, notes that the other prominent supporters of Jaʿfar b. al-Hādī's succession, Yazīd b. Mazyad and ʿAlī b. ʿĪsā b. Māhān, were given no important appointments for the next decade. According to Jahshiyārī, 135, al-Khayzurān at first wanted to execute all those who had opposed al-Rashīd's succession, but Yaḥyā al-Barmakī dissuaded her, suggesting instead that they should be given dangerous military commands and, as with David's appointment of Uriah the Hittite, placed in the battle line with a good chance of finding death anyway (on Jahshiyārī as a source for the events of al-Rashīd's reign, see Sourdel, "La valeur littéraire et documentaire du 'Livre des Vizirs' d'al-Ǧahšiyārī d'après le chapitre consacré au califat de Hārūn al-Rašīd," *Arabica*, II [1955], 193–210).

366. As emerges from Ibn Abī Ṭāhir Ṭayfūr, 133, and Ṭabarī, III, 1065, see II, 684 (below, 224, n. 771), Abū Salamah Sallām (the full name in Jahshiyārī, 187) was a eunuch (*abrash*, more usually applied to animals = "mottled, speckled," doubtless in allusion to his skin). He later recovered favor and was employed by al-Rashīd for various confidential missions, including duties during the arrest of the Barmakīs and the confiscation of their property; see Ṭabarī, III, 684.

367. Jahshiyārī, 135, who says that Yaḥyā's intercession with al-Rashīd secured for Ibrāhīm the post of secretary to Muḥammad b. Sulaymān.

368. Grandson of al-Rashīd's great-great-grandfather ʿAlī b. ʿAbdallāh b. al-ʿAbbās.

Friday, the thirteenth of Shawwāl of this year (April 7, 787),[369] whilst al-Ma'mūn was born before him, on the night of Friday (i.e., of Thursday-Friday), the sixteenth of Rabīʿ I (September 15, 786).[370]

In this year, al-Rashīd appointed Yaḥyā b. Khālid as his vizier and told him, "I have invested you with responsibility for the subjects' affairs and have transferred the burden from myself to you. So exercise authority in this with what you consider to be sound judgement; appoint as your subordinate governors whom
[604] you think fit; and conduct affairs as you consider best." At the same time, he handed his seal ring over to him. Concerning this event, Ibrāhīm al-Mawṣilī recited,

Have you not seen that the sun was sickly,
 but when Hārūn assumed power, its light gleamed forth.
Through the auspicious effects of the trusted one of God, Hārūn, the munificent one?
 For Hārūn is its ruler, and Yaḥyā its vizier.[371]

Al-Khayzurān was the one who had the oversight of affairs; Yaḥyā used to lay matters before her and do things on her advice.[372]

In this year, Hārūn gave orders concerning the share of the Prophet's kindred (i.e., the share from the poor-tax to the *dhawū al-qurbā*), and it was divided out among the Hāshimites in equal portions.

In this year, he gave a guarantee of safe-conduct to those who had fled or who had gone into concealment, with the exception of a group of the dualist infidels [*al-zanādiqah*], including Yūnus b. Farwah and Yazīd b. al-Fayḍ.[373] Among the Ṭālibids who came

---

369. Actually, a Saturday.

370. Yaʿqūbī, *Ta'rīkh*, II, 491–2; Ṭabarī-Balʿamī, tr., IV, 456–7; Azdī, 262; Ibn al-Athīr, VI, 107; Palmer, 35; Gabrieli, "La successione di Hārūn ar-Rašīd e la guerra fra al-Amīn e al-Ma'mūn," *RSO*, XI (1926–8), 344.

371. Masʿūdī, *Murūj*, VI, 288–9 = ed. Pellat, § 2494; Iṣfahānī, *Aghānī*, ed. Būlāq, V, 41 = ed. Cairo, VI, 242; Ibn Khallikān, VI, 221, tr. IV, 105. Cf. Palmer, loc. cit.; Abbott, 113; Sourdel, *Vizirat*, I, 134–5, who notes that similar laudatory verses are attributed to Abān al-Lāḥiqī.

372. Jahshiyārī, 134; *K. al-ʿUyūn*, 291; Ibn al-Athīr, VI, 107–8.

373. Yazīd b. al-Fayḍ was a former secretary of al-Manṣūr, who had been arrested by al-Mahdī in 167/783–4, but had contrived to escape (Jahshiyārī, 115–16; Ṭabarī, III, 519–20), only, it seems, to have been recaptured; see Vajda, "Les zindîqs au pays d'Islam," 186.

into the open were Ṭabāṭabā, that is, Ibrāhīm b. Ismāʿīl,[374] and ʿAlī b. al-Ḥasan b. Ibrāhīm b. ʿAbdallāh b. al-Ḥasan.[375]

In this year, al-Rashīd detached the whole of the Byzantine marches [*al-thughūr*] from al-Jazīrah and Qinnasrīn, and made them into a single (administrative) region called "the frontier strongholds" [*al-ʿawāṣim*].[376]

In this year, Tarsus[377] was rendered prosperous and populous through the efforts of Abū Sulaym Faraj al-Turkī the eunuch [*al-khādim*],[378] and people settled there.[379]

In this year, Hārūn al-Rashīd led the Pilgrimage from the City of [605]
Peace. He gave the people of the two sanctuaries (i.e., Mecca and Medina) numerous gifts and divided out among them a huge sum of money.[380] It has been said that he both performed the Pil-

374. I.e., the Ḥasanid Ibrāhīm b. Ismāʿīl Ṭabāṭabā al-Rassī, father of the subsequent Zaydī Imām in Yemen al-Qāsim, died in 246 (860); Ibrāhīm fought with al-Ḥusayn b. ʿAlī in the rising which ended at Fakhkh. See Iṣfahānī, *Maqātil,* 297, 304; Öhrnberg, Tables 20, 22–3.

375. Ibn al-Athīr, VI, 108.

376. Ibid.; M. A. Shaban, *Islamic history. A new interpretation. 2. A.D. 750–1055 (A.H. 132–448),* 28–9. See on this region of the "frontier strongholds," Yāqūt, *Muʿjam,* IV, 165–6; Le Strange, *Lands,* 128 ff.; Canard, 226–35; *EI*² s.v. al-ʿAwāṣim (Canard).

377. Town and fortress of Cilicia. See Yāqūt, *Muʿjam,* IV, 28–9; Le Strange, *Lands,* 132–4; Canard, 282; *EI*¹ s.v. Ṭarsūs (F. Buhl).

378. Mawlā of al-Rashīd; see Crone, 190. As Ayalon has pointed out (*The military reforms of Caliph al-Muʿtaṣim,* 3–4), the role of the eunuchs in affairs increases perceptibly during al-Rashīd's caliphate; Masrūr was one of his closest confidants, and he and others of the court eunuchs were present at the Caliph's deathbed (Ṭabarī, III, 738, below, 303). As with Faraj here, eunuchs were prominent as military commanders, especially on the Byzantine frontiers. The eunuch al-Mufaḍḍal was invited to lead an ʿAbbāsid force at Mecca in 169 (786) against the ʿAlid al-Ḥusayn b. ʿAlī (Ṭabarī, III, 558, above, 25). Such instances make nonsense of the assertion by Shaban, 139, that the eunuch "certainly cannot lead armies or rule governments" (on the latter point, cf. the skillful rule in Egypt of Kāfūr as Regent for the Ikhshīdids).

379. Balādhurī, 168; Azdī, 262; Ibn al-Athīr, VI, 108–9; Brooks, *EHR,* XV (1900), 740; Canard, in *Cambridge medieval history, IV. The Byzantine empire. Part 1, Byzantium and its neighbours,* 706; Shaban, 29. In Khalīfah, *Taʾrīkh,* II, 711, and Yaʿqūbī, *Taʾrīkh,* II, 495, this work of restoration by Faraj al-Khādim, with the building of five gates and eighty-seven towers for the town, is placed in the year 171 (787–8).

380. Yaʿqūbī, *Taʾrīkh,* II, 592, who states that Hārūn actually deputed Mūsā b. ʿĪsā to lead the Pilgrimage when he first acceded to the throne, but then decided to lead it himself; Khalīfah, *Taʾrīkh,* II, 709; Muḥammad b. Ḥabīb, 38; Dīnawarī, 387; Azdī, 266, Ibn al-Athīr, VI, 109; Shaban, 27.

grimage and led an expedition against the infidels in this same year. Dāwūd b. Razīn[381] has recited concerning this,

Through Hārūn, the light has shone forth in every region,
and the straight path has become established by the justness of his conduct.
(He is) a leader who has ordered his affairs[382] through attention to God's requirements,
and whose greatest concern is with raiding the infidels and the Pilgrimage.
People's eyes are unable to endure the brilliance of his face,
when his resplendent aspect appears to them.
Indeed, the trusted one of God, Hārūn, the munificent one,
gives the one who has hope of his bounty several times more than what he hopes.

In this year, Sulaymān b. ʿAbdallāh al-Bakkāʾī led the summer raid.[383]

In this year, the governor of Medina was Isḥāq b. Sulaymān al-Hāshimī; of Mecca and al-Ṭāʾif, ʿUbaydallāh b. Qutham; of al-Kūfah, Mūsā b. ʿĪsā, with his deputy there being his son al-ʿAbbās b. Mūsā; and of al-Baṣrah, Baḥrayn, the Gulf littoral ports, al-Yamāmah and the administrative districts of Ahwāz and Fārs, Muḥammad b. Sulaymān b. ʿAlī.[384]

---

381. Poet of Wāsiṭ, whose poems are largely lost; he died at some point after this date. See *GAS,* II, 455.

382. The text here is better (cf. de Goeje's comment in *Addenda et emendanda,* p. DCCLX) than the *aṣbaḥa shughaluhu* of the Cairo text, VIII, 234.

383. Ibn al-Athīr, loc. cit.

384. Ibid.

The Events of the Year 171

(June 22, 787–June 10, 788)

Among the events taking place during this year was the arrival of Abū al-ʿAbbās al-Faḍl b. Sulaymān al-Ṭūsī in the City of Peace, returning from Khurāsān.[385] At the time of his arrival, the seal ring of the caliphate was in the hands of Jaʿfar b. Muḥammad b. al- [606]
Ashʿath (al-Khuzāʿī),[386] but then when Abū al-ʿAbbās al-Ṭūsī arrived, al-Rashīd took it from Jaʿfar and transferred it to Abū al-ʿAbbās.[387] Shortly afterwards, however, Abū al-ʿAbbās died, so he handed over the seal ring to Yaḥyā b. Khālid. Thus, Yaḥyā now combined the two vizierial functions [*al-wizāratayn*].[388]

---

385. Dīnawarī, loc. cit. According to Ḥamzah al-Iṣfahānī, *T. Sinī mulūk al-arḍ wa-al-anbiyāʾ*, 164, al-Faḍl had arrived in Khurāsān in Rabīʿ I 166 (October 782).

386. Soon afterwards to be nominated governor of Khurāsān, which he governed 170–3 (787–9). See Ḥamzah, loc. cit.; Ṭabarī, III, 609 (below, 108); Ibn al-Athīr, VI, 114, 120.

387. According to Jahshiyārī, 134, the *dīwān al-khātam*, thus given to Abū al-ʿAbbās, was the only government department not entrusted immediately to Yaḥyā al-Barmakī on al-Rashīd's accession; cf. Sourdel, *Vizirat*, I, 136–7. Jahshiyārī, 135, further relates that Yaḥyā became exasperated at Abū al-ʿAbbās's dilatoriness and his making heavy weather over the sealing of letters, hence he started to take measure with his own hands over correspondence with provincial governors.

388. I.e., of the financial *dīwān al-kharāj* and the *dīwān al-khātam* for official

In this year, Hārūn had Abū Hurayrah Muḥammad b. Farrūkh, who was governor of al-Jazīrah, executed. Hārūn sent Abū Ḥanīfah Ḥarb b. Qays to him, who brought Abū Ḥurayrah back to the Caliph at the City of Peace; he was then decapitated in the Khuld Palace.[389]

In this year, Hārūn ordered the expulsion of all the Ṭālibids in the City of Peace to the City of the Messenger (of God) (i.e., al-Madīnah), with the exception of al-ʿAbbās b. al-Ḥasan b. ʿAbdallāh b. ʿAlī b. Abī Ṭālib; the latter's father al-Ḥasan b. ʿAbdallāh was nevertheless among those whom the Caliph sent off.[390]

Al-Faḍl b. Saʿīd al-Ḥarūrī rebelled, but Abū Khālid al-Marwarrūdhī killed him.[391]

In this year, Rawḥ b. Ḥātim (al-Muhallabī) arrived in Ifrīqiyah.[392]

In this year, al-Khayzurān set out in the month of Ramaḍān for Mecca, and she stayed there until the time for the Pilgrimage, and then she performed it.[393]

In this year, ʿAbd al-Ṣamad b. ʿAlī b. ʿAbdallāh b. al-ʿAbbās[394] led the Pilgrimage.[395]

---

correspondence. On this title, see Goldziher, "Ueber Dualtitel," *WZKM*, XIII (1899), 323–4 = *Gesammelte Schriften*, IV, 197–8; Sourdel, *Vizirat*, I, 137–8.

389. Azdī, 267, with detail on Abū Hurayrah's governorship in al-Jazīrah; Ibn al-Athīr, VI, 114.

390. Op. cit., VI, 114–15.

391. Op. cit., VI, 115, records a further Khārijite revolt during this year, that of al-Ṣaḥṣaḥ in al-Jazīrah against the local governor Abū Hurayrah; possibly his difficulties over this were a cause of al-Rashīd's having him executed during this year, as mentioned above.

392. The detailed background to this appointment (the governorship of his nephew Dāwūd b. Yazīd b. Ḥātim, his unsatisfactory conduct, a revolt of the Ibāḍiyyah Khārijites and his replacement by Rawḥ) is given by Yaʿqūbī, *Ta'rīkh*, II, 496, and Ibn al-Athīr, VI, 108, 113–14, 115.

393. Her Pilgrimage and her extensive benefactions in the Ḥaramayn are placed by the *K. al-ʿUyūn*, 291, in 172 (788–9). For details of these charitable works, see Abbott, 117–20.

394. See on him, Ṭabarī, III, 573 (above, 49, and n. 196).

395. Khalīfah, *Ta'rīkh*, II, 711, also recording that it was Sulaymān b. ʿAbdallāh al-Aṣamm who led the annual expedition against the Byzantines; Muḥammad b. Ḥabīb, 38; Azdī, 267.

The Events of the Year 172

(June 11, 788–May 30, 789)

Among the events taking place during this year was al-Rashīd's setting out for Marj al-Qalʿah,[396] seeking there a residence (or, an encampment, *manzil*) where he might stay.

Mention of the reason for that. It has been mentioned that the motive behind his journey thither was that he found the City of Peace intolerable—he used to call it "the steamy place" [*al-bukhār*]—so he set off for Marj al-Qalʿah; but he fell ill there, hence he turned back homewards.[397]. That particular journey was called "the journey of the seeker." [607]

In this year, al-Rashīd dismissed Yazīd b. Mazyad from the governorship of Armenia, and gave it to ʿUbaydallāh b. al-Mahdī.[398]

---

396. "The pasture-ground of the fortress," the district around the town of Karind in Jibāl, on the Khurāsānian highway between Ḥulwān and Kirmān-shāh where, it is mentioned, the ʿAbbāsid Caliphs kept their studs of horses. See Yāqūt, *Muʿjam*, V, 101; Le Strange, *Lands*, 192; Schwarz, 491–2.

397. Hence, he never seems to have used this new palace.

398. Yaʿqūbī, *Taʾrīkh*, II, 515–16, with the background details of this appointment; Azdī, 269; Ibn al-Athīr, VI, 118.

In this year, Isḥāq b. Sulaymān b. ʿAlī led the summer raid [*al-ṣāʾifah*].[399]

In this year, Yaʿqūb b. Abī Jaʿfar al-Manṣūr led the Pilgrimage.[400]

In this year, Hārūn lifted from the shoulders of the inhabitants of the Sawād the tithe which used to be taken from them after the tax of a half (of their produce).[401]

---

399. Azdī, 270; Ibn al-Athīr, loc. cit.; but according to Yaʿqūbī, *Taʾrīkh*, II, 522, the leader was Muḥammad b. Ibrāhīm, and according to Khalīfah, *Taʾrīkh*, II, 712, it was Ẓufar b. ʿAṣim al-Hilālī together with his son ʿAbd al-ʿAzīz.

400. Khalīfah, loc. cit.; Ibn al-Athīr, loc. cit.

401. Ibid.; cf. Shaban, 32–3.

The Events of the Year 173

(May 31, 789–May 19, 790)

The Death of Muḥammad b. Sulaymān and the Confiscation of His Fortune

Among the events taking place during this year was the death of Muḥammad b. Sulaymān[402] at al-Baṣrah a few nights before the end of Jumādā II (mid-November 789). It has been mentioned that when Muḥammad b. Sulaymān died, al-Rashīd despatched an agent for every category of what Muḥammad b. Sulaymān had left behind, ordering him to select the best items from it. Thus, he sent for the precious metals which he had left behind a man from the staff of his head treasurer; for the clothing, likewise; and for the carpets and coverings, for the slaves, for the riding beasts, including horses and camels, for the perfumes and aromatic substances, for the jewels and for every utensil, a man from the staff of each of these categories of possessions. So they came to al-Baṣrah and then sequestrated the whole of Muḥammad's property which might be

402. The senior ʿAbbāsid prince and victor at Fakhkh, see Ṭabarī, III, 557 ff. (above, 23 ff. and n. 90).

valuable to the caliphate, leaving behind nothing except the worthless remnants which were of no possible use to the Caliphs. They acquired on the Caliph's behalf sixty million (dirhams' worth), and transported it back together with all the rest which was brought
[608] back. When it arrived in the boats, al-Rashīd was informed about the position of the boats which had conveyed that consignment, and he ordered the whole of it to be placed in his treasuries, with the exception of the actual money. He ordered authorizations for payment [*ṣikak*][403] (regarding this last) to be prepared, and they were written out for the boon-companions (at court), whilst the singers received authorizations for smaller sums, which were not put through the *dīwān* (i.e., through the normal accounting procedure). Then he handed over to each person a draft for the amount which he thought fit to give that person; these persons then sent their agents to the boats, and took the whole of the money, according to what the Caliph had awarded them in the drafts, not a single dīnār or dirham entering the Caliph's treasury. The Caliph also selected what he wanted from Muḥammad b. Sulaymān's estates, including one called Barashīd (?) in Ahwāz, which brought in a considerable amount of revenue.[404]

ʿAlī b. Muḥammad has mentioned from his father, saying: When Muḥammad b. Sulaymān died, there was recovered from his treasury all his clothing from the time when he was a boy in the Qurʾān school till the time when he died, covering a period of many years; some of this clothing even had ink stains on it. He related: They brought out of his treasury what had been given to him as presents from the land of Sind, Makrān, Kirmān, Fārs, Ahwāz, al-Yamāmah, al-Rayy and ʿUmān, including fine gifts, unguents and balms, musk,[405] grain, cheese and such-like, but the

---

403. For this technical term of the financial departments of the administration, sing. *ṣakk*, see Bosworth, "Abū ʿAbdallāh al-Khwārazmī on the technical terms of the secretary's art," 125–6.

404. Khalīfah, *Taʾrīkh*, II, 713; Masʿūdī, *Murūj*, VI, 289–92 = ed. Pellat, §§ 2496–7; Azdī, 270; Qāḍī Ibn al-Zubayr, 221–2, §§ 308–9; *K. al-ʿUyūn*, 292; Ibn al-Athīr, VI, 119; cf. Kennedy, 118. Among Muḥammad b. Sulaymān's estates resumed by the Caliph was that of the town of Bālis on the Euphrates above al-Raqqah, on the borders of Syria and al-Jazīrah; formerly the possession of Maslamah b. ʿAbd al-Malik, al-Saffāḥ had given it to Sulaymān b. ʿAlī; see Balādhurī, 151, and Yāqūt, *Muʿjam*, I, 328.

405. Following the reading of Ibn ʿAsākir for the text's *al-samak* "fish."

greater part of all this was found to have become spoilt. Also included in that were five hundred *kanʿadah* fish[406] which were thrown out of the house of Jaʿfar and Muḥammad into the street and which then became a nuisance.[407] He related: For some time, we were unable to pass by al-Mirbad[408] because of its stench.

In this year, al-Khayzurān, mother of Hārūn al-Rashīd and Mūsā al-Hādī, died.

The Time of al-Khayzurān's Death and Her Burial

Yaḥyā b. al-Ḥasan has mentioned that his father transmitted the information to him, saying: I saw al-Rashīd on the day when al-Khayzurān died—this being in the year 173—wearing a Saʿīdī robe [*jubbah*][409] and a patched and ragged *ṭaylasān* which was tied [609]
around his waist, gripping the framework of the funeral bier and walking barefoot through the mud until he reached the Cemetery of Quraysh.[410] He washed his feet and then called for a pair of boots, prayed over her corpse and went down into her grave. When he came away from the cemetery, a stool was set down for him, and he sat down on it. He summoned al-Faḍl b. al-Rabīʿ and said to him, "By the right of al-Mahdī!"—and he never used to swear such an oath except when he was expressing himself forcefully—"For some time now [*min al-layl*], I have been intending to confer on you some administrative charge or similar responsibility, but my mother has (hitherto) been restraining me and I have accordingly been obedient to her command; but now, take over the seal ring from Jaʿfar (b. Yaḥyā al-Barmakī)." Al-Faḍl b. al-Rabīʿ said to Ismāʿīl b. Ṣubayḥ, "I have too much respect for Abū al-Faḍl (i.e., Yaḥyā, father of Jaʿfar and al-Faḍl) that I should write to him and

---

406. See for this term, *WbKAS*, I, 390b.

407. Despite the recommendation in the *Addenda et emendanda*, p. DCCLX, of the reading *malā*, the original reading of the text here (and that of the Cairo one, VIII, 238), *balāʾ*, seems preferable.

408. The celebrated commercial quarter on the western side of al-Baṣrah (literally, "place where dates are spread to dry, where camels and sheep are herded together"). See Pellat, *Le milieu baṣrien*, 11–12, and *EI*² s.v.

409. For the term *Saʿīdī*, see Lane, *Lexicon*, s.v., and BGA, IV, *Glossarium*, 260; for the *jubbah* as a garment, see Ahsan, 40.

410. This was situated on the western bank of the Tigris opposite al-Ruṣāfah. See Le Strange, *Baghdad*, 157–8, 193; Lassner, *Topography*, 111, 253–4, 285–6.

take it away from him; but perhaps he might, if he thinks fit, convey it to me?" He related: He (i.e., the Caliph) gave al-Faḍl charge of the public and privy expenditure and of Bādurayā[411] and al-Kūfah, comprising five *ṭassūjs*. His power and prestige thus began to increase, up to the year 187 (803). It has been said that the deaths of Muḥammad b. Sulaymān and al-Khayzurān took place on the same day.[412]

In this year, al-Rashīd recalled Jaʿfar b. Muḥammad b. al-Ashʿath from Khurāsān, and he entrusted it to his son al-ʿAbbās b. Jaʿfar b. Muḥammad b. al-Ashʿath.[413]

In this year, Hārūn himself led the Pilgrimage. It has been mentioned that he set out from the City of Peace observing the taboos and wearing the ritually clean garments of the Pilgrimage [*muḥrim*[an]].[414]

---

411. The district to the west of Baghdad on the Nahr ʿĪsā. See Yāqūt, *Muʿjam*, I, 317–18; Le Strange, *Lands*, 66–7; idem, *Baghdad*, 50–1.

412. Jahshiyārī, 145; Qāḍī Ibn al-Zubayr, 235, § 343; *K. al-ʿUyūn*, 292; Ibn al-Athīr, VI, 119; Abbott, 125–8; Sourdel, *Vizirat*, I, 138; idem, *EI*² s.v. al-Faḍl b. al-Rabīʿ. If she died at the same time as Muḥammad b. Sulaymān, her death must also be placed in late Jumādā II (November 789). As Sourdel remarks, the information given here by Ṭabarī and by Jahshiyārī does not imply, as some modern historians (e.g., Abbott, 126–7) have asserted, that al-Faḍl took charge of the office of the seal at this point; this seems to have been retained by Jaʿfar till 180 (796), when al-Rashīd transferred it to his father Yaḥyā (Ṭabarī, III, 644, below, 162).

413. Ṭabarī-Balʿamī, tr., IV, 457; Ibn al-Athīr, VI, 120. Jaʿfar b. Muḥammad had replaced in this governorship Abū al-ʿAbbās Faḍl b. Sulaymān al-Ṭūsī; see Ṭabarī, III, 605, 740, and Barthold, *Turkestan*, 203. According to Ḥamzah, 164, the governorship had been briefly given to al-Ḥasan b. Qaḥṭabah before Jaʿfar.

414. Khalīfah, *Taʾrīkh*, II, 713; Muḥammad b. Ḥabīb, 38; Azdī, 270, 274; Ibn al-Athīr, loc. cit. Khalīfah and Azdī also record that ʿAbd al-Malik b. Ṣāliḥ b. ʿAlī led the summer raid.

The Events of the Year

174

(May 20, 790–May 9, 791)

Among the events taking place during this year was the factional strife [ʿ*aṣabiyyah*] which took place in Syria.[415]

In this year, al-Rashīd appointed Isḥāq b. Sulaymān al-Hāshimī governor of Sind and Makrān.[416]

In this year, al-Rashīd appointed Yūsuf b. Abī Yūsuf as judge whilst his father was still alive.[417]

In this year, Rawḥ b. Ḥātim perished.[418]

In this year, al-Rashīd set out for Bāqirdā and Bāzabdā,[419] and [610]
built a palace at Bāqirdā.[420] A poet has said concerning that,

---

415. It is possible that this is the rebellion raised by the people of Damascus against their governor Sulaymān b. Abī Jaʿfar al-Manṣūr over a crystal vessel [*qullah billawr*] kept in the *miḥrāb* (presumably of the Umayyad Mosque) mentioned, without a clear date, in Yaʿqūbī, *Taʾrīkh,* II, 494–5. Dīnawarī, 387, attributes the strife to the usual rivalry of Muḍar and Yaman.

416. Yaʿqūbī, *Taʾrīkh,* II, 493.

417. I.e., the son of one of the founders of the Ḥanafī law school, Abū Yūsuf. The son Yūsuf became deputy judge for his father over the western side of Baghdad and died in 192 (808); see *EI*² s.v. Abū Yūsuf (J. Schacht).

418. Yaʿqūbī, *Taʾrīkh,* II, 496; Ibn al-Athīr, VI, 121; Kennedy, 192.

419. These were districts on the eastern and western banks, respectively, of the

At Qirdā[421] and Bāzabdā are places where one finds hospitality and a site for residence,
a source of sweet, cool water, which resembles al-Salsabīl (i.e., the fountain in Paradise).
Whereas Baghdad, how can one describe Baghdad? On the one hand, its soil
is pure excrement, and on the other, its heat is intense.[422]

ʿAbd al-Malik b. Ṣāliḥ led the summer raid.[423]

In this year, Hārūn al-Rashīd led the Pilgrimage. He began by visiting al-Madīnah and distributed a great deal of money among its people. During this year, an outbreak of plague hit Mecca, hence Hārūn held back from entering it. Then he did actually enter on the "Day of Refreshment" and made the circumambulation of the Kaʿbah and the running (between al-Ṣafā and al-Marwah) without however staying in Mecca.[424]

---

upper Tigris near Jazīrat Ibn ʿUmar, in the eastern part of Diyār Bakr. See Yāqūt, *Muʿjam,* I, 321, 327; Le Strange, *Lands,* 93–4.

420. Ibn al-Athīr, loc. cit. Al-Rashīd seems nevertheless not to have used this new palace to any known extent; cf. Kennedy, 120.

421. According to Yāqūt, *Muʿjam,* I, 327, quoting this hemistich, Qirdā or Qardā was the popular pronunciation of Bāqirdā.

422. Both verses cited (with minor variants) in op. cit. I, 321, s.v. Bāzabdā.

423. Khalīfah, *Taʾrīkh,* II, 714; Azdī, 274; Ibn al-Athīr, loc. cit.; Brooks, *EHR,* XV (1900), 740. According to Yaʿqūbī, *Taʾrīkh,* II, 522, Sulaymān b. Abī Jaʿfar al-Manṣūr was the leader.

424. Khalīfah, *Taʾrīkh,* loc. cit.; Yaʿqūbī, *Taʾrīkh,* II, 521; Ibn al-Athīr, loc. cit.

The Events of the Year 175

(May 10, 791–April 27, 792)

Among the events taking place during this year was al-Rashīd's formal designation, in the City of Peace, of his son Muḥammad as heir to the rule over the Muslims, his receiving the oath of allegiance to that arrangement on Muḥammad's behalf from the commanders and the troops, and his giving him the honorific title of al-Amīn, the latter being at that time five years old.[425] Salm al-Khāsir has said,

> God has bestowed His favor on the Caliph when he made firm the structure of the caliphate for the nobly-born, fair-of-face one.

---

425. Yaʿqūbī, *Taʾrīkh,* II, 493; Dīnawarī, 390; Ṭabarī-Balʿamī, tr. IV, 457–8, 459; *K. al-ʿUyūn,* 292; Ibn al-Athīr, VI, 122; Gabrieli, "Successione," 344–5. Gabrieli points out that this designation of Muḥammad al-Amīn cannot have been viewed by al-Rashīd as definitive, in the light of the unfolding, over the course of time, of the respective characters and abilities of Muḥammad and his brother ʿAbdallāh al-Maʾmūn, leading him to make the fresh succession arrangements at Baghdad and al-Raqqah in 182 (802), see Ṭabarī, III, 647 (below, 167). The reports in Dīnawarī, 387–9, and Masʿūdī, *Murūj,* VI, 317 ff. = ed. Pellat, §§ 2520 ff., of the subsequent doubts in al-Rashīd's mind over his two sons' capabilities tend to confirm this.

For he is the Caliph in descent from his father and his grandfather; both of them have testified to this, on the basis of external appearance and inner qualities.
The two weighty creations (i.e., men and jinn) have given their allegiance, in the seat of divine guidance (i.e., in Baghdad) to Muḥammad son of Zubaydah, the daughter of Jaʿfar (b. al-Manṣūr).[426]

The Reasons for al-Rashīd's Exacting Allegiance to Muḥammad al-Amīn as Heir

[611] According to what Rawḥ, the mawlā of al-Faḍl b. Yaḥyā b. Khālid has mentioned, the reason behind this was that he had noted that ʿĪsā b. Jaʿfar had gone along to al-Faḍl b. Yaḥyā and had said to him, "I adjure you by God to work[427] for allegiance to be given to my sister's son"—he meant Muḥammad b. Zubaydah bt. Jaʿfar b. al-Manṣūr—"for he is in effect a child of yours and his caliphate will be in effect your rule." Al-Faḍl promised him that he would do that. Al-Faḍl directed his efforts at securing it, at a time when a group of the ʿAbbāsids had openly shown their ambitions (literally, "had stretched forth their necks") for the caliphate after al-Rashīd, since he had not yet designated his heir. When he did in fact settle the succession on Muḥammad, they rejected (or: disapproved of, *ankarū*) giving him allegiance on account of his youthfulness.[428]

He related: When al-Faḍl had become governor of Khurāsān, he had resolved to secure recognition of Muḥammad as heir. Muḥammad b. al-Ḥusayn b. Muṣʿab has mentioned that when al-Faḍl b. Yaḥyā went to Khurāsān he divided out among the people there sums of money and gave the troops successive allotments of pay.

---

426. Von Grunebaum, "Three Arabic poets of the early Abbasid age. V. Salm al-Ḫâsir," 66–7, no. XVII = *Shuʿarāʾ ʿAbbāsiyyūn*, 100, no. 17; Azdī, 274–5, adding also verses by Abān al-Lāḥiqī.

427. *Lammā ʿamilta*; for *lammā* = *illā* after verbs of beseeching and adjuring, see W. Wright, *Arabic grammar*, Cambridge, 1896–8, I, 294, II, 340; H. Reckendorf, *Arabische Syntax*, Heidelberg 1921, 512 § 262.12.

428. Cf. the doubts of several members of the Hāshimite family because of Muḥammad al-Amīn's youthfulness, expressed in Yaʿqūbī, *Taʾrīkh*, loc. cit., and *K. al-ʿUyūn*, loc. cit.; Yaʿqūbī reports that ʿAbd al-Ṣamad b. ʿAlī, Hārūn's great-great-uncle, tried to assuage their fears by saying, "O people, don't let his tender age delude you, for this is indeed the blessed tree whose roots are vigorously growing and whose branches stretch up to the heavens"; cf. Gabrieli, "Successione," 345.

Then he proclaimed openly the matter of allegiance to Muḥammad b. al-Rashīd as heir, and as a result, the people gave their allegiance and addressed Muḥammad as al-Amīn.[429] (Manṣūr) al-Namarī said concerning this,

At Marw, with God's favor and through the agency of al-Faḍl,
the hands of both Persians and Arabs have become clasped together.
In an act of allegiance to the designated heir to the throne, which he (i.e., al-Faḍl) has made firm
with his sincere advice, his solicitude and his benevolence.
Al-Faḍl has made secure an affirmation of allegiance which cannot be broken,
to a chosen and selected one of the ʿAbbāsid house.[430]

He related: When the news about that finally reached al-Rashīd, and the people of the East had given their allegiance to Muḥammad, he (formally) hailed Muḥammad as heir to the throne and [612] wrote to all the provinces and the great cities. Abān (b. ʿAbd al-Ḥamīd) al-Lāḥiqī[431] said concerning this,

O Commander of the Faithful, you have determined upon the right path
by means of a judgment based on divine guidance, so praise be to God, the One worthy of praise!

In this year, al-Rashīd dismissed al-ʿAbbās b. Jaʿfar from the governorship of Khurāsān and gave it to his maternal uncle al-Ghiṭrīf b. ʿAṭāʾ.[432]

In this year, Yaḥyā b. ʿAbdallāh b. Ḥasan proceeded to Daylam and became active there (i.e., in rebellion).[433]

---

429. *K. al-ʿUyūn,* loc. cit.

430. *Shiʿr Manṣūr al-Namarī,* ed. al-Ṭayyib al-ʿAshshāsh, 71. On this eulogist of al-Rashīd (who died at some uncertain date in that Caliph's reign), see Iṣfahānī, *Aghānī,* ed. Būlāq, XII, 16–26 = ed. Cairo, XIII, 140–57; *GAS,* II, 541–2; *EI*[2] s.v. (T. Achèche).

431. Eulogist of al-Rashīd and the Barmakīs, who died ca. 200 (815–16). See Pellat, *Le milieu baṣrien,* 179–80; *GAS,* II, 541–2; *EI*[2] s.v. (S. M. Stern).

432. Khalīfah, *Taʾrīkh,* II, 745; Dīnawarī, 387; Yaʿqūbī, *Taʾrīkh,* II, 488; Ḥamzah al-Iṣfahānī, 164; Ibn al-Athīr, VI, 122; Daniel, 169; *EI*[2] Suppl. s.v. al-Ghiṭrīf b. ʿAṭāʾ. Cf. also Ṭabarī, III, 590–1, above, 73.

433. Ṭabarī-Balʿamī, tr. IV, 458; Abū al-Faḍl Bayhaqī, *Taʾrīkh-i Masʿūdī,* 414; Ibn al-Athīr, loc. cit.; and see below, 115–20, for a full account of this episode.

In this year, ʿAbd al-Raḥmān b. ʿAbd al-Malik b. Ṣāliḥ led the summer raid and reached as far as Iqrīṭiyah (i.e., Crete).[434] Al-Wāqidī has related, that it was ʿAbd al-Malik b. Ṣāliḥ who led the summer raid in this year.[435] He related: During the course of this raid, they encountered severely cold weather, which made their hands and feet drop off (i.e., from frostbite).[436]

In this year, Hārūn al-Rashīd led the Pilgrimage.[437]

---

434. Khalīfah, *Ta'rīkh,* II, 715; Ibn al-Athīr, loc. cit; Brooks, *EHR,* XV (1900), 740; cf. *EI*[2] s.v. Iḳrīṭish (Canard).

435. Thus in Yaʿqūbī, *Ta'rīkh,* II, 522.

436. Brooks, loc. cit.

437. Khalīfah, *Ta'rīkh,* loc. cit.; Muḥammad b. Ḥabīb, 38; Yaʿqūbī, *Ta'rīkh,* II, 521; Ibn al-Athīr, loc. cit.

The Events of the Year 176

(April 28, 792–April 17, 793)

Among the events taking place during this year was al-Rashīd's appointment of al-Faḍl b. Yaḥyā as governor of the districts of Jibāl, Ṭabaristān, Dunbāwand, Qūmis, Armenia and Azerbaijan.[438]

In this year, Yaḥyā b. ʿAbdallāh b. Ḥasan b. Ḥasan b. ʿAlī b. Abī Ṭālib appeared in Daylam.[439]

Yaḥyā b. ʿAbdallāh b. Ḥasan's Uprising and His Role in These Events [613]

Abū Ḥafṣ al-Kirmānī has mentioned, saying: The first reports about Yaḥyā b. ʿAbdallāh b. Ḥasan b. Ḥasan b. ʿAlī b. Abī Ṭālib were that he had appeared in Daylam, that his military strength had grown, that his power had increased and that people from the great cities and the provincial districts had gone over to his side.[440] Al-

---

438. Ṭabarī-Balʿamī, tr. loc. cit.; Azdī, 277; Bayhaqī, *Taʾrīkh-i Masʿūdī,* 414–15.

439. I.e., the inland mountain region of the western part of the Elburz mountains, the hinterland of Gīlān, a region at this time hardly Islamized. See *EI*² s.v. (Minorsky).

440. For this episode of the adventures of Yaḥyā, half-brother of the "Pure Soul"

Rashīd became much distressed over this, and during these days refrained from drinking any date wine. He then invited al-Faḍl b. Yaḥyā to march against him with fifty thousand men, accompanied by the stoutest commanders, and he appointed al-Faḍl over the regions of Jibāl, al-Rayy, Jurjān, Ṭabaristān, Qūmis, Dunbāwand and al-Rūyān, and quantities of money were taken along with him. He then allotted the various regions among his commanders. He made al-Muthannā b. al-Ḥajjāj b. Qutaybah b. Muslim[441] governor over Ṭabaristān and ʿAlī b. al-Ḥajjāj al-Khuzāʿī[442] over Jurjān, and he ordered that he should be given five hundred thousand dirhams. He encamped at al-Nahrabīn.[443] The poets sang his praises, for which he rewarded them profusely. People sought to ingratiate themselves with him through their poetry, and he distributed great sums of money among them.

Al-Faḍl b. Yaḥyā set off, and left behind as his representative at the Commander of the Faithful's court Manṣūr b. Ziyād,[444] with the responsibility of personally conveying al-Faḍl's letters and of transmitting the answers to the letters to al-Faḍl. They (i.e., the Barmakīs) used to have complete trust in Manṣūr and his son

---

Muḥammad and of Idrīs, founder of the Idrīsid line in Morocco (see Ṭabarī, III, 561–2; above, 28–30), see also of the primary sources, Jahshiyārī, 145–6; Yaʿqūbī, *Taʾrīkh*, II, 492–3; Masʿūdī, *Murūj*, VI, 193, 300–1 = ed. Pellat, §§ 2405, 2505; Iṣfahānī, *Maqātil*, 308–23; *K. al-ʿUyūn*, 292–4, 306–7; Ibn al-Athīr, VI, 122, 125–6; Ibn al-Ṭiqṭaqā, 176, tr. 190–1. Of the secondary sources, see Palmer, 57–61; Bouvat, 58–9; Van Arendonck, 65–70; Marquet, "Le Šīʿisme au IXe siècle," 109–10; Kennedy, 119–20, 206–7. After the failure of the revolt of al-Ḥusayn b. ʿAlī (at the time of which Yaḥyā had been a guarantor for the good conduct of the Ḥasanid al-Ḥasan b. Muḥammad b. ʿAbdallāh, see Ṭabarī, III, 552, above, 16) at Fakhkh in 169 (786), Yaḥyā had fled like his brother Idrīs and had travelled clandestinely throughout the Islamic world from the Maghrib to Transoxania, but had finally sought refuge in the Caspian region of Persia. His stay in Daylam, though brief, seems to have paved the way for Zaydī Shīʿī activity in the Caspian provinces a century or so later (see Madelung, in *Cambridge history of Iran*, IV, 206 ff).

441. Ibn Isfandiyār, tr. 132. Al-Muthannā was another of the descendants of the Umayyad governor Qutaybah b. Muslim al-Bāhilī who prospered greatly under the early ʿAbbāsids; see Crone, 137.

442. According to Muḥammad b. Ḥabīb, 375, ʿAlī was at one time commander of the police [*shurṭah*] for al-Rashīd.

443. Restored by the editor from the text's *al-nahrayn* and presumably a form of the Nahr Bīn/Bīl of Yāqūt, *Muʿjam*, V, 318, a *ṭassūj* or rural administrative district of the Sawād of Baghdad.

444. According to Jahshiyārī, 135 (cf. Sourdel, *Vizirat*, I, 142), Manṣūr was very close to Yaḥyā's confidence, to the extent that people desiring his help would seek it through Manṣūr's intercession.

regarding all their affairs, because of Manṣūr's long-established association with them and his attitude of respectfulness and solicitude for them. Then al-Faḍl set out from his military encampment. Al-Rashīd's letters came to him in a continuous stream, expressing kindness and benevolence, and with presents and robes of honor. He (i.e., al-Faḍl) then wrote to Yaḥyā, treating him with consideration, conciliating him, exhorting him, giving him warnings, offering him advice, and enlarging his hopes. Al-Faḍl encamped at al-Ṭālaqān in the vicinity of al-Rayy[445] and at Dastabā in a place called Ashabb.[446] The weather was extremely cold and very [614]
snowy; concerning this, Abān b. ʿAbd al-Ḥamīd al-Lāḥiqī says,

Indeed, the habitations of former days at al-Dawlāb,[447]
    where the irrigation canal winds along
Are dearer to me than the habitations
    of Ashabb, when they are covered in snow.

He related: Al-Faḍl remained in this spot. He sent a series of letters to Yaḥyā, and wrote to the ruler of Daylam offering him a million dirhams on condition that he should facilitate Yaḥyā's reversion to his previous state of obedience. This sum was transported to him, and Yaḥyā responded to the offer of peace and agreed to come forth under his (i.e., al-Faḍl's) auspices provided that al-Rashīd would personally and in his own hand write out for him a guarantee of safe-conduct which he (i.e., al-Faḍl) would forward to him. So al-Faḍl wrote to al-Rashīd about that; this made him rejoice, and al-Faḍl's status rose in his sight. The Caliph wrote out a guarantee of safe-conduct for Yaḥyā b. ʿAbdallāh and had it witnessed by the religious lawyers and judges and by the leading figures and shaykhs of the Hāshimites, including ʿAbd al-Ṣamad b. ʿAlī, al-ʿAbbās b. Muḥammad, Muḥammad b. Ibrāhīm,[448] Mūsā b.

---

445. For this al-Ṭālaqān on the borders of Jibāl and Daylam (to be distinguished from the one in northern Afghanistan), see Yāqūt, *Muʿjam*, IV, 7–8; Le Strange, *Lands*, 225; Schwarz, 733–5; *EI*[1] s.v. (Huart).

446. *K. al-ʿUyūn*, 293; Ibn al-Athīr, VI, 125; Bouvat, 58. On Ashabb, see Schwarz, 734–5. Dastabā probably lay to the south of Qazwīn, see Le Strange, *Lands*, 220.

447. Literally, "water-wheel, contrivance for raising water," but also the name of at least one place in the Baghdad area, as is intended by the contrast here. See Yāqūt, *Muʿjam*, II, 485; Le Strange, *Baghdad*, 190, 321.

448. I.e., Muḥammad b. Ibrāhīm b. Muḥammad b. ʿAlī, first cousin of al-Mahdī, governor on various occasions of Mecca and Medina, died in 185 (801).

ʿĪsā, and others like them. He forwarded it, together with presents, marks of respect and benevolence, and gifts. Al-Faḍl in turn sent these on to Yaḥyā b. ʿAbdallāh, who then came to him; al-Faḍl then brought him to Baghdad. Al-Rashīd presented him with everything which he desired, ordered him to be given a large sum of money, allotted to him on a regular basis munificent living allowances, and installed him in a fine house after he had stayed for some days in Yaḥyā b. Khālid's house. He was supervising all these arrangements for Yaḥyā b. ʿAbdallāh personally, and would not delegate these to anyone else. He further ordered people (i.e., the leading men in the state and at court) to go to him after his move from Yaḥyā (b. Khālid)'s house and to present their greetings to him. Al-Rashīd also exerted himself to the utmost in showing honor to al-Faḍl.[449] Concerning this, Marwān b. Abī Ḥafṣah says,

You gained the victory, and may a Barmakī arm never lose its power!
with it you closed up the breach which was between (the members of) Hāshim (i.e., between the ʿAbbāsid al-Rashīd and the ʿAlid Yaḥyā b. ʿAbdallāh).
[615] At a time when repairing it proved impossible for those who (normally) close up breaches,
so that they gave up the attempt, protesting that the breach was irreparable.
But then you came along, and your hands accomplished a glorious deed, whose renown will endure through all the seasons of the Pilgrimage.
The contest-arrow of royal authority (i.e., of the Caliph) will continue to come out the winner
for you whilst ever the contestant's[450] arrows are gathered together.[451]

He related: Abū Thumāmah al-Khaṭīb[452] recited to me a poem of his own authorship, including the lines,

---

449. Jahshiyārī, 145–6; Yaʿqūbī, *Taʾrīkh,* II, 492; Azdī, 277; Abū al-Faḍl Bayhaqī, *Taʾrīkh-i Masʿūdī,* 415; *K. al-ʿUyūn,* loc. cit.; Ibn al-Athīr, loc. cit.; Bouvat, 58–9; Sourdel, *Vizirat,* I, 144–5, 164; Kennedy, 119–20.

450. Following the reading of the Cairo text, VIII, 243, *al-musāhim.*

451. Munierah al-Rasheed, 168; *Shiʿr Marwān b. Abī Ḥafṣah,* ed. ʿAṭawān, 103 no. 65; Harley, "Abu's-Simṭ Marwān b. Abī Ḥafṣah," 84–5.

452. There is a bare mention of him in Marzubānī, 508.

Al-Faḍl secured the victory on the day of al-Ṭālaqān, and before that,
on a day when he deployed his forces against Khāqān.[453]
There have never been two days like al-Faḍl's ones, in which there followed successively
two battles in the course of two campaigns.
He stopped up the breaches, and restored harmony among Hāshim
after it was split apart, so that its divisions are now brought closely together again.
His judgment has made the whole body of Hāshim secure
from the unsheathing of two (opposing) swords among its ranks.[454]
That judgment [*ḥukūmah*] is not of the kind whose confused nature
gave rise to momentous reports, and the two arbiters [*al-ḥakamān*] dispersed.[455]

As a result, al-Faḍl gave him one hundred thousand dirhams and presented him with a robe of honor, and Ibrāhīm (al-Mawṣilī) made a song out of the verses.

Aḥmad b. Muḥammad b. Jaʿfar has mentioned from ʿAbdallāh b. Mūsā b. ʿAbdallāh b. Ḥasan b. Ḥasan, saying: When Yaḥyā b. ʿAbdallāh arrived from Daylam, I went to him, at a time when he was staying in the house of (the descendants of) ʿAlī b. Abī Ṭālib, and said to him, "O my paternal uncle, there is no one after you who can bring news, and no one after me who is so well-informed about the news (i.e., no one knows all the news better than we two; between us we know all the news!), so tell me all the news about yourself." He replied, "O my nephew, I am, by God, merely just as Ḥuyayy b. Akhṭab said,

By your life, Ibn Akhṭab did not reproach himself,
but he whom God forsakes is completely forsaken.
He exerted[456] himself until he justified his high opinion of himself

453. Cf. Ṭabarī, III, 631 ff. (below, 143 ff.).

454. These two verses in Azdī, loc. cit.

455. Alluding to the arbitration [*ḥukūmah*] at Ṣiffīn in 37 (657) between Muʿāwiyah's supporter ʿAmr b. al-ʿĀṣ and ʿAlī's one Abu Mūsā al-Ashʿarī, the "two arbiters."

456. Following the text of the Cairo edition, VIII, 244, *la-jāhada*, also the reading in Ibn Hishām (see next note).

(literally, "until he made his self reach the point of praise of itself")
and he stormed onwards to the utmost in pursuit of glory.[457]

Yaḥyā b. ʿAbdallāh al-ʿAlawī's Altercation with Bakkār b. ʿAbdallāh al-Zubayrī

[616] Al-Ḍabbī[458] has mentioned that a shaykh of the Nawfalīs[459] said: We went into ʿĪsā b. Jaʿfar's presence, at a moment when long cushions had been laid out for him, one on top of the other, and he himself was in a propped-up position, reclining on his side with them at his back. Moreover, at this particular point he was laughing to himself at something and displaying wonder at it. We said, "What is causing the Amīr to laugh, may God make his joy perpetual?" He replied, "Today, a feeling of joy has come over me such as I have never experienced before." We said, "May God complete the Amīr's joy and increase him in it!" He replied, "By God, I can only recount the story to you in a propped-up position (i.e., because of his fit of laughing)," and he reclined on his side on the mattress, remaining in a propped-up position.

He then began, "Today I was with the Commander of the Faithful al-Rashīd. He sent for Yaḥyā b. ʿAbdallāh, and he was brought forth from the prison loaded with iron fetters.[460] The Caliph had

457. Ḥuyayy was a leading figure of the Jewish tribe of Qurayẓah in al-Madīnah and strenuous opponent of the Prophet; see Ibn Hishām, *Sīrat al-Nabī*, passim; in the *Sīra*, III, 252, tr. A. Guillaume, 464, the poem quoted here (uttered on the occasion of Ḥuyayy's execution) is attributed to the contemporary Jewish Medinan poet Jabal b. Jawwāl al-Thaʿlabī.

458. On chronological grounds, it seems impossible that this should be the famous Kūfan philologist and *rāwī* al-Mufaḍḍal b. Muḥammad al-Ḍabbī, who died ca. 170 (786–7).

459. Since Nawfal was, with Hāshim, al-Muṭṭalib and ʿAbd Shams, one of the sons of ʿAbd Manāf of Quraysh in pre-Islamic Mecca, the clan of Nawfal claimed a kinship with the house of the Prophet as fellow-Manāfis.

460. Al-Rashīd's initial favor to Yaḥyā on his arrival from Daylam in the capital under the guarantee of *amān* had speedily turned into suspicion and hostility, leading to his imprisonment (on four separate occasions, according to Ṭabarī, III, 624; below, 131). See Iṣfahānī, *Maqātil*, 313–4; *K. al-ʿUyūn*, loc. cit.; Ibn al-Athīr, VI, 125–6; Van Arendonck, 69–70; Sourdel, *Vizirat*, I, 164–5. According to *Maqātil*, 313, al-Rashīd welcomed Yaḥyā hypocritically and intended all the time to procure his downfall, and issued a mendacious and false letter allegedly from a partisan of Yaḥyā's to secure this.

with him Bakkār b. ʿAbdallāh b. Muṣʿab b. Thābit b. ʿAbdallāh b. al-Zubayr.[461] Bakkār had a violent hatred for the house of ʿAlī b. Abī Ṭālib and used to send reports to Hārūn about them and put the worst construction on information about their doings. Also, al-Rashīd had appointed him as governor of Medina and ordered him to press hard on the ʿAlids. He related: When Yaḥyā was summoned, al-Rashīd said to him with an appearance of laughter, "Go away! Go away! Does this man allege too that we have poisoned him?"[462] Yaḥyā replied, "What do you mean by 'allege?' Just look at what is wrong with my tongue!" He related: And he put out his tongue, which was as dark as beetroot. He related: Hārūn scowled and became extremely angry. Yaḥyā said, "O Commander of the Faithful, we have a bond of relationship and kinship between us, and we (i.e., the ʿAlids) are not Turks or Daylamīs. O Commander of the Faithful, we and you are members of a single house, and I remind you of God and our common relationship to the Messenger of God, that you should not imprison and ill-treat me."[463]

He related: Hārūn then felt compassion towards him. But al-Zubayrī came up to al-Rashīd and said, "O Commander of the Faithful, don't let this man's words delude you, for he is a dissident and rebel and this is mere trickery and deceit; indeed, this fellow has introduced an element of evil into our own city (i.e., Medina, the home of the Prophet after the *hijrah*) and has manifested rebellion there." He related: Yaḥyā then went up to him, but by God, he did not ask the Commander of the Faithful for permission to speak before he said, "*I* am introducing evil into *your* city! And who are you, anyway, may God grant you good health?" Al- [617]
Zubayrī retorted, "This is what he says to your face, so what do

461. Father of the genealogist of Quraysh, al-Zubayr b. Bakkār (on whom see *EI*[2] s.v. Ibn al-Zubayr [J. F. P. Hopkins]). Bakkār was governor of Medina for al-Rashīd at a date subsequent to 183 (799), see Ṭabarī, III, 739 (below, 304). His hatred for the ʿAlids would be explicable in the light of the ancient hostility between the two Meccan leading Companions ʿAlī and al-Zubayr, dating back at least to the time of the Battle of the Camel in which ʿAlī's forces killed al-Zubayr, and their descendants.

462. From the time of the Second Imām al-Ḥasan onwards, it was frequently alleged by the Shīʿah when their leaders died that they had in fact been poisoned.

463. *K. al-ʿUyūn*, 294. In Iṣfahānī, *Maqātil*, 315 ff., Yaḥyā attacks the Zubayrids for various aspects of their lukewarmness as Muslims in the early days of Islam.

you think he says when he is away from you? He says, 'And who are you, anyway?' thereby refering to us contemptuously." He related: Yaḥyā then came up to him and said, "Yes, and just who are you, may God grant you good health? Was Medina the place of refuge [*muhājar*] sought by ʿAbdallāh b. al-Zubayr[464] or by the Messenger of God? And who are you to say, 'He has introduced evil into our city,' when it was only through my forefathers and the forefathers of this person (i.e., the Caliph) that your forefather (i.e., al-Zubayr) migrated for refuge to Medina?"

Then he went on to say, "O Commander of the Faithful, the true founders of Islam [*al-nās*] are ourselves and your family; if we come out in revolt against you, we can say (in extenuation), 'You have eaten, but have left us hungry; you have clothed yourselves, but have left us naked; you have gone off on your mounts, but have left us to go on foot.' We have derived grounds of complaint against you from that, and you have derived grounds of complaint against us from our rebelling against you. Thus, the two complaints balance each other out, and the Commander of the Faithful will renew his favor upon his own house. O Commander of the Faithful, why do this man and his likes dare to impugn the people of your own house [*ahl baytika*]? He bears slanderous reports to you about them. Indeed, by God, he doesn't bear slanderous reports to you about us as an act of good counsel to you on his part, and indeed, he comes to us and brings slanderous reports to us about you without any intention thereby of providing us with good counsel; he only wishes to introduce an element of separation between us and inflict injury on both parties to his own satisfaction. By God, this man came to me, O Commander of the Faithful, when my brother Muḥammad b. ʿAbdallāh was killed,[465] and said, 'May God curse the one who killed him!' and he recited to me an elegy on him, uttering about twenty verses of it.[466] He also said, 'If you make a move in this affair (i.e., join in the rebellion), I will be the first to give allegiance to you. What is there to prevent you

---

464. I.e., Bakkār's great-great-grandfather, anti-Caliph in Mecca and Medina during ʿAbd al-Malik's caliphate, died in 73 (692); see EI^2 s.v. (Gibb).

465. I.e., the "Pure Soul" 's death in battle, see above, 15, n. 61.

466. Isfahani, *Maqātil*, 316–17, gives nine verses of the poem in his account of these exchanges between Yaḥyā and Bakkār, and Masʿūdī, *Murūj*, VI, 297 = ed. Pellat, § 2503, a single verse.

going to al-Baṣrah, and then our forces will be joined together with yours?' "

He related: Al-Zubayrī's face became transformed and grew dark. Hārūn went up to him and said, "What is this man saying?" He replied, "(He is) lying, O Commander of the Faithful, not a word of what he is saying really happened." He related: The Caliph went up to Yaḥyā b. ʿAbdallāh and asked, "Can you recite the ode in which he eulogized him (i.e., Muḥammad b. ʿAbdallāh)?" He replied, "Certainly, O Commander of the Faithful, may God guide you uprightly!" The Caliph said, "Then recite that ode of his!" Al-Zubayrī protested, "O Commander of the Faithful, by God, than whom there is no God but He"—and he went on until he came to the end of the mendacious oath [*al-yamīn al-ghamūs*][467]—"there [618] is nothing at all in what he says, and he has falsely accused me[468] of what I didn't in fact say." He related: Al-Rashīd came up to Yaḥyā b. ʿAbdallāh and said, "He has sworn an oath; now is there any testimony (from people) who heard him recite this elegy?" He replied, "No, O Commander of the Faithful, but I will make him swear to what I desire." He said, "Go ahead and make him swear."

He related: So he went up to al-Zubayrī and said, "Say, 'May I be deprived of God's strength and power, and abandoned to my own strength and power only, if I really did say that!' " Al-Zubayrī said, "O Commander of the Faithful, what sort of an oath is this? I swear to him by God, the Unique God, yet he makes me swear by a formula which is meaningless to me." Yaḥyā b. ʿAbdallāh retorted, "O Commander of the Faithful, if he is speaking the truth, what is preventing him from swearing by what I am asking him to swear?" So Hārūn said, "Swear to him, woe upon you!" He related: Al-Zubayrī then said, "May I be deprived of God's strength and power, and abandoned to my own strength and power only!" He related: He became agitated by these words and reduced to a state of trembling, and said, "O Commander of the Faithful, I don't know

467. Etymologically, an oath made firm by dipping the hands [*ghamasa*] into blood, perfume, date or fruit syrup, etc., according to J. Wellhausen, *Reste arabischen Heidentums*², 128–9; hence, originally "a firm, binding oath," still with this sense in Ṭabarī, III, 1903, in connection with the Zanj rebellion. The sense of a false or perjured oath, as here, developed later; see J. Pedersen, *Der Eid bei den Semiten*, 26, 192 n. 1, 217 n. 2.

468. Following the Cairo text, VIII, 246, *taqawwala ʿalayya.*

what this oath which he is making me swear is all about, and I have already sworn to him by God the Mighty One, the Mightiest of all things." He related: Hārūn nevertheless said to him, "You must certainly swear to him, or if not, I shall indeed attach credence (to his words) against you and shall punish you." He related: So he pronounced the formula "May I be deprived of God's strength and power, and abandoned to my own strength and power only, if I really did say that!" He related: He then went forth from Hārūn's presence, God thereupon afflicted him with a paralytic stroke, and he died instantly.[469]

He related: ʿĪsā b. Jaʿfar said, "By God, what gives me joy is that Yaḥyā did not omit a single word of what passed between the two of them, nor did he cut short any part at all of what he addressed to him."

He related: As for the members of the Zubayrid family, however, they assert that his wife killed him, she being a descendant of ʿAbd al-Raḥmān b. ʿAwf. Isḥāq b. Muḥammad al-Nakhaʿī has mentioned that al-Zubayr b. Hishām transmitted the information to him from his father that Bakkār b. ʿAbdallāh married a woman who was a descendant of ʿAbd al-Raḥmān b. ʿAwf,[470] and he had a place dear to her heart. But then he took to himself a slave con-
[619] cubine, to her detriment, and aroused her jealousy. Hence, she said to two black slaves of his, "This evildoer (i.e., her husband) is planning to kill you both," and she cajoled and led them on,[471] "so will you help me to kill him?" They replied, "Certainly!" So she went into his presence whilst he was asleep, accompanied by the two slaves, and the two of them sat down on top of his face until he died. He related: She then gave them date wine to drink until they vomited all over and around the bed furnishings. Then she dismissed them and placed by his head a wine flask. When next morning came, his household assembled together and she said,

469. Masʿūdī, *Murūj*, VI, 298–300 = ed. Pellat, § 2505; Iṣfahānī, *Maqātil*, 317–18; *K. al-ʿUyūn*, 294; Ibn al-Ṭiqṭaqā, 176–7, tr. 191–2. The Shīʿī sources give lurid details of his death from leprosy [*judhām*], swelling and blackening of the body, etc., and the impossibility of filling in his grave with earth so that it had to be roofed over with planks of teak.

470. Companion of the Prophet and member, after ʿUmar's death, of the *Shūrā* or council which elected ʿUthmān as Caliph; see *EI*² s.v. (M. Th. Houtsma, W. M. Watt).

471. Following *Addenda et emendanda*, p. DCCLX, *lāṭafat-humā*.

"He got drunk and then vomited and choked, and thus died." But the two slaves were seized and savagely beaten, to the point that they confessed to his murder and that she had ordered them to do it. She was accordingly ejected from the house and excluded from inheriting anything.

Al-Rashīd's Repudiation of Yaḥyā b. ʿAbdallāh's Guarantee of Safe-Conduct

Abū al-Khaṭṭāb[472] has mentioned that Jaʿfar b. Yaḥyā b. Khālid transmitted the information to him one night whilst he was engaged in his nocturnal storytelling session, saying: Today, al-Rashīd summoned Yaḥyā b. ʿAbdallāh b. Ḥasan, there being already present with him the judge Abū al-Bakhtarī[473] and Muḥammad b. al-Ḥasan the religious lawyer,[474] the disciple [*ṣāḥib*] of Abū Yūsuf.[475] He produced the guarantee of safe-conduct which he had given to Yaḥyā, and then said to Muḥammad b. al-Ḥasan, "What do you say concerning this guarantee, is it legally valid?" He replied, "It is valid." Al-Rashīd then argued and disputed with him over that. Muḥammad b. Ḥasan said to him, "What are you going to do about the guarantee? If he were to make war, and then renounce the struggle, he would still have a guarantee of security." Al-Rashīd showed his anger towards Muḥammad b. al-Ḥasan because of his words. Then he asked Abū al-Bakhtarī to examine the guarantee. Abū al-Bakhtarī reported, "This is invalid, on such-and-such counts." Al-Rashīd said, "You are the supreme judge [*qāḍī al-quḍāt*], and you are the person most knowledgeable about that." He thereupon tore up the guarantee and Abū al-Bakhtarī spat on it.[476]

---

472. I.e., Ḥamzah b. ʿAlī, a *rāwī* frequently cited by Ṭabarī.

473. I.e., Wahb b. Wahb, traditionist, genealogist and judge of ʿAskar and then of Medina, died in 200 (815–16). See *GAS,* I, 267.

474. I.e., the great lawyer and pupil of, among others, Abū Ḥanīfah, al-Shaybānī, died in 189/805. See *GAS,* I, 421–33; *EI*[1] s.v. (W. Heffening).

475. The famed lawyer, died in 182 (798). See *GAS,* I, 419–21; *EI*[2] s.v. (Schacht). In Iṣfahānī, *Maqātil,* 314, these persons are included in "a group of Ḥijāzīs" who instituted the calumnies against Yaḥyā and who persuaded al-Rashīd that the guarantee of *amān* was invalid. See Van Arendonck, 69–70, and Sourdel, *Vizirat,* I, 165 n. 1, outlining the various forms of this story in the different sources.

476. Iṣfahānī, *Maqātil,* 318–19; Ibn al-Athīr, VI, 125–6.

More Accusations from the Zubayrī Family against Yaḥyā b. ʿAbdallāh al-ʿAlawī

Bakkār b. ʿAbdallāh b. Muṣʿab happened to be present at the court session, and he went up to Yaḥyā b. ʿAbdallāh, confronting him face-to-face, and said, "You have separated yourself from the community of Muslims (literally, "you have split the staff") and have abandoned the majority body [*al-jamāʿah*] (i.e., the majority Sunnī
[620] community); you have opposed our doctrine and have planned designs on our Caliph, and you have acted in regard to us as is well-known." Yaḥyā replied, "Who are you, may God have mercy on you?" Jaʿfar related: By God, al-Rashīd could not prevent himself from laughing heartily.[477] He related: Yaḥyā rose up in order to go back to the prison, when al-Rashīd said to him, "Go free! Don't you (i.e., the courtiers around him) perceive signs of sickness in him? If he dies at this moment, people will say, 'They poisoned him.'" Yaḥyā replied, "Not at all! I have been continuously ill since I have been in prison, and before then I was ill also." Abū al-Khaṭṭāb related: Yaḥyā only remained one month after this before he died.

Abū Yūnus Isḥāq b. Ismāʿīl has mentioned, saying: I heard ʿAbdallāh b. al-ʿAbbās b. al-Ḥasan b. ʿUbaydallāh b. al-ʿAbbās b. ʿAlī,[478] who was known as al-Khaṭīb, saying: One day, my father and I were at al-Rashīd's gate, and on that particular day there was present such a number of troops and commanders as I have never seen the like at any Caliph's gate either before then or since. He related: Al-Faḍl b. al-Rabīʿ came out to my father and said to him, "Come in!" and he remained for a while and then came out to me and said, "Come in too!" so I went in. Behold, there I was with al-Rashīd, who had with him a woman with whom he was talking. My father made signs to me by moving his head, (conveying the sense) that "He does not want anyone to come in today, but I asked permission for you to enter because of the great press of people that I saw crowding round the gate; and if you come in by this entrance, that will increase your prestige in the eyes of the people."

477. Masʿūdī, *Murūj*, VI, 296 = ed. Pellat, § 2503.

478. Descendant of ʿAlī's son al-ʿAbbās (killed with al-Ḥusayn at al-Ṭaff or Karbalā') by his wife Umm al-Banīn bt. Ḥizām al-Kilābiyyah. See Yaʿqūbī, *Ta'rīkh*, II, 253; Ṭabarī, I, 3471; Masʿūdī, *Tanbīh*, 298, tr. 388.

We did not wait very long before al-Faḍl b. al-Rabīʿ came along and said, "ʿAbdallāh b. Muṣʿab al-Zubayrī seeks permission to enter." The Caliph replied, "I don't want anyone to be allowed to come into my presence today." Al-Faḍl stated, "He has said, 'I have something (important) to mention.'" The Caliph retorted, "Tell him to say it to you!" Al-Faḍl said, "I told him that, but he asserts [621]
that he can only tell it to you personally." The Caliph said, "Bring him in, then," and al-Faḍl went out to bring him in. The woman returned, and the Caliph became immersed in talking to her. My father came up to me and said, "He hasn't really got anything to mention. Al-Faḍl only means by this to convey the idea to all those at the gate that the Commander of the Faithful hasn't allowed us to enter because of some special matter for which we have been specifically singled out; he has merely allowed us to enter because of some request we have to make of him (i.e., of the Caliph), just as this al-Zubayrī has entered."

Al-Zubayrī appeared and said, "O Commander of the Faithful, here is something which I must mention." The Caliph said to him, "Speak on!" Al-Zubayrī said to him, "It's a secret!" The Caliph said, "We have no secrets from al-ʿAbbās." I got up (as if to go), but he said, "Nor from you, my dear fellow," so I sat down again. The Caliph then said, "Now speak!" Al-Zubayrī said, "By God, I have become fearful for the Commander of the Faithful on account of his wife and daughter, the slave girl who sleeps by his side, his slave attendant who hands him his clothes, and both the most intimate of mankind with him from among his commanders and those more distant from him" (i.e., there is virtually no one who should not be regarded with suspicion). He related: I saw that his (i.e., the Caliph's) color changed, and he said, "What's this about?" Al-Zubayrī replied, "The summons to the cause of Yaḥyā b. ʿAbdallāh b. Ḥasan came to me, and I realized that it must not have reached me—in view of the enmity between us (i.e., the Zubayrids) and them (i.e., the ʿAlids)—until he had not left anyone at your gate (i.e., at court) without bringing him into opposition against you."[479]

479. I.e., as the least likely person to adhere to the ʿAlid cause, a Zubayrid would be the very last person to be invited to join it; hence, all the less intransigent foes of the ʿAlids must already have been invited!

The Caliph said, "Will you say this to him to his face?" He replied, "Yes." Al-Rashīd said, "Bring him in." He came in, and he repeated the words which he had said to the Caliph. Yaḥyā b. ʿAbdallāh then replied, "O Commander of the Faithful, he has by God brought forward something which, if it were said to a person of lower status than you in regard to a person of higher status than me, and he had the controlling power over him, he would never escape (from the accusation) at all. I have a bond of kinship and relationship; so why do you not either lay aside this matter or else dispose of it quickly? It may be that you will be relieved of the burden of me by some hand or tongue other than your own; or you may well find that you will sever the bond of kinship without your being aware of it! I will contend with him in argument in your presence, bringing down the curse of God on whomever is proved wrong, if you will be patient for a little while."

The Caliph said, "O ʿAbdallāh, arise and perform the worship, if
[622] you judge that appropriate." Yaḥyā arose and faced towards the *qiblah*, and performed two shortened (literally, "light") *rakʿah*s,[480] and ʿAbdallāh likewise performed two *rakʿah*s. Then Yaḥyā knelt down and said (to ʿAbdallāh), "Kneel," and then he intertwined his own right hand with ʿAbdallāh's one and said, "O God, if you have known that I summoned ʿAbdallāh b. Muṣʿab to rebelliousness on the basis of this"—and he place his (other) hand on the intertwined right hands and pointed to them—"then destroy me with an act of Your divine punishment, and abandon me to my own strength and power alone. But if the contrary is true, then abandon him to his own strength and power alone, and destroy him with an act of Your divine punishment. Amen, O Lord of the Worlds!" ʿAbdallāh also repeated, "Amen, O Lord of the Worlds!" Yaḥyā b. ʿAbdallāh then said to ʿAbdallāh b. Muṣʿab, "Say the words which I have just said." ʿAbdallāh accordingly said, "O God, if you have known that Yaḥyā b. ʿAbdallāh did not summon me to rebelliousness on the basis of this, then abandon me to my own strength and power alone, and destroy me with an act of Your divine punishment. But if the contrary is true, then abandon him to his own strength and power alone, and destroy him with an act of Your divine punishment. Amen, O Lord of the Worlds!" On that, the two of them parted.

480. *Rakʿatayn khafīfatayn,* i.e., consisting only of the *Fātiḥah* plus a short sūrah or portion of the Qurʾān, a permissible abridgment of the *ṣalāt*; cf. Jahshiyārī, 218, *fa-khaffafa al-rajul ṣalātahu.*

Orders were then given for Yaḥyā to be imprisoned in an out of the way part of the palace. When he went back there and ʿAbdallāh b. Muṣʿab went away, al-Rashīd came up to my father and said, "I have done so-and-so for him and I have done so-and-so for him," and then he enumerated his favors to him. My father addressed him with a couple of words which were so innocuous as not to have scared away a sparrow, out of fear for his own safety. The Caliph commanded us to depart, so we departed homewards.

I entered (the house) with my father, taking off from him his black robes, as was my wont. Whilst I was unloosing his girdle, the slave boy suddenly burst into his presence and said, "ʿAbdallāh b. Muṣʿab's messenger (is here)!" He replied, "Bring him in!" When the messenger entered, he said to him, "What's the reason behind your coming?" The messenger said, "My master says to you, 'I adjure you by God, please come to me!' " My father said to the slave, "Tell him that I have been with the Commander of the Faithful right up till this very moment, but I am just sending ʿAbdallāh to you; whatever you wish to communicate to me, deliver the message to him," and he further told the slave, "Set off, and he (i.e., ʿAbdallāh) will follow on your tracks."

My father remarked to me, however, "He has only summoned
me in order to seek assistance from me in the furtherance of the [623]
lies which he has put forward. If I help him, I shall sever my bond of relationship with the Messenger of God; and if I oppose him, he will spread slanderous reports about me. Yet people can use their children as shields and protect themselves against unpleasant occurences by means of them; so go along to him, and to everything which he says to you make your reply, 'I will inform my father.' I am sending you, without however feeling confident about your safety." My father had told me when he returned homewards (from the palace)—that (delay) having arisen because we were kept back with al-Rashīd—"Did you not observe the slave strategically placed to block the way out of the palace? He did not, by God, dismiss us until he had finished with him"—he meant Yaḥyā—"Indeed we belong to God and to Him we shall be returning, and we expect our reward from God (i.e., ultimately, and not immediately)!"[481]

---

481. Following the *ʿinda Allāh* of the Cairo text, VIII, 251, for the Leiden text's *ʿAbdallāh.*

I accordingly set off with the messenger. When I had gone some distance along the way, disturbed in my mind at what I was about to embark on, I said to the messenger, "Woe upon you! What is he up to, and what has disquieted him into sending to my father at this time?" He replied, "When he came back from the palace, the very moment he alighted from his mount he cried out, 'My belly, my belly!'" ʿAbdallāh b. ʿAbbās related: I did not attach much significance to these words of the slave's nor pay much attention to him. But when we came to the gate of the house, which was in a cul-de-sac, the two doors were thrown open[482] and behold, the womenfolk had come forth with their hair flowing loose, girt with cords around their waists, beating their faces and crying out in lamentation. The man had just died!

I said (to myself), "I have never seen anything more remarkable than this," and I pulled at my mount's reins to turn it round homewards, galloping at a pace I had never galloped at previously nor ever did subsequently. The slaves and retainers were meanwhile awaiting me (anxiously), because of the strength of the shaykh's (i.e., his father al-ʿAbbās's) attachment to me. Hence, when they saw me, they ran into the house. He came out to meet me in a state of agitation, wearing only his shirt and a towel (round his waist) and crying, "What sort of situation have you left behind, my dear son?" I replied, "He is dead!" He exclaimed, "Praise be to God, who has brought about his death and has freed you and ourself of him!"

He had not finished his words when one of al-Rashīd's eunuchs
[624] arrived, ordering my father to ride forth and me with him. My father observed, while we were travelling along the road, "If it were permissible for a gift of prophecy to be attributed to Yaḥyā, then his family (i.e., ʿAbdallāh b. Muṣʿab's)—may God have mercy on him!—might well claim that to be so! We reckon him to have earned a recompense from God! By God, we cannot doubt but that he has been struck dead!" We proceeded onwards until we entered al-Rashīd's presence. When he looked up at us he said, "O ʿAbbās b. al-Ḥasan, have you not heard the news?" My father replied, "Yes indeed, O Commander of the Faithful, and praise be to God who has struck him down through the words of his own tongue, and

482. Following the emendations recommended in n. *c*.

may God protect you, O Commander of the Faithful, from the severance of your bonds of relationship!" Al-Rashīd said, "By God, the man (i.e., Yaḥyā) is perfectly free to do what he likes!" and he drew aside the curtain. Yaḥyā came in and, by God, I discerned clearly the shaykh's joy.

When al-Rashīd looked at him he cried out, "O Abū Muḥammad, have you not yet realized that God has destroyed your enemy, the tyrant!" He (i.e., Yaḥyā) exclaimed, "Praise be to God who has made clear to the Commander of the Faithful his enemy's mendacity against me and who has spared him from severing the bonds of his relationship! By God, O Commander of the Faithful, even if this matter (i.e., Yaḥyā's alleged bid for power and assumption of the rule) were something which I seek, and am suitable for and earnestly desire, how (could I achieve it?). In fact, I don't seek or earnestly desire it! And (even if) attaining it could only be achieved by enlisting his (i.e., ʿAbdallāh b. Muṣʿab's) help and then there was no one left in the world except myself, yourself and him, I would never overpower you by means of his help. Also, this man, by God"—and he pointed to al-Faḍl b. al-Rabīʿ—"is one of the misfortunes which you are afflicted with. By God, even if you were to give him ten thousand dirhams, and then he had an avid desire for one single date from me, he would sell you to me for that date" (i.e., he is totally mercenary). The Caliph replied, however, "As for al-ʿAbbāsī,[483] don't say anything but good about him." He ordered Yaḥyā to be given that very day one hundred thousand dīnārs, having imprisoned him for just part of a day. Abū Yūnus related: Hārūn had imprisoned him on three occasions in addition to this spell of imprisonment and had presented him with four hundred thousand dīnārs.

In this year, factional strife [*ʿaṣabiyyah*] was stirred up in Syria between the Nizārīs and Yamānīs (i.e., the North and South Arabs), the head of the Nizārīs being at that time Abū al-Haydhām.[484]

---

483. The name which al-Rashīd was wont to give al-Faḍl, presumably referring to his clientage [*walā*ʾ] to the ʿAbbāsid family.

484. This person must be the Abū al-Haydhām ʿĀmir b. ʿUmārah who, according to Yaʿqūbī, *Ta*ʾ*rīkh*, II, 495, and Azdī, 279, was head of the Nizārīs and who rebelled in the Ḥawrān in this year, slaughtering the Yamānīs; the Caliph sent against him, these sources continue, al-Sindī (b. al-Shāhik? See Ṭabarī, III, 580, above, 59), who

[625]

*The Internecine Strife [*fitnah*] among the North and South Arabs in Syria*

It has been mentioned that this internecine strife was stirred up in Syria at the time when Mūsā b. ʿĪsā[485] was governor there on behalf of the ruling power. A large number of people were killed among the Nizārīs and Yamānīs on account of the factional strife between them. So al-Rashīd appointed Mūsā b. Yaḥyā b. Khālid as governor over Syria,[486] and strengthened his power by attaching to him a body of commanders, troops and senior secretaries. When he reached Syria, this body of retainers was halted and accommodated [*uḥillat*] for his entry into (the house of) Ṣāliḥ b. ʿAlī al-Hāshimī.[487] Mūsā then remained there until he had restored peace among its people, the strife had died down and affairs in Syria became settled and on an even keel. The news about this reached al-Rashīd in the City of Peace, and he awarded jurisdiction over the people of Syria to Yaḥyā; the latter forgave them and overlooked the violence that had raged between them and brought them (i.e, the leaders of the Syrian factions) to Baghdad. Concerning this, (Abū Yaʿqūb) Isḥāq b. Ḥassān al-Khuraymī[488] says,

---

killed Abū al-Haydhām and scattered his forces. In Ibn al-Athīr, VI, 127 ff., we have a highly detailed and original account of this factional strife and of the activities of the *Zawāqīl* or banditry, including the fighting of Abū al-Haydhām al-Murrī with the Yamānī faction, placed under the year 176 (792–3) but giving a connected narrative of events up to Abū al-Haydhām's death, placed in 182 (798), hence, encompassing also the account of the unrest in Syria given by Ṭabarī, III, 639–41. Cf. further Yaʿqūbī, *Taʾrīkh*, II, 494–5; Palmer, 63–4; P. von Sievers, "Military, merchants and nomads: the social evolution of the Syrian cities and countryside during the classical period, 780–969/164–358," *Isl.*, LVI (1979), 220–1.

485. It is stated in Ṭabarī, III, 626, below, 134, that Mūsā was governor of Egypt around this time. His governorship in Syria may have followed after his second spell of power in Egypt, ending in Ṣafar 176 (June 792); see below, loc. cit., n. 494.

486. Cf. Bouvat, 49.

487. The text here, as the editor notes, is evidently corrupt. The present tentative translation is an attempt to make sense of it on the lines suggested by the editor (and, in regard to the vocalization *uḥillat*, by the Cairo text, VIII, 251), including the insertion of a word like *dār* before the name of Ṣāliḥ b. ʿAlī b. ʿAbdallāh, the former ʿAbbāsid governor of Syria and father of ʿAbd al-Malik b. Ṣāliḥ, who had himself been dead since 152 (769).

488. Eulogist of al-Rashīd and the Barmakīs, and supporter of al-Amīn in the Civil War, died ca. 206/821–2 (the *nisbah* to be read thus according to Pellat, and not "al-Khuzaymī" as here in the text). See *GAL*, S I, 111–12; *GAS*, II, 550–1; *EI*[2] s.v. Abū Yaʿḳūb al-Khuraymī (Pellat).

Who will go as a messenger to Yaḥyā, when before meeting up with him
lie the thickets of every valiant lion?
O shepherd of Islam, who is not neglectful of his duties,
(at this moment residing) in the pleasant circumstances of a contented way of life and the fragrance of sweet-smelling perfumes.
Its watering places are sweet and wholesome, and you are given water to drink,
whilst it (i.e., the camel bearing the messenger to him) spends the nights in the hills and mountain ridges,
Until it lays down its forequarters, striking (the ground) with the upper
part of its neck, and its tethering ropes become firmly fixed in an abode of peace.
Every gap in the frontiers has a guard, through his forethought,
and in regard to the bright gleams of a glance, no one who raises his eyes is rendered weak.[489]

Another poet, in addition to Abū Yaʿqūb (i.e., al-Khuraymī), has said,

Syria raged with unrest
such as to make the hair of a child turn white!
Then Mūsā was unleashed upon it, [626]
with his cavalry and his detachment of troops.
So that Syria submitted (to him), when
he came with the auspiciousness of his unique presence.[490]
He is the generous one, and every other
generous person is surpassed by his generosity.
The generosity of his father Yaḥyā
and that of his forefathers has passed to him,
So that Mūsā b. Yaḥyā has become generous
with both recently acquired liberality and his hereditary qualities,

489. *Dīwān*, ed. ʿAli Jawād al-Ṭāhir and Muḥammad Jabbār al-Muʿaybid, 58 no. 47.
490. The Cairo text, VIII, 252, has "when he brought his unique presence."

And indeed, Mūsā reached the zenith of glory
when he was still a young child in his cradle.
I have singled him out for my eulogies,
both eulogies in prose and those in the form of poetic odes.
He has a branch from (i.e., is a scion of) the Barmakīs,
and how noble is his branch!
They have acquired possession of the whole of poetry,
that in the *khafīf* metre and that in the *madīd* one!

In this year, al-Rashīd dismissed al-Ghiṭrīf b. ʿAṭāʾ from the governorship of Khurāsān and appointed Ḥamzah b. al-Haytham al-Khuzāʿī, who had the nickname of "the Bride,"[491] over it.[492]

In this year, al-Rashīd appointed Jaʿfar b. Yaḥyā b. Khālid b. Barmak over Egypt, and the latter appointed (as his deputy) there ʿUmar b. Mihrān.[493]

The Reason behind al-Rashīd's Appointment of Jaʿfar al-Barmakī over Egypt and the Latter's Appointment of ʿUmar b. Mihrān (as His Deputy) over It

Muḥammad b. ʿUmar has mentioned that Aḥmad b. Muḥammad b. Mihrān transmitted the information to him that the news reached al-Rashīd that Mūsā b. ʿĪsā, the governor in Egypt at that time,[494] had resolved to throw off allegiance.[495] Al-Rashīd ex-

---

491. Son of the *naqīb* prominent in the ʿAbbāsid Revolution and commander of guard for al-Manṣūr and al-Mahdī, died in 181 (797–8). See Crone, 181; Kennedy, 81.

492. Ṭabarī-Balʿamī, tr. IV, 459; Ḥamzah, 165; Azdī, 277.

493. Bouvat, 68; Sourdel, *Vizirat*, I, 148–9. Jahshiyārī, 146, states that in this year there was something like a division of the empire into two governorships for Yaḥyā's sons, and with Jaʿfar taking over all the lands west of Anbār and al-Faḍl all the lands east of al-Nahrawān. In fact, al-Faḍl's stay in Khurāsān was only brief, 178–9 (794–5), see Ṭabarī, III, 631–7 (below, 143–51), and Jaʿfar's must have been nominal, for he stayed in Baghdad over the next years, apart from his expedition to quell a revolt in Syria, see Ṭabarī, III, 639 ff. (below, 155 ff.).

494. According to Kindī, 132, 134, 137, the member of the ʿAbbāsid family Mūsā b. ʿĪsā b. Mūsā b. Muḥammad (a second cousin of al-Rashīd's) was governor of Egyt on three separate occasions, the one mentioned here being the second governorship al-Muḥarram 175–Ṣafar 176 (May 791–June 792). Kindī does not, however, give this episode of ʿUmar b. Mihrān's surprise arrival in Egypt and deposition of Mūsā.

495. More feasible as a reason for al-Rashīd's displeasure are the reports of Mūsā b. ʿĪsā's oppressions in Egypt, as adduced, e.g., by Jahshiyārī, 171.

claimed, "By God, I'll replace him with the most insignificant person at my court! Search out for me such a man!" Hence, the name of ʿUmar b. Mihrān, who was at that time functioning as secretary for al-Khayzurān,[496] and had no experience of acting thus for anyone else, was mentioned (to him). ʿUmar had a squint [627]
and an unprepossessing face; he wore inferior-quality clothes, the most valuable part of his clothing being his *ṭaylasān* which was worth thirty dirhams. He used to tuck up his robes and roll up his sleeves; he used to ride a mule, with a halter and an iron bridle, and with his slave boy mounted behind him.[497] Al-Rashīd now summoned him and then appointed him governor over Egypt, with responsibility for its finances, the caliphal estates there, and the conduct of warfare there. ʿUmar said, "O Commander of the Faithful, I will act as governor there on one condition." He replied, "And what is that?" ʿUmar said, "That I may make the decision myself about laying down office; when I have restored peace to the land, I shall depart." So al-Rashīd granted him that condition.

ʿUmar b. Mihrān made his way to Egypt, and his tenure of the governorship followed immediately upon that of Mūsā b. ʿĪsā. The latter was expecting ʿUmar's arrival. ʿUmar b. Mihrān then entered Egypt, mounted on a mule, with his slave boy Abū Durrah[498] riding on a baggage mule. He sought out Mūsā b. ʿĪsā's house, at a moment when Mūsā had a throng of people around him, went in and sat down among the people at the back. When the people attending the session dispersed, Mūsā b. ʿĪsā enquired of ʿUmar, "Is there anything you want, O shaykh?" ʿUmar replied, "Yes, may God guide the Amīr uprightly!" Then he stood up with the documents (i.e., those he had brought with him, containing his own letter of appointment) and handed them over to him. Mūsā said, "Abū Ḥafṣ—may God preserve him!—is coming?" ʿUmar replied, "I am Abū Ḥafṣ." Mūsā exclaimed, "Are you really ʿUmar b. Mihrān?" He replied, "Yes." Mūsā commented, "May God curse Phar-

496. Cf. Abbott, 121–4.

497. ʿUmar's unprepossessingness and his shabby clothes are emphasized in Jahshiyārī, loc. cit.

498. Specified in ibid. as black; hence, with the name "Father of the pearl" by antiphrasis, as often in the names of slaves.

aoh when he says, 'Is not the kingdom of Egypt mine?' "[499] Then he handed over to him the administrative charge of the province and departed.[500]

ʿUmar b. Mihrān went up to his slave boy Abū Durrah and instructed him, "Don't accept any presents except those which can be put into a bag (i.e., small ones, or those in cash form); don't accept any riding beast, slave girl, or slave boy." The people now began to send their presents. He (i.e., Abū Durrah) for his part began to send back the larger presents in kind but would accept presents of money and clothing and would take them along to ʿUmar, who would then record on them the names of the donors. At this point, ʿUmar began the process of collecting the taxes. Now there was in Egypt a group of people who were accustomed to put off payment of the taxes due and evade them. ʿUmar made a start with one of these persons, but he pleaded inability to pay him. ʿUmar thereupon exclaimed, "By God, you're going to have to
[628] pay the taxation due from you at the public treasury in the City of Peace itself, if you live to tell the tale!" The man said, "I'll pay it," and then begged for his indulgence and intercession. But ʿUmar said, "I have sworn an oath and I cannot break it," so he despatched the man under an escort of two soldiers. Provincial governors were at this time able to correspond directly with the Caliph,[501] hence ʿUmar sent with them a letter to al-Rashīd in the following terms:

"I summoned so-and-so, son of so-and-so, and demanded payment of the taxation due from him, but he refused to pay me and asked for a delay; so I gave him a respite. Then I summoned him again, but he put off paying once more, and looked like refusing payment altogether. Whereupon I swore that he should only pay it at the public treasury in the City of Peace. The total sum due from him is such-and-such, and I have sent him forward under the escort of so-and-so, son of so-and-so, and so-and-so, son of so-and-

---

499. Qur'ān, XLIII, 50/51.

500. Jahshiyārī, 171–3; *K. al-ʿUyūn*, 294–5; Ibn al-Athīr, VI, 126; Ibn Taghrībirdī, *al-Nujūm al-zāhirah*, II, 78–81, discussing at length why mention of ʿUmar b. Mihrān apparently dropped out of mention among the governors of Egypt; Palmer, 61–2.

501. I.e., without having to go through the central *Dīwān* of the Seal, a concession obtained from the Caliph by al-Faḍl b. Yaḥyā because of the administrative tardiness of the then head of that department, Abū al-ʿAbbās al-Faḍl al-Ṭūsī. See Jahshiyārī, 135; Sourdel, *Vizirat*, I, 137.

so, from the section of the Commander of the Faithful's army under the command of so-and-so, son of so-and-so. If the Commander of the Faithful thinks fit to write back to me confirming his arrival, then, if God Most High so wills, perhaps he would kindly do so?"

He related: No one now pleaded inability to pay him any part of the taxation due, so he sought payment of the taxation for the first stipulated period, and then the second one. But when it was time for the third instalment, demands for payment had to be made and people put off payment. ʿUmar accordingly summoned the taxpayers and the traders, and pressed them for payment; they put off payment and complained of indigence. ʿUmar thereupon ordered those presents which had been sent to him to be brought in, looked into the bags and summoned the assayer and valuer [*jahbadh*].[502] He weighed out their contents and used them as payments toward the sums required from their original donors. He sent for baskets, and had the sale of their contents publicly proclaimed; he sold them and used the price gained towards settling the original donors' tax liabilities. Then he said, "O group of men, I kept back from you your presents for the time when you would need them. So hand over to us now the remainder of the taxation due to us." They duly handed it over to him until the whole of the taxation of Egypt was gathered in. Then he departed; it is not known that anyone else except ʿUmar ever succeeded in collecting by the end of the fiscal year the whole of the taxation of Egypt due [*aghlaqa māla Miṣr*][503] and then departed. So he set out on a mule, with Abū Durrah on another mule, he himself having made the decision to lay down office.[504]

---

502. On the functions of this official in the financial administration of the mediaeval caliphate, see *EI*[2] s.v. (W. J. Fischel).

503. For the technical term of the financial departments *ighlāq,* see Bosworth, "Abū ʿAbdallāh al-Khwārazmī on the technical terms of the secretary's art," 135. The difficulties of collecting taxation in Egypt are well-known to us, through, *inter alia,* the papyri from there; see E. Ashtor, *A social and economic history of the Near East in the Middle Ages,* 67–9.

504. Jahshiyārī, 173–4; *K. al-ʿUyūn,* 295–6; Ibn al-Athīr, VI, 127; Ibn Taghrībirdī, II, 80–1; Palmer, 61–3; Abbott, 122–4. According to Kindī, 134–5, followed by Ibn Taghrībirdī, II, 83, Mūsā's successor after this second governorship of his was another ʿAbbāsid prince, Ibrāhīm b. Ṣāliḥ b. ʿAlī b. ʿAbdallāh (a first cousin twice removed of al-Rashīd's), himself serving as governor for the second time.

In this year, ʿAbd al-Raḥmān b. ʿAbd al-Malik led the summer raid and captured a fortress.[505]

[629] In this year, Sulaymān b. Abī Jaʿfar al-Manṣūr led the Pilgrimage, and according to what al-Wāqidī has mentioned, Hārūn's wife Zubaydah and with her her brother[506] also made the Pilgrimage.[507]

---

505. Brooks, *EHR*, XV (1900), 740. According to Yaʿqūbī, *Taʾrīkh*, II, 522, Hāshim b. al-Ṣalt, but according to Khalīfah, *Taʾrīkh*, II, 716, there was no summer raid this year.

506. Presumably, her full brother Ibrāhīm b. Jaʿfar b. al-Manṣūr.

507. Khalīfah, *Taʾrīkh*, loc. cit.; Muḥammad b. Ḥabīb, 38; Yaʿqūbī, *Taʾrīkh*, II, 521; Abbott, 242.

The Events of the Year 177

(April 18, 793–April 6, 794)

Among the events taking place during this year was al-Rashīd's dismissal, according to what has been mentioned, of Jaʿfar b. Yaḥyā from the governorship of Egypt and his appointment to Egypt of Isḥāq b. Sulaymān;[508] also, al-Rashīd's dismissal of Ḥamzah b. Mālik from Khurāsān and his appointment of al-Faḍl b. Yaḥyā to there, together with al-Rayy and Sijistān, in addition to the provinces which he was already governing.[509]

In this year, ʿAbd al-Razzāq b. ʿAbd al-Ḥamīd al-Taghlibī led the summer raid.[510]

---

508. According to Kindī, 136, governor after the second governorship of Ibrāhīm b. Ṣāliḥ, from Rajab 177 to Rajab 178 (October 793–October 794). Isḥāq b. Sulaymān b. ʿAlī b. ʿAbdallāh was in fact a first cousin of his predecessor.

509. Jahshiyārī, 146, placing the appointment in 176; Ḥamzah, 165; *K. al-ʿUyūn*, 296; Ibn al-Athīr, VI, 140; Ibn Tiqtaqā, 183, tr. 199; Bouvat, 59–60; Sourdel, *Vizirat*, I, 145–6; Daniel, 169. Al-Faḍl did not actually set out for Khurāsān till the following year, see Ṭabarī, III, 631 (below, 143).

510. Ibn al-Athīr, loc. cit.; Brooks, *EHR*, XV (1900), 741. According to Yaʿqūbī, *Taʾrīkh*, II, 522, however, the leader was Dāwūd b. al-Nuʿmān on behalf of ʿAbd al-Malik b. Ṣāliḥ (who, according to Khalīfah, *Taʾrīkh*, II, 717, was the actual leader, with Sulaymān b. Rāshid al-Thaqafī the leader of an apparently successful winter raid (the event recorded by Ṭabarī, III, 637, under the year 178?).

In this year, according to what al-Wāqidī has mentioned, there occurred a (violent) wind, and overshadowing (of the heavens) and a redness (in the sky), on the night of Sunday (i.e., the night of Saturday-Sunday), the twenty-sixth of al-Muḥarram[511] (May 13, 793).[512] Then there was a further overshadowing (of the heavens) of the heavens on the night of Wednesday (i.e., the night of Tuesday-Wednesday), the twenty-eighth of al-Muḥarram (May 15, 793), and then a violent wind and intense overshadowing of the heavens on Friday, the second of Ṣafar[513] (May 19, 793).[514]

In this year, Hārūn al-Rashīd led the Pilgrimage.[515]

---

511. Actually, a Monday, which would fit correctly with the next-mentioned day of Wednesday, the twenty-eighth of al-Muḥarram.

512. Ibn al-Athīr, loc. cit.

513. Actually, a Sunday.

514. Ibn al-Athīr, loc. cit.

515. Muḥammad b. Ḥabīb, 38; Yaʿqūbī, *Ta'rīkh,* II, 521; Ibn al-Athīr, loc. cit.

The Events of the Year 178

(April 7, 794–March 26, 795)

Among the events of this year was the uprising of the Arab tribesmen of the Ḥawf[516] in Egypt, comprising the Qays,[517] Quḍāʿah and
others, against al-Rashīd's governor there, Isḥāq b. Sulaymān, their
fighting with him, and al-Rashīd's despatching to him of Harthamah b. Aʿyan, in company with a group of commanders attached
to him as reinforcements for Isḥāq b. Sulaymān, until the tribes- [630]
men of the Ḥawf submitted, returned to their obedience and handed over the taxes due to the central government which were incumbent upon them. Harthamah was at that moment al-Rashīd's
governor over Palestine. When the episode of the Ḥawf tribesmen
was settled, Hārūn removed Isḥāq b. Sulaymān from the governorship of Egypt and appointed in his stead Harthamah for about a
month; then he removed him and appointed ʿAbd al-Malik b. Ṣāliḥ
over Egypt.[518]

---

516. Literally, "the flank," the region stretching from the eastern Nile delta to the fringes of Sinai; see Yāqūt, *Muʿjam,* II, 322.

517. On the influx of North Arab tribesmen into Egypt from 109 (727) onwards, see C. H. Becker, *Beitrage zur Geschichte Ägyptens unter dem Islam,* II, 121 ff.

518. Kindī, 136; Ibn al-Athīr, VI, 141; Ibn Taghrībirdī, II, 87–8; Palmer, 64–5; Becker, II, 132–3.

Harthamah b. Aʿyan Restores Order in Ifrīqiyah

In this year occurred the uprising of the people of Ifrīqiyah against ʿAbdawayh al-Anbārī and the troops of the army who were with him there. As a result, al-Faḍl b. Rawḥ b. Ḥātim was killed and the members of the house of al-Muhallab there were expelled.[519] So al-Rashīd sent Harthamah b. Aʿyan against them, and they returned to their obedience. It has been mentioned that, when this ʿAbdawayh seized control of Ifrīqiyah and threw off allegiance to the central government, his power grew and the number of his supporters swelled and the people of the outlying areas rushed to join him. Al-Rashīd's vizier at that particular moment was Yaḥyā b. Khālid b. Barmak, and the latter sent Yaqṭīn b. Mūsā and his secretary Manṣūr b. Ziyād against ʿAbdawayh.[520] Yaḥyā b. Khālid kept continuously despatching letters to ʿAbdawayh, encouraging him to return to his obedience, putting him in fear of the consequences of rebellion, going to great lengths in exhorting him, giving him hopes of future bounty and promises, until he accepted a guarantee of safe-conduct and returned to his obedience and came to Baghdad. Yaḥyā implemented his guarantee of ʿAbdawayh and treated him handsomely;[521] he secured a guarantee of safety on his behalf from al-Rashīd, gave him presents and appointed him to high office.[522]

---

519. According to Yaʿqūbī, *Taʾrīkh,* II, 496, and Ibn al-Athīr, VI, 135–6, al-Faḍl had succeeded Naṣr b. Ḥabīb al-Muhallabī (Ibn al-Athīr, Ḥabīb b. Naṣr), arriving in Ifrīqiyah in al-Muḥarram 177 (April –May 793). In Ibn al-Athīr's detailed account, VI, 135–9, it is described how the Ifrīqiyan troops rebelled under ʿAbdawayh against the bad conduct of the Muhallabī governors there, with ʿAbdawayh extending his power from Tunis to Qayrawān and killing al-Faḍl b. Rawḥ; but at VI, 137, the further revolt of a section of ʿAbdawayh's army against its leader is placed immediately after the killing of al-Faḍl and, by implication, made into a result of this killing.

520. According to Ibn al-Athīr, VI, 138, Yaḥyā was sent on ahead by Harthamah to negotiate because of his influence and standing with the Khurasanian troops who formed a good proportion of the garrison of Ifrīqiyah.

521. Bouvat, 49. Ibn al-Athīr, VI, 139, says however that he was imprisoned [*uʿtuqila*] at Baghdad.

522. In Yaʿqūbī's detailed account of events in Ifrīqiyah, *Taʾrīkh,* II, 496, the leader of the revolt is given as ʿAbdallāh b. al-Jārūd, but with Harthamah as the pacifier of the country before his return to Egypt in 179 (795–6); the equally detailed account of Ibn al-Athīr, VI, 135–9, combines the two names as "ʿAbdallāh b. al-Jārūd, known as ʿAbdawayh al-Anbārī." This same account makes clear that

In this year, al-Rashīd entrusted all his affairs to Yaḥyā b. Khālid b. Barmak.[523] [631]

In this year, al-Walīd b. Ṭarīf the Khārijite[524] rebelled in al-Jazīrah and proclaimed there the doctrine of *taḥkīm*;[525] he fell upon Ibrāhīm b. Khāzim b. Khuzaymah at Nisībīn,[526] and then moved from there into Armenia.[527]

Al-Faḍl b. Yaḥyā's Governorship in Khurāsān and the Poetic Eulogies of Him

In this year, al-Faḍl b. Yaḥyā set out for Khurāsān as governor over it. He behaved in a praiseworthy way there, building mosques and *ribāṭ*s and making raids into Transoxania. Khārākharah (?), the ruler of Ushrūsanah,[528] submitted to him, having previously refused allegiance. It has been mentioned that al-Faḍl b. Yaḥyā formed in Khurāsān an army of the local population [*al-ʿAjam*] which he called "partisans of the ʿAbbāsids" [*al-ʿAbbāsiyyah*], attaching them as clients [*jaʿala walāʾahum*] to the ʿAbbāsids. (It

---

the complex military operations in Ifrīqiyah extended at least up to the year 180 (796–7), for Harthamah did not return from Ifrīqiyah till Ramaḍān 181 (November 797), after a governorship there of two and a half years. See also Palmer, 67–72; Marçais, *La Berbérie musulmane et l'Orient au Moyen Age*, 52–3; Kennedy, 192–3.

523. Azdī, 280; Ibn al-Athīr, VI, 145; cf. Bouvat, 49.

524. In Khalīfah, *Taʾrīkh*, Azdī, 283, the *K. al-ʿUyūn* and Ibn al-Athīr (see below, n. 527), he is given the *nisbah* of "al-Taghlibī," but in Iṣfahānī, *Aghānī*, ed. Būlāq, XI, 9 = ed. Cairo, XII, 94, and the biography given by Ibn Khallikān, VI, 31–4, tr. III, 668–71, that of "al-Shaybānī." This must be correct, in the light of the verses given by Ṭabarī, III, 638 (below, 153, see n. 564), unless we amend "al-Taghlibī" to "al-Thaʿlabī," for Thaʿlabah was the forebear of Shaybān of the great group of Bakr b. Wāʾil; see *EI*[2] s.v. (W. Caskel).

525. Echoing the slogan of the early Khārijites at the time of their secession from ʿAlī's army at Ḥarūrā in protest at the Caliph's acceptance of the idea of arbitration between himself and Muʿāwiyah; from this slogan "no judgment [*ḥukm*] except by God" arose the alternative name for the sect of *al-Muḥakkimah*.

526. A town of upper al-Jazīrah on the Hirnās river. See Yāqūt, *Muʿjam*, V, 288–9; Le Strange, *Lands*, 94–5; Canard, *H'amdânides*, 103; *EI*[1] s.v. (Honigmann).

527. Khalīfah, *Taʾrīkh*, II, 718; Yaʿqūbī, *Taʾrīkh*, II, 495, placing the beginning of al-Walīd's revolt in 179 (795–6); Azdī, 280; *K. al-ʿUyūn*, 296; Ibn al-Athīr, VI, 141. Ṭabarī considers the later stages of this revolt under the year 179; see III, 638 (below, 153–54).

528. I.e., the Afshīn; for this ancient Iranian title, see *EI*[2] s.v. (Barthold-Gibb). The name of the ruler given here is perhaps identical with the name Kh.rākh.rāf (?) in Maqdisī, *Aḥsan al-taqāsīm*, 274.

has also been mentioned) that these troops numbered as many as five hundred thousand, that twenty thousand of them went on to Baghdad, being known there as *K.r.n.biyyah*,[529] and that al-Faḍl left the remainder of them in Khurāsān, registered according to their names and entries in the pay-registers.[530] Concerning this event, Marwān b. Abī Ḥafṣah says,

Al-Faḍl is none other than a brilliant shooting star that sets not
in battles when other stars set.
A protector over the realm of a house whose share of power is resplendent,[531]
through inheritance, having a connection (i.e., with the Prophet, as descendants of the Prophet's paternal uncle al-ʿAbbās) in their possession.
An access of strength has been formed for the sons of the one who provided the pilgrims with water to drink (i.e., for the descendants of Hāshim, grandfather of al-ʿAbbās[532]), made up of squadrons of cavalry who have no other allegiance except to them.
Squadrons of cavalry for the descendants of al-ʿAbbās; the latter have recognized
what al-Faḍl has brought together of these troops, both non-Arabs and Arabs.

---

529. In Jāḥiẓ, *K. al-Bukhalāʾ*, 69, *kurunbiyyah* = "a dish made with cabbage"; cf. *WbKAS*, I, 150b. But could this usage here be an opprobrious designation, "cabbage [*kurunb*] eaters"? The penchant of the Khurāsānians for their own regional dishes, even when they were resident in Baghdad, appears from Ṭabarī, III, 1046.

530. Jahshiyārī, 146–7; Yaʿqūbī, *Taʾrīkh*, II, 292 (mentioning a rebellion of the people of Ṭālaqān [i.e., of Ṭālaqān in Ṭukhāristān]; see Yāqūt, *Muʿjam*, IV, 6–7; Le Strange, *Lands*, 423–4; *EI*[1] s.v. [Huart]); Ḥamzah al-Iṣfahānī, 165; Ṭabarī-Balʿamī, tr. IV, 459; Azdī, 280; *K. al-ʿUyūn*, 296; Ibn al-Athīr, VI, 145; Ibn Khallikān, IV, 29, tr. II, 460–1; Barthold, *Turkestan*, 202–3; Bouvat, 60–2; Daniel, 169; Pipes, 137; Kennedy, 120, 181. Shaban, 31, 36, explains al-Faḍl's concessions on tax arrears and other financial matters in Khurāsān—unusual in a family so keen on exacting all the state's dues—as measures to ensure a continued flow of recruits for the troops at that time being raised in Khurāsān.

531. Vocalizing here *gharra sahmuhum*; the Cairo text, VIII, 257, has *ʿazza sahmuhum* "whose share of power is exalted," with a similar meaning.

532. Hāshim had the right of *siqāyah*, supplying water to the pilgrims in Mecca during pre-Islamic times, a right confirmed by the Prophet at the conquest of Mecca in 8 (630). See M. Gaudefroy-Demombynes, *Mahomet*, 64, 173; idem, *Le pèlerinage à la Mekke*, 89 ff.

He set down of their numbers, five hundred [632]
thousands, which the registers have enumerated for you,
Who go forth in defence of a group of persons who are the closest to
Aḥmad (i.e., to the Prophet Muḥammad)
(who figures) in the Holy Book [*al-Furqān*],[533] if their genealogy is traced back.
Indeed, in regard to the munificent one, the son of Yaḥyā, al-Faḍl,
neither silver coins
nor gold ones remain for very long, through the lavish generosity of his two hands.
Not a single day of his life has elapsed since he girded up his
loincloth (i.e., prepared for action in the Caliph's service)
without people becoming rich from what he bestows in gifts.
How many utmost efforts in munificence and valor has he guarded
closely
for those who seek their furthest extent, to such a degree that
one experiences fatigue before that extent is reached!
He lavishes handsome presents, when even the (ordinarily) generous person does not give them, and he does not
shrink back when the sharp, slender[534] Indian swords are
unsheathed.
Neither the desire for approbation—and the desire for God's approbation is his supreme aim—
nor anger impels him to anything unjust.
Your liberality has flowed forth in floods, to the point that no
life-giving rain nor sea with swelling waves equals it.[535]

He related: Marwān b. Abī Ḥafṣah had recited the following to al-Faḍl in his military encampment before the latter set out for Khurāsān:

Have you not seen that generosity passed down from Adam
till it reached al-Faḍl's palm?

---

533. A Qur'ānic term with connotations of "deliverance, redemption; separation (of the believers from the unbelievers)," often applied to the Qur'ān as a whole; see *EI*[2] s.v. Furḳān (R. Paret).

534. Following the *al-quḍub* of *Addenda et emendanda,* p. DCCLX, and the Cairo text, VIII, 257.

535. Munierah al-Rasheed, 101, no. 8; *Shiʿr Marwān b. Abī Ḥafṣah,* ed. ʿAṭawān, 18–19, no. 3; Harley, "Abu's-Simṭ Marwān b. Abī Ḥafṣah," 85.

When Abū al-ʿAbbās's heavens become favorable and open (i.e., when al-Faḍl bestows his largesse),
what fine continuous rain and heavy downpours (i.e., of bounty) you experience![536]

[633] He also said:

When her child's hunger makes a child's mother fearful,
she calls him by the name of al-Faḍl and the child finds security.
Islam is given new life through you, for you are indeed its strength and glory,
and you stem from a family whose youngest one is fully mature (i.e., in wisdom and power).[537]

Muḥammad b. al-ʿAbbās has mentioned that al-Faḍl b. Yaḥyā ordered one hundred thousand dirhams to be given to him (i.e., to Marwān), and presented him with fine clothes and a she-mule as a mount. He related: I heard him say, "From this visit of mine to the court I netted seven hundred thousand dirhams." He further says concerning al-Faḍl,

I have selected for praise the son of Yaḥyā b. Khālid,
and this is sufficient for me; and I have not acted wrongfully in thus choosing.
He habitually spreads forth justice and munificence
to the leading men of Qaḥṭān and of those attaching themselves to Nizār (i.e., of the South and North Arabs).
He has travelled to the pulpit (i.e., the commanding position of an Islamic leader) of the eastern lands, and he has always had
a father who takes up the lofty position on a dais and a pulpit.
He is accounted with Yaḥyā al-Barmakī, and is never seen
as anything but a military leader or as one appointed to a position of power.[538]

Salm al-Khāsir also eulogized him, saying,

---

536. Munierah al-Rasheed, 163, no. 152; *Shiʿr,* 92, no. 58; Harley, 84–5.
537. Jahshiyārī, 142; Munierah al-Rasheed, 162, no. 151; *Shiʿr,* 86, no. 53; Harley, 85.
538. Munierah al-Rasheed, 126, no. 76; *Shiʿr,* 45, no. 26.

How can you fear any misfortune in a place
 which the Barmakīs, the munificent ones, have encompassed with their protection?
And a people who include al-Faḍl b. Yaḥyā,
 a group of warriors who hurl themselves into the fray and whom no other group of warriors can withstand (or: can equal, *yuwāzinuhu*)?
He has two days, one for munificence and one for valor in battle, [634]
 as if Time were a captive between them.
When one of the Barmakīs reaches the age of ten years,
 his ambition is to become a vizier or an amīr.[539]

Al-Faḍl b. Isḥāq al-Hāshimī has mentioned that Ibrāhīm b. Jibrīl[540] set out with al-Faḍl b. Yaḥyā for Khurāsān, with Ibrāhīm reluctant to depart; this consequently made al-Faḍl angry with him. Ibrāhīm related: One day, he sent for me, having paid no attention to me for a while. I went into his presence, and when I stood before him, I greeted him, but he failed to return the salutation. So I said to myself, "By God, this portends something unpleasant." He was all this time reclining, but now sat upright and then said, "Let not your mind be troubled (or: let your fear be dispelled), O Ibrahim, for the fact of my power over you restrains me from doing anything to you." He related: Then he conferred the governorship of Sijistān upon me, and when I brought in the province's taxation, he thereupon gave it back to me and gave me five hundred thousand dirhams additionally. (Al-Faḍl b. Isḥāq) related: Ibrāhīm was the commander of al-Faḍl b. Yaḥyā's police force and personal guard. Al-Faḍl sent him against Kābul; he conquered it and took immense booty.[541]

---

539. Von Grunebaum, "Three Arabic poets of the early Abbasid age. V. Salm al-Ḫâsir," 67, no. XIX = *Shuʿarāʾ ʿAbbāsiyyūn*, 101, no. 19.

540. Son of a Khurasanian Jibrīl b. Yaḥyā al-Bajalī, who had probably taken part in the ʿAbbāsid *daʿwah* in Khurāsān; as noted below, Ibrāhīm was in charge of the *shurṭah* and *ḥaras* for al-Faḍl. See Crone, 179–80.

541. This operation of al-Faḍl in eastern Afghanistan and Sīstān, penetrating as far as Zābulistān, Kābul and Bāmiyān, was important for the extension of Muslim arms in these regions. See Jahshiyārī, 148; Yaʿqūbī, *Buldān*, 289–91, tr. 102–3, 106–7; anon., *Taʾrīkh-i Sīstān*, 154–5, tr. M. Gold, 122; Sourdel, *Vizirat*, I, 146; Bosworth, *Sīstān under the Arabs, from the Islamic conquest to the rise of the Ṣaffārids (30–250/651–864)*, 85–6; Kennedy, 181.

He related: Al-Faḍl b. al-ʿAbbās b. Jibrīl, who was with his paternal uncle Ibrāhīm, transmitted the information to me, saying: As a result of that episode, Ibrāhīm acquired seven million (dirhams), at a time when he already had in his possession four million dirhams from the money collected in taxation. When he came back to Baghdad and built the house for himself at al-Baghayīn,[542] he invited al-Faḍl to pay him a visit so that he might show al-Faḍl the results of the latter's benevolence towards him. He prepared for al-Faḍl presents, rare and costly gifts, and vessels of gold and silver, and he ordered four million (dirhams) to be placed in a certain part of the house. He related: When al-Faḍl b. Yaḥyā seated himself, Ibrāhīm offered him the presents and the rare and costly gifts, but al-Faḍl refused to accept a single one of
[635] them and told him, "I haven't come to you in order to despoil you!"[543] Ibrahim replied, "O Amīr, it is really your own munificence." Al-Faḍl said, "You can count on further munificence from us (in the future)." He related: Out of all that, al-Faḍl only accepted a Sijzī whip, saying, "This is part of the equipment of real cavalrymen (i.e., of outstanding warriors)." Ibrāhīm then told him, "This money is the money collected in taxation." Al-Faḍl replied, "It is all meant for you." Ibrāhīm repeated his protest to him a second time. Then al-Faḍl said, "Haven't you a house big enough for it?" Then he made all that over to Ibrāhīm and departed homewards.[544]

He related: When al-Faḍl b. Yaḥyā arrived back from Khurāsān, al-Rashīd proceeded to the Garden of Abū Jaʿfar, going forth to meet him ceremonially, and the Hāshimites and a great crowd of the military commanders, secretaries, and nobles [*ashrāf*] met him. He began to offer presents to people of a million (dirhams) and of five hundred thousand (dirhams),[545] and Marwān b. Abī Ḥafṣah eulogized him, saying:

We give praise to the One who has safely brought back Ibn Yaḥyā,

---

542. The quarter on the west bank of the Tigris just below the Upper Bridge. See Le Strange, *Baghdad*, 108; Lassner, *Topography*, 68.

543. Following *Addenda et emendanda*, p. DCCLXI, the Cairo text, VIII, 259, and Bayhaqī, *Maḥāsin*, ed. Schwally, 197 = ed. Ibrāhīm, I, 297: *li-uslubaka.*

544. Jahshiyārī, 148; Bayhaqī *Maḥāsin*, loc. cit.

545. Jahshiyārī, 147; Ḥamzah al-Iṣfahānī, 165; *K. al-ʿUyūn*, 296; Ibn Khallikān, IV, 29, tr. II, 461.

and with his advent
the birds are flying back to us with portents of great fortune.
Our eyes did not sink into a state of calm until they beheld him,
nor did they cease to be suffused with tears until he returned.
His cavalrymen and his foot soldiers came to us in the morning,
led by a man exciting intense admiration, who outstrips all other people in valor and commanding authority.[546]
He drove the foe away from Khurāsān, just as the morning sunshine
dispells the enveloping garment of night, so that it has vanished away.
The one whose route was in the evening at Marw has returned
to us, and people have said, "Our throng of people (or: host of warriors, *shaʿbunā*) has now dispersed!"
On the occasion when he dashed down the padlock of every act of wrong,
and with his forgiveness set free the captive loaded with fetters,
And he distributed among them, without arousing a sense of obligation and with fairness,
beneficent gifts, perpetually enduring and repeated ones.
In this way, he dispelled from them the causes of fear which alarmed, [636]
and instituted and completed among them highly desired security and peace.
Moreover, he lavished his bounty upon the orphans among them,
to such an extent that he was more caring and more beneficial (to them) than real fathers.
If people wish to attain the extremity of al-Faḍl's generosity
and valor, they will find it farther away than the stars.
Yaḥyā and Khālid have become elevated through al-Faḍl
to every high and noble aim.
He acts with clemency towards the one who gives the Caliph his obedience,
but gives the sharp-bladed Indian sword to drink the rebel's blood.

546. The Cairo text, VIII, 259, has ". . . a man who has subdued people with his valor and eminence."

His swords have brought low hypocrisy in religion, together with polytheism,
yet they have been a source of everlasting might and glory to the followers of the faith.
The one who, in addition to (or: because of, *ʿalā*) his own excellence, has been invested with the companionship of the Caliph,
has acquired strength through his allegiance to the Chosen One (i.e., the Prophet Muḥammad, al-Muṣṭafā),
The contender with the Prophet in excellence, the one who inaugurates affairs and finishes them, through whom
God bestows all beneficence and cuts it off.
You made the mountains of the ruler of Kābul lawful spoil and you did not leave
there any hearth (or: any fuel, *mūqad*) for the fires of error;[547]
And then you let them experience (the impact of) cavalrymen who trampled down their massed forces,
(leaving them) as slain ones, captives and routed troops in disarray.
[637] Your benevolence was shown again to Ibn al-Barm[548] after
he had humbled himself, as one rendered forsaken by God, who sees death face-to-face, standing alone.[549]

Al-ʿAbbās b. Jarīr has mentioned that Ḥafṣ b. Muslim,[550] the brother of Rizām b. Muslim the mawlā of Khālid b. ʿAbdallāh al-Qasrī,[551] transmitted the information to me, saying: I went into al-Faḍl b. Yaḥyā's presence at the time of his return from Khurāsān, and he had scattered about bags of money, with their seals still intact; not a single one of these bags had its seal broken. Whereupon I recited,

547. Referring to the expedition sent against Kābul under Ibrāhīm b. Jibrīl by al-Faḍl in this year, see Ṭabarī, III, 634 (above, 147).

548. I.e., the son of the Khurasanian rebel Yūsuf b. al-Barm, executed by al-Mahdī in 170 (786–7), see Ṭabarī, III, 563 (above, 32, and n. 135).

549. Munierah al-Rasheed, 114, no. 43; *Shiʿr Marwān b. Abī Ḥafṣah*, 31–2, no. 15; Harley, 85–6.

550. Abū Muqātil Ḥafṣ b. Muslim al-Fazārī is mentioned as a *rāwī* by Yāqūt, *Muʿjam*, III, 249, s.v. Samarqand, in a tradition stemming from Anas b. Malik and in material taken from Samʿānī.

551. I.e., the Umayyad governor of Iraq during Hishām's caliphate, died in 126 (743–4); see *EI*[2] s.v. (G. R. Hawting).

Through al-Faḍl b. Yaḥyā b. Khālid
and the liberality of his hands, God has compensated for the avarice of every miser.

He related: Marwān b. Abī Ḥafṣah said to me, "I wish I had forestalled you in reciting this verse, and I am ready to pay ten thousand dirhams!" (i.e., for the use of this verse).

In this year, Muʿāwiyah b. Zufar b. ʿĀṣim[552] led the summer raid, and Sulaymān b. Rāshid led the winter one, accompanied by Elpidius [*Albīd*], the Patricius of Sicily.[553]

In this year, Muḥammad b. Ibrāhīm b. Muḥammad b. ʿAlī, who was governor of Mecca, led the Pilgrimage.[554]

---

552. Member of a North Arab family of al-Jazīrah, whose grandfather ʿĀṣim al-Hilālī had been killed in the ʿAbbāsid Revolution fighting for the last Umayyad Caliph Marwān II; see Crone, 166.

553. Ibn al-Athīr, VI, 145; Brooks, *EHR*, XV (1900), 741. According to Khalīfah, *Taʾrīkh*, II, 718, al-Bakhtarī b. Sharīk b. ʿAlāʾ al-ʿAbsī led the raid under ʿAbd al-Malik b. Ṣāliḥ, but according to Yaʿqūbī, *Taʾrīkh*, II, 522, Yazīd b. Ghazwān led it. Elpidius had been *strategos* of Sicily, but had rebelled there and then in 782 fled to the Arabs in North Africa. This particular expedition penetrated as far north as Amisus (i.e. Samsun) on the Black Sea coast. See M. V. Anastos and Canard, in *Cambridge medieval history. IV. The Byzantine empire. Part 1*, 83, 707.

554. Khalīfah, *Taʾrīkh*, loc. cit.; Yaʿqūbī, *Taʾrīkh*, II, 521; Azdī, 281; Ibn al-Athīr, loc. cit.

The Events of the Year 179

(March 27, 795–March 15, 796)

Among the events of this year was the return home from Khurāsān of al-Faḍl b. Yaḥyā and his appointment as his deputy there of ʿAmr b. Shuraḥbīl.[555]

[638] In this year, al-Rashīd appointed as governor of Khurāsān Manṣūr b. Yazīd b. Manṣūr al-Ḥimyarī.[556]

In this year, Ḥamzah b. Atrak al-Sijistānī led a Khārijite rebellion [*sharā*] in Khurāsān.[557]

In this year, al-Rashīd dismissed Muḥammad b. Khālid b. Bar-

555. Jahshiyārī, 147, calls ʿAmr "ʿUmar b. Jamīl," resembling the "ʿAmr b. Ḥ.m.l" of Ḥamzah al-Iṣfahānī, 165.

556. Manṣūr had been governor of Yemen for al-Mahdī, his father being a maternal uncle of that Caliph. See Yaʿqūbī, *Taʾrīkh*, II, 481, 515; Ṭabarī, III, 502–3, 518; Ḥamzah al-Iṣfahānī, loc. cit.; Ibn al-Athīr, VI, 146; Crone, 255, n. 580.

557. Yaʿqūbī, *Buldān*, 304, tr. 133; Gardīzī, *K. Zayn al-akhbār*, ed. ʿAbd al-Ḥayy Ḥabībī, 131–3; Ibn al-Athīr, VI, 147. On the very serious revolt of Ḥamzah b. Adharak (thus correctly for Ṭabarī's Atrak) or ʿAbdallāh, which disturbed Khurāsān and Sīstān for some thirty years, till his death in 213 (828), see Palmer, 108–9; Bosworth, *Sīstān under the Arabs*, 87–104; idem and B. Scarcia Amoretti, in *Cambridge history of Iran*, IV, 96–7, 108–9, 510–12; R. N. Frye, *The golden age of Persia, The Arabs in the East*, 119.

mak from the office of court chamberlain and gave the job to al-Faḍl b. al-Rabīʿ.[558]

In this year, al-Walīd b. Ṭarīf the Khārijite returned to al-Jazīrah, and his military might grew strong and his partisans numerous.[559] Hence, al-Rashīd sent against him Yazīd b. Mazyad al-Shaybānī.[560] Yazīd enticed al-Walīd onwards and then met him in battle above Hīt,[561] when the latter was unprepared, and killed him and a numerous group of his followers, the remainder of them dispersing.[562] The poet has said in this connection,[563]

One group of Wā'il[564] is slaughtering another group of themselves;
only the steel (of a sword blade) can make notches in another sword blade.

Al-Fāriʿah, the sister of al-Walīd, said,

O trees of the Khābūr, what are you doing, putting forth leaves,
as if you felt no grief for Ibn Ṭarīf?

---

558. Jahshiyārī, 184; cf. Sourdel, *Vizirat,* I, 144. Muḥammad b. Khālid had been given the post in 172 (788–9), according to Jahshiyārī, 143.

559. The early stages of this revolt are recorded by Ṭabarī, in the events of the previous year, at III, 631 (above, 143).

560. According to Yaʿqūbī, *Ta'rīkh,* II, 496, the Caliph had previous to this sent two other commanders against the rebel. Iṣfahānī, *Aghānī,* ed. Būlāq, XI, 9 = ed. Cairo, XII, 95, and Ibn al-Athīr, VI, 142, emphasize the Barmakīs' hostility to Yazīd regarding this appointment; this stemmed of course from Yazīd's support for the succession of Jaʿfar b. al-Hādī in the last days of al-Hādī's caliphate, see Ṭabarī, III, 572 (above, 45).

561. Town on the Euphrates to the west of Baghdad. See Yāqūt, *Muʿjam,* V, 420–1; Le Strange, *Lands,* 64–5; *EI*² s.v. (M. Streck).

562. Jāḥiẓ, *al-Bayān wa-al-tabyīn,* I, 342; Ibn Qutaybah, 382; Khalīfah, *Ta'rīkh,* II, 720–3; Iṣfahānī, *Aghānī,* ed. Būlāq, XI, 9–10 = ed. Cairo, XII, 94–6; Azdī, 281–2; *K. al-ʿUyūn,* 296–7; Ibn al-Athīr, VI, 141–3; Ibn Khallikān VI, 31–4, 327–9, tr. III, 668–71, IV, 218–20; Palmer, 65–7. Khalīfah, Azdī, Ibn al-Athīr, and Ibn Khallikān give considerable detail about what was clearly a serious and prolonged outbreak of some two years affecting not only al-Jazīrah and Armenia but also parts of Diyārbakr and western Persia; cf. Kennedy, 121.

563. Identified in Khalīfah, *Ta'rīkh,* II, 723, as Ibn al-Naṭṭāḥ, i.e., Muḥammad b. Ṣāliḥ b. Mihrān, called Ibn al-Naṭṭāḥ, historian and traditionist of Baṣrah, died in 252 (866). See *GAL,* S I, 216; *GAS,* I, 317.

564. Shaybān, to which both al-Walīd and Yazīd belonged, were a component of Bakr b. Wā'il, see *EI*² s.v. (Caskel). In Ibn al-Athīr, VI, 142, and Ibn Khallikān, VI, 31, tr. III, 668, the Barmakīs, hostile to Yazīd, allege that the latter was not prosecuting the war against al-Walīd energetically enough because of the tribal kinship bond between them.

A noble youth, who prefers provision for a journey only in the form
of piety,[565]
and wealth only in the form of spears and swords.[566]

In this year, in the month of Ramaḍān, al-Rashīd performed the ʿUmrah as an act of thanksgiving to God for the benevolence which He had vouchsafed to him regarding al-Walīd b. Ṭarīf. Then when he had completed the ʿUmrah, he returned to Medina and he remained there till the time for the Pilgrimage. Then he led the people in the Pilgrimage and traveled on foot from Mecca to Minā and thence to ʿArafāt. He visited on foot the various places involved in the rites of the Pilgrimage and then came back home-
[639] wards along the Baṣrah road. Al-Wāqidī, however, states that when al-Rashīd had completed the ʿUmrah, he remained at Mecca until he led the people in the Pilgrimage.[567]

565. Echoing Qur'ān, II, 193/197.

566. Khalīfah, *Ta'rīkh*, II, 723; Iṣfahānī, *Aghānī*, ed. Būlāq, XI, 8–11 = ed. Cairo, XII, 92–9, giving eleven verses of this elegy plus verses by the poet Muslim b. al-Walīd Sarīʿ al-Ghawānī, who accompanied Yazīd b. Mazyad on the final campaign against al-Walīd and eulogized him for his victory; Azdī, 282–3; *K. al-ʿUyūn*, 297; Ibn al-Athīr, VI, 142–3; Ibn Khallikān, VI, 32–3, tr. III, 669, giving eighteen verses of the elegy of al-Fāriʿah plus five more from another *marthiyah*; Kaḥḥālah, *Aʿlām al-nisā'*, IV, 20.

567. Muḥammad b. Ḥabīb, 38; Khalīfah, *Ta'rīkh*, II, 719; Azdī, 284; *K. al-ʿUyūn*, 297.

The
Events of the Year
180
(March 16, 796–March 4, 797)

Among the events of this year was the factional strife which raged in Syria between its people.

The Outcome of the Factional Strife in Syria and the Poetic Eulogies of Jaʿfar b. Yaḥyā, Restorer of Order There

It has been mentioned that, when this factional strife took place in Syria between its people and the state of affairs became grave, al-Rashīd grew disturbed about what was happening among them; so he invested Jaʿfar b. Yaḥyā with control of Syria and told him, "Either you go forth (to settle affairs there) or I'll go myself." Jaʿfar exclaimed to him, "Nay, I will protect you personally," so he set out with a numerous host of military commanders, horses and armaments, and appointed al-ʿAbbās b. Muḥammad b. al-Musayyab b. Zuhayr[568] as commander of his police force and

568. Grandson of a Khurasanian, al-Musayyab al-Ḍabbī, prominent as a deputy *naqīb* in the ʿAbbāsid *daʿwah*; he remained in charge of the *shurṭah* until al-Maʾmūn's arrival in Baghdad in 204 (819). See Crone, 187–8.

Shabīb b. Ḥumayd b. Qaḥṭabah[569] as commander of his personal guard. He went to them (i.e., to the warring factions), arranged peace between them, killed the *Zawāqīl*[570] and brigands in their ranks and did not leave there a single lance or horse (i.e., any matériel for future warfare). Thus, they returned to a state of security and tranquillity, and he extinguished that rancor.[571] Manṣūr al-Namarī recited when Jaʿfar set out,

The fires of civil strife have been kindled in Syria,
but this is now the time in Syria when its fire will be allayed.
When the waves of the sea of the house of Barmak rose high
over it, its blazing flames and sparks became extinguished.
The Commander of the Faithful has launched an assault upon this civil strife by means of Jaʿfar,
and through the latter there have come together both the suppression of the trouble and then restoration of the damage (or: both its damaged part and the restored part).
He (i.e., the Caliph) has launched an attack on this civil strife by means of one auspicious in his nature, a noble one,

---

569. Grandson of the *naqīb* and outstanding figure in the *daʿwah*, Qaḥṭabah al-Ṭāʾī, and subsequently head of al-Maʾmūn's *ḥaras* for a time. See Crone, 188–9; Kennedy, 79–80.

570. This group (the etymology of whose name remains obscure; in Yāqūt, *Muʿjam*, II, 523, s.v. Dayr al-ʿAdhārā, we have the collective form *Zāqūlah*) is an intriguing one. The definition in *Glossarium*, p. CCLXXVIII, "non-Arab soldiers of Syria (and Mesopotamia)," is not appropriate. From mentions like the present one and that in the passage dealing with fighting at al-Raqqah in al-Amīn's reign, in 196 (811–12) (see Ṭabarī, III, 843, 845), it is clear that the *Zawāqīl* were Arabs, predominantly of the North Arab Qays or Muḍar group, for their chiefs were the heads of such prominent tribes as ʿUqayl, Hilāl and Sulaym. Their being linked with brigands (here, *mutalaṣṣiṣah*) and other lawless elements (as emerges, e.g., from Jāḥiẓ's mention of the *Zawāqīl al-Shām* in his *K. al-Bukhalāʾ*, 49, among such notorious predators as the Kurds, the Zuṭṭ and the Qufṣ) presumably arose from their anti-ʿAbbāsid stance in this period; their head Naṣr b. Shabath al-ʿUqaylī led a prolonged rebellion against the caliphate in al-Maʾmūn's reign, see Ṭabarī, III, 1045–6, 1069–72. From all this, we discern that the *Zawāqīl* were a social group rather than an ethnic or sectarian or confessional one. For a detailed consideration of the *Zawāqīl*, see Ayalon, *The military reforms of Caliph al-Muʿtaṣim*, 18–20.

571. Jahshiyārī, 162–3, and Yaʿqūbī, *Taʾrīkh*, II, 495, giving the (differing) texts of a *khuṭbah* or oration which Jaʿfar pronounced to the people of Syria, presumably at Damascus, after completing his operation there; Ṭabarī-Balʿamī, tr. IV, 459–60; Azdī, 289; Ibn al-Athīr, VI, 151; Bouvat, 68–9; Sourdel, *Vizirat*, I, 149; K. S. Salibi, *Syria under Islam: empire on trial, 634–1097*, 37; Kennedy, 122.

a man with whom both the Qaḥṭān and Nizār factions of Syria have become content.[572]

A hard, Barmakī rock has come down upon them, [640]
whose onslaught penetrates as far as the brains in the skulls of those who have broken their trust.

You have set out in the morning, driving forward a dense mass of troops, on whose heads are
the gleaming stars of the Pleiades and whose fruit is death.

When their banners flutter and the wind murmurs gently
through them, their sudden, dazzling appearance strikes fear into those who hear them.

So say to the people of Syria, "Do not let
either long-term or immediate hopes deprive you of your native intelligence.

For indeed, the Commander of the Faithful is coming to you in person, and
if not in person, then his personal choice."

He (i.e., Jaʿfar) is the wielder of authority, whose beneficence and piety are hoped for,
and against whose battle assaults no one can stand firm.

The Caliph's helper, sword
and spearshaft; and in warfare, their blades become stained with blood!

Some persons have the Caliph's secrets kept from them,
but you are their repository and the place where they are held safe.

You have fulfilled your trust, and have never acted treacherously
towards any group of people with a covenant of protection,
and you have never come near to any matter whose dishonorable aspects have reached you.

A physician, in bringing fresh life to affairs; when necks become contorted
through the onslaughts of time, you are their healing splint.

When momentous strokes of ill fate come upon the son of Yaḥyā, Jaʿfar, [641]
the most serious of them do not affright him.

---

572. This eulogy of Jaʿfar's pacifying role among both South and North Arabs confirms that the *Zawāqīl* were a component element of the local Syrian Arabs.

There has arisen in Syria, from your approach, a cloud,
whose gifts are eagerly hoped for but whose destructiveness is feared.
So well for the people of Syria, but woe for their mother!
Either life-giving rain has come to it, or else destruction for it!
If they agree to peace, it will be the cloud of a lavish giver
and abundant rain; but if not, then its rain will be composed of blood!
Your father is the father of those wielding authority, Yaḥyā b. Khālid,
the one who is characterized by liberality and beneficence; even the small acts of beneficence which he does are great ones (i.e., by other people's standards) (or: even the great acts of liberality are [for him] small ones).
How many acts of generosity do you see among the Barmakīs,
and how many of their rushing-forward battle horses, whose dust cannot be penetrated!
The person who alights with his baggage by you comes with auspicious stars,
and a band of people having you as their protector is rendered strong.
My defender (or: excuser, *ʿadhīrī*) from the attacks of fate; can its determined actions
and its acts of constraint keep me back from Jaʿfar?
Hence, the eye of sorrowfulness is continually fixed from fear of separation from him;
my soul is attached to him, and its recollection does not allow any sleep.[573]

Jaʿfar b. Yaḥyā's Return from Syria and His Address of Thanks to the Caliph

Jaʿfar b. Yaḥyā appointed Ṣāliḥ b. Sulaymān governor of the Balqāʾ[574] and adjoining regions, and appointed as his deputy in

573. *Shiʿr Manṣūr al-Namarī,* 92–3, no. 23.

574. The hilly district, still thus known today, east of the Jordan. See Yāqūt, *Muʿjam,* I, 489; Le Strange, *Palestine,* 34–5; *EI*² s.v. (J. Sourdel-Thomine).

Syria ʿĪsā b. al-ʿAkkī,[575] and then returned homewards. Al-Rashīd heaped further honors on him. When he came to al-Rashīd, he went into his presence, according to what has been mentioned, and kissed his hands and feet. Then he stood respectfully before him[576] and said, [642]

"O Commander of the Faithful, praise be to God who has put my fearfulness at ease, answered my prayers, shown mercifulness in regard to my supplications and prolonged my predetermined span of life so that He has let me see the face of my master! He has honored me with proximity to him, He has bestowed favor on me by allowing me to kiss his hand, and He has brought me back to his service. By God, if I were indeed to mention my absence from him, the occasion of my going away and the strokes of destiny which have disquieted me, then know that they were the result of sins against God which overtook me and errors which encompassed me. If my absence from you were to prove long, O Commander of the Faithful—may God make me your ransom!—I would be afraid of my reason giving way out of anxious solicitude for your presence and sorrowfulness at being separated from you, and afraid that violent yearning to see you would speedily turn me away from giving ear to you! So praise be to God, who has preserved me safe during the period of my absence, has let me enjoy sound health, has taught me to respond readily, has held me fast to obedience and has stepped in to keep me back from embarking on courses of disobedience. For I only set out in accordance with your judgment, and I have only come back with your express permission and command; and death has not intervened to cut me off before I could reach you. By God, O Commander of the Faithful—and there is no mightier oath than one sworn by God—I have experienced directly things regarding which, if the whole of the present world were set out before me, I would nevertheless prefer over it being close to you, and would not indeed consider it a fair exchange for staying close to you."

---

575. Cf. Sourdel, *Vizirat,* I, 149 n. 2.

576. On these customs of respectful greeting, see Sourdel, "Questions de cérémoniale ʿabbaside," 136–8. It was humiliating to have to stand thus for an inordinately long time.

Then Jaʿfar said to al-Rashīd immediately after the previous speech and on the same spot,

"O Commander of the Faithful, God has not ceased to confer favors upon you in your caliphate, inasmuch as He knows your intentions and lets you see in your subjects the full extent of your hopes. He sets their community aright for you, He brings together their social cohesion and He repairs the disorder of their affairs, as an act of preserving your power among them and as an act of mercifulness for them. All this is only in order (for them) to hold firmly to obeying you and to preserve the bond of your favor; God is the One deserving of praise and merit for this. O Commander of the Faithful, I have left the people of various districts of Syria in a state of obedience to your command, remorseful over their previous rebelliousness against you, holding fast to their allegiance to you, placing themselves within your sphere of authority, seeking your forgiveness, feeling assured of your magnanimity, hopeful of
[643] your graciousness and secure against the manifestations of your anger. Their condition in their present state of unity and agreement is exactly as it was in their (former) state of mutual dissension, and their condition in their present state of harmony is exactly as it was in their (former) state of refractoriness and rebellion. The Commander of the Faithful's pardon and forgiveness towards them is bestowed before they actually plead their extenuating circumstances, and his conciliatory approach to them and favorable attitude towards them is vouchsafed in advance by him before their actually seeking (forgiveness).

"God's oath, O Commander of the Faithful, if it is true that I have set out homewards from them, and that God has allayed the sparks of their violence, extinguished their blazing, expelled their rebellious ones, set on the upright way the mass of them, bestowed on me a fortunate outcome in my dealings with them and given me the upper hand over them, all that stems only from your charismatic power, your auspiciousness, your victorious strength, the perpetuation of your happy, fortunate and enduring ruling authority, and their fearfulness of you, combined at the same time with hopefulness of favor from you. By God, O Commander of the Faithful, I only marched against them in accordance with your instructions, I only dealt with them strictly according to your command, and I only went among them in exact conformity with what you indicated and delineated to me and gave me the resources to achieve; and by God, it was only because of your summons, because of God's singling you out to use as His instrument and because of their fear of your severity, that they submitted.

"That which I myself have accomplished—even though I have exerted myself to the utmost and reached the farthest extent of my powers—has not fulfilled a part of the duty which I owe to you. Nay, your beneficence towards me has only increased in intensity as I myself have increased in inability and sense of weakness to render you thanks. God has not created a single person out of your subjects who has striven further than myself in stimulating within himself the desire to fulfill the obligations due to you. My sole desire is to expend my life blood in obedience to you and in everything which brings (me) nearer to conformity with your will. But I experience your acts of benevolence towards me on a scale which I experience from no one else. Moreover, how can I thank you enough, when I have become unique among my contemporaries in regard to what you have done for me and through me? Or how can I thank you enough, when I am only able to give thanks to you through your own acts of beneficence to me? Or how can I thank you enough, when, even if God were to set my act of thanks among the enumeration of the acts of generosity which you have vouchsafed to me, the abundance of these from me would not reach to that? Or how can I thank you enough, when you are my [644]
refuge to the exclusion of any other refuge which I might have? Or how can I thank you enough, when you do not accept what I want for myself (i.e., the Caliph knows what is good for him better than he does himself)? Or how can I thank you enough, when you renew your acts of beneficence to me to an extent which exceeds everything bestowed on me previously by you? Or how can I thank you enough, when you make me forget all your earlier favors to me by the renewed favors which you heap upon me (at present)? Or how can I thank you enough, when, through your bounty, you set me in the foremost place above my peers? Or how can I thank you enough, when you are my patron and master [*waliyyī*]? Or how can I thank you enough, when you are the bestower of honors upon me? I beseech God, who has bestowed that upon me through you, without any just claims (of mine) to it—for thankfulness is impotent to attain the conveying of a part of that, nay, a part of the tenth

of a tenth of it—that He will take charge of recompensing you on my behalf with what He is more able to accomplish and more powerful to attain, and that He will fulfill, on my behalf, the obligations justly due to you and (the requiting of) the great extent of your favor. For all that lies within the power of His hand, and He is the One able to bring it about!"

Various Items of Information

In this year, al-Rashīd took away the seal ring from Jaʿfar b. Yaḥyā and handed it over to his father Yaḥyā b. Khālid.[577]

In this year, Jaʿfar b. Yaḥyā was appointed governor of Khurāsān and Sijistān. He appointed as his deputy over them Muḥammad b. al-Ḥasan b. Qaḥṭabah.[578]

In this year, al-Rashīd set out from the City of Peace, intending to travel to al-Raqqah via the Mawṣil road. When he encamped at al-Baradān, he appointed ʿĪsā b. Jaʿfar governor of Khurāsān and dismissed Jaʿfar b. Yaḥyā from it. Jaʿfar b. Yaḥyā's tenure of power over it was twenty days (literally, "nights") only.[579]

In this year, Jaʿfar b. Yaḥyā was appointed commander of the guard.[580]

[645] In this year, al-Rashīd had the walls of al-Mawṣil demolished because of the Khārijites who had raised rebellions from there.[581] Then he proceeded to al-Raqqah; he encamped there, and made it one of his homes.[582]

In this year, he dismissed Harthamah b. Aʿyan from Ifrīqiyah and

577. Ibn al-Athīr, VI, 152; Bouvat, 69; Sourdel, *Vizirat,* I, 138.

578. Khalīfah, *Taʾrīkh,* II, 686; Ḥamzah al-Iṣfahānī, 165; Ibn al-Athīr, loc. cit.; Bouvat, loc. cit. Muḥammad was a grandson of the *naqīb* Qaḥṭabah al-Ṭāʾī, see Ṭabarī, III, 639 (above, 156, n. 569), and Crone, 188.

579. Ibn al-Athīr, loc. cit.; Bouvat, loc. cit.; Sourdel, *Vizirat,* I, 149.

580. Ibid.

581. Dīnawarī, 390; Azdī, 279–80, 284–7; Ibn al-Athīr, VI, 152–3. The Khārijite rebel is named here as al-ʿAṭṭāf b. Sufyān al-Azdī, who according to Azdī began his rebellion in the Mawṣil region as far back as 177 (793–4) and who eventually escaped to Armenia.

582. Azdī, 289; Ibn al-Athīr, VI, 153. Al-Raqqah became in fact al-Rashīd's favored residence rather than Baghdad, possibly because, Shaban has suggested, the Barmakīs' effective methods of collecting taxation were detested by the Abnāʾ of Baghdad. See Shaban, 30, 37; Kennedy, 120.

brought him back to the City of Peace. Jaʿfar b. Yaḥyā then appointed him as his deputy over the guard.[583]

In this year, there was a severe earthquake in Egypt, and as a result, the top of the Pharos at Alexandria fell down.[584]

In this year, Khurāshah (b. Sinān) al-Shaybānī proclaimed a Khārijite revolt [*ḥakkama . . . wa-sharā*] in al-Jazīrah, but Muslim b. Bakkār b. Muslim al-ʿUqaylī killed him.[585]

In this year, the "wearers of red" [*al-muḥammirah*][586] rebelled in Jurjān. At this, ʿAlī b. ʿĪsā b. Māhān[587] wrote that the person who had stirred up that outbreak against him was ʿAmr b. Muḥammad al-ʿAmrakī and that he was a dualist infidel [*zindīq*];[588] so al-Rashīd ordered him to be killed, and he was executed at Marw.[589]

In this year, he dismissed al-Faḍl b. Yaḥyā from Ṭabaristān and al-Rūyān and appointed as governor there ʿAbdallāh b. Khāzim (b. Khuzaymah). He also dismissed al-Faḍl from al-Rayy; Muḥammad b. Yaḥyā b. al-Ḥārith b. Shikhkhīr[590] became governor there, and Saʿīd b. Salm (b. Qutaybah) became governor over al-Jazīrah.[591]

---

583. Ibn al-Athīr, VI, 152.

584. *K. al-ʿUyūn*, 301; Ibn al-Athīr, loc. cit. The Pharos was frequently affected by earthquakes, but remained in use till the 5th (11th) century; see *EI*² Manār, Manāra (J. Sadan and J. Fraenkel).

585. Ibn al-Athīr, loc. cit. Khalīfah, *Taʾrīkh*, II, 724–7, gives a detailed account of this revolt, which began in 179 (795–6) and affected western Persia and central Iraq rather than al-Jazīrah; al-Faḍl b. Yaḥyā sent Ibrāhīm b. Jibrīl to suppress it in this year. Azdī, 279, places this revolt under the year 176, and at p. 291, as continuing into the year 181. For Muslim b. Bakkār, member of an al-Jazīrah family whose members served both the Umayyads and the ʿAbbāsids, see Crone, 106–7.

586. This is the name later given to the partisans of Bābak al-Khurramī. These must have been the neo-Mazdakites who had already risen in Gurgān in 162 (779) in conjunction with the Khurramiyyah or Abū-Muslimiyyah (Ṭabarī, III, 493). See on both these revolts, Scarcia Amoretti, in *Cambridge history of Iran*, IV, 505; Daniel, 147; *EI*² s.v. Khurramiyya (Madelung).

587. ʿAlī b. ʿĪsā had been appointed governor of Khurāsān in 180 (796–7) in place of al-Faḍl b. Yaḥyā al-Barmakī's deputy Manṣūr b. Yazīd, an appointment not actually noted by Ṭabarī,. See Jahshiyārī, 180; Dīnawarī, 390; Ḥamzah al-Iṣfahānī, 165; Gardīzī, 131; Daniel, 170; Crone, 178; Kennedy, 121.

588. Presumably a Manichaean.

589. Ibn al-Athīr, VI, 152; Daniel, loc. cit.

590. The *Addenda et emendanda*, p. DCCLXI, suggest for this last component B.sh.khīr in the light of Iṣfahānī, *Aghānī*, ed. Būlāq, XVII, 74 = ed. Cairo XVIII, 301 (here read as Buskhunnar).

591. Ibn al-Athīr, loc. cit.

In this year, Muʿāwiyah b. Zufar b. ʿĀṣim led the summer raid.[592]

In this year, al-Rashīd went to al-Baṣrah on his return from Mecca. He reached it in al-Muḥarram of this year and then encamped at al-Muḥdathah[593] for some days before transferring thence to the palace of ʿĪsā b. Jaʿfar[594] at al-Khuraybah.[595] Then he sailed on the Sayḥān Canal, which Yaḥyā b. Khālid had dug out,[596] with the aim of inspecting it and the weir [*sikr*] across the Ubullah Canal and the Maʿqil Canal,[597] until (as a result of that) the condition of the Sayḥān (Canal) was put in good order. Then he set out
[646] from al-Baṣrah on the eighteenth of al-Muḥarram and arrived at the City of Peace. Then he set out for al-Ḥīrah;[598] he established himself there, had residences built there and allotted parcels of building land [*khiṭaṭ*] for his retinue, remaining there about forty days. The people of al-Kūfah rose up against him and made his position in the neighborhood uncomfortable, so he traveled to the City of Peace.[599] From there, he set out for al-Raqqah, appointing as his deputy in the City of Peace at this time Muḥammad al-Amīn, to whom he entrusted the governorship of the two Iraqs (i.e., Mesopotamia and ʿIrāq ʿAjamī, western Persia).

In this year, Mūsā b. ʿĪsā b. Mūsā b. Muḥammad b. ʿAlī led the Pilgrimage.[600]

---

592. Ibid.; Brooks, *EHR*, XV (1900), 741. According to Yaʿqūbī, *Taʾrīkh*, II, 522, Ismāʿīl b. al-Qāsim led the raid.

593. "The newly founded," presumably a new suburb of the expanding city of al-Baṣrah.

594. I.e., the ʿAbbāsid prince, grandson of al-Manṣūr, at this time governor of al-Baṣrah; see Ṭabarī, III, 559 (above, 26–27, n. 109).

595. A place in al-Baṣrah, according to Yāqūt, *Muʿjam*, II, 363–4.

596. Balādhurī, 363; Yāqūt, *Muʿjam*, III, 293–4; Pellat, *Le milieu baṣrien*, 64. The surroundings of this canal seem to have been noisome, judging by the poetry on it.

597. For these canals, see Balādhurī, 358–63; Yāqūt, *Muʿjam*, V, 363–4; Le Strange, *Lands*, 46–8; Pellat, 16–19.

598. Town of central Iraq, the ancient capital of the pre-Islamic Lakhmid kings, but in Islamic times gradually eclipsed by the nearby military camp of al-Kūfah. See Yāqūt, *Muʿjam*, II, 328–31; Le Strange, *Lands*, 75–6; *EI*² s.v. (I. Shahîd).

599. Ibn al-Athīr, VI, 152–3.

600. Muḥammad b. Ḥabīb, 38; Khalīfah, *Taʾrīkh*, II, 720; Yaʿqūbī, *Taʾrīkh*, II, 522; Azdī, 290; Ibn al-Athīr, VI, 153.

The Events of the Year 181

(March 5, 797–February 21, 798)

Among the events taking place in this year was al-Rashīd's leading a raid into the Byzantine lands. He captured by force of arms the fortress of al-Ṣafṣāf.[601] Marwān b. Abī Ḥafṣah accordingly recited,

Indeed, the Commander of the Faithful, the Chosen One,
has left al-Ṣafṣāf a desert plain [*qāʿan ṣafṣafā*]![602]

In this year, ʿAbd al-Mālik b. Ṣāliḥ led a raid against the Byzantines; he reached as far as Anqirah and captured Maṭmūrah.[603]

---

601. Dīnawarī, 390 (with "Maʿṣūf" for "Ṣafṣāf"); Yaʿqūbī, *Taʾrīkh*, loc. cit.; Ṭabarī-Balʿamī, tr. IV, 460; Azdī, 290; Ibn al-Athīr, VI, 158; Palmer, 75. This fortress ("The Willows") lay beyond the northern end of the Cilician Gates, on the Constantinople road, near Loulon or Luʾluʾah. See Yāqūt, *Muʿjam*, III, 413; Le Strange, *Lands*, 134–5, 139; Honigmann, 42; Canard, *Hʾamdânides*, 284; idem, in *Cambridge medieval history*, IV/1, 707; Shaban, 31–2.

602. Munierah al-Rasheed, 143, no. 119. This *rajaz* verse utilizes the same play on words as v. 4 of the complete ode in the *ṭawīl* metre given by Ṭabarī, III, 741–3 (below, 306–8).

603. Ibn al-Athīr, loc. cit.; Brooks, *EHR*, XV (1900), 741. Anqirah is the modern Ankara; see Yāqūt, *Muʿjam*, I, 271–2; Le Strange, *Lands*, 149; and *EI*[2] s.v. Anḳara (F. Taeschner). Maṭmūrah, or its plural form Maṭāmīr, lay in Cappadocia north of

In this year, al-Ḥasan b. Qaḥṭabah and Ḥamzah b. Mālik both died.[604]

In this year, the "wearers of red" gained control of Jurjān.

In this year, at the time of his establishment at al-Raqqah, al-Rashīd introduced as the opening formula of his official documents the words "Blessings [*al-ṣalāt*] be upon Muḥammad, may God bless him and grant him peace!"[605]

In this year, Hārūn al-Rashīd led the Pilgrimage.[606] He led the people in the Pilgrimage rites, and then he turned back in haste. Yaḥyā b. Khālid remained behind, but then caught up with al-Rashīd at al-Ghamrah.[607] He begged to be excused from his official post, hence, al-Rashīd released him from the charge. Yaḥyā therefore gave back the seal ring to al-Rashīd and asked the Caliph for permission to remain in Mecca. Al-Rashīd gave him this, so Yaḥyā returned to Mecca.[608]

---

the Taurus range. See Le Strange, *Lands,* 138; Honigmann, 46; *EI*[2] s.v. (Ed.). According to the *K. al-ʿUyūn,* 301, it was ʿAbd al-Razzāq (b. ʿAbd al-Ḥamīd al-Taghlibī, see Ṭabarī, III, 629, above, 139) who led the summer raid; Yaʿqūbī, *Taʾrīkh,* II, 522, makes al-Rashīd its leader.

604. Azdī, 290; Ibn al-Athīr, VI, 159.

605. Ibn al-Athīr, loc. cit. Hilāl al-Ṣābiʾ mentions innovations in the *invocatio* of official letters from the caliphate of al-Maʾmūn, with wording similar to this (*wa-asʾaluhu an yuṣalliya ʿalā Muḥammad*[in] *ʿabdihi wa-rasūlihi*); see his *Rusūm dār al-khilāfah,* 106, tr. Elie A. Salem, 83.

606. Muḥammad b. Ḥabīb, loc. cit.; Khalīfah, *Taʾrīkh,* II, 728; Yaʿqūbī, *Taʾrīkh,* loc. cit.; Azdī, 292; *K. al-ʿUyūn,* loc. cit.; Ibn al-Athīr, loc. cit.

607. The stage on the Pilgrimage route from Mecca to Iraq which conventionally marked the transition from the lowland Tihāmah to the upland Najd. See Bakrī, III, 1003–4; Yāqūt, *Muʿjam,* IV, 212–13; Al-Wohaibi, 135, 381; Saad A. Al-Rashid, *Darb Zubaydah. The Pilgrim Road from Kufa to Mecca,* 136, 138.

608. Sourdel, *Vizirat,* I, 138–40.

The Events of the Year 182

(February 22, 798–February 11, 799)

Among the events taking place during this year was al-Rashīd's [647]
return from Mecca and his journeying to al-Raqqah. He exacted there homage to his son ʿAbdallāh al-Maʾmūn in succession after his other son al-Amīn, and secured allegiance to him from the army at al-Raqqah. He confided al-Maʾmūn to the care of Jaʿfar b. Yaḥyā, and then despatched him to the City of Peace, accompanied by the members of the ʿAbbāsid family Jaʿfar b. Abī Jaʿfar al-Manṣūr[609] and ʿAbd al-Malik b. Ṣāliḥ, and by the military commander ʿAlī b. ʿĪsā. Homage was given to al-Maʾmūn at the City of Peace when he arrived there, and his father appointed him governor of Khurāsān and its dependencies as far (west) as Hamadhān, and gave him the honorific of "al-Maʾmūn."[610]

---

609. Governor of al-Baṣrah for al-Rashīd, died in 186 (802); see Ṭabarī, III, 651 (below, 179).

610. Jahshiyārī, 165 (without specifying the date); Ṭabarī-Balʿamī, tr. IV, 460; Azdī, 293; *K. al-ʿUyūn*, 301; Ibn al-Athīr, VI, 161. These events are, however, placed by Yaʿqūbī, *Taʾrīkh*, II, 500–1, in the following year 183 (799–800), which accords with Ṭabarī's also placing them, III, 652 (below, 180) in 183. This later year for al-Maʾmūn's nomination seems to be the one favored by Gabrieli, "Successione,"

In this year, the daughter of the Khāqān, ruler of the Khazars, was brought to al-Faḍl b. Yaḥyā, but she died at Bardhaʿah,[611] Saʿīd b. Salm b. Qutaybah al-Bāhilī being governor of Armenia at that time. The Khazar nobles [*al-ṭarākhinah*[612]] who had been accompanying her went back to her father and told him that his daughter had been slain by treachery. He accordingly grew enraged on account of this, and began making preparations for war against the Muslims.[613]

In this year, Yaḥyā b. Khālid returned to the City of Peace.

In this year, ʿAbd al-Raḥmān b. ʿAbd al-Malik b. Ṣāliḥ led the summer raid[614] and reached as far as Ephesus [*D.fsūs*, read *Afsūs*], the town of the Companions of the Cave.[615]

In this year, the Byzantines blinded their ruler Constantine, son of Leo, and set up as ruler his mother, Irene [*Rīnī*], who was called by the honorific of "Augusta."[616]

344–5; but Bouvat, 69, and Sourdel, *Vizirat*, I, 151, favor 182. See also Abbott, 181–2, and Kennedy, 124. Jaʿfar was regarded at the time as the main proponent of al-Maʾmūn's claims as second heir, as is expressed in the poetry cited in Masʿūdī, *Murūj*, VI, 367 = ed. Pellat, § 2564.

611. The main town of Arrān in eastern Transcaucasia. See Yāqūt, *Muʿjam*, I, 379–81; Le Strange, *Lands*, 177–8; *EI*² s.v. (D. M. Dunlop); *EIr* s.v. Bardaʿa (Bosworth).

612. Sing. *ṭarkhān* (Tkish. *tarqan, tarkhan, terken*), a title used among the ancient Turks to denote a princely status just below that of the Qaghan. See Sir Gerard Clauson, *An etymological dictionary of pre-thirteenth century Turkish*, 544; and for its use among the Khazars, Dunlop, *The history of the Jewish Khazars*, 72, 180 n. 43, and among their neighbors the Oghuz, A. Z. V. Togan, *Ibn Faḍlāns Reisebericht*, text 16–17, tr. 30–1, and Excursus § 36a, 143–4.

613. Azdī, 294; Ibn al-Athīr, VI, 161. Dunlop, 180–1, 183–5, believes that the episode of the Khazar Khaqan's daughter placed in 182–3 (798–9) is a confusion with the events of 145 (762–3), when the Khazars did invade the Muslim lands after the death of a Khazar princess who had married the governor of Armenia Yazīd b. Usayd al-Sulamī; the confusion may have arisen from the similarity of this latter name with that of the governor of Armenia in 183, Yazīd b. Mazyad.

614. Azdī, 293; Ibn al-Athīr, loc. cit.; Brooks, loc. cit.; Canard, in *Cambridge medieval history*, IV/1, loc. cit.

615. I.e., of the Qurʾānic Aṣḥāb al-Kahf or Sleepers of Ephesus (Qurʾān, XVIII, 9–25/10–26; see *EI*² s.v. (Paret).

616. *K. al-ʿUyūn*, loc. cit.; Ibn al-Athīr, loc. cit.; Brooks, loc. cit. Constantine VI, son of Leo IV, was blinded in 797 by his mother, Irene, when he achieved his majority so that she might retain control of the real power, and she held this till she was deposed in the revolution of 802, as the last of the Isaurian dynasty, by Nicephorus I. See A. A. Vasiliev, *History of the Byzantine empire 324–1453*, I, 234–5; Anastos and Canard, in *Cambridge medieval history*, IV/1, 88–91, 706.

In this year, Mūsā b. ʿĪsā b. Mūsā b. Muḥammad b. ʿAlī led the Pilgrimage.[617]

---

617. Muḥammad b. Ḥabīb, 38; Khalīfah, *Ta'rīkh*, II, 729; Yaʿqūbī, *Ta'rīkh*, II, 522; Azdī, 294.

The Events of the Year 183

(February 12, 799–January 31, 800)

[648] *The Khazar Invasion of Armenia*

Among the events taking place during this year was the invasion of the Khazars through Bāb al-Abwāb,[618] on account of the Khāqān's daughter, their sweeping down on the Muslims and the Protected Peoples [*ahl al-dhimmah*] there, and their capture and enslavement—according to what has been mentioned—of more than 100,000 persons. They perpetrated a monstrous deed, whose like had never been heard of previously in Islam. Hence, al-Rashīd appointed Yazīd b. Mazyad as governor of Armenia, together with Azerbaijan, reinforced him with the army and sent him forward, and he stationed Khuzaymah b. Khāzim at Niṣībīn as a supporting force for the troops of Armenia.[619]

---

618. The later town of Darband on the western shore of the Caspian Sea, guarding a celebrated pass between the Sea and the Caucasus mountains; see *EI*[2] s.v. Bāb al-Abwāb (Dunlop).

619. Dīnawarī, 390; *K. al-ʿUyūn*, 301–2; Ibn al-Athīr, VI, 163. The appointment of Yazīd over Armenia and Arrān, and subsequently of his sons Asad and Khālid (see Crone, 170), established a connection of the family with the Transcaucasian region

A differing account of the reason behind the Khazar's invasion of Armenia has, however, been related. This is what Muḥammad b. ʿAbdallāh has mentioned, to the effect that his father transmitted the information to him that the reason for the Khazars' invasion of Armenia in Hārūn's reign was that Saʿīd b. Salm had executed, by the axe, al-Munajjim al-Sulamī.[620] His son thereupon went to the land of the Khazars and asked them for military assistance against Saʿīd. Hence, they invaded Armenia through the breach.[621] Saʿīd was defeated and fled, and the Khazars raped the Muslims' womenfolk and remained there—according to what I believe is the truth—for seventy days. Hārūn then sent Khuzaymah b. Khāzim and Yazīd b. Mazyad to Armenia, until the two of them restored the position which Saʿīd had brought to such a parlous state and expelled the Khazars. The breach was thus closed up.[622]

Various Items of Information

In this year, al-Rashīd wrote to ʿAlī b. ʿĪsā b. Māhān, who was at that time (governor) in Khurāsān, to come to him. The reason for his despatch to ʿAlī with these instructions was that a rumor had been brought to his notice and he had been informed that ʿAlī had determined upon an act of rebelliousness. So ʿAlī b. ʿĪsā appointed

---

which later led to the rule in Sharvān of a line of Yazīdī Sharvān-Shāhs, in the course of time largely Iranized; see Minorsky, *A history of Sharvān and Darband in the 10th–11th centuries*, 116 ff.

620. Probably to be identified with the local ruler of Bāb al-Abwāb or Darband, al-Najm b. Hāshim, mentioned in Yaʿqūbī, *Taʾrīkh*, II, 518, as being executed by Saʿīd, whereupon his son Ḥayyūn rebelled and appealed to the Khazars for aid; cf. Dunlop, *The history of the Jewish Khazars*, 183–4.

621. I.e., the Caspian Gate.

622. Azdī, 294–5; Ibn al-Athīr, loc. cit.; Kennedy, 122–3. This is the version of events concerning the Khazar invasion accepted by Dunlop, loc. cit., as the correct one, i.e., as having no connection with the death of a daughter of the Khazar ruler but rather with internal events in Armenia and Transcaucasia. As Yaʿqūbī's detailed account of events there in al-Rashīd's caliphate (*Taʾrīkh*, II, 515–19) shows, these regions had been continuously in turmoil during the earlier part of his reign, partly, it seems, because of an influx of North Arab tribesmen brought in by North Arab governors into regions prevously largely settled by Yamanī tribesmen. Salm's governorship had begun peacefully, but then relations with the local aristocracy [*al-baṭāriqah*] had deteriorated. The situation was restored, after the retreat of the Khazars, by punitive measures of al-Rashīd's new governors and the achievement of a balance between Nizār and Yaman there.

[649] his son Yaḥyā as his deputy in Khurāsān, a procedure confirmed by al-Rashīd, and then came to the Caliph, bringing to him an immense sum of money. Al-Rashīd thereupon sent him back to Khurāsān as governor responsible to his own son al-Ma'mūn, with the task of combatting Abū al-Khaṣīb; so at this, he returned.[623]

In this year, Abū al-Khaṣīb Wuhayb b. ʿAbdallāh al-Nasāʾī, mawlā of (the tribe of) al-Ḥarīsh,[624] rebelled at Nasā' in Khurāsān.[625]

In this year, there died at Baghdad Mūsā b. Jaʿfar b. Muḥammad[626] and the judge Muḥammad b. al-Sammāk.[627]

In this year, al-ʿAbbās b. Mūsā al-Hādī b. Muḥammad b. ʿAbdallāh b. Muḥammad b. ʿAlī led the Pilgrimage.[628]

---

623. Ibn al-Athīr, loc. cit. Ḥamzah, 165, places ʿAlī b. ʿĪsā's journey to al-Rashīd at al-Rayy in Jumādā I, 184 (June, 800).

624. I.e., the Banū al-Ḥarīsh b. Kaʿb b. Rabīʿah b. ʿĀmir, see Ibn Durayd, *K. al-Ishtiqāq*, 297–8, 300–1.

625. Ṭabarī-Balʿamī, tr. IV, 460; Ibn al-Athīr, VI, 164; Daniel, 171, noting that Abū al-Khaṣīb was possibly the governor of Abīward in northern Khurāsān, since Yaʿqūbī, *Buldān*, 305, tr. 133, says that he rebelled there. Nasā was a town of northern Khurāsān. See *Ḥudūd al-ʿālam*, tr. 103, comm. 326; Yāqūt, *Muʿjam*, V, 281–2; Le Strange, *Lands*, 394; *EI*[1] s.v. (Minorsky).

626. I.e., the Seventh Imām Mūsā al-Kāẓim who, in spite of his apolitical stance, had been imprisoned by al-Rashīd in Baghdad. See Yaʿqūbī, *Ta'rīkh*, II, 499–500; Masʿūdī, *Murūj*, VI, 309–11, 329–30 = ed. Pellat, §§ 2512–13, 2532; Iṣfahānī, *Maqātil*, 332–6; *K. al-ʿUyūn*, 302; Ibn al-Athīr, loc. cit.; Ibn Khallikān, V, 307–10, tr. III, 463–6; *EI*[1] s.v. Mūsā al-Kāẓim (Strothmann).

627. I.e., Abū al-ʿAbbās Muḥammad b. Sabīḥ, described also as a *mudhakkir* or homilist. See Azdī, 295; al-Khaṭīb al-Baghdādī, V, 368–73, no. 2895; Ibn al-Athīr, VI, 165.

628. Muḥammad b. Ḥabīb, 38; Khalīfah, *Ta'rīkh*, II, 730; Yaʿqūbī, *Ta'rīkh*, II, 522; Azdī, loc. cit.; Ibn al-Athīr, VI, 164.

The Events of the Year 184

(February 1, 800–January 19, 801)

Among the events taking place during this year was Hārūn's entering the City of Peace in Jumādā II, returning thither from al-Raqqah by boat down the Euphrates.[629] When he reached the City of Peace, he instituted punitive measures against the people regarding arrears of taxation from previous years [*al-baqāyā*[630]], and, according to what has been mentioned, ʿAbdallāh b. al-Haytham b. Sām assumed the task of extracting these arrears, by imprisonment and flogging.[631] Ḥammād al-Barbarī was governor of Mecca and the Yemen;[632] Dāwūd b. Yazīd b. Ḥātim al-Muhallabī was governor over Sind; Yaḥyā (b. Saʿīd) al-Ḥarashī was

629. Dīnawarī, 390.
630. This technical term of the financial departments, "arrears of taxation from previous years," seems to have been distinguished from *al-bāqī* "taxation of the current year still uncollected"; see Bosworth, "Abū ʿAbdallāh al-Khwārazmī on the technical terms of the secretary's art," 135.
631. Dīnawarī, loc. cit.; Yaʿqūbī, *Taʾrīkh*, II, 501.
632. Ḥammād was a slave and mawlā of the Caliph whom al-Rashīd had freed at the opening of his reign (Yaʿqūbī, *Taʾrīkh*, II, 498–9). See Crone, 191; Ṭabarī, III, 712 (below, 267, and n. 923).

governor over al-Jabal;[633] and Mahrūyah (or Mahrawayh) al-Rāzī was governor over Ṭabaristān. Ibrāhīm b. al-Aghlab took charge of affairs in Ifriqīyah, and then al-Rashīd (formally) appointed him governor there.[634]

In this year, the Khārijite [*al-Shārī*] Abū ʿAmr rebelled, so the Caliph sent against him Zuhayr al-Qaṣṣāb, and the latter killed Abū ʿAmr at Shahrazūr.[635]

In this year, Abū al-Khaṣīb sought a grant of safe-conduct, so ʿAlī b. ʿĪsā gave it to him. Abū al-Khaṣīb came to meet ʿAlī at Marw, and the latter received him honorably.[636]

[650] In this year, Ibrāhīm b. Muḥammad (al-Mahdī) b. ʿAbdallāh b. Muḥammad b. ʿAlī led the Pilgrimage.[637]

---

633. Member of a family from northern Syria prominent in the early ʿAbbāsid period who, like his (?) brother Saʿīd al-Ḥarashī, filled various governorships; see Crone, 145.

634. Yaʿqūbī, *Ta'rīkh*, II, 494, 497–8; *K. al-ʿUyūn*, 302–3; Ibn Isfandiyār, tr. 140; Ibn al-Athīr, VI, 166.

635. Azdī, 299; Ibn al-Athīr, loc. cit.

636. Ibn al-Athīr, loc. cit.; Daniel, 171.

637. Muḥammad b. Ḥabīb, loc. cit.; Khalīfah, *Ta'rīkh*, II, 731; Yaʿqūbī, *Ta'rīkh*, II, 522; Azdī, 300; Ibn al-Athīr, loc. cit.

The Events of the Year 185

(January 20, 801–January 5, 802)

Among the events taking place during this year was the people of Ṭabaristān's killing the governor of that province, Mahrūyah al-Rāzī. Al-Rashīd now appointed in his place ʿAbdallāh b. Saʿīd al-Ḥarashī.[638]

In this year, ʿAbd al-Raḥmān al-Abnāwī[639] killed the rebel (or: the Khārijite, *al-khārijī*) Abān b. Qaḥṭabah at Marj al-Qalʿah.[640]

In this year, the Khārijite [*al-Shārī*] Ḥamzah wrought mischief in the Bādhghīs region of Khurāsān. ʿĪsā b. ʿAlī b ʿĪsā[641] then swept down on ten thousand of Ḥamzah's partisans and killed them, and penetrated as far as Kābul, Zābulistān and al-Qandahār.[642] Abū al-ʿUdhāfir[643] has recited concerning these events,

---

638. Ibn Isfandiyār, tr. 140–1; Ibn al-Athīr, VI, 168. ʿAbdallāh, son of the prominent commander and (?) brother of the Yaḥyā b. Saʿīd mentioned in Ṭabarī, III, 649 (above, 173–74), later fought for al-Amīn; see Crone, 144–5.

639. Following the *Addenda et emendanda*, p. DCCLXI, and the Cairo text, VIII, 273, instead of the text's al-Anbārī, this last followed by Ibn al-Athīr.

640. Ibn al-Athīr, loc. cit.

641. I.e., the son of the governor of Khurāsān; see Crone, 178–9.

642. This seems to be a conflation of a complex and protracted series of events

ʿĪsā has almost become Alexander the Great;
he has reached the two Easts and the two Wests.[644]
He has not left untouched Kābul or Zābulistān,[645]
and then the surrounding regions as far as the two al-Rukh-khajs.[646]

In this year, Abū al-Khaṣīb revolted at Nasā' a second time. He seized control of it and of Abīward,[647] Ṭūs and Naysābūr. He marched at a measured pace on Marw and surrounded it, but was repulsed, and then proceeded towards Sarakhs,[648] with his power becoming mighty.[649]

In this year, Yazīd b. Mazyad died at Bardhaʿah, and Asad b. Yazīd was appointed governor in his place.[650]

In this year, Yaqṭīn b. Mūsā died at Baghdad.[651]

---

which involved western Afghanistan (including Herat and Bādhghīs, where the local governor ʿAmr b. Yazīd al-Azdī was involved in fighting Ḥamzah before his death) and Sīstān but not, so far as is known, eastern Afghanistan. See Gardīzī, 131; *Ta'rīkh-i Sīstān,* 156–60, tr. 123–6; Bosworth, *Sīstān under the Arabs,* 94–5. Yaʿqūbī, *Buldān,* 305, tr. 133, states that ʿAlī b. ʿĪsā killed Ḥamzah at Kābul; in fact, Ḥamzah continued his rebellion for a further quarter-century.

643. Following for the name Abū al-ʿUdhāfir *Addenda et emendanda,* loc. cit. This poet is in fact Ward b. Saʿd al-ʿAmmī, poet of al-Baṣrah and Baghdad in al-Rashīd's time; see *GAS,* II, 524. Azdī, 303, makes the poet Abū al-ʿIdām al-Qummī and the occasion ʿAlī b. ʿĪsā's killing of Abū al-Khaṣīb (see Ṭabarī, III, 651, below, 178).

644. Cf. Qur'ān, LV, 16–17.

645. The region of eastern Afghanistan around Ghaznah; see *Ḥudūd al-ʿālam,* tr. 112, comm. 346.

646. The region of eastern Afghanistan around Qandahār, classical Arachosia; see ibid., tr. 111, comm. 346. It was from this region that the mawlā Faraj al-Rukhkhajī, prominent in the service of al-Rashīd and al-Ma'mūn, was captured; see Crone, 190.

647. Town of northern Khurāsān, on the edge of the Qara Qum desert, also known as Bāward. See *Ḥudūd al-ʿālam,* tr. 103, comm. 326; Yāqūt, *Muʿjam,* I, 86–7, 333; Le Strange, *Lands,* 394–5; *EI²* s.v. (Minorsky); *EIr* s.v. (Bosworth).

648. Town adjacent to Nasā and Abīward and also on the northern edge of Khurāsān. See *Ḥudūd al-ʿālam,* tr. 104, comm. 327; Yāqūt, *Muʿjam,* III, 208–9; Le Strange, *Lands,* 395–6; *EI¹* s.v. (J. Ruska).

649. Khalīfah, *Ta'rīkh,* II, 733 (placing this under the year 186); Daniel, 171.

650. Azdī, 300–1; Ibn al-Athīr, VI, 169–71; Ibn Khallikān, VI, 338, tr. IV, quoting a lengthy elegy on Yazīd by Abū Muḥammad ʿAbdallāh b. Ayyūb al-Taymī (correct Ibn al-Athīr's "al-Tamīmī" thus). Ibn Khallikān cites also a further elegy on him by Muslim b. al-Walīd (cf. Iṣfahānī, *Aghānī,* ed. Būlāq, XVIII, 237–8 = ed. Cairo, XIX, 42–3).

651. Ibn al-Athīr, VI, 169.

In this year, in Jumādā II, ʿAbd al-Ṣamad b. ʿAlī died at Baghdad, never having lost his front milk teeth; he was placed in his grave with the teeth of a child, not lacking a single one of them.[652]

In this year, al-Rashīd set out for al-Raqqah via the al-Mawṣil road.[653] [651]

In this year, Yaḥyā b. Khālid sought al-Rashīd's permission to perform the ʿUmrah and to spend some time in the Holy City, and the Caliph gave him his consent. So Yaḥyā went forth in Shaʿbān and performed the ʿUmrah in the month of Ramaḍān. Then he passed his time in pious exercises [*rābaṭa*] at Juddah till it was time for the Pilgrimage, and then he performed that.[654] A thunderbolt struck the Sacred Mosque and killed two men.

In this year, Manṣūr b. Muḥammad (al-Mahdī) b. ʿAbdallāh b. Muḥammad b. ʿAlī led the Pilgrimage.[655]

---

652. Khalīfah, *Ta'rīkh*, II, 732; Azdī, 300; Ibn al-Athīr, loc. cit., stigmatizing ʿAbd al-Ṣamad as "the base one [*quʿdud*] of the Banū ʿAbd Manāf" and approximating him to the hated Yazīd b. Muʿāwiyah in this.

653. Dīnawarī, 390; Azdī, loc. cit.; Ibn al-Athīr, loc. cit., but making al-Rashīd set out from al-Raqqah for Baghdad.

654. Ibn al-Athīr, VI, 168.

655. Muḥammad b. Ḥabīb, 38; Khalīfah, *Ta'rīkh*, loc. cit.; Yaʿqūbī, *Ta'rīkh*, II, 522; Ibn al-Athīr, VI, 169. Khalīfah records that there was no summer raid against the Byzantines this year.

◈

The Events of the Year 186

(January 6, 802–December 29, 802)

Among the events taking place during this year was ʿAlī b. ʿĪsā b. Māhān's setting out from Marw for Nasāʾ in order to combat Abū al-Khaṣīb. He killed the latter there, and captured and took over his wives and progeny, and Khurāsān became peaceful once more.[656]

In this year, al-Rashīd imprisoned Thumāmah b. Ashras because of his coming to know about al-Rashīd's lying in the matter of Aḥmad b. ʿĪsā b. Zayd.[657]

---

656. Khalīfah, *Taʾrīkh,* II, 733; Yaʿqūbī, *Buldān,* 305, tr. 133; Azdī, 303; Ibn al-Athīr, VI, 174; Daniel, 171.

657. Abū Maʿn Thumāmah b. Ashras al-Numayrī, who died ca. 213 (828), was a Muʿtazilī of al-Baṣrah and a leading participant in the theological and intellectual symposia of the Barmakīs, al-Rashīd and al-Maʾmūn; see Watt, *The formative period of Islamic thought,* 178, 197, 222. Aḥmad b. ʿĪsā, great-grandson of the Fourth Imām ʿAlī Zayn al-ʿĀbidīn and member of the Zaydī branch of the Ḥusaynid Shīʿah (see Öhrnberg, Table 91), was subsequently, in 188 (804), arrested by al-Rashīd and imprisoned at al-Rāfiqah but succeeded in escaping and then disappeared underground at al-Baṣrah, according to Yaʿqūbī, *Taʾrīkh,* II, 512, see Van Arendonck, 62 n. 1, and Marquet, 110 (this episode not however mentioned by Ṭabarī or Masʿūdī). Given Thumāmah's close connections with the Barmakīs, and the accusations later brought against Yaḥyā b. Khālid and Jaʿfar b. Yaḥyā of tenderness towards and clandestine support for the ʿAlids (see Sourdel, *Vizirat,* I, 158, 168–9), the Caliph's animus against him is not surprising.

In this year, Jaʿfar b. Abī Jaʿfar al-Manṣūr died whilst with Harthamah, and al-ʿAbbās b. Muḥammad died at Baghdad.[658]

Al-Rashīd's Succession Arrangements for His Three Sons

In this year, Hārūn al-Rashīd led the Pilgrimage. He set out from al-Raqqah on the Pilgrimage in Ramaḍān of this year (September, 802). He passed through (or: by, *bi-*) al-Anbār and did not enter the City of Peace, but encamped at a halting-place on the banks of the Euphrates called al-Dārāt,[659] seven farsakhs from the City of Peace. He left behind Ibrāhīm b. ʿUthmān b. Nahīk (al-ʿAkkī)[660] in charge of al-Raqqah, and took with him his two sons Muḥammad al-Amīn and ʿAbdallāh al-Maʾmūn, his two designated heirs. He began at Medina, and its people were given three sums of money as gifts. They would come forward to him, and he would give them a gift of money. Then they would come forward to Muḥammad, and he would give them a second gift of money. Then they would come to al-Maʾmūn, and he would give them a third gift of money. [652]
Then he proceeded onward to Mecca, and gave its people a gift of money. All this amounted to one million and fifty thousand dīnārs.[661]

According to what Muḥammad b. Yazīd (al-Tamīmī) has mentioned from Ibrāhīm b. Muḥammad al-Ḥajabī,[662] al-Rashīd had conferred the succession on his son Muḥammad on a Thursday in

---

658. See for these two ʿAbbāsid princes, above, p. 167, n. 609, and p. 7, n. 19. Ibn al-Athīr, loc. cit., has for the second deceased prince his son ʿAlī b. ʿAbbās b. Muḥammad, apparently incorrectly.

659. Literally, "the encampments, settlements," not mentioned, it seems, by the geographers, but clearly lying to the south of the capital.

660. ʿUthmān b. Nahīk had been a deputy *naqīb* at the time of the ʿAbbāsid Revolution. Ibrāhīm acted as al-Rashīd's commander of police (*shurṭah*) (Muḥammad b. Ḥabīb, 375), but because of his closeness to the Barmakīs was executed by the Caliph in 187 (803). See Ṭabarī, III, 699–701 (below, 245–47); Crone, 189; Sourdel, *Vizirat*, I, 151 n. 3.

661. Khalīfah, *Taʾrīkh*, II, 733; Yaʿqūbī, *Taʾrīkh*, II, 501; Dīnawarī, 390; Azdī, 302; Masʿūdī, *Murūj*, VI, 326 = ed. Pellat, § 2527; *K. al-ʿUyūn*, 303; Ibn al-Athīr, VI, 173; Azraqī, in *Die Chroniken der Stadt Mekka*, I, 159–60; Abbott, 189.

662. Samʿānī, IV, 70, refers this *nisbah* to the right of *ḥijābat al-bayt al-muʿaẓẓam*, which was traditionally held by the clan of ʿAbd al-Dār of Quraysh, a right confirmed by Muḥammad at the conquest of Mecca. See Watt, *Muhammad at Medina*, 69; *EI*[1] s.v. Shayba, Banū (Gaudefroy-Demombynes).

Shaʿbān 173 (December 789–January, 790) and had given him the honorific title of al-Amīn,[663] and he had made over to him the governorships of Syria and Iraq in 175 (791–2). Then he designated ʿAbdallāh al-Maʾmūn as his (second) heir at al-Raqqah in 183 (799–800) and appointed him governor of the regions from the limits of Hamadhān to the farthest ends of the East.[664] Salm b. ʿAmr al-Khāsir recited concerning this,

Hārūn, the Imam of guidance, has had allegiance done
    to the sagacious one, the one with an excellent moral character,
(To) the one who replaces his wealth and expends it prodigally,
    and the one who assumes responsibility for the heavy burdens of the person bearing a load,
(To) the one who is learned and penetrating[665] in his knowledge,
    and the one who is the excellent and equitable dispenser of justice,
(To) the one with supreme power to bring together and to disjoin the bond of guidance,
    and the one who speaks the word of truth and acts efficaciously,
To the best (of the sons) of ʿAbbās, when they are enumerated in the registers (or: when they are gathered together, *ḥuṣṣilū*),
    and the one who bestows favors and brings sufficiency for the person burdened with a family,
(To) the most assiduous of them in piety and the speediest of them in conferring beneficence when calamities befall,
To the one who resembles al-Manṣūr in his kingly power,
    when the darkness of falsehood spreads its covering.
The light of divine guidance has become complete through al-Maʾmūn,
    and ignorance has been dispelled from the ignorant one.[666]

---

663. This is actually recorded by Ṭabarī, III, 610 (above, 111–12), under the events of 175 (791–2), which must be correct; cf. Gabrieli, "Successione," 344.

664. Actually recorded by Ṭabarī, III, 647 (above, 167), under the events of 182 (798–9), cf. Ṭabarī-Balʿamī, tr. IV, 461; but Yaʿqūbī, *Taʾrīkh*, II, 550–1, confirms the date of 183. Cf. Gabrieli, loc. cit.

665. Following the reading *al-nāfidh* of *Addenda et emendanda*, p. DCCLXI.

666. Von Grunebaum, "Three Arabic poets of the early Abbasid age. V. Salm al-Ḫāsir," 73, no. XLI = *Shuʿarāʾ ʿAbbāsiyyūn*, 110–11, no. 41.

Al-Ḥasan b. Quraysh has mentioned that al-Qāsim b. al-Rashīd[667] was under the tutelage of ʿAbd al-Malik b. Ṣāliḥ. When al-Rashīd had allegiance done to Muḥammad and al-Maʾmūn as heirs to the succession, ʿAbd al-Malik b. Ṣāliḥ wrote to him (as follows),

O monarch, who,
    if he were a star would be an auspicious one,
Have an oath of allegiance sworn to Qāsim,
    and strike sparks with a fire-stick for him in the kingdom!
God is a Unique, Sole One,
    so make the heirs to the succession a unique group!

These verses were the factor which first impelled al-Rashīd to proclaim allegiance to al-Qāsim. He then had allegiance done to his son al-Qāsim, gave him the honorific of al-Muʾtaman and conferred on him the governorship of al-Jazīrah and the frontier regions and defensive fortresses [*al-thughūr wa-al-ʿawāṣim*].[668] He (i.e., ʿAbd al-Malik b. Ṣāliḥ) recited in this connection, [653]

Love for the Caliph is a love which the person who has rebelled against God,
    causing dissension and strife, does not hold as an act of faith.
God invested Hārūn with the direction of our affairs
    when He chose him (as ruler) and thereby gave fresh life to the faith and the Sunnah.
Hārūn has, out of his compassion for us, invested
    a trusted one [*amīn*], a trustworthy one [*maʾmūn*] and a trusty one [*muʾtaman*] with the whole earth.[669]

He related: When he divided the earth between his three sons, some of the masses of the common people said, "He has made the fabric of the state firm," but others said, "On the contrary, he has

667. Al-Rashīd's son by a slave concubine Qaṣif; see Abbott, 141.

668. Dīnawarī, 391; Ṭabarī-Balʿamī, tr., loc. cit.; Azdī, 302–3; *K. al-ʿUyūn*, 303–4; Ibn al-Athīr, loc. cit.; Abbott, 188. Gabrieli, "Successione," 346 n. 2, points out that Masʿūdī, *Murūj*, VI, 328 = ed. Pellat, § 2530, places al-Qāsim's nomination as third heir in the next year, 187 (803), suggesting that this was an afterthought; certainly, Yaʿqūbī does not mention it in his account of the events leading up to and surrounding the Meccan Agreements. Cf. also Kennedy, 125.

669. Azdī, 303.

given full rein to their propensities for clashing among themselves, and the result of his arrangements concerning that will be a source of trepidation for the subjects."[670] The poets composed verses on this topic, and one of them recited,

I say to the feeling of grief within my spirit,
 at a time when the tears in my eyes are flowing freely,
Take suitable provision against the forthcoming dread, with resoluteness;
 you will encounter that which will keep you from all sleep!
For if you are spared alive, you will see a momentous affair
 which will cause you prolonged distress and sleeplessness.
A really skillful and experienced monarch would have seen the ill judgment
 in his action of dividing up the caliphate and the land.
He would have discerned a course of action which, if he were to examine critically its consequences,
 would turn snow-white the black hair on the partings of his hair.
He intended, by doing this, that he might remove from among his sons
 the causes of dissension, and that they might give free rein to amicableness.
But he has implanted unremitting enmity
 and has bequeathed a legacy of divisiveness and separation to the unity of their family solidarity,
And he has sown among them recurring warfare,
 and has made easy the way for their avoidance of each other (i.e., their separation).
So woe to the subjects, in the near future!
 He has presented them with a fatal gift of violent distress,
And he has clothed them with a garment of permanent affliction,
 and has made inevitable for them humiliation (or destruction, *taḍaʿḍuʿ*) and corruption!
[654] Swollen seas of their blood will flow,
 for which they will see no end.

670. *K. al-ʿUyūn*, 304; Abbott, 189.

And as a result, the burden of their sufferings will be for ever upon him;
was that (decision) the result of error or right guidance [*rashād*]?[671]

The Taking of the Solemn Oaths in the Ka'bah by the Two Princes

He related: Hārūn made the Pilgrimage, accompanied by Muḥammad and 'Abdallāh and by his military commanders, ministers and judges, in the year 186 (802). He left behind at al-Raqqah Ibrāhīm b. 'Uthmān b. Nahīk al-'Akkī in charge of his womenfolk, the treasuries and material wealth, and the army, and he despatched his son al-Qāsim to Manbij[672] and then installed him there with the military commanders and soldiers whom he had attached to al-Qāsim's side.

When he had accomplished the rites of the Pilgrimage, he composed for his son 'Abdallāh al-Ma'mūn two letters, over the composition of which the religious lawyers and judges had expended intensively their intellectual efforts. One of them comprised stipulations laid upon Muḥammad setting forth the conditions which Hārūn had imposed on him regarding Muḥammad's faithful adherence to the arrangements in the document concerning the handing over of the administrative regions for which 'Abdallāh was to assume responsibility, and he conveyed to him estates, sources of revenue, jewels, and wealth. The other was the documentary text of the oath of allegiance which the Caliph had extracted from the nobles and commoners alike, and that of the obligations due to 'Abdallāh and incumbent upon both Muḥammad himself and those nobles and commoners.

He placed the two documents in the Holy House after he had

---

671. The latter nine verses are translated by Gabrieli, op. cit., 349. The last hemistich clearly contains a play on words with the Caliph's name al-Rashīd "the Rightly Guided One." A verse similarly prophesying dissension and bloodshed as a result of the Caliph's measures, uttered by a Bedouin of Hudhayl, is given in Mas'ūdī, *Murūj*, VI, 326–7 = ed. Pellat, § 2528.

672. A town of northern Syria, classical Hierapolis, and facing the Byzantine marches. See Yāqūt, *Mu'jam*, V, 205–7; Le Strange, *Palestine*, 500–2; idem, *Lands*, 107–8; Canard, *H'amdânides*, 87, 233–4; *EI*[2] s.v. (N. Elisséeff).

extracted the oath of allegiance to Muḥammad and after he had called to witness in his favor regarding the terms of the oath, God, His angels and all those who were with him in the Kaʿbah, comprising the rest of his children, his family, his mawlās, his military commanders, his ministers, his secretaries, and so forth. The act of witness to the succession oath and the (other) document took place in the Holy House, and he ordered the doorkeepers to guard the two documents and to prevent anyone from taking them away and making off with them. ʿAbdallāh b. Muḥammad, Muḥammad b. Yazīd al-Tamīmī, and Ibn al-Ḥajabī have mentioned that al-Rashīd was present and that he summoned the leading members of the Hāshimite family, the military commanders and the religious lawyers. They were taken into the Holy House, and he ordered the document to be read out to ʿAbdallāh and Muḥammad, and made the whole of those present bear witness to the attestation of the two of them to the document. Then he thought it fitting to hang up the document in the Kaʿbah, but when it was lifted up in order to attach it for suspension, it fell down, and people commented that this arrangement would speedily be dissolved before it could be carried through completely.[673]

The text of the document was as follows:[674]

---

673. Muḥammad b. Ḥabīb, 38; Jahshiyārī, 175; Khalīfah, *Taʾrīkh,* II, 733; Yaʿqūbī, *Taʾrīkh,* II, 501–10; Azdī, 302; Masʿūdī, *Murūj,* VI, 326–8 = ed. Pellat, §§ 2527–2530; idem, *Tanbīh,* 345, tr. 444; *K. al-ʿUyūn,* 304–5; Ibn al-Athīr, VI, 173; Ibn al-Ṭiqṭaqā, 193, tr. 211; Azraqī, in *Die Chroniken der Stadt Mekka,* I, 160–1 = ed. Milḥas, I, 231–4; Palmer, 114–16; Abbott, 189–91; Gabrieli, op. cit., 346–7; Sourdel, *Vizirat,* I, 151–2; Shaban, 39–40; Kennedy, 123–7. Azdī adds the detail that the documents were placed in silver tubes and then hung up. On the placing or hanging of solemn undertakings and covenants, as here in the Kaʿbah, see Pedersen, 144.

674. The texts of the documents attested by the two brothers, the first of which, written out by Muḥammad al-Amīn, now follows, exist in two forms, one somewhat shorter, in Yaʿqūbī, *Taʾrīkh,* II, 502–9 (also given in Azraqī, in *Die Chroniken der Stadt Mekka,* I, 161–8 = ed. Milḥas, I, 235–41), and the slightly fuller one given here by Ṭabarī. As Gabrieli states in his discussion about the authenticity of these and other documents pertaining to the struggle between al-Amīn and al-Maʾmūn ("Documenti relativi al califfato di al-Amīn in aṭ-Ṭabarī," *RCAL,* Classe di Scienze Morali, Storiche e Filologiche, Serie sesta, Vol. III [1927], 192–3), there seems no reason to doubt their essential authenticity, even if this cannot be irrefutably demonstrated.

A new attempt at analyzing the significance of the documents, concentrating on Ṭabarī's production of a version of these differing from that given by Yaʿqūbī and Azraqī, has recently been made by R. A. Kimber in his "Hārūn al-Rashīd's Meccan

In the name of God, the Merciful, the Compassionate One. This [655] is a document composed by the servant of God Hārūn the Commander of the Faithful, which Muḥammad son of Hārūn the Commander of the Faithful has written out in a state of soundness of mind and full exercise of his powers, willingly and unconstrainedly. The Commander of the Faithful has appointed me as his successor after him and has imposed acknowledgement of allegiance to me on the whole of the Muslims. He has appointed ʿAbdallāh the son of Hārūn the Commander of the Faithful as his successor and as caliph and as the one responsible for all the affairs of the Muslims after myself, with my full agreement and freely conceded by me, willingly and unconstrainedly. He has given responsibility for Khurāsān, its frontier regions and its districts, for the conduct of warfare there and its army, its land tax, its official textile workshops [*ṭuruz*],[675] its postal relay system, its public treasuries, its poor-tax, its religious tithe, the sums collected as tribute,[676] and all its administrative divisions, both during his own (i.e., Hārūn's) lifetime and afterwards.[677] I have accepted the

---

settlement of AH 186/AD 802," in *University of St. Andrews, School of Abbasid Studies, Occasional Papers* 1, 55–79. His article has the merit of distinguishing clearly between the first stage of the Meccan settlement, based on mutuality of obligations between the two princes al-Amīn and al-Maʾmūn and dating from 186 (802), and the subsequent modifications of three years later, when al-Rashīd travelled eastwards to Khurāsān with his forces to investigate the unrest caused by ʿAlī b. ʿĪsā b. Māhān's exactions (the new Qarmāsīn and Baghdad settlement of 189 [205]; see Ṭabarī, III, 666–7 [below, 200]). Kimber is right to emphasize the clear worsening by then of al-Amīn's legal position as successor to his father, with the introduction of provision for the third brother al-Qāsim as al-Maʾmūn's successor should the latter favor this, effectively excluding the possibility of al-Amīn's progeny ever controlling the caliphate. His final conclusion, *pace* most modern historians who have seen in al-Rashīd's policy one of a deliberate division of the overextended empire into a western and an eastern wing, is that the Caliph gradually moved in the last years of his life toward a policy of making al-Maʾmūn in effect his sole heir. See also below, n. 677.

675. See on these, *EI*[1] s.v. Ṭirāz (A. Grohmann).

676. *ʿUshrahā wa-ʿushūrahā,* the latter possibly, in de Goeje's conjecture, the tribute collected from the Dhimmīs, see *Glossarium,* p. CCCLXIII.

677. As Gabrieli points out, "Successione," 347–8, that al-Maʾmūn, as governor of the East, should have total control of all military, administrative and financial affairs there, with complete freedom to nominate his own officials and district governors (as set forth below, 187) and to have total control over the judicial system (below, 188), was unprecedented in the grants to members of the ruling family by either the Umayyads or the early ʿAbbāsids, and must reflect al-Rashīd's doubts and fears about the future and his resolve to secure an unshakable position for his

obligation laid on me by the servant of God Hārūn the Commander of the Faithful with my full agreement and a contented mind, that I will faithfully fulfill and hand over to my brother ʿAbdallāh b. Hārūn the right of succession, the executive power, the caliphate and the affairs of the whole of the Muslims, which Hārūn the Commander of the Faithful has granted to him after me. (I further undertake to hand over to him) the governorship of Khurāsān and the whole of its administrative divisions which the Caliph has made over to him, together with the grants of land [*qaṭīʿah*] which the Commander of the Faithful has assigned to him, or any revenue-yielding property or estate of his which he may have given to him or which he may have purchased, and together with whatever the Caliph has given him during his own lifetime and in his state of sound health, comprising money, ornaments of precious metal, jewels, possessions, clothing, residences, and riding-beasts, whether it be small or large: all this shall be handed over in its entirety to ʿAbdallāh the son of Hārūn the Commander of the Faithful. I have duly acknowledged this, item by item.

[656] If the accident of death should befall the Commander of the Faithful and the caliphate should pass (subsequently) to Muḥammad the son of the Commander of the Faithful, then it will be incumbent upon Muḥammad to give effect to what Hārūn the Commander of the Faithful has commanded him regarding the investiture of ʿAbdallāh son of Hārūn the Commander of the Faithful as governor of Khurāsān and its frontier regions and the appointment of those members of the Commander of the Faithful's family whom he (i.e., Hārūn) attached to his (i.e., ʿAbdallāh's) entourage at Qarmāsīn.[678] And if ʿAbdallāh son of the Commander of

first-born son. Al-Maʾmūn's position was to be virtually that of an independent sovereign, only limited by a vague formula of obedience to al-Amīn (in Azraqī's version of al-Maʾmūn's document, *Die Chroniken der Stadt Mekka,* I, 166–7 = ed. Milḥas, I, 240) and by a more specific promise to furnish troops when required by al-Amīn to fend off enemy attacks (Ṭabarī, III, 661, below, 193). Such an attenuation of caliphal control was to facilitate the status of virtual autonomy soon to be achieved by the Aghlabids in Ifrīqiyah and then the Ṭāhirids in Khurāsān.

678. Gabrieli, op. cit., 349 n. 3, suggests that the mention of the members of the ʿAbbāsid family and the mention in Ṭabarī, III, 657 (below, 189), of the commanders sent to join al-Maʾmūn at Qarmāsīn or Kirmānshāh (on which town of western Persia see Yāqūt, *Muʿjam,* IV, 330–1; Le Strange, *Lands,* 186–8; Schwarz, 480–2;

the Faithful should proceed to Khurāsān and al-Rayy and the districts which the Commander of the Faithful enumerated, in whatever part of the Commander of the Faithful's military encampment ʿAbdallāh the son of the Commander of the Faithful himself may be, or any others of those dependent on the Commander of the Faithful's authority or all those whom the Commander of the Faithful has attached to ʿAbdallāh's side, (proceeding) wherever he wishes, from al-Rayy to the farthest administrative division of Khurāsān, then Muḥammad the son of the Commander of the Faithful must not transfer from ʿAbdallāh's control any military commander or subordinate nor a single person from among those companions of his which the Commander of the Faithful attached to his side. Nor must he transfer ʿAbdallāh the son of the Commander of the Faithful from the administrative charges which Hārūn the Commander of the Faithful has entrusted to him, namely, the frontier regions of Khurāsān and the whole of its component administrative divisions, from the region of al-Rayy bordering on Hamadhān to the farthest fringes of Khurāsān, its frontier regions, its districts and its dependencies. Nor must Muḥammad compel ʿAbdallāh to come to him[679] (i.e., by forcible means, thus controlling and interfering with him), nor remove any single member of his entourage and military commanders from him, nor appoint anyone over him, nor despatch over his head, or over the heads of any of his own financial officials and executives, any agent purchasing taxes collected in kind [*bundār*],[680] accounting officer or financial official. Nor must he introduce any damaging element into any of ʿAbdallāh's affairs, whether small or great. Nor must he interfere, with his own views

---

Barthold, *An historical geography of Iran*, 195–8; *EI*² s.v. Kirmānshāh [A. K. S. Lambton]) are two interpolations in the text referring to the events of 189 (805) at Qarmāsīn, in which al-Rashīd renewed the succession pledge to al-Ma'mūn and arranged that the whole of his weapons, war matériel, and wealth was to go to al-Ma'mūn on his own death (thus according to Ṭabarī, III, 666–7; in III, 765, cf. 772, the army commanders and troops were obviously included in the adjuration to travel from Iraq and join al-Ma'mūn in Khurāsān).

679. Reading instead of the text's *wa-lā-shakhṣuhu ilayhi* either the Cairo text's (VIII, 278) *wa-lā yushkhiṣ-hu ilayhi* or Gabrieli's ("Documenti relativi al califfato di al-Amīn in aṭ-Ṭabarī," 195 n. 1) *wa-lā ishkhāṣuhu ilayhi.*

680. For this (originally) Persian term, see *Glossarium*, pp. CXLI–CXLII, and Lokkegaard, 124, 244 n. 110.

and his own ways of proceeding, in any aspect of ʿAbdallāh's affairs here. Nor must Muḥammad molest or impede any person of those whom the Commander of the Faithful has attached to ʿAbdallāh's side, including his family, his companions, his judges, his financial
[657] officials, his secretaries, his military commanders, his slaves, his mawlās, and his troops, by means of anything which aims at introducing an element of violence or unpleasantness for them, whether for themselves or for their kinsfolk, mawlās or progeny, which touches any part of their physical safety, sources of wealth, estates, houses, abodes, possessions, slaves, and mounts, whether it be a small or a grave matter; nor must any (other) person act thus on his (i.e., Muḥammad's) orders, or according to his judgment or arbitrary act of will, or according to any permission granted by him regarding that or any stratagem on his part in the affair, with any human being whatsoever. Neither Muḥammad nor any of his judges, financial officials or anyone connected with him, is to exercise any legal jurisdiction in any of their affairs (i.e., those of ʿAbdallāh's dependents) without the express authority and judgment of ʿAbdallāh the son of the Commander of the Faithful or the judgment of his own judges.

Moreover, if any person out of those whom the Commander of the Faithful attached to ʿAbdallāh the son of the Commander of the Faithful's side, from among the Commander of the Faithful's family, his companions, his military commanders, his financial officials, his secretaries, his slaves, his mawlās, and his troops, goes over to his (i.e., Muḥammad's) side and repudiates his due dependent status (literally, "his name"), his military obligations[681] and his position with ʿAbdallāh the son of the Commander of the Faithful, displaying rebelliousness towards him or acting against his interests, then Muḥammad the son of the Commander of the Faithful must send him back to ʿAbdallāh the son of the Commander of the Faithful in humiliation and ignominy, so that ʿAbdallāh may put into execution his decision and decree concerning him.

If Muḥammad the son of the Commander of the Faithful should attempt to remove ʿAbdallāh the son of the Commander of the

681. *maktabahu,* cf. *Glossarium,* p. CDXVI "military status," apparently to be connected with the command of, or the place where is stationed, a *katībah* or military unit.

Faithful from his right of succession after himself (i.e., after Muḥammad), or if he should attempt to remove ʿAbdallāh the son of the Commander of the Faithful from the governorship of Khurāsān, its frontier regions, its administrative divisions, its province which runs up to the boundaries adjacent to Hamadhān and the districts specifically named by the Commander of the Faithful in this document of his, or if he should attempt to dismiss any of his military commanders who came to Qarmāsīn and whom the Commander of the Faithful attached to ʿAbdallāh's side, or if he should attempt to deprive him of either a small or a great part of what the Commander of the Faithful has granted to him, in any [658] manner whatsoever or by any stratagem whatsoever, be it insignificant or momentous, then the caliphate after the Commander of the Faithful shall pass (directly) to ʿAbdallāh the son of Hārūn the Commander of the Faithful, and he shall come before Muḥammad the son of the Commander of the Faithful and be the one invested with power (immediately) after the Commander of the Faithful.

(In this case,) all the military commanders of the Commander of the Faithful Hārūn, comprising the men of Khurāsān and those in receipt of official stipends [*ahl al-ʿaṭāʾ*], and all the Muslims in all the army units and garrison cities, are to give their obedience to ʿAbdallāh the son of the Commander of the Faithful. They are to stand by his side, combat those in rebellion against him, give aid to him and defend him whilst ever they have life. None of them, whoever he may be or wherever he may find himself, is to rebel against him, defy him or throw off obedience to him, nor is he to give any obedience to Muḥammad the son of the Commander of the Faithful in removing ʿAbdallāh the son of the Commander of the Faithful (from the succession) and in diverting the succession after himself from ʿAbdallāh to anyone else, nor is he to deprive ʿAbdallāh of any single part of what the Commander of the Faithful Hārūn has granted to him during his lifetime and in full possession of his bodily health and has stipulated in the document written in his own hand which he required him to draw up in the Holy House[682] and in this present document; and ʿAbdallāh the

682. I.e., the document written out by al-Maʾmūn, whose text now follows this present one written out by al-Amīn; cf. Gabrieli, op. cit., 196 n. 1.

son of the Commander of the Faithful is the one whose word is accounted veracious.

You (i.e., the Muslims in general) are to be released from the oath of allegiance to Muḥammad the son of Hārūn the Commander of the Faithful which is at present incumbent on you if the latter diminishes any part of what the Commander of the Faithful Hārūn has made over to ʿAbdallāh; Muḥammad the son of Hārūn the Commander of the Faithful is to show himself submissive to ʿAbdallāh the son of the Commander of the Faithful Hārūn and hand over to him the caliphate.

Muḥammad and ʿAbdallāh, the sons of the Commander of the Faithful Hārūn, are not to deprive al-Qāsim son of the Commander of the Faithful Hārūn of his rights (as third heir to the throne), nor are they to usurp his precedence in favor of anyone of their own children, kindred or indeed any member of the human race at all. However, when the caliphate passes to ʿAbdallāh the son of the
[659] Commander of the Faithful, then the choice will be open to him of putting into execution the succession arrangements which the Commander of the Faithful established in al-Qāsim's favor, or else of deflecting these from him in favor of one of his own (i.e., ʿAbdallāh's) children or brothers, as he may deem fit.[683] He may give preference over al-Qāsim to whomever he desires, and place al-Qāsim the son of the Commander of the Faithful after any other person to whom he has given preference over al-Qāsim; he may come to a decision regarding this according to his own preference and judgment.

O Muslims, you are to put into execution that which the Commander of the Faithful has laid down in this document of his, has stipulated for them (i.e., his three sons) and has commanded to be done. You are to give hearing and obedience to the Commander of the Faithful in the duties which he has prescribed and made incumbent upon you in regard to ʿAbdallāh the son of the Commander of the Faithful, and upon you is laid the covenant of God and His agreement of protection, His messenger's agreement of protection and the agreements of protection of the Muslims, and

683. This possibility of choice for al-Ma'mūn regarding al-Qāsim's succession is confirmed in Masʿūdī, *Murūj*, VI, 328 = ed. Pellat, § 2530, and idem, *Tanbīh*, 345, tr. 444.

the covenants and solemn undertakings which God has made with the angels of His brought near to the throne [*al-malā'ikah al-muqarrabīn*],[684] the prophets and those sent with a message, and which He has imposed upon the believers and the Muslims. You are to fulfill faithfully towards the servant of God the Commander of the Faithful what he has laid down specifically, and towards Muḥammad, ʿAbdallāh and al-Qāsim the sons of the Commander of the Faithful what he has laid down specifically and prescribed in this document of his and made incumbent upon you, and which you have for your part agreed personally to accept. If you alter or change any part of it, or if you fail to fulfill your undertaking or go against what the Commander of the Faithful has commanded you and made incumbent upon you in this present document of his, then God's agreement of protection, the agreement of protection of His messenger Muḥammad and the agreements of protection of the believers and the Muslims, shall be null and void in respect of you. Moreover, all the wealth which each one of you possesses at this present moment, or will acquire up to a period of fifty years from now, shall be given in alms to the poor. Each one of you shall make the Pilgrimage on foot to God's Holy House at Mecca fifty times as a compulsory vow of expiation, whose fulfillment God will require absolutely from such a person. Every slave which each of you possesses, or will possess over the next fifty years, shall be set free. Every wife whom such a person has, shall be divorced with
the threefold repudiation, definitively, the divorce of sinfulness [660]
[*ṭalāq al-ḥaraj*][685] and the one which admits of no possibility of exception. God is the guarantor over you and curator regarding that, and He is sufficient as a reckoner (of men's virtues and sins)![686]

684. I.e., the cherubim; see *EI*² s.v. Malā'ika. 1. In the Ḳur'ān and Sunnī Islam (D. B. Macdonald).

685. Literally, "a divorce implying a sinful act, *ḥaraj*," in which the woman may resume the liaison; Gabrieli, op. cit., 197, translates *con divorzio implicante peccato* [*ove la donna venga ripresa*].

686. Tr. Gabrieli, op. cit., 193–7, who notes, however (p. 193) that the preciosity and floridity of the Arabic style of this and the following documents make absolute certainty in translation impossible. Yaʿqūbī, *Ta'rīkh*, II, 506–7, and Azraqī, in *Die Chroniken der Stadt Mekka*, I, 167–8 = ed. Milḥas, I, 238–9, add a list of those witnesses attesting the document.

Text of the Document Laying Down Conditions Which ʿAbdallāh Son of the Commander of the Faithful Wrote Out in His Own Hand in the Kaʿbah

This is a document composed by the servant of God Hārūn the Commander of the Faithful which ʿAbdallāh son of Hārūn the Commander of the Faithful has written out for him in a state of soundness of mind, full exercise of his powers, sincerity of intention in what he has set down in this document, and recognition of the excellence and soundness of its contents for himself, the members of his family and the whole community of Muslims:

The Commander of the Faithful Hārūn has designated me as successor in the caliphate and in all the affairs of the Muslims under his authority after my brother Muḥammad son of Hārūn. He has during his own lifetime appointed me governor of the frontier regions of Khurāsān, its districts and all its administrative and financial divisions, and he has stipulated to Muḥammad son of Hārūn that he should faithfully observe what he (i.e., Hārūn) has made over to me, comprising the caliphate and direction of the affairs of the people and the lands after him (i.e., after Muḥammad), and the governorship of Khurāsān and all its administrative and financial divisions. He is not to interfere with me nor contest with me over any part of the estates, revenue-yielding properties, and dwellings which the Commander of the Faithful has assigned to me or purchased for me, or which I have purchased from him, nor in regard to any of the material wealth, jewels, clothing, possessions, riding-beasts, slaves, and so forth, which the Commander of the Faithful has given to me. Nor is he ever to interfere with or molest me or any of my financial officials and secretaries on the pretext of making an audit or accounting, nor is he ever to pursue me or any of my officials over that, nor is he to perpetrate against me, against those officials, or against any of my retainers and persons in general whom I have called upon to assist me, any
[661] unpleasant act involving person, blood, hair, or flesh (i.e., act of physical violence and bloodshed inflicted on the person), or involving questions of property or indeed any matter, great or small.

He (i.e., Muḥammad) has agreed to this and has acknowledged it, and has written out for him (i.e., Hārūn) a document in which he has bound himself to observe these conditions. The Commander of the Faithful Hārūn was pleased at this, accepted it, and recognized the sincerity of his intentions in this matter.

I, for my part, have undertaken to the Commander of the Faithful and have laid upon myself the obligation that I will hear and obey Muḥammad and not act rebelliously against him; that I will give him sincere advice and not deceive him; that I will fulfill the oath of allegiance to him and acknowledge his authority, and not betray him or break my oath; and that I will put into effect his official instructions and commands, will cheerfully give him help and combat his enemies within my own territories. (All this) in such a manner as will fulfill towards me the obligations which he undertook to the Commander of the Faithful to observe regarding me and which he listed specifically in the document which he wrote out (personally) for the Commander of the Faithful and with which the Commander of the Faithful was satisfied; and (in such a manner as) will not hound and discommode me in any of those matters and will not break any of the undertakings to which the Commander of the Faithful made him agree regarding me.

If ever Muḥammad the son of the Commander of the Faithful requires a military force and writes to me, ordering me to despatch it to him or to any region or against any of his enemies who may have rebelled against him or sought to impair any part of his authority or part of my own authority which the Commander of the Faithful has assigned to us and has given us official responsibility for it, then I undertake to carry out his commands and not oppose him or fall short in the performance of any matter about which he has written to me. If Muḥammad wishes to appoint as successor to the caliphate after me one of his own children, then he has the right to do so, provided that he has at the same time fulfilled to me the obligations towards me which the Commander of the Faithful laid upon him and stipulated as due to me from him and which he himself undertook to fulfill regarding me. I undertake to carry out all that and to fulfill that faithfully to him; I will not diminish or change or alter any part of it, and I will not give premier place over him to any of my own children nor to any close or distant person whatsoever, unless the Commander of the Faith- [662]
ful Hārūn should appoint any (other) one of his children as successor to the caliphate after me and then compel me and Muḥammad to give fidelity to him.

I have taken upon myself the obligation of fidelity to the Commander of the Faithful and to Muḥammad according to what I have contracted to perform and have listed specifically in this document written out by me, as long as Muḥammad fulfills all the obligations towards me which the Commander of the Faithful has stipulated to me as incumbent upon him in my regard and all the items which the Commander of the Faithful has granted to me and which are specifically listed in this document which he wrote down for me.

I take upon myself (observance of) God's charge and covenant, together with the contractual agreements of my forefathers and those of all the believers, the most binding of the solemnly pledged charges and covenants which God has laid upon the prophets and messengers from all his creatures, and with the solemn oaths concerning which God has commanded fidelity and has forbidden their being broken or altered.

If I break a single item of what I have undertaken to observe and have specifically listed in this document of mine, or if I alter or change or fail to observe or act deceitfully (regarding it), then may I be cut off from God, He is exalted and magnified, from His protection and religion and from Muḥammad the Messenger of God, and may I meet God face-to-face on the Day of Resurrection as an unbeliever and polytheist. Every wife whom I have at this moment or may marry within the next thirty years, shall be divorced with the threefold repudiation, definitively, the divorce of sinfulness.[687] Every slave which I possess at this moment or may possess within the next thirty years shall be set free out of the love of God. I promise to make the Pilgrimage on foot to God's Holy House at Mecca thirty times, as a compulsory vow of expiation laid upon me, barefoot and walking, whose fulfillment God will require from me absolutely. All the wealth which I possess at this moment or may possess within the next thirty years shall be pledged as a gift intended for the Kaʿbah. Everything which I have undertaken towards the Commander of the Faithful and have obligated myself in this document of mine to fulfill, is binding upon me, and I will not conceive in my mind or determine upon anything else. Sulaymān the son of the Commander of the Faithful, so-and-so and so-

687. Gabrieli, op. cit., 199: *col ripudio del peccato.*

and-so have borne witness to this, and it has been written out in Dhū al-Ḥijjah, 186 (December, 802).[688]

The Text of the Letter of Hārūn b. Muḥammad, al-Rashīd, to the Provincial Governors[689] [663]

In the name of God, the Merciful, the Compassionate. As follows: God is the patron [*walī*] of the Commander of the Faithful, the patron of what he has endowed him with as ruler, the guardian of the caliphate and the authority which He has entrusted to his care and has honored him with, and the One who favors him in all the affairs of his which he initiates or relinquishes. He is the One who bestows upon him aid and succor in both the eastern and the western parts of the earth, the One who guards and protects and the One who is sufficient against the whole of His creation. He is the One who is to be praised for all His favors, the One responsible for the bringing to completion of the good things of His decrees which He has put into execution for the Commander of the Faithful and of His laudable customary actions for him; (He is likewise responsible for) the inspiring of what is agreeable to Him; and He makes incumbent upon him for the achievement of this the finest augmentation of His grace.

Among the favors of God, He is exalted and magnified, which He has vouchsafed to the Commander of the Faithful, to you and to the generality of Muslims, is what God has arranged with regard to Muḥammad and ʿAbdallāh the two sons of the Commander of the Faithful by His conveying to them the best of what the Muslim community has hoped for and has hastened eagerly towards. God has cast into the hearts of the mass of the populace love and affection for these two princes, peace of mind stemming from confidence in them and reliance upon them because of the firmness of their faith, the uprightness of their affairs, their mutual harmony and the rectitude of their mien. God has kept away from them fearful and unpleasant things making for disunity and di-

688. Tr. Gabrieli, op. cit., 197–200. Again, Yaʿqūbī, *Taʾrīkh*, II, 509, and Azraqī, in *Die Chroniken der Stadt Mekka*, I, 168 = ed. Milḥas, I, 241, note that the same witnesses who attested al-Amīn's document attested this one also.

689. Cf. Gabrieli, "Successione," 346–7; the text of this letter is not given in any other early source, i.e., one not repeating Ṭabarī's text.

visiveness, to the point that people have entrusted to the two of them the reins of power over themselves and have given to them their pledges of allegiance and solemnly sworn oaths by means of covenants, contractual agreements, and firm oaths strenuously impressed on them. God has expressed His will thus, and there is no one who can gainsay Him; he has put it into effect, and none of His creatures can controvert it or render it invalid, or can deflect Him from what He desires and wills or from what He has previously formed the intention in His mind of doing.

The Commander of the Faithful hopes for the completion of
[664] beneficence upon himself and his two sons regarding that and upon the whole Muslim community; there is no one who can put back God's command, no one who can reverse His decree and no one who can set up a substitute for His ordinance.

Since the Muslim community agreed with one mind upon settling the succession on Muḥammad the son of the Commander of the Faithful after the Commander of the Faithful himself and then on ʿAbdallāh the son of the Commander of the Faithful after Muḥammad the son of the Commander of the Faithful, the Commander of the Faithful has continuously exercised his thought, judgment, mind, and powers of reflection[690] on what will give benefit to them both and to the whole of the subjects; will bring harmony to their discussions; will repair the disorder of affairs; will dispel those things making for disunity and divisiveness; will cut off short the wiles of the enemies of divine favor, comprising the infidels, the hypocrites, those harboring rancor and those sowing dissension; and will cut short the hopes of these last on every occasion when they hope to achieve these aims and seize appropriate opportunities against the two princes by impairing their just rights. The Commander of the Faithful asks God's blessing for all that and begs Him to grant him resolution of purpose for following the best course for the two princes and the whole Muslim community. (He asks Him for) strength in fulfilling God's command and His due rights; in reconciling their divergent notions and working out the best course for them mutually; and in preserving them

---

690. Reading with the Cairo text, VIII, 284, *rawiyyatihi* for the Leiden text's *ru'yatihi.*

both from the wiles of the enemies of divine favor, repelling their enviousness, deceitful stratagems, injuriousness, and endeavors to sow evil between the two of them.

Accordingly, God implanted in the Commander of the Faithful the determination to despatch them both to God's House; to take from them the oath of allegiance to the Commander of the Faithful by hearing and obeying and by putting into effect his command; and to have written down the set of obligations upon each of them towards the Commander of the Faithful and towards each other by the strongest of covenants and agreements and the firmest of oaths and undertakings. (He also determined upon) requiring an undertaking from each one of them to the other regarding what the Commander of the Faithful sought to secure in the way of their mutual harmony, their mutual affection, their mutual accord, assistance to each other and protection for each other in conformity with a favorable regard for their own mutual interests and those of the Commander of the Faithful's subjects, whom he has entrusted to their care as rulers. (The Commander of the Faithful also sought to secure) unity for the furtherance of the religion of God, He is exalted and magnified, His book and the exemplary practices [*sunan*] of His Prophet; (to bring about) holy warfare [*jihād*] against the enemies of the Muslims, whoever and wherever they may be; and (to secure) the suppression of the ambitious schemes of every enemy who openly manifests hostility or secretly harbors it, of every hypocrite and deviant from the faith, of those persons holding heretical opinions who are themselves deluded and who delude others, who stem from a group which plots to bring about an evil stratagem between them and to bring about [665]
discord between them. (He has also sought to secure the suppression of) that which God's enemies, the enemies of the divine favors and the enemies of His religion, seek to bring about—violence among the Muslim community, endeavors to wreak corruption in the earth and an invitation to unlawful innovations [*bida*ʿ] and error. (All these endeavors come) from a solicitude on the part of the Commander of the Faithful for God's religion, His subjects and the community of His Prophet Muḥammad, from a policy of giving good counsel for the furtherance of God's interests and for all the Muslims, and from defending God's authority which he has pre-

pared[691] and for which he has devoted himself solely in regard to the burden with which He has charged him (i.e., the caliphate). (God has also implanted in the Caliph a determination to make) strenuous endeavors in everything which brings nearness to God and by means of which His favor is achieved and access gained to His presence.

When he arrived in Mecca, he made manifest to Muḥammad and ʿAbdallāh his intention regarding this and what he envisaged for them in it. They both assented to everything which he called upon them to undertake in firmly binding themselves to its acceptance, and they wrote out for the Commander of the Faithful, in the heart of God's Holy House, in their own handwriting and in the assembly of those members of the Commander of the Faithful's family, his military commanders, his retainers, and his judges who were present for the Pilgrimage, and the doorkeepers of the Kaʿbah, and with their attestation to the two persons swearing (these obligations), two documents, which the Commander of the Faithful entrusted to the safekeeping of the doorkeepers and commanded that they should be hung up inside the Kaʿbah.

When the Commander of the Faithful had completed all this inside God's Holy House and the interior of the Kaʿbah, he commanded his judges, who had borne witness to them both and had been present at their writing out (i.e., the documents), that they should inform all those present for the Pilgrimage season, comprising those who had come to perform the Pilgrimage and the ʿUmrah and the delegations from the great cities, about the conditions which the two princes had taken upon themselves and which they had written out, and to which they (i.e., the judges) had borne witness. (He further ordered) the reading out of that to them (i.e., to the assembled people in Mecca) in order that they might comprehend it, keep it in their minds, come to know it, learn the texts by heart, and communicate it to their comrades and the people of their lands and cities. They accordingly did that, and the two contractual agreements were read out to them *in extenso* in the Holy Mosque. Then they went back. The reports about all this

691. Translation here conjectural; the text's reading here *qaddarahu* is very dubious.

having been already widely disseminated among them, they confirmed its attestation and they realized the Commander of the Faithful's intention and his solicitude for their welfare, the prevention of bloodshed among them, the repairing of their disorder, and the extinguishing of the blazing brand of God's enemies and the enemies of His religion, His book and the whole community of Muslims, from among them. They offered up prayers for the Commander of the Faithful and thanks for what he had arranged in [666]
respect of all this.

The Commander of the Faithful has transcribed for you those two contractual agreements which the Commander of the Faithful's two sons Muḥammad and ʿAbdallāh wrote down for him in the interior of the Kaʿbah, at the foot of this writing of his being the words:

So praise God, He is exalted and magnified, profusely for what He has wrought for Muḥammad and ʿAbdallāh, the two designated successors to rule over the Muslims, and give copious thanks to Him for His favor in regard to the Commander of the Faithful, to the two bearers of the succession for the Muslims, to you (i.e., the governor receiving the copy of this letter) and to the whole of the community of Muḥammad. Have the Commander of the Faithful's letter read out to the Muslims under your authority, make them understand it, take responsibility for it among them, have it set down firmly in the *dīwān* which is under your control and that of the military commanders of the Commander of the Faithful and his subjects under your charge, and write back to the Commander of the Faithful concerning anything which may take place regarding this, if God wills. God is our sufficiency, and how good a guardian of our interests! In Him is power and strength and might!

Ismāʿīl b. Ṣubayḥ wrote this on Saturday, the twenty-third of al-Muḥarram, 187[692] (January 21, 803).

He related: Hārūn al-Rashīd ordered 100,000 dīnārs to be given to ʿAbdallāh al-Maʾmūn, and this sum was brought for him to Baghdad from Raqqah.

---

692. Read thus (as Gabrieli points out in op. cit., 347 n. 1) for the text's date of 186, which does not give the correct correspondence of day and date.

Al-Rashīd's Subsequent Renewal of the Succession Pledges to al-Ma'mūn and al-Qāsim at Qarmāsīn

He related: At a period of time after the killing of Ja'far b. Yaḥyā,[693] al-Rashīd went to al-Raqqah and then came to Baghdad, complaints about 'Alī b. 'Īsā b. Māhān having reached him continuously from Khurāsān and much adverse talk about 'Alī having come to his ears. Hence, he decided upon dismissing him from Khurāsān, and preferred to have 'Alī near him.[694] So when he went to Baghdad, he set out from there after a while towards Qarmāsīn; this was in the year 189 (805). He further despatched to Qarmāsīn a number of persons, comprising judges and others, and made them bear witness that the whole of what he had with him in his army—wealth, treasuries, weapons, horses and mules, and so forth, in its entirety—was to go to 'Abdallāh al-Ma'mūn, and that he would retain nothing of it for himself, small or great, for any motive or pretext. He renewed the succession pledge to al-Ma'mūn from
[667] those who were with him, and he sent Harthamah b. A'yan, the commander of his guard, to Baghdad. Then he once again exacted the succession pledge to 'Abdallāh and al-Qāsim from Muḥammad the son of Hārūn the Commander of the Faithful and those in his circle, according to the terms of the document to which al-Rashīd had required his assent at Mecca. He relegated the question of al-Qāsim, whether he was to be removed from his designated role as third heir or confirmed in it, to 'Abdallāh's decision when the caliphate should pass to him.[695]

Ibrāhīm al-Mawṣilī recited concerning Hārūn's securing adhesion to the succession of his two sons in the Ka'bah,

The best of affairs for having a good conclusion
    and the most likely affair to achieve completion
Is an affair whose firm constituting the Merciful One
    has decreed in the Holy House.[696]

---

693. Actually, some two years later, the fall of the Barmakīs being in Ṣafar, 187 (January, 803).

694. This was the occasion of al-Rashīd's journeying to al-Rayy, where 'Alī b. 'Īsā's amassment of wealth for his master sufficiently impressed the Caliph to confirm 'Alī in his governorship; see Ṭabarī, III, 702–4 (below, 250–54).

695. Ibn al-Athīr, VI, 173, 191; Gabrieli, op. cit., 349.

696. *K. al-'Uyūn*, 305.

The Events of the Year 187

(December 30, 802–December 19, 803)

Among the events taking place during this year was al-Rashīd's killing of Jaʿfar b. Yaḥyā b. Khālid and his swooping down on the Barmakīs.[697]

---

697. The other main sources for this celebrated episode of mediaeval Islamic history are as follows:

Jahshiyārī, 185–211; Yaʿqūbī, *Taʾrīkh*, II, 510–12; Ṭabarī-Balʿamī, tr. IV, 461–9; Masʿūdī, *Murūj*, VI, 386–414 = ed. Pellat, §§ 2588–2618; Azdī, 304–6; *K. al-ʿUyūn*, 305–9; Ibn al-Athīr, VI, 175–80; Ibn Khallikān, I, 328–46, tr. I, 301–19 (Jaʿfar b. Yaḥyā), IV, 27–36, tr. II, 459–68 (al-Faḍl b. Yaḥyā), VI, 219–29, tr. IV, 103–14 (Yaḥyā b. Khālid); Ibn al-Ṭiqṭaqā, 190–2, tr. 207–10.

However, virtually every chronicler of the caliphate touched on this topic, which clearly fascinated mediaeval Muslims as an example of overweening pride and immense riches brought low at a single stroke and as an object lesson in the dangers of servants endeavoring to rise above their masters in splendor of life and munificence. Special works were even composed on the episode, especially in the Persian cultural world, which was perhaps attracted to the subject through the Barmakīs' Persian origins and which may have been tempted to view the Barmakīs (as have some modern authors) as upholders of the Persian traditions of government and culture in the caliphate. Bouvat notes, e.g., two works of the eighth (fourteenth) century, the Indo-Muslim historian Ḍiyāʾ al-Dīn Baranī's *Akhbār-i Barmakiyān* and ʿAbd al-Jalīl Yazdī's *Taʾrīkh-i āl-i Barmak* (Bouvat, 9–10; cf. C. A. Storey, *Persian literature, a bio-bibliographical survey*, I, 1082–3).

Modern writers have likewise been attracted by the enigmatic aspects of the

The Reason for al-Rashīd's Killing of Jaʿfar al-Barmakī, the Manner of His Killing, and What al-Rashīd Did to Him and the Members of His Family

Concerning the reason for al-Rashīd's anger against him, occasioning the Caliph's killing of him, there are varying accounts.[698] One of them is what is mentioned from Bukhtīshūʿ b. Jibrīl,[699] who had it from his father, that the latter related: I was sitting in al-Rashīd's court circle when Yaḥyā b. Khālid appeared. It had always been the practice previously that he should enter without seeking formal permission. Now, when he entered, drew near to al-Rashīd and greeted him, the latter returned only a perfunctory salutation. Yaḥyā then realized that their relationship (or: the position of the Barmakī family, *amrahum*) had changed.

He related: Then al-Rashīd came up to me and said, "O Jibrīl, does anyone enter upon your presence, without your permission, when you are in your house?" I replied, "No, and no one would presume to do that." He commented, "Why, then, should we have
[668] to put up with intrusions upon us without permission?" Yaḥyā rose and explained, "O Commander of the Faithful, may God bring my term of life to an end before yours! By God, I haven't inaugurated this practice at this very moment, and it is no more than an honor with which the Commander of the Faithful has favored me and has thereby increased my prestige, to the extent that I used to come into his presence when he was in his bed, at times garmentless, or at other times just dressed in one of his loincloths. I did not realize that the Commander of the Faithful (now) disliked what he

---

Barmakīs' fall and the motives impelling al-Rashīd to such savagery against the family when he burst out of their tutelage. A bibliography of earlier studies can be found in Bouvat, 127–31, Appendix II. For subsequent works, see Bouvat's own monograph, 74–101, and now the profounder analysis of motives at work in the Caliph's mind, material and psychological considerations, by Sourdel, *Vizirat*, I, 151–81. See also Palmer, 81–106; Shaban, 35–9; Sourdel, in *Cambridge history of Islam*, I, 115–16; Kennedy, 127–9; *EI*² s.v. Barāmika (Sourdel).

698. As acknowledged by most of the sources, e.g., Yaʿqūbī, *Taʾrīkh*, II, 510: "Most authorities hold divergent views about the causes of his anger against them."

699. Member of a celebrated Christian family of physicians from Jundīshāpūr, several members of which personally served the ʿAbbāsid Caliphs and who died in 256 (870). His father, Jibrīl b. Bukhtīshūʿ b. Jurjīs, died in 212 (827), was physician to Jaʿfar b. Yaḥyā and, in the words of Jahshiyārī, 178, their protégé, *ṣanīʿat al-Barāmikah*. See *GAS*, III, 226–7; *EI*² s.v. Bukhtīshūʿ (Sourdel).

used to approve. But now that I have realized it, in future I will take my place in the second or third rank of those seeking permission to enter, if my master so commands." He related: Al-Rashīd was thereupon ashamed—among all the Caliphs, he related, al-Rashīd had one of the mildest countenances—and he remained with his eyes to the ground, not looking upwards at Yaḥyā. Then he said, "I didn't intend anything to discomfit you, but people are talking." He related, I had the impression that al-Rashīd had not been able to think of a satisfactory reply on the spur of the moment, and hence had answered him thus. Al-Rashīd refrained from saying any more to Yaḥyā, and Yaḥyā departed.[700]

It has been mentioned from Aḥmad b. Yūsuf that Thumāmah b. Ashras said: The first occasion when Yaḥyā b. Khālid felt uneasy about his position was when Muḥammad b. al-Layth[701] presented an epistle to al-Rashīd in which he gave the Caliph a warning and mentioned that "Yaḥyā b. Khālid will not in any way absolve you of your responsibilities towards God. You have made him preeminent in matters which are between yourself and God alone. What will be your position when you stand before God (i.e., at the Last Judgement) and He asks you about what you have achieved among His servants and His lands, and you reply, 'O Lord, I committed the responsibilities of the affairs of Your servants entirely to Yaḥyā'? Do you imagine that you will be able to adduce a plea of extenuation acceptable to God?" (He said all this) in a speech full of blame and upbraiding.[702] Al-Rashīd accordingly sent for Yaḥyā, to whom news of the epistle had already arrived, and he said, "Do you know Muḥammad b. al-Layth?" Yaḥyā replied, "Yes." Al-Rashīd said, "What sort of a man is he?" He replied, "A man whose Islamic faith is suspect." Al-Rashīd thereupon commanded that Muḥammad b.

---

700. Ibn al-Athīr, VI, 177; Palmer, 89–90.

701. Presumably, the official whom Yaʿqūbī, *Ta'rīkh*, II, 483, lists as a minister of al-Mahdī's, known for his eloquence; cf. Sourdel, *Vizirat*, I, 111–12, 143 n. 6, 176 n. 2. In Ṭabarī-Balʿamī, tr. IV, 463, he is given the patronymic of Abū Rabīʿah and described as a popular ascetic and religious figure of al-Raqqah, and in his denunciation of the Barmakīs to the Caliph he accuses them of infidelity and atheism.

702. This is the moment when Ṭabarī gets to the explanation favored by so many of the sources, that the Barmakīs had arrogated to themselves executive and judicial powers proper to the Caliph only. See, e.g., Jahshiyārī, 164; Yaʿqūbī, *Ta'rīkh*, II, 510–11; Ibn al-Ṭiqṭaqā, 190, tr. 207; Ibn Khaldūn, *Muqaddimah*, tr. F. Rosenthal, I, 30–2; Abbott, 193–5.

al-Layth should be incarcerated in the Maṭbaq prison indefinitely.[703] But when al-Rashīd's attitude towards the Barmakīs had changed for the worse, he remembered Muḥammad. He ordered him to be brought forth, and Muḥammad was set before him. Al-Rashīd said to him after a long speech, "O Muḥammad, do you love me?" He replied, "By God, O Commander of the Faithful, no!" He said, "You really mean this?" He replied, "Yes, certainly! You
[669] have put fetters on my legs, and have come between me and my family (i.e., deprived me of contact with them), when I have committed no sin or grave crime, all on the word of an envious one who is plotting against Islam and the Muslims and who loves heresy and its practitioners. How can I possibly love you?" Al-Rashīd said, "You have spoken truly," and he ordered him to be set free. Then he asked, "O Muḥammad, do you love me now?" He replied, "By God, O Commander of the Faithful, no, although the hard feelings in my breast have gone away." So al-Rashīd ordered him to be given one hundred thousand dirhams. He was brought before him again, and al-Rashīd asked, "O Muḥammad, do you love me now?" He replied, "Now, at last, yes; you have been munificent and generous towards me!" Al-Rashīd said, "May God take vengeance upon the one who has wronged you, and may He take upon Himself the fulfillment of your just rights from the one who incited me against you!" He related: People started talking at length to the discredit of the Barmakīs, and this occasion was the first manifestation of the change in their fortunes.[704]

Muḥammad b. al-Faḍl b. Sufyān, the mawlā of Sulaymān b. Abī Jaʿfar, transmitted the information to me, saying: Yaḥyā b. Khālid went into al-Rashīd's presence after this, and the slaves [*al-ghilmān*] stood up when he entered. But al-Rashīd told the eunuch Masrūr, "Give the slaves the order not to stand up in Yaḥyā's presence when he enters the palace." He related: Yaḥyā came in, and no one stood up in his presence; Yaḥyā became ashen faced at this. He related: Subsequently, when the slaves and doorkeepers

703. Ṭabarī-Balʿamī, tr. IV, 463.

704. The sources retail various stories concerning the Barmakīs' premonitions of al-Rashīd's changed attitude and his intention to overthrow them. See, e.g., the verses which al-Rashīd made a Kūfan storyteller repeat continually to him one night, the news of which alarmed Jaʿfar b. Yaḥyā, in Bayhaqī, *Maḥāsin*, ed. Schwally, 401–2 = ed. Ibrāhīm, II, 80–1.

saw him, they turned away from him. He related: Yaḥyā used on occasion to ask for a drink of water or something, and they would not give it to him; or rather, if it happened that they did in the end provide him with a drink, it was only after he had called for it several times.

Jaʿfar's Alleged Connivance with the Release of the ʿAlid Yaḥyā b. ʿAbdallāh b. Ḥasan

Abū Muḥammad al-Yazīdī[705]—and according to what is said, he was one of the persons most knowledgeable about the story of the Barmakīs—has mentioned, saying: "If anyone says that al-Rashīd killed Jaʿfar b. Yaḥyā for any other reason but over Yaḥyā b. ʿAbdallāh b. Ḥasan, don't believe him!"[706] The story here is that al-Rashīd handed over Yaḥyā to Jaʿfar, who thereupon imprisoned him. Then, one night, Jaʿfar summoned Yaḥyā and interrogated him about some aspects of his affairs and position, and Yaḥyā gave him suitable answers, until he said, "Show piety towards God in my regard, and don't lay yourself open to the possibility that [670] Muḥammad may speak unfavorably against you in the future (i.e., on the Last Day), for by God, I have not introduced any heretical

705. Yaḥyā b. Mubārak, died in 202 (817), was a poet and later aspirant to al-Ma'mūn's court circle (see Ṭabarī, III, 1156–8), and a member of a well-known poetic family; see Sezgin, *GAS*, II, 610.

706. The adducing of such a reason as the prime one for the downfall of the Barmakīs is nevertheless farfetched; cf. Bouvat, 75, and Kennedy, 128. But it does seem that at various points in his career as commander and minister for al-Rashīd, al-Faḍl did not regard the ʿAlids as mortal enemies and, following in the footsteps of al-Mahdī, favored a policy of conciliation toward them, ill according with al-Rashīd's violently anti-ʿAlid views; cf. his generosity toward the Imām Muḥammad b. Ibrāhīm, Ibn Ṭabāṭabā (Jahshiyārī, 151–2; Ibn al-Ṭiqṭaqā, 185–6, tr. 201–2; Bouvat, 64; Sourdel, *Vizirat*, I, 166) and his general attitude of leaving ʿAlids in the remoter parts of the empire alone, as being less harmful there to the state, as is emphasized by Sourdel, op. cit., I, 164–6, idem, "La politique religieuse du calife ʿabbaside al-Ma'mūn," *REI*, XXX (1962), 28–9, and Kennedy, 119–20. In Jahshiyārī, 194, Yaḥyā b. Khālid is accused by al-Rashīd of giving a financial subsidy to Yaḥyā b. ʿAbdallāh in Daylam so that his strength might increase, and then al-Faḍl b. Yaḥyā would have all the greater honor for suppressing the revolt—a puerile argument that Yaḥyā b. Khālid easily disposes of. In Abū al-Faḍl Bayhaqī, *Ta'rīkh-i Masʿūdī*, 415, Yaḥyā acknowledges that he is suspect in al-Rashīd's eyes for his ʿAlid sympathies, which may be a characteristic touch of the Persian sources on the Barmakīs and their fall.

innovations nor have I given shelter to any perpetrator of such misdeeds!" So Jaʿfar relented towards him and told him, "Go forth into wherever you like of God's lands!" But Yaḥyā replied, "How can I go forth, when I have no assurance that I shall not be arrested after a short while and sent back to you or someone else?" Hence, Jaʿfar sent along with Yaḥyā someone who could conduct him to a secure place for him. The news of this reached al-Faḍl b. al-Rabīʿ through a spy of his within the inner circle of Jaʿfar's servants (or: eunuchs, *khadamihi*) whom he had over Jaʿfar.

Al-Faḍl made a full investigation into the matter; he found it to be perfectly true, and it was fully revealed to him. So he went into al-Rashīd's presence and informed him. The latter indicated to al-Faḍl ostensibly that he was uninterested in his information, and said, "What's the matter got to do with you, may you be deprived of your mother? For all you know, this may be at my express command!" At this, al-Faḍl was crushed. Jaʿfar now came to al-Rashīd. The latter called for food; the two of them ate together, and the Caliph began to put tasty morsels of food into Jaʿfar's mouth and to converse with him, until finally, at the end of their session together, al-Rashīd asked, "What has Yaḥyā b. ʿAbdallāh been up to?" Jaʿfar replied, "He is just as he was before, O Commander of the Faithful, in a cramped prison cell, loaded with fetters." Al-Rashīd commented, "By my life!" At this, Jaʿfar—who had one of the acutest intelligences and soundest perceptions among all mankind—drew back, and realized within himself that the Caliph in fact knew something about the affair. So he then said, "Nay, by your life, my lord, in reality I set him free, having learnt that there was nothing to be gained by holding him and that he was completely harmless." The Caliph replied, "You did well! You have done exactly what was in my own mind!" (literally, "you have not gone beyond what was in my own mind"). But when Jaʿfar went out, al-Rashīd followed him with his gaze until Jaʿfar became almost hidden from his sight, and then he burst out, "May God
[671] slay me with the sword of right guidance for having committed an erroneous act if I don't kill you!" What subsequently happened regarding him is well-known.[707]

707. Ṭabarī-Balʿamī, tr. IV, 464; *K. al-ʿUyūn*, 306–7; Ibn al-Athīr, VI, 176; Ibn Khallikān, I, 334–5, tr. I, 308–9; Ibn al-Ṭiqṭaqā, 191, tr. 208; Ibn Khaldūn, tr. I, 31–2; Palmer, 85; Bouvat, 83; Abbott, 196–7.

Idrīs b. Badr has transmitted the information,[708] saying: A man presented himself before al-Rashīd (or: presented a petition to al-Rashīd, *ʿaraḍa li-al-Rashīd*) whilst the latter was engaged in a discussion with Yaḥyā (al-Barmakī), with the words, "O Commander of the Faithful, a word of advice (for you), so summon me before you!" Al-Rashīd said to Harthamah, "Take this man aside with you, and ask him about this piece of advice of his." Harthamah questioned him (about it), but he refused to tell him, saying, "It is a secret meant for the Caliph's ear alone." Harthamah informed al-Rashīd of what the man had said, and the Caliph replied, "Don't let him leave the palace gate until I have a chance to speak with him privately." He related: When it was midday, all those who had been with the Caliph departed, and the Caliph summoned the man. The man said, "Accord me complete privacy." So Hārūn turned to his sons and said, "Please go away, lads!" and they sprang up (and left). Khāqān and Ḥusayn remained standing by his head. The man looked at them. Al-Rashīd told them, "Retire from my presence," and they did so. Then al-Rashīd went up to the man and said, "Now tell me what is in your mind." The man replied, "Provided that you grant me a promise of personal security and safe conduct." The Caliph said, "I undertake to grant you such a promise of personal safety and to treat you well."

The man said, "I was at Ḥulwān, in one of the caravanserais there, when I realized that I was in the presence of Yaḥyā b. ʿAbdallāh, who was wearing a coarse, open-fronted tunic [*durrāʿah*][709] of wool and a coarse, green-colored woolen cloak. He was accompanied by a group of persons who encamped whenever he encamped and who travelled on whenever he travelled on and who took up a position near him, (nevertheless) giving the impression to anyone who saw them that they did not know Yaḥyā although they were in reality his aides. Each one of them had a chit [*manshūr*][710] guaranteeing him safe-conduct, should he be stopped." Al-

---

708. There is a complete *isnād* for this story back to Idrīs b. Zayd in Iṣfahānī, *Maqātil*, 309–10.

709. For this long gown, see Dozy, *Dictionnaire détaillée des noms de vêtements chez les arabes*, 177–81; Agius, 217–20.

710. See for this early use of the term (in later times a more grandiose document of appointment for officials), *EI*[2] s.v. Diplomatic. i. Classical Arabic. Section 3.c (h) (W. Björkman): a pass for peasants in Egypt, designed to impede movement away from the land.

Rashīd said, "Do you know Yaḥyā b. ʿAbdallāh, then?" He replied, "I have known him for a long time, and it was this which made certain my recognition of him the other day." Al-Rashīd said, "Describe him to me." The man replied, "(He is) a man with an appearance of well-being, slightly swarthy in complexion, with receding hair at the temples, pleasant eyes, and a substantial paunch." Al-Rashīd retorted, "You have spoken truly, he is just like that," and went on to say, "What did you hear him say?" The man replied, "I
[672] didn't hear him say anything, except that I saw him performing the worship. I also saw one of his slaves, whom I used previously to know, sitting at the gate of the caravanserai. When Yaḥyā had finished his act of worship, the slave brought him a freshly laundered robe. He threw it over Yaḥyā's shoulders and took away the woolen gown. After the sun began to decline from its zenith, he performed another act of worship which was, I think, the afternoon one [*al-ʿaṣr*]. I was meanwhile watching him closely, and he performed the opening sections of the two acts of worship in a protracted, measured fashion, but the closing sections of the two acts of worship in a light and speedy fashion."[711]

Al-Rashīd exclaimed, "May God bless your father! How excellently have you remembered all this! Yes indeed, that would be the afternoon worship, and that would be the appropriate time for it in the view of people in general. May God grant you a handsome reward and thank you appropriately for your efforts! But who exactly are you?" The man replied, "I stem from the progeny of the 'sons of the dynasty';[712] my family origin is from Marw and my birthplace is the City of Peace." The Caliph said, "Is your house, then, there?" He replied, "Yes." The Caliph remained silent, with his eyes to the ground, for a considerable period and then said, "How would you be able to endure an unpleasant experience, which you would have to suffer, as an act of obedience to me?" The man said, "I would undergo the unpleasantness of that inasmuch as the Commander of the Faithful wishes it." The Caliph said, "Stay where you are until I come back," and he darted quickly into

711. Following here the Cairo text, VIII, 290, *al-ūlayayni* and *al-ukhrayayni*, for the Leiden text's *al-awwalatayni* (sic) and *al-ākhiratayni* (presumably referring to the four *rakʿah*s which make up the *ṣalāt al-ẓuhr* and the *ṣalat al-ʿaṣr*).

712. I.e., from the *Abnāʾ al-Dawlaḥ*, the original backing of the ʿAbbāsids from the Arabs of the Khurāsānian garrison cities.

a chamber[713] which was just at his back and pulled out a purse containing two thousand dīnārs. He said, "Take this, and let me put into operation a plan which I have thought up concerning you." The man accordingly took the money and wrapped his robes over it. Then the Caliph called out, "O slave!" and Khāqān and Ḥusayn answered the call. He said, "Strike this son of a stinking, uncircumcised whore [*ibn al-lakhnāʾ*]!" so the two of them punched him about a hundred times. Then the Caliph said, "Take him out to those who are still in the palace precincts, with his turban round his neck, and proclaim, 'This is the reward of the person who brings slanderous accusations against the Commander of the Faithful's courtiers and retainers!' " They did all that, and the people talked about the man and what had happened to him, but no one knew about the man's real role nor about what he had communicated to al-Rashīd until the fall of the Barmakīs eventually took place.[714]

The Barmakīs' Wealth and Ostentation as a Reason for Their Fall

Yaʿqūb b. Isḥāq (al-Iṣfahānī)[715] has mentioned that Ibrāhīm b. al-Mahdī transmitted the information to him, saying: I visited Jaʿfar b. Yaḥyā in that palace of his which he had built. He said to me, [673]
"Aren't you astonished at Manṣūr b. Ziyād?"[716] He said: I replied, "In what connection?" He said, "I asked him whether he discerned any defect at all in my palace, and he replied, 'Yes, it doesn't contain any sun-dried brick or pine trunk (in its construction).' " Ibrāhīm related: I said, however, "What renders it faulty, in my view, is that you have expended on it around twenty million dirhams, and this is a thing concerning which I would not guarantee your personal security, at some future date, in the Caliph's eyes." He retorted, "He knows well that he has given me in presents more

---

713. Following the reading of the *Addenda et emendanda*, P. DCCCLXII, *faṭafara fī ḥujratin*.

714. Iṣfahānī, *Maqātil*, 309–11; Sourdel, *Vizirat*, I, 164 n. 3.

715. Also mentioned as a *rāwī* by Ṭabarī, III, 759 (below, 328), 965.

716. Manṣūr's closeness to the Barmakīs (Ṭabarī, III, 613, above, 116, and n. 444) was such that just before their fall, the Caliph attacked them indirectly by mulcting Manṣūr of an enormous sum, with the penalty of death for nonpayment, which Manṣūr had to obtain from the Barmakīs. See Jahshiyārī, 175–7; Sourdel, *Vizirat*, I, 172–3.

than that, and as much as that again, in addition to what he has left open for me to acquire [*mā ʿarraḍanī lahu*]." He related: I remarked, "An enemy has only to go to the Caliph over this with the intention of saying to him, 'O Commander of the Faithful, since he has been able to expend twenty million dirhams on a single palace, what about his ordinary expenditure? And all the gifts he bestows? And (provision against) all the eventualities and misfortunes which may assail him? Moreover, O Commander of the Faithful, what do you think about expenditure beyond all that? This is a sum which can speedily be disbursed, but getting oneself into a position to acquire it is difficult.' "[717] Jaʿfar replied, "If he hears anything (critical) about me, I shall respond, 'The Commander of the Faithful has bestowed many favors on people who have displayed ingratitude for these favors by concealing them or by outwardly displaying only a small part from a great number of these favors. I, on the other hand, am a man who has considered the Caliph's bounty to me; as a result, I have placed it on a mountain top and then instructed the people, "Come forth and gaze on it!" ' "

The Barmakīs' Growing Fears of the Caliph's Threatening Intentions

Zayd b. ʿAlī b. Ḥusayn b. Zayd (al-ʿAlawī)[718] has mentioned that Ibrāhīm b. al-Mahdī transmitted the information to him that Jaʿfar b. Yaḥyā said to him one day—Jaʿfar b. Yaḥyā being Ibrāhīm's patron and sponsor [*ṣāḥibahu*] at al-Rashīd's court and the one who had brought him into the Caliph's circle of intimates—"I have begun to feel suspicious regarding this man's—he meant al-Rashīd's—attitude, and I have got the idea that this stems from some previous action of his which has affected me. Hence, I wished to examine that in the light of another person's opinion; now you are that person. So keep an eye on that point as you go

717. In Ibn al-Athīr, VI, 176, Jaʿfar's expenditure of twenty million dirhams on his palace is specifically adduced as one of the causes of al-Rashīd's vengeance on him.

718. Ḥusaynid *rāwī* and great-grandson of the Zayd b. ʿAlī killed at al-Kūfah in 121 (739), cited three times by Ṭabarī for events in al-Rashīd's reign, see also III, 692, 746 (below 235, 311).

about today's business, and let me know what you observe regarding him." He related: In the course of my day's activities, I did that. [674]
When al-Rashīd rose up from his court session, I was the first of his companions to rise up and leave him. I then went along to a clump of trees along the road which I was wont to take and went inside it, together with my attendants, and ordered them to extinguish the candles. The Caliph's boon-companions began to pass by where I was, one by one. I could see them, but they could not see me. Finally, all of them had gone, when suddenly Jaʿfar appeared in view. When he came through the clump of trees he called out, "Come forth, my dear friend!" He related: So I came forth. He said, "Well, what information have you got?" I replied, "Not till you tell me how you knew I was here!" He said, "I was aware of your solicitude over what I am worried about and aware that you are not the sort of person who would go home without informing me of what you observed in him. I also know that you would not like to be seen standing about at this sort of hour. There is no better place for concealment along the road than this one, so I decided that you must be here in it." I said, "Yes, true." He said, "Now let's hear what you have learnt!" I replied, "I observed a man who jests when you speak seriously, and who becomes serious when you jest." He said, "That is exactly how he appears to me, so go homewards, my dear friend." He related: I then went home.[719]

He related: ʿAlī b. Sulaymān transmitted the information to me, that he heard Jaʿfar b. Yaḥyā saying one day, "This present mansion of ours (i.e., our present life) is without defect, except that the owner has only a short spell of existence in it," alluding to himself.

It is mentioned from Mūsā b. Yaḥyā that he said: My father set out to make the circumambulation (of the Kaʿbah) [*al-ṭawāf*] during the year in which disaster struck him, with myself, from among his children, accompanying him. He began to grip the coverings of the Kaʿbah and repeatedly to utter supplications, saying, "O God, my sins are numerous and momentous; only You can number them and only You can know them. O God, if You punish me, then make my punishment in this present world, even if that punishment involves my senses of hearing and sight, my

---

719. Cf. Sourdel, *Vizirat*, I, 157. Various of the sources stress al-Rashīd's suspiciousness and vacillations.

wealth and children, until You are fully satisfied, and do not make my punishment one in the next world!"

He related: Aḥmad b. al-Ḥasan b. Ḥarb transmitted the information to me, saying: I saw Yaḥyā at a time when he had stood facing the (Holy) House and had gripped the coverings of the Kaʿbah and
[675] was saying, "O God, if it is Your good pleasure to deprive me of Your goodness vouchsafed to me, then deprive me! O God, if it is Your good pleasure to deprive me of my family and children, then deprive me, O God, but leave me al-Faḍl!" He related: Then he turned round in order to go on his way. When he drew near to the door of the mosque, he wheeled round rapidly and repeated his previous actions and began to say, "O God, it is unseemly for the like of myself to make supplication to You and then ask You to make an exception. O God, (take) al-Faḍl (also)!"[720]

He related: When they returned from the Pilgrimage, they encamped at al-Anbār, whilst al-Rashīd halted at al-ʿUmr,[721] accompanied by the two heirs to the throne, al-Amīn and al-Maʾmūn. Al-Faḍl lodged with al-Amīn, whilst Jaʿfar lodged with al-Maʾmūn; Yaḥyā was in the same dwelling as his secretary Khālid b. ʿĪsā;[722] Muḥammad b. Yaḥyā was in the same dwelling as Ibn Nūḥ, the head of the state embroidery workshops [*al-ṭirāz*]; whilst Muḥammad b. Khālid was with al-Maʾmūn at al-ʿUmr with al-Rashīd.[723]

He related: Al-Rashīd spent the nights in the sole company of al-Faḍl, then he bestowed robes of honor on him, gave him a jewelled collar and commanded him to set off homeward with Muḥammad al-Amīn. He sent for Mūsā b. Yaḥyā, and then displayed his favor to him. Previously, on the outward journey, at al-Ḥīrah, he had displayed anger at Mūsā because ʿAlī b. ʿĪsā b. Māhān had made him an object of suspicion in al-Rashīd's eyes in connection with the affairs of Khurāsān and had told the Caliph about the people of

720. Ibn al-Athīr, loc. cit.; Palmer, 101–2.

721. The site of a monastery, the Dayr ʿUmr Mar Yūnān, on the banks of the Euphrates, described by Shābushtī, 258–64, as extensive, with many monks, well-fortified like a castle and much-celebrated in verse as a pleasure haunt.

722. According to Yaʿqūbī, *Taʾrīkh*, II, 511, Yaḥyā lodged in the monastery of al-ʿUmr and was there shown, by one of the priests, a poetic inscription set up by the founder; when he read this, Yaḥyā derived from it an omen of impending doom, and found that the priest had disappeared into thin air.

723. Yaʿqūbī, *Taʾrīkh*, loc. cit.; Masʿūdī, *Murūj*, VI, 394 = ed. Pellat, § 2596; *K. al-ʿUyūn*, 305.

Khurāsān's sincere obedience to Mūsā and their love for him, and that he was in correspondence with him and making plans for slipping away to them and for mounting an attack on him (i.e., the Caliph) in collusion with them. All that made a profound impression on al-Rashīd's mind to Mūsā's detriment, and made the Caliph apprehensive of him. Mūsā was one of the great and courageous heroic leaders, so when ʿAlī b. ʿĪsā spread these calumnies about him, they found an immediate response in al-Rashīd and just a small part of them had an effect on him.[724]

At that point, Mūsā became liable for a debt and he concealed himself from his creditors. As a result of this, al-Rashīd imagined that he had gone to Khurāsān, as had been related to him. Hence, when al-Rashīd came to al-Ḥīrah on this Pilgrimage, Mūsā met him from Baghdad. Al-Rashīd then imprisoned him in the custody of al-ʿAbbās b. Mūsā at al-Kūfah. This was the first impairment of [676] their position which the Barmakīs suffered. Al-Faḍl b. Yaḥyā's mother rode forth to intervene in Mūsā's plight; al-Rashīd used never to refuse her anything. Al-Rashīd therefore said, "His father must stand guarantor for him, since accusatory reports about him have reached me." Yaḥyā accordingly stood as guarantor for him, and al-Rashīd handed Mūsā over to him. Then al-Rashīd showed his favor towards Mūsā and bestowed on him robes of honor. Before this, al-Rashīd had become angry and reproachful at al-Faḍl b. Yaḥyā, and had found al-Faḍl's company uncongenial because al-Faḍl had given up drinking wine with him. Al-Faḍl used to say, "Even if I knew that water was detrimental to my manly honor [*muruwwatī*], I wouldn't drink it (i.e., wine)."[725] He was, however, passionately devoted to listening to music and singing [*al-samāʿ*]. He related: Jaʿfar used to take part in al-Rashīd's convivial sessions as a boon-companion, to the point that his father forbade him to participate further and ordered him to cease from familiar contacts with the Caliph; but Jaʿfar would brush aside his father's com-

724. Ibn al-Athīr, VI, 177.

725. Jahshiyārī, 150. This last author also notes, 167, that the ʿAbbāsid prince ʿAbd al-Malik b. Ṣāliḥ, whom al-Rashīd was later to imprison (Ṭabarī, III, 688–94, below, 230–38), was likewise generally refused admission to the circle of the Caliph's boon-companions because of his refusal to drink *nabīdh*, as did the Caliph; cf. A. S. Tritton, *The Caliphs and their non-Muslim subjects*, 193–4.

mand and would enthusiastically join the Caliph in whatever the latter invited him to.

It has been mentioned from Saʿīd b. Huraym that, when he was unable to exert any further efforts to dissuade Jaʿfar, Yaḥyā wrote to him, "I have only let you go on in your own way so that the passage of time might bring you into a difficult position which might make you realize what you are involved in, even though I strongly fear that this difficult position might be a far from trifling one." He related: Yaḥyā had already addressed these words to al-Rashīd, "O Commander of the Faithful, I disapprove, by God, of Jaʿfar's mingling intimately with you and your affairs, and I am not sure that the outcome of all this may not rebound on me through your agency. If only you would let someone else have a turn instead of him[726] and would restrict him to devoting himself to the important administrative tasks for you which he is undertaking, that would be much more in accordance with my own desires and make you feel more confident regarding me."[727] Al-Rashīd replied, "O my father, this is not your real reason; in reality, you merely wish to manoeuvre al-Faḍl into a superior position over Jaʿfar."[728]

The Alleged Misconduct between Jaʿfar and the Caliph's Sister ʿAbbāsah

Aḥmad b. Zuhayr—I think from his paternal uncle Zāhir b. Ḥarb[729]—transmitted the information to me that the reason behind the destruction of Jaʿfar and the Barmakīs was that al-Rashīd could not bear to be away from the company of Jaʿfar and of his own sister ʿAbbāsah bt. al-Mahdī.[730] He used to invite them both to be present when he had one of his drinking sessions, this being

726. Following the Leiden text's *fa-law aʿqabtahu*; the Cairo text, VIII, 293, has *fa-law aʿfaytahu* "if only you would dismiss him."

727. Jahshiyārī, 178: "would make me feel more confident over his safety."

728. Ibid.

729. These two were possibly kinsmen of the *rāwī* Aḥmad b. al-Ḥasan b. Ḥarb mentioned by Ṭabarī, III, 674 (above, 212).

730. Half-sister of al-Rashīd, being the daughter of al-Mahdī by a slave girl Raḥīm, and already three times married and widowed; she must accordingly have been middle-aged, rather than "in the vigor of youth," as Ṭabarī says, at the time of this alleged liaison with Jaʿfar. According to the Qāḍī Ibn al-Zubayr, 235, § 342, she died in 182 (798) and left behind a large fortune. See Abbott, 21, 156; *EI*[2] s.v. (J. Horovitz).

after he had told Jaʿfar how little able he was to endure Jaʿfar's and ʿAbbāsah's absence from him. He said to Jaʿfar, "I will give her to you in marriage so that it will be licit for you to look on her when I [677] invite her to my court sessions," and he ordered him not to touch her (i.e., sexually) or do anything at all of what a man usually does with his wife. So al-Rashīd gave her to him in marriage on these conditions. He used to invite them both to his circle when he held a drinking session, then he would get up from the circle and leave the two of them together. They would then become intoxicated with the wine, and both of them being in the vigor of youth, Jaʿfar would make for her and copulate with her. Subsequently, she became pregnant by him and gave birth to a boy. She was afraid of her own safety from al-Rashīd, if he should get to know about that, so she sent the newly born child, accompanied by nurses for him from among her own slaves, to Mecca. The matter remained concealed from Hārūn until some bad blood arose between ʿAbbāsah and a certain slave girl of hers, and this latter thereupon communicated the story of her affair and the matter of the child to al-Rashīd, informing him at the same time of the child's whereabouts, of the slave girls of ʿAbbāsah who were looking after him, and of the ornaments with which his mother had adorned him. So when Hārūn performed this particular Pilgrimage, he sent to the place where the slave girl had told him the child was someone who would bring back to him the child and the nurses looking after him. When they were brought before him, he questioned the women who were caring for the child, and they told him substantially the same story which ʿAbbāsah's delator had told him. It is alleged that he wanted to kill the child but then restrained himself from that.[731]

Now whenever al-Rashīd made the Pilgrimage, Jaʿfar used to

731. Ṭabarī-Balʿamī, tr. IV, 464–6; Masʿūdī, *Murūj*, VI, 387–94 = ed. Pellat, §§ 2588–90; *K. al-ʿUyūn*, 307–8; Ibn al-Athīr, VI, 175; Ibn Khallikān, I, 332–8, tr. I, 306–8; Palmer, 83–5, 91–2, 98–9; Bouvat, 113–19; Abbott, 156–7, 196–7. This alleged reason for al-Rashīd's anger against Jaʿfar, which so caught the imagination of later chroniclers, does not appear in such early sources as Jahshiyārī and Yaʿqūbī. Ibn Khaldūn, tr. I, 28–30, rejected its authenticity, and the words of the executioner Masrūr to an enquirer at a later time, in al-Mutawakkil's reign, indicate that "women's tales," *amr al-marʾah*, were already circulating by then around the causes of the Barmakīs' fall (Jahshiyārī, 204; cf. Sourdel, *Vizirat*, I, 158). Of modern writers, Bouvat, 70, 74, and Horovitz, *EI*² s.v. ʿAbbāsa, regard it as legend, as does Sourdel, op. cit., I, 167; only Abbott, loc. cit., gives it credence.

organize a feast for him at ʿUsfān,[732] in order to show him hospitality when he returned from Mecca and set off in the direction of Iraq. When the time came round in this year, Jaʿfar prepared the feast there, as was his wont, and then requested al-Rashīd to visit him (for the feast). But the latter adduced an excuse to him, and did not attend the feast. Jaʿfar (nevertheless) remained with him until he halted at his encampment at al-Anbār, and then there took place the events involving him and his father which I am about to relate, if God Most High wills.

The Killing of Jaʿfar

[678] Al-Faḍl b. Sulaymān b. ʿAlī has mentioned that al-Rashīd performed the Pilgrimage in the year 186 (802), and that he returned homewards from Mecca and reached al-Ḥīrah in al-Muḥarram, 187 (December, 802–January, 803) on his return journey from the Pilgrimage. He stayed for a few days at the palace of ʿAwn al-ʿIbādī[733] and then set out by boat until he stopped at al-ʿUmr in the vicinity of al-Anbār. When it was the night of Saturday, the thirtieth of al-Muḥarram (the night of Friday-Saturday, January 27–8, 803), he sent the eunuch Masrūr,[734] together with Abū ʿIṣmah Ḥammād b. Sālim[735] and a detachment of troops. They encircled Jaʿfar b. Yaḥyā's (lodging) by night, and Masrūr burst in on him. Jaʿfar had with him (Jibrīl) Ibn Bukhtīshūʿ the physician and Abū Zakkār al-Kalwādhānī the blind singer,[736] and was engaged in a convivial session. Masrūr dragged him out roughly and hustled him along until he brought him to the lodging where al-Rashīd

---

732. According to Yāqūt, *Muʿjam,* IV, 121–2, this lay two stages away from Mecca; the modern village of this name is some thirty miles to the north-east of Mecca. See Bakrī, III, 942–3; Al-Wohaibi, 284–9.

733. ʿAwn is mentioned in Masʿūdī, *Murūj,* VI, 305–6 = ed. Pellat, § 2511, as the governor or chief [*ṣāḥib*] of al-Ḥīrah who at one point entertained al-Rashīd in his residence there.

734. Abū Hāshim Masrūr, the eunuch employed by al-Rashīd as confidential agent and executioner, who died in al-Mutawakkil's reign; see Crone, 192–3.

735. Clearly not the Abū ʿIṣmah executed by al-Rashīd on his accession; see Ṭabarī, III, 602 (above, 95).

736. Described also in Masʿūdī, *Murūj,* VI, 395 = ed. Pellat, § 2596, as *ṭunbūrī,* player of the pandore, as well as a singer; his *nisbah* refers to the town of Kalwādhā situated on the Tigris to the southeast of Baghdad. See Yāqūt, *Muʿjam,* IV, 477–8; Le Strange, *Lands,* 32; *EI*[2] s.v. (Ed.).

was. He imprisoned him, bound him up with a rope used for hobbling asses, and informed al-Rashīd that he had arrested Jaʿfar and had brought him back. Al-Rashīd then ordered Jaʿfar to be beheaded, and Masrūr did that.[737]

It is mentioned from ʿAlī b. Abī Saʿīd that Masrūr the eunuch communicated the information to him, saying: Al-Rashīd sent me to bring back to him Jaʿfar b. Yaḥyā when he had decided to kill him. I came to Jaʿfar, and he had with him Abū Zakkār the blind singer, who was at that moment singing the verse

Go not far away, for death will come upon
every brave youth, whether by night or in the morning!

He related: I said to him, "O Abū al-Faḍl, what I have come for is indeed something of that kind (i.e., death); by God, it has come to you by night! Give an account of yourself to the Commander of the Faithful!"[738] He related: He raised his arms and fell at my feet, kissing them, and said, "(Give me some time) until I can go back into my lodging and make my last testament." I replied, "There's no possibility of your going back inside, but make your last dispositions (here and now) with whatever arrangements you wish." So he gave the appropriate orders in his testament for the effecting of his wishes, and freed his slaves. At that point, messengers came to me from the Commander of the Faithful urging me to deal with him speedily. He related: So I took Jaʿfar along with me to his lodging and informed him (about this). The Caliph said to me—being [679]
himself at that moment in his bed—"Bring me his head!" I went back to Jaʿfar and told him that. He exclaimed, "O Abū Hāshim, O God, O God! By God, he wouldn't order you to do that if he were not drunk! Put off killing me till the morning, or else go and consult with him about me a second time!" So I went back to consult al-Rashīd. But when he heard my whispered words of intercession [*ḥissī*], he burst out, "O you who suck your mother's clitoris! Bring me Jaʿfar's head!" So I returned to Jaʿfar and told him. He thereupon said, "Go back to him on my behalf a third time!" I went back to al-

737. Ibn Khallikān, I, 336–7, tr. I, 310.

738. The incident of the verses foreshadowing Jaʿfar's violent death is given in Jahshiyārī, 187; Ṭabarī-Balʿamī, tr. IV, 466–7; Azdī, 304; Iṣfahānī, *Aghānī*, ed. Būlāq, XI, 54–5 = ed. Cairo, XII, 191–2; *K. al-ʿUyūn*, 305; Ibn al-Athīr, VI, 177–8; Ibn Khallikān, I, 345, tr. I, 312; cf. Masʿūdī, *Murūj*, loc. cit.

Rashīd, but he struck me with a staff and exclaimed, "May I be excluded from (the offspring of) al-Mahdī! If you come back to me and don't bring Jaʿfar's head, I shall certainly send to you someone who will first of all bring back to me your head and, secondly, Jaʿfar's!" He related: So I went forth and brought back to him Jaʿfar's head.[739]

He related: That same night, al-Rashīd ordered men to be sent who would seize Yaḥyā b. Khālid and all his children, mawlās, and everyone in any way connected with them; not one of those who were present there escaped. Al-Faḍl b. Yaḥyā was removed by night and then imprisoned in a wing of one of al-Rashīd's residences. Yaḥyā b. Khālid was imprisoned in his own house.[740] He confiscated all the wealth, estates, possessions, and so forth, which they were found to have, [741] and the soldiers did not allow a single person (i.e., of the Barmakīs' households) to go forth to the City of Peace or anywhere else.[742] That same night, he despatched the eunuch Rajāʾ to al-Raqqah with orders to seize their wealth and possessions (there) and to arrest all their slaves, mawlās and retainers. He gave Rajāʾ complete charge in dealing with them. That same night, he sent out letters to all the governors and chief officials in the various regions and administrative divisions of the provinces (ordering them) to seize the Barmakīs' wealth and arrest their agents.[743]

When morning came, he sent Jaʿfar b. Yaḥyā's corpse with Shuʿ-

---

739. Jahshiyārī, 186–7; Ṭabarī-Balʿamī, tr. IV, 467–8; *K. al-ʿUyūn*, 305–6; Ibn al-Athīr, loc. cit.; Palmer, 94–8. Masʿūdī, *Murūj*, VI, 395–8 = ed. Pellat, §§ 2596–9 (also in Ibn Khallikān, I, 338–9, tr. I, 312—13) has a somewhat fanciful version of this story in which the executioner of Jaʿfar is a eunuch called Yāsir al-Rikhlah, who is then himself killed by al-Rashīd. Iṣfahānī, *Aghānī*, loc. cit., gives this account from Masrūr via another *rāwī* and adds that Abū Zakkār expressed a wish to die with his patron and benefactor Jaʿfar but was spared and rewarded by al-Rashīd; cf. Bouvat, 87, 90.

740. Presumably, the residence in the district of the Shammāsiyyah Gate quarter called Suwayqah, granted to Khālid b. Barmak by al-Mahdī, which Yaḥyā had built and which was known as the Qaṣr al-Ṭīn; see Jahshiyārī, 145.

741. The wealth which the various members of the Barmakī family were found to have is enumerated in Qāḍī Ibn al-Zubayr, 224–5, §§ 314–15.

742. Yaʿqūbī, *Taʾrīkh*, II, 510. Jahshiyārī, 188, cf. Sourdel, *Vizirat*, I, 175 n. 2, relates that al-Rashīd had given al-Sindī b. Shāhik (see below) instructions a whole year previously secretly to appoint sequestrators [*wukalāʾ*] of the Barmakīs' palaces and possessions.

743. Jahshiyārī, 186–7.

bah al-Khaftānī, Harthamah b. Aʿyan and Ibrāhīm b. Ḥumayd al-Marwarrūdhī,[744] and he sent after them a number of his slaves and [680] trusty retainers, including the eunuch Masrūr, to Jaʿfar b. Yaḥyā's house; Ibrāhīm b. Ḥumayd and the eunuch Ḥusayn to al-Faḍl b. Yaḥyā's house; Yaḥyā b. ʿAbd al-Raḥmān[745] and Rashīd the eunuch[746] to the house of Yaḥyā and Muḥammad b. Yaḥyā. He sent Harthamah b. Aʿyan with him (i.e., with Rashīd the eunuch) and ordered him to seize all their wealth, and he wrote to al-Sindī b. Shāhik[747] to send Jaʿfar's corpse to the City of Peace, to set up his head on the Middle Bridge and to cut up his body and gibbet each piece of it on the Upper and Lower Bridges.[748] Al-Sindī did that. The eunuchs performed the duties they had been sent to do. A number of the young children of al-Faḍl, Jaʿfar, and Muḥammad were brought to al-Rashīd, and he ordered them to be released. He ordered proclamation to be made regarding all the Barmakīs, that there would be no quarter for anyone sheltering them, apart from Muḥammad b. Khālid, his children, his family, and his retainers, whom he exempted from this order because of the manifestly good advice which Muḥammad had given him and because he recognized that Muḥammad had had no part in what the rest of the Barmakīs had been involved.[749]

Before al-Rashīd set out from al-ʿUmr, he set Yaḥyā free,[750] but over al-Faḍl, Muḥammad and Mūsā the sons of Yaḥyā and over Abū al-Mahdī their relative by marriage he appointed custodians [*ḥafaẓah*], who were responsible to Harthamah b. Aʿyan until he should

---

744. Son of a commander who had fought under Qaḥṭabah in the ʿAbbasid *daʿwah,* and governor of Sīstān for al-Manṣūr; see Crone, 175.

745. On Abū Ṣāliḥ Yaḥyā b. ʿAbd al-Raḥmān, described by Jahshiyārī, 135, as one of Yaḥyā b. Khālid's protégés, shortly after this to be appointed by al-Rashīd to take charge of the property confiscated from the Barmakīs, see Sourdel, *Vizirat,* I, 142–3.

746. The role in all this of eunuchs, often employed for confidential missions, is notable here. It is not, however, known that there was any special enmity existing between the Caliph's body of eunuchs and the Barmakī family.

747. Following the suggested reading of the *Addenda et emendanda,* p. DCCLXII.

748. Jahshiyārī, 186, 188, 190; *K. al-ʿUyūn,* 306; Ibn al-Athīr, VI, 178. For the Tigris bridges, see Le Strange, *Baghdad,* index, s.v. "Bridge," and Lassner, *Topography,* index, s.v. "Jisr."

749. The fanciful account in Ṭabarī-Balʿamī, tr. IV, 468, records a general massacre of all the Barmakīs with the exception of Muḥammad b. Khālid.

750. This release must have been only temporary.

bring them to al-Raqqah. Al-Rashīd ordered the execution of Anas b. Abī Shaykh[751] on the day he reached al-Raqqah, Ibrāhīm b. ʿUthmān b. Nahīk[752] being in charge of his killing; his corpse was then gibbeted. Yaḥyā b. Khālid, together with al-Faḍl and Muḥammad, was then kept in confinement in the Dayr al-Qāʾim,[753] with custodians responsible to Masrūr the eunuch and to Harthamah b. Aʿyan set over them; he made no distinction in treatment between them and a number of their slaves, nor over necessities for them.[754]
[681] He despatched together with them Zubaydah bt. Munīr, al-Faḍl's mother, Yaḥyā's slave girl Danānīr,[755] and a number of their servants (or eunuchs, *khadam*) and slave girls. They were well treated until al-Rashīd grew angry with ʿAbd al-Malik b. Ṣāliḥ; then, on account of his anger, they were all subjected to rough treatment. Al-Rashīd's suspicions against both him and them were reawakened, and as a result, he made their confinement more unpleasant.[756]

---

751. Secretary and favorite of Jaʿfar b. Yaḥyā's, whose corpse was also gibbeted. See Jahshiyārī, 189–91; Ibn Qutaybah, 382; Sourdel, *Vizirat*, I, 154.

752. Ibrāhīm had been left in charge of al-Raqqah during al-Rashīd's Pilgrimage of 186 (802), see Ṭabarī, III, 651 (above, 179).

753. According to Yāqūt, *Muʿjam*, II, 526, the Dayr al-Qāʾim al-Aqṣā lay on the road from al-Raqqah towards Baghdad, on the banks of the Euphrates, and was so-called because there was there a lofty watchtower which had marked the Byzantine-Persian frontier; it is not mentioned by Shābushtī.

754. But cf. the words of Jahshiyārī, 191, cited below, n. 756.

755. The celebrated singer Danānīr al-Barmakiyyah, mentioned in several places in Iṣfahānī's *Aghānī*, who had been freed by Yaḥyā, whose arrest she now shared. See Bouvat, 52–4; Farmer, 135; Abbott, 138–40, 198 n. 75.

756. Jahshiyārī, 195 (followed by Bayhaqī, *Maḥāsin*, ed. Schwally, 562–4 = ed. Ibrāhīm, II, 326–8; Masʿūdī, *Murūj*, VI, 405–13 = ed. Pellat, §§ 2609–15; Ibn Khallikān, IV, 33–4, tr. II, 464–5), states that al-Rashīd ill-treated the Barmakīs in an attempt to ferret out all their wealth and ordered Masrūr to flog al-Faḍl with two hundred lashes; cf. Bouvat, 92, and Sourdel, *Vizirat*, loc. cit. When first arrested, the children of Yaḥyā had been well-treated and well-supplied with food and clothing and had not been fettered like the Barmakīs' servants and retainers, according to Jahshiyārī, 191. This same author likewise states, 195–6, that al-Rashīd offered to release Yaḥyā and to allow him to live wherever he wished, but Yaḥyā chose to remain with his family—hence, in jail at al-Rāfiqah—until his death from natural causes in al-Muḥarram, 190 (November–December, 805), aged 64 (Jahshiyārī, 210; *K. al-ʿUyūn*, 308; Ibn Khallikān, IV, 33, VI, 228; tr. II, 464, IV, 112; Sourdel, *Vizirat*, I, 155). Al-Faḍl died from a paralytic stroke in jail at al-Raqqah in al-Muḥarram, 193 (October–November, 808), aged 45 (Jahshiyārī, loc. cit.; *K. al-ʿUyūn*, loc. cit.; Ibn Khallikān, IV, 36, tr. II, 466; Sourdel, *Vizirat*, I, 155–6). Jahshiyārī, 196 ff., gives several anecdotes about the Barmakīs in prison.

Al-Zuhayr b. Bakkār[757] has mentioned that Jaʿfar b. al-Ḥusayn al-Lahbī communicated the information to him that Anas b. Abī Shaykh was brought before al-Rashīd on the morning after the night in which Jaʿfar b. Yaḥyā was killed. Talk was bandied between them, and then al-Rashīd pulled out a sword from beneath the coverings he had been lying on and ordered Anas to be beheaded, at the same time reciting an appropriate verse which had previously been composed concerning Anas's killing,

The sword is eager with desire to taste (the blood of) Anas;
the sword looks on, whilst Fate is waiting (i.e., for his death).

He related: He was executed, and the blood spurted out before the sword had cut through. Al-Rashīd exclaimed, "May God have mercy on ʿAbdallāh b. Muṣʿab!"[758] People commented that the sword had belonged to al-Zubayr b. al-ʿAwwām. Others have mentioned that ʿAbdallāh b. Muṣʿab had acted as an intelligence agent and spy over the people for al-Rashīd, and had denounced Anas to the Caliph as a heretic, for which Anas had killed him. He (i.e., Anas) was one of the Barmakīs' retainers.[759]

Muḥammad b. Isḥāq (al-Hāshimī) has mentioned that Jaʿfar b. Muḥammad b. Ḥakīm al-Kūfī communicated the information to him, saying that al-Sindī b. Shāhik had given him the information, saying: One day, I was sitting, when suddenly at my side there appeared a servant, who had arrived by the *barīd* service, and he handed me a slim letter. I broke open the seal, and lo, it was a letter from al-Rashīd, in his own handwriting, running as follows: "In the name of God, the Merciful, the Compassionate. O Sindī, when you examine this letter of mine, if you happen to be sitting, then arise, and if are already standing, then don't sit down again until you come to me."

Al-Sindī related: I accordingly called for my riding-beasts and got [682]

---

757. Descendant of the Companion of the Prophet al-Zubayr b. al-ʿAwwām mentioned below (see on him, *EI*[1] s.v. [A. J. Wensinck]); al-Zubayr b. Bakkār was a historian and genealogist, nephew of al-Muṣʿab al-Zubayrī (see above, 75, n. 292) and like him author of a *K. Nasab Quraysh,* who died in 256 (870). See *GAL,* I[2], 146–7, SI, 215–6; *GAS,* I, 317–8.

758. The grandfather of the narrator al-Zubayr b. Bakkār, see his *nasab* in Sezgin, loc. cit.

759. See Ṭabarī, III, 680 (above, 220, and n. 751); Bouvat, 86.

on my way. Al-Rashīd was at that moment at al-ʿUmr. Al-ʿAbbās b. al-Faḍl b. al-Rabīʿ (later) told me, "Al-Rashīd sat in his gondola [*zaww*][760] on the Euphrates awaiting you. A cloud of dust became visible, and he said to me, 'O ʿAbbās, that must be al-Sindī and his attendants!' I replied, 'O Commander of the Faithful, it is very likely he!'" He related, "Then you came in sight." Al-Sindī continued the story: I dismounted from my steed and stood there. Al-Rashīd sent a messenger for me, and I therefore went to him. I remained standing before him for a while. He told his servants who were with him to arise and go, which they did, so there only remained al-ʿAbbās b. al-Faḍl and myself. After an interval he said to al-ʿAbbās, "Go forth, and order the seatboards arranged in the boat to be lifted out," and he did that. Then he said to me, "Come near to me," so I drew near to him. He said to me, "You know why I sent the message to you?" I replied, "No, by God, O Commander of the Faithful." He said, "I have sent for you concerning an affair which, if the buttons of my own shirt knew about it, I would throw the shirt into the Euphrates! O Sindī, who is the most trustworthy of my commanders here within my entourage?" I replied, "Harthamah." He said, "You have spoken truly. Who, then, is the most trustworthy of my servants here within my entourage?" I replied, "Masrūr the Elder."[761] He said, "You have spoken truly! Get on your way immediately and ride flat out until you reach the City of Peace. Gather together your trusty retainers and watchmen and order them and their aides to get themselves ready. Then when the groups are ready, go off to the houses of the Barmakīs, station at every one of their gates one of the watchmen appointed to keep public order [*ṣāḥib al-rabʿ*].[762] Order him not to let anyone enter or leave—with the exception of the gate of Muḥammad b. Khālid—until my further orders reach you." He (i.e., Muḥammad b. Isḥāq) related: At this point of time, he had not yet moved against the Barmakīs (literally, "stirred them up," *ḥarraka*). Al-Sindī continued the story: I began to ride off furiously until I reached the City of

760. See *Glossarium*, p. CCLXXX; Kindermann, 36–7; al-Nukhaylī, 58–9. A possible etymology for the term is from Persian *zūd* "swift."

761. As factors in their trustworthiness, Harthamah was the Caliph's mawlā, whilst Masrūr was a black eunuch, totally isolated socially and hence very dependent on his master; see Ayalon, "On the eunuchs in Islam," 69–72.

762. See on this term, *Glossarium*, p. CCLVII.

Peace, and there I gathered my retainers together and did what he had commanded me. He related: Very soon Harthamah b. Aʿyan came up to me, accompanied by (the body of) Jaʿfar b. Yaḥyā on the [683] back of a mule, without a pack-saddle, and with its head severed, and lo, there was the Commander of the Faithful's letter ordering me to chop Jaʿfar's body into halves and gibbet him on three bridges (i.e., with the head for the third bridge).[763] He related: I did what he commanded me.[764]

Muḥammad b. Isḥāq related: Jaʿfar's corpse remained gibbeted until al-Rashīd decided to set out for Khurāsān. I went along and looked at it. When al-Rashīd went to the eastern side (of Baghdad), by the Gate of Khuzaymah b. Khāzim,[765] he sent for al-Walīd b. Jusham[766] al-Shārī (i.e., the Khārijite) from prison, and gave orders to his executioner Aḥmad b. al-Junayd al-Khuttalī, and the latter beheaded al-Walīd. Then al-Rashīd turned to al-Sindī and said, "This"—meaning Jaʿfar's corpse—"must be burnt." When he had gone on his way, al-Sindī gathered together thorny brushwood and firewood for this purpose and burnt the corpse.[767]

Muḥammad b. Isḥāq related: When al-Rashīd executed Jaʿfar b. Yaḥyā, someone said to Yaḥyā b. Khālid, "The Commander of the Faithful has killed your son Jaʿfar." He replied, "His own son will be killed likewise." He related: Someone also said to him, "Your dwellings have become desolate." He replied, "Their houses (i.e., those of the ʿAbbāsids) will become desolate."[768]

(Abū Ḥafṣ) al-Kirmānī has mentioned that Bashshār al-Turkī transmitted the information to him that al-Rashīd set out hunting, whilst he was at al-ʿUmr, on the day at whose close he had Jaʿfar executed. That day happened to be Friday, and Jaʿfar b. Yaḥyā accompanied him, al-Rashīd having insisted on being alone with

763. I.e., the pieces of the corpse were to be exhibited on the Upper, Main, and Lower Bridges across the Tigris.

764. Jahshiyārī, 186, 188, 190; Azdī, 305.

765. The *qaṭīʿah* and palace of Khuzaymah (on whom see Crone, 180) were in the Mukharrim quarter of the East Bank; see Le Strange, *Baghdad*, 218, and Lassner, *Topography*, 171. Possibly the adjacent Bāb al-Ṭāq, at the Mukharrim end of the Main Bridge, is intended.

766. The "al-Walīd b. Ḥ.sh.m" of Yaʿqūbī, *Taʾrīkh*, II, 515, should be read thus.

767. Jahshiyārī, 188; Dīnawarī, 391; Yaʿqūbī, *Taʾrīkh*, II, 514–15; Ṭabarī-Balʿamī, tr. IV, 468; *K. al-ʿUyūn*, 306.

768. Jahshiyārī, 204; Azdī, 306; Ibn al-Athīr, VI, 179.

him, without the presence of the heirs to the throne. He went along with Jaʿfar, having placed his hand on Jaʿfar's shoulder and having, a little while before that, anointed him with precious unguents with his own hand. He remained with Jaʿfar all the time, never leaving his side, until he went back at sunset (or: at the time of the sunset prayer). When he was about to enter his lodging, the Caliph clasped Jaʿfar to himself and told him, "If it were not for the fact that I shall be spending tonight with my womenfolk, I would not part from you. But you yourself, remain in your own house, drink wine too and enjoy entertainment so that you may have as pleasurable a
[684] time as I shall be having." Jaʿfar replied, "No, by God, I only desire to do that in your company." Al-Rashīd told him, "By my life, (I beseech you) to drink."[769] Then he left him for his own residence. For hour after hour, al-Rashīd's envoys kept continuously coming to Jaʿfar with comestibles to accompany the wine [*al-anqāl*],[770] fragrant incense, and aromatic herbs, until the night was spent. Then he sent Masrūr to him. Jaʿfar was held prisoner in the Caliph's residence, and he ordered Jaʿfar's execution. He imprisoned al-Faḍl, Muḥammad and Mūsā, and sent Sallām al-Abrash as guard over Yaḥyā b. Khālid's gateway.[771] He did not, however, harm Muḥammad b. Khālid nor any of his children and retainers.[772]

He related: Al-ʿAbbās b. Bazīʿ communicated the information to me from Sallām, who said: When I went into Yaḥyā's presence at that time, his hangings and furnishings having all been torn open to the public gaze and his belongings piled up together, he said to me, "O Abū Salamah, it will be just like this on the Last Day!" Sallām related: I passed on these words to al-Rashīd after I had returned to him, and he thereupon became silent and downcast, wrapped in thought.[773]

---

769. *lammā sharibta*; on this use of *lammā* = *illā* in oaths and supplications, see above, 112, n. 427.

770. The Cairo text, VIII, 299, has *al-anfāl* "presents," whilst Jahshiyārī, 186, has *al-alṭāf* "presents." For *nuql,* pl. *anqāl,* "hors d'oeuvres," see Rodinson, "Recherches sur les documents arabes relatifs à la cuisine," 133, and Ahsan, 112–13.

771. Cf. Jahshiyārī, 186, 187. Eunuchs were not infrequently employed as guards and jailers; see Ṭabarī, III, 461, where Nuṣayr al-Waṣīf becomes jailer of the ʿAlid al-Ḥasan b. Ibrāhīm b. ʿAbd Allāh.

772. Jahshiyārī, 185–6; Azdī, 305.

773. Jahshiyārī, 187; Azdī, loc. cit.; Ibn al-Athīr, loc. cit.

He related: Ayyūb b. Hārūn b. Sulaymān b. ʿAlī communicated the information to me, saying: I used to have a relationship of ease and trustfulness with Yaḥyā.[774] When they all halted at al-Anbār, I went out to him and spent that evening with him which marked the end of their period of power. He had earlier gone to the Commander of the Faithful in his river craft [*ḥarrāqah*].[775] He entered his presence by the door for the intimates and nobility [*ṣāḥib al-khāṣṣah*] and he spoke with the Caliph about various requests and petitions from the people and other things, including the topics of putting the frontier regions with the Byzantines into a state of order and the mounting of raids by sea, and then he came out. He told the people waiting there, "The Commander of the Faithful has commanded that your requests be granted," and he sent to Abū Ṣāliḥ Yaḥyā b. ʿAbd al-Raḥmān giving him instructions to put those measures into effect. Then he engaged continuously in conversation with us about Abū Muslim and his sending of Muʿādh b. Muslim,[776] until he went into his own lodging after the sunset prayer. At dawn, the news of the killing of Jaʿfar and the fall of the Barmakīs' power reached us. He related: I wrote a letter of consola- [685]
tion to Yaḥyā (on Jaʿfar's death) and he wrote back to me, "I am content with God's decree and recognizant of His choice; God only punishes his servants for their own sins, 'Your Lord does not act unjustly towards (His) servants,'[777] and what God pardons is greater (than what He punishes), so praise be to God!"[778]

He related: Jaʿfar b. Yaḥyā was killed on the night of Saturday (i.e., the night of Friday-Saturday),[779] the first of Ṣafar, 187 (January

774. Doubtful reading, but apparently interpretable as *sakanī*, rather than the *suknayya* of the *Addenda et emendanda*, p. DCCLXII, which would mean "my habitation, dwelling."

775. See Kinderman, 22–3, and al-Nukhaylī, 32–7, who point out that the meaning "fire-ship" (which the term certainly bears in the Crusading, Ayyūbid and Mamlūk periods) is clearly not appropriate here, where a light craft, not one used for war, is intended.

776. Possibly referring to the part of Muʿādh b. Muslim (on whom see Ṭabarī, III, 558, above, 25, n. 102) in the attack of the rebel Ustadhsīs on the Arab garrison of Marw al-Rūdh in 149 (766) (Ṭabarī, III, 354); this was long after Abū Muslim's death; otherwise, the reference seems obscure.

777. Qurʾān, XLI, 46.

778. Jahshiyārī, loc. cit.

779. The exact correspondence of the night the first of Ṣafar would have to be Saturday-Sunday night.

29, 187), when he was thirty-seven years old, their vizierate having lasted seventeen years.[780] Concerning this, al-Raqāshi[781] has said,

O Saturday, O worst of Saturdays in regard to its morning,
and ill-omened Ṣafar, you have never brought a more inauspicious one (or: what you have brought is the most inauspicious possible)![782]
Saturday has come with the momentous occurrence which has shattered our cornerstone,
and in Ṣafar has come the catastrophe in a decisive fashion (literally, "like a blow which has penetrated as a sword does to the bone").

He related: It has been mentioned from Masrūr that he informed al-Rashīd that Jaʿfar had begged him just to see him, but al-Rashīd had said, "No, for he knows that if my eye falls on him, I will not be able to kill him."

Poetry Written on the Fall of the Barmakīs

Al-Raqāshi says concerning the Barmakīs (but it has also been mentioned that this poem is by Abū Nuwās[783]),

We have now come to rest, and our mounts have taken rest,
and the camel which is urged along and the one who used to urge the camels along by his singing have now ceased doing this.[784]
So say to the camels, "You no longer have to travel through the

---

780. Khalīfah, *Taʾrīkh,* II, 734; Jahshiyārī, 186; Ibn al-Athīr, loc. cit.

781. Al-Faḍl. b. ʿAbd al-Ṣamad, *mājin* poet of Baghdad, who died before 207 (822) and whose verses were gathered into a *dīwān* by the Barmakīs; see *GAS,* II, 516.

782. Ṣafar was notoriously regarded in Arabic lore as the most inauspicious month of the year. *Inter alia,* it was held to be the month in which God expelled Adam from the Garden of Eden, whilst for the Shīʿah, various unpleasant events affecting the Imāms al-Ḥasan and al-Ḥusayn took place in it; see Bess A. Donaldson, *The wild rue, a study of Muhammadan magic and folklore in Iran,* 123–5.

783. Abū Nuwās certainly endeavored to secure the patronage of the Barmakīs, but does not seem to have been particularly successful; see Wagner, *Abū Nuwās,* 52–9.

784. Jahshiyārī, 187, and the Cairo text, VIII, 300, have for this second hemistich "and he who lavishes gifts and he who used to seek gifts have been silenced" (i.e., *yujdī* and *yajtadī* here for the Leiden text's *yuḥdā* and *yaḥtadī*).

night
and traverse the deserts, desolate waste after desolate waste."
Say too to Death, "You have laid hold of Jaʿfar,
and you will never after him lay hold of such a great leader!"
Say too to munificence, "After Faḍl, cease completely!" [686]
and say to calamities, "Manifest yourselves anew every day!"
(You see) before you a Barmakī Indian sword,
which has been shattered by a Hāshimite Indian sword![785]

He also speaks about them in a lengthy poem of his,

If perfidious Time betrays us, well, it has
betrayed Jaʿfar and Muḥammad,
To the point that, when daylight gleamed bright, it revealed
the killing of the noblest one who has ever perished and who had not yet been laid in his grave.
Were it not that the gleaming white blades were expressly commanded (to be brought into action),
the cutting edge of one Indian sword would not have been notched by another Indian sword.
O house of Barmak, how many a gift and act of munificence of yours
have there been, as abundant as grains of sand, given ungrudgingly!
It is very true that the Caliph was your brother (through foster-relationship),
but he was not born of Barmakī stock.
You have disputed with him over being suckled together by the noblest of free women
ever created from gems and chrysolite.
(You were) a wielder of power who had a hand ever-flowing with bounty,
which was perpetually wont to be generous with newly acquired things and anciently inherited possessions alike.
It was a hand ever-disposed to bountifulness, until a decree of Fate fettered it,
so that bountifulness was prevented from dispensing largesse.

785. Jahshiyārī, loc. cit.; Masʿūdī, *Murūj*, VI, 402 = ed. Pellat, § 2603; Azdī, 305; *K. al-ʿUyūn*, 308–9; Ibn al-Athīr, VI, 179; Ibn Khallikān, I, 346, tr. I, 314.

[687] Sayf b. Ibrāhīm[786] says concerning them,

The stars of munificent gifts have set, the hand of bountifulness has dried up,
and the seas of liberality have become scanty after the Barmakīs.
Stars of the sons of Barmak have set,
by which the camel driver used to know the direction of the way (i.e., to the Barmakīs' liberality).[787]

Ibn Abī Karīmah[788] has said,

Every borrower who has had high rank lent to him
is, after the noble youth of Barmak, in peril.
A blow from Fate has come down heavily upon him,
the same hand by means of which he himself came down on people!

Abū ʿAbd al-Raḥmān al-ʿAṭawī[789] has said,

By God, were it not for the denunciation of a slanderer
and an eye of the Caliph's which never sleeps,
We would circumambulate the gibbet[790] on which you are nailed and kiss it,
just as the pilgrims kiss the (Black) Stone!
Farewell to the whole world and its inhabitants,
and to the period of power of the Barmakī house![791]

Abū al-ʿAtāhiyah[792] has said concerning the killing of Jaʿfar,

---

786. Unidentified.

787. Masʿūdī, *Murūj*, VI, 403 = ed. Pellat, § 2605, attributes these two verses to Salm al-Khāsir; Azdī, loc. cit., to a "certain poet." Von Grunebaum notes the two lines in this "Three Arabic poets of the early Abbasid age. V. Salm al-Ḫāsir," 72, no. XXXVI = *Shuʿarāʾ ʿAbbāsiyyūn*, 108, no. 36, but states that Ṭabarī's attribution to (the otherwise unknown) Sayf b. Ibrāhīm must be correct, since Salm died before the fall of the Barmakīs (actually in 186 [802]).

788. In his *K. al-Ḥayawān*, II, 367–73, Jāḥiẓ quotes at length an ode by Aḥmad b. Ziyād b. Abī Karīmah on hunting with dogs and with cheetahs.

789. Muḥammad b. ʿAbd al-Raḥmān al-ʿAṭawī was a poet of al-Baṣrah and a Muʿtazilī theologian, who died in 240 (854); see *GAS*, II, 518.

790. I.e., as if making the *ṭawāf* round the Kaʿbah in the Pilgrimage.

791. These two verses are attributed in Iṣfahānī, *Aghānī*, ed. Būlāq, XV, 36 = ed. Cairo, XVI, 249, followed by Ibn Khallikān, I, 346, tr. I, 314, to al-Raqāshī also.

Say, ye twain, to the one who hopes for (enduring) life, is there not
a warning example in Jaʿfar and Yaḥyā?
They were the two ministers of God's Caliph, Hārūn;
do you know who they were? They were his two close friends!
Now, here is Jaʿfar, (secured) by a worn piece of rope,
with his head and the two halves (of his body) up in a high place,
While as for the shaykh Yaḥyā, the minister, he (i.e., the Caliph) has
banished him from his presence and sent him far away.
Their compact position has been scattered into pieces after being solidly united, [688]
and they have wandered off confusedly through the lands.
In this way, God recompenses the person who angers God
by doing what pleases the servant (i.e., pleases himself, to the exclusion of God).
All praise to the One to whom rulers give submission;
I bear witness that there is no God but He!
A happy lot for the one who turns to God after being heedless,
and who repents before death, happy is he![793]

He related: In this year, factional strife raged in Damascus between the partisans of Muḍar and Yaman. Hence, al-Rashīd despatched Muḥammad b. Manṣūr b. Ziyād,[794] and the latter arranged peace between them.[795]

In this year, al-Maṣṣīṣah[796] was struck by an earthquake. Part of its wall collapsed, and the inhabitants' water supply disappeared into the earth for a period during the night.[797]

---

792. Ismāʿīl b. al-Qāsim, together with Bashshār b. Burd and Abū Nuwās the most celebrated poet of the early ʿAbbasid period. See *GAS*, II, 534–5; *EI*² s.v. (A. Guillaume).

793. *Abū al-ʿAtāhiyah, ashʿāruhu wa-akhbāruhu*, ed. Shukrī Fayṣal, 667; Azdī, 305–6.

794. Son of Manṣūr b. Ziyād, Yaḥyā b. Khālid's confidant; see Ṭabarī, III, 613 (above, 116, n. 444).

795. Ibn al-Athīr, VI, 189.

796. Town in Cilicia, the classical Mopsuestia. See Yāqūt, *Muʿjam*, V, 144–5; Le Strange, *Palestine*, 505–7; idem, *Lands*, 130–1; *EI*² s.v. (Honigmann).

797. Ibn al-Athīr, loc. cit.

In this year, ʿAbd al-Salām rebelled at Āmid[798] and proclaimed Khārijite doctrines [*ḥakkama*]. Yaḥyā b. Saʿīd al-ʿUqaylī (subsequently) killed him.[799]

In this year, Yaʿqub b. Dāwūd died at al-Raqqah.[800]

In this year, al-Rashīd sent his son al-Qāsim to lead the summer expedition (against the Byzantines). He devoted him to God's service, made him an offering and means of access to God's favor, and he gave him charge of the frontier fortresses [*al-ʿawāṣim*].[801]

In this year, al-Rashīd became angry with ʿAbd al-Malik b. Ṣāliḥ and imprisoned him.[802]

Al-Rashīd's Anger against ʿAbd al-Malik b. Ṣāliḥ and His Consequent Imprisonment

Aḥmad b. Ibrāhīm b. Ismāʿīl[803] has mentioned that ʿAbd al-Malik b. Ṣāliḥ had a son called ʿAbd al-Raḥmān, who was one of the leading figures among the people of the time and from whom ʿAbd

---

798. The chief town of Diyār Bakr and the modern city of that name, classical Amida. See Yāqūt, *Muʿjam*, I, 56–7; Le Strange, *Lands*, 108–11; Canard, *H'amdânides*, 79–81; *EI*² s.v. Diyār Bakr. iii (Canard and Cahen).

799. Ibn al-Athīr, loc. cit.

800. Chief minister, hence, a proto-vizier, to al-Mahdī, but later imprisoned by him. See Ibn Khallikān, VII, 19–26, tr. IV, 352–9; E. Köcher, "Yaʿqūb b. Dā'ūd," *Mitteilungen des Instituts für Orientforschung*, III (1955), 378–420; Sourdel, *Vizirat*, I, 103–11; Omar, "Some observations on the reign of the Abbasid Caliph al-Mahdī 775–785 A.D.," in *ʿAbbāsiyyāt*, 97–8; *EI*² s.v. Abū ʿAbd Allāh Yaʿḳūb (Moscati).

801. Khalīfah, *Ta'rīkh*, II, 734; Yaʿqūbī, *Ta'rīkh*, II, 522; Brooks, *EHR*, XV (1900), 742. These events are dealt with in more detail by Ṭabarī at III, 694–5 (below, 238–39).

742. These events are dealt with in more detail by Ṭabarī at III, 694–5 (below, 000).

802. On this episode in general, see Jahshiyārī, 211–12; Khalīfah, *Ta'rīkh*, II, 735; Yaʿqūbī, *Ta'rīkh*, II, 513–14; Masʿūdī, *Murūj*, VI, 302–5 = ed. Pellat, §§ 2509–10; *K. al-ʿUyūn*, 328; Ibn al-Athīr, VI, 180–4; Kennedy, 74–5, 118. As Kennedy notes, ʿAbd al-Malik's father Ṣāliḥ had taken over most of the former Umayyad lands in Syria and had built up a powerful position there. ʿAbd al-Malik represented the "Syrian interest" at al-Rashīd's court, which he was later, on that Caliph's death, able to bring over to al-Amīn's side (see Ṭabarī, III, 841 ff.; *K. al-ʿUyūn*, loc. cit.; Ibn al-Athīr, VI, 257–8), and was the supporter of al-Qāsim's claims ultimately to share in his father's inheritance, just as Jaʿfar b. Yaḥyā al-Barmakī was al-Ma'mūn's supporter. Yaʿqūbī, *Ta'rīkh*, II, 513, makes the specific accusation against ʿAbd al-Malik that he was allegedly in treacherous correspondence with the tribal leaders in Syria and al-Jazīrah who were intending to mount an insurrection against the Caliph, but this does not seem to be supported in other sources.

803. See Ṭabarī, III, 597, and above, 85, n. 338.

al-Malik derived his patronymic. This son of his ʿAbd al-Raḥmān had a speech impediment and stuttered over the letter *fāʾ*. In [689] complicity with Qumāmah,[804] he set himself up in hostility to his father, and the two of them denounced him to al-Rashīd and told him that ʿAbd al-Malik was seeking after and avidly aspiring to the caliphate.[805] Hence, al-Rashīd arrested ʿAbd al-Malik and had him imprisoned in the custody of al-Faḍl b. al-Rabīʿ. It has been mentioned that ʿAbd al-Malik b. Ṣāliḥ was brought before al-Rashīd when the latter became angry against him, and al-Rashīd said to him, "(Is this) out of ingratitude for beneficence and (interpretable as) a rejection of outstanding favors and honorable treatment?" He replied, "O Commander of the Faithful, in that case, I would have acknowledged the need for contrition and would have exposed myself to the just necessity of punishment; but all this is nothing but the unjust accusation of an envious one who has contended with me before you over the bonds of affection stemming from kinship and over the appointments to positions of authority. O Commander of the Faithful, you are the successor of the Messenger of God over his community and his faithful trustee of the interests of his own family. The obligation of obedience and the provision of sincere advice to you are incumbent upon them (i.e., the community of subjects); in turn, you have the obligation of meting out justice among them fairly, of patiently investigating the accidents of fate which may come upon them and of forgiving their sinful acts." Al-Rashīd said to him, "Are you calming me

---

804. Yaʿqūbī, *Taʾrīkh,* II, 513, adds to this name ". . . b. Yazīd," but Jahshiyārī, 211–12, 214, has the correct form ". . . b. Abī Yazīd." According to Jahshiyārī, 211–12, Qumāmah was a mawlā of the ʿAbbāsid Sulaymān b. ʿAlī and a noted stylist, whose family had been in the service of the ʿAbbāsids since their residence at al-Ḥumaymah. He now took ʿAbd al-Malik b. Ṣāliḥ's place as secretary and tutor to al-Qāsim b. al-Rashīd; see Jahshiyārī, 214, and Sourdel, *Vizirat,* I, 188 n. 5.

805. The later Persian writer on the Barmakīs, Yazdī (see above, 201, n. 697), states that Jaʿfar b. Yaḥyā had supported pretensions to the caliphate not of ʿAbd al-Malik but of his son ʿAbd al-Raḥmān. There seems to be no evidence whatsoever for this, and as Sourdel suggests, *Vizirat,* I, 168–9, it seems to be an aspect of the evolution of the "Persian" version of the fall of the Barmakīs influenced by Jaʿfar's alleged tenderness to the ʿAlid Yaḥyā b. ʿAbdallāh (see Ṭabarī, III, 669–70, and above, 205, n. 706). That there was deep hostility between ʿAbd al-Malik and his son is shown by the fact that in the Civil War shortly afterwards, ʿAbd al-Raḥmān was in Marw with al-Maʾmūn and became one of his commanders (Ṭabarī, III, 772; Ibn al-Athīr, VI, 223), whilst his father brought Syria behind al-Amīn.

down with your tongue, whilst rising up against me in your heart? This is your secretary Qumāmah, who is giving information about your secret hatred and the evilness of your intentions, so listen to his words!" ʿAbd al-Malik replied, "He has given you something which he has no competence to provide; it may well turn out that he is unable to slander me and revile me over something which he has not in fact known me to commit."

Qumāmah was then summoned. Al-Rashīd said to him, "Speak out fearlessly and without feeling overawed." Qumāmah said, "I assert that he is bent on acting treacherously towards you and on setting himself up in opposition to you." ʿAbd al-Malik said, "Is it really like that, O Qumāmah?" Qumāmah replied, "Yes, you have planned to deceive the Commander of the Faithful." ʿAbd al-Malik said, "How should he not tell lies about me behind my back, when
[690] he slanders me directly to my face?" Al-Rashīd said to him, "This, moreover, is your own son ʿAbd al-Raḥmān who is providing information to me about your disobedience and the evilness of your intentions; if I wanted to adduce against you any argument, I could not find a juster one than (the testimony of) these two persons against you. On what grounds, then, do you reject their accusations against you?" ʿAbd al-Malik b. Ṣāliḥ said, "Either he is acting under someone else's orders or else he is an ingrate towards his parents, driven on by an idée fixe [*ʿāqq majbūr*[806]]. If the first, then he can be excused; but if he is rebellious against his parents, then he is an ungrateful evildoer, whose hostile attitude God, He is magnified and exalted, has mentioned and against whom He has given a warning when he says, 'Among your wives and children, there is an enemy to you, so beware of them.' "[807] He related: Al-Rashīd then arose, at the same time saying, "This affair of yours has now become clear, but I shall not act precipitately until I know what God's good pleasure will be regarding you, for He is the supreme arbiter between you and me." ʿAbd al-Malik replied, "I am satisfied with God as arbiter and with the Commander of the Faithful as judge, for I know that he will prefer the Book of God over his own inclinations and God's command over his own personal satisfaction."[808]

---

806. Alternatively, one might read with ms. C, *majnūn* "mentally deranged."
807. Qur'ān, LXIV, 14.
808. Yaʿqūbī, *Ta'rīkh*, loc. cit.; Palmer, 131–3.

He related: Sometime after that, the Caliph held another court session. ʿAbd al-Malik greeted the Caliph with the *taslīm* when he entered, but the Caliph did not return the salutation. So ʿAbd al-Malik said, "This is not a day for me to indulge in legal pleading or to contend with an adversary or opponent." The Caliph enquired, "Why is that?" He replied, "The opening has not gone according to the *Sunnah*, hence, I am fearful of its latter part." The Caliph said, "How was that?" ʿAbd al-Malik said, "You didn't return my salutation to you; act in the correct way here, just as the mass of people do." The Caliph said "Peace be upon you!" in conformity with the *Sunnah*, choosing the just way and using the accepted practice for a greeting, then he turned towards Sulaymān b. Abī Jaʿfar and recited, addressing himself to ʿAbd al-Malik with his words,

I desire his (long) life, but he desires my being killed . . .
(and so on to the end of the verse).[809]

Then he continued, "Well then, by God, it is as if I were looking at a heavy rainstorm (i.e., extensive bloodshed) which has fallen, whose clouds have shown forth lightning flashes; and it is as if I were in the presence of a threat (of punishment) which has kindled [691] a rapidly spreading fire and has then let fall fingerjoints without wrists and heads without necks. So gently, gently (O Hāshimites[810])! For by God, it is through me that the rough ground has been made smooth for you and the turbid waters have become clear for you, and the power of conducting your own affairs has been given to you. So guard yourselves, guard yourselves, before an overwhelming disaster comes down (upon you), striking the ground with its forefeet, galloping with its hindfeet raised in the air!"

ʿAbd al-Malik retorted, "Fear God, O Commander of the Faithful, in regard to the power which He has entrusted to you and in regard to the subjects whom He has asked you to watch over! Do not set ingratitude in the place of thankfulness, or punishment in the place of reward! I have given you disinterested advice and have

809. The second hemistich of this verse, "(this is) your requiter for your friend from Murād," completes the verse allegedly uttered by ʿAlī b. Abī Ṭālib when he saw his future assassin Ibn Muljam; it is given in Ibn al-Athīr, VI, 182, and Ibn al-Ṭiqṭaqā, 90, tr. 96.

810. This vocative phrase added in Masʿūdī, *Murūj*, VI, 303 = ed. Pellat, § 2509, and Ibn al-Athīr, loc. cit.

vouchsafed to you sincere obedience. I have strengthened the sacred rights of your royal power with what is firmer than the two bastions [*ruknay*] of Yalamlam,[811] and I have left your enemy preoccupied with affairs (i.e., and thus unable to attack you). So I adjure you by God not to sever the bonds of kinship with your family, after you have made them close, through suspiciousness, whose calumny the (Holy) Book has made explicit for me,[812] or through the wrongful accusation of an evilwisher which gnaws the flesh and laps up the blood. By God, I have made smooth for you the rough places, and I have made affairs tractable for you, and I have brought together the hearts in people's breasts into obedience of you. Through how many complete nights have I endured hardships on your behalf, and in how many narrow places have I stood firm for you! (I have endured these trials) just as the member of the tribe of Jaʿfar b. Kilāb has said,[813]

Out of how many a narrow place of battle have I fought a way,
with my hand (literally, "fingertips") and my tongue and fierceness in battle!
[692] If the elephant or its driver were to take up their position,
they would run swiftly from a battle-place like mine and retreat.[814]

He related: Al-Rashīd said to him, "By God, if it were not for sparing the blood of the Hāshimites, I would cut off your head!"[815]

---

811. Yalamlam was a place in the lowlands of Yemen, mentioned several times by Hamdānī, and described by him, 326, as "the meeting-place of the people of the Tihāmah" (i.e., the rendezvous for the Pilgrims). There is clearly here a reference to some popular proverb about hardness and firmness (the editor here, in n. *g*, compares it with Maydānī, *Majmaʿ amthāl al-ʿArab*, tr. Freytag, I, 271), strengthening the idea that Yalamlam was also the name of a hill or rock; cf. Yāqūt, *Muʿjam*, V, 441.

812. I.e., in the Qur'ānic quotation above.

813. I.e., the pre- and early Islamic poet Labīd b. Rabīʿah, as stated specifically in Ibn al-Athīr, VI, 183.

814. *Dīwān*, ed. Brockelmann, text 16, German tr. 29.

815. Jahshiyārī, 211–12; Yaʿqūbī, *Ta'rīkh*, II, 513–14; Masʿūdī, *Murūj*, VI, 303–4 = ed. Pellat, § 2509, giving this story on the authority of Aṣmaʿī, who was present at the court session in question; Ibn al-Athīr, VI, 181–3; Palmer, 133–4. Masʿūdī, *Murūj*, and Ibn al-Athīr, loc. cit., add that ʿAbd al-Malik was then sent back to his prison cell. In the version of this episode in Bayhaqī, *Maḥāsin*, ed. Schwally, 546–7 = ed. Ibrāhīm, II, 302–4, al-Rashīd repents of his suspicions of ʿAbd al-Malik b. Ṣāliḥ.

Zayd b. ʿAlī b. al-Ḥusayn al-ʿAlawī has mentioned, saying: When al-Rashīd imprisoned ʿAbd al-Malik b. Ṣāliḥ, ʿAbdallāh b. Mālik (al-Khuzāʿī), who was at that moment al-Rashīd's commander of the police guard, came into the Caliph's presence and said, "May I have leave to speak?" He replied, "Speak on!" ʿAbdallāh said, "Nay, by the Almighty God, O Commander of the Faithful, I only know ʿAbd al-Malik as a faithful counsellor; why then have you imprisoned him?" He replied, "Woe upon you! Something reached me about him which disquieted me, and I did not trust him not to stir up dissension between these two sons of mine"—he meant al-Amīn and al-Maʾmūn—"but if you have come to the opinion that we should release him from prison, we will set him free." He said, "Since you have thus imprisoned him, O Commander of the Faithful, I don't think it wise to release him in the immediate future; but I do consider that you should keep him in custody in an honorable fashion, as befits someone of your position imprisoning someone of his status." The Caliph replied, "I will certainly do that." He related: Al-Rashīd then summoned al-Faḍl b. al-Rabīʿ and said, "Go to ʿAbd al-Malik b. Ṣāliḥ in his prison cell and ask him, 'Think about what you have need of in your prison cell, and then give orders for it, so that it may be arranged for you.'" ʿAbd al-Malik accordingly mentioned his requests and what he sought.[816]

He related: Al-Rashīd said to ʿAbd al-Malik b. Ṣāliḥ one day, in the course of some conversation he had with him, "You're not descended from Ṣāliḥ!" He enquired, "Who am I descended from, then?" The Caliph said, "From Marwān al-Jaʿdī." He replied, "I don't care which of these two notable warriors is more prominent in my ancestry."[817] Al-Rashīd had him imprisoned in the custody of al-Faḍl b. al-Rabīʿ, and he remained there until al-Rashīd died.

---

816. Ibn al-Athīr, VI, 183.

817. Ibid.; Palmer, 134–5. Jahshiyārī, 212, explains that ʿAbd al-Malik's father, Ṣāliḥ, took over a slave girl from Marwān b. Muḥammad, the last Umayyad Caliph, when the latter was killed in Egypt, and she became ʿAbd al-Malik's mother; but some people said that she was at that time pregnant by Marwān, so that ʿAbd al-Malik's real father was the Umayyad. As well as having the by-name of *al-Ḥimār* "the wild ass," Marwān had the further *laqab* of *al-Jaʿdī* from his mawlā Jaʿd b. Dirham, allegedly a pioneer exponent of the doctrine of the createdness of the Qur'ān; see Watt, *The formative period of Islamic thought*, 242–3, and Madelung, "The origins of the controversy concerning the creation of the Koran," *Orientalia hispanica sive studia F. M. Pareja octogenario dicata*, I/1, 505–6.

Muḥammad (al-Amīn) then released him and appointed him governor of Syria; he used to have his residence at al-Raqqah. He gave Muḥammad a solemn undertaking and covenant, sworn upon God, that if Muḥammad were killed and he himself were still alive, he would never give his obedience to al-Ma'mūn. But in fact, he died
[693] before Muḥammad,[818] and was buried in one of the buildings of the complex of government headquarters [*dār min dūr al-imārah*]. When al-Ma'mūn set out with the intention of raiding the Byzantine lands, he sent an order to one of ʿAbd al-Malik's sons, "Take your father away from my residence!" Hence, his bones were disinterred and transferred (elsewhere). ʿAbd al-Malik had told Muḥammad, "If you are fearful about anything, seek refuge with me, for by God, I will certainly protect you!"[819]

It has been mentioned that one day, al-Rashīd sent to Yaḥyā b. Khālid the following message: "ʿAbd al-Malik b. Ṣāliḥ has planned to rebel and to contest with me my royal authority, and you are fully aware of this. So tell me everything you know about him (or, about the affair), for if you are completely frank with me, I will restore you to your former elevated state." He replied, "O Commander of the Faithful, I have not learned anything of that sort about ʿAbd al-Malik, and if I had learned something (and had not informed you), then I would have become his confederate to the exclusion of my loyalty to you.[820] For your royal authority has been my royal authority and your power my power, and the good and bad elements in it have been my responsibility and attributable to me. How then, can it be possible for ʿAbd al-Malik to have designs on the power with my assistance? Moreover, if I did do that on his behalf, could he do more for me than you yourself have done? I beg you to seek refuge in God from harboring this sort of suspicion about me! It is simply that he is a patient and forbearing man, and it gives me joy that there should be a person like him in your family. You appointed him to office because you admired his conduct (or: his way of thinking, *madhhabihi*), and you showed

---

818. According to Masʿūdī, *Murūj*, VI, 437 = ed. Pellat, § 2644, in 197 (812–13), but according to Ṭabarī, III, 846, and Ibn al-Athīr, VI, 259, in 196 (811–12).

819. Ibn al-Athīr, VI, 183.

820. ʿAbd al-Malik is mentioned as having close relations with Jaʿfar (Jahshiyārī, 167–8), but not with Yaḥyā.

him favor because of his learning and his patience and forbearingness."[821]

He related: When the messenger went back to al-Rashīd with this reply, al-Rashīd sent a further message to him with the threat, "Unless you affirm as being true these intentions of his, I shall kill your son al-Faḍl."[822] He told him, "You have complete authority over us, so do what you will—but with the proviso that if there is anything in this accusation, then the fault is mine, so how can al-Faḍl come into it?" The messenger said to al-Faḍl, "Arise, for I must execute the Commander of the Faithful's orders regarding you." Al-Faḍl was certain that al-Rashīd was about to have him killed. So he bade farewell to his father and said, "Are you displeased with me?" He replied, "On the contrary, I am indeed pleased, and God is pleased with you." Al-Rashīd then kept them apart from each other for three days, but when he was unable to find any substance for his accusations against Yaḥyā, he brought them together again as they had been before.[823]

Meanwhile, there kept coming to them from al-Rashīd messages couched in the harshest possible terms, because the Barmakīs' enemies were carrying slanderous accusations concerning them to al-Rashīd about the affair. When Masrūr took al-Faḍl's hand for the purpose which he had informed him about (i.e., to kill
him), Yaḥyā was carried away by distress, and he blurted out what [694]
was in his mind, telling Masrūr, "Say to the Caliph, 'Your own son will be killed just like al-Faḍl.' " Masrūr related: When al-Rashīd's anger abated, he said, "How did Yaḥyā express himself?" I then repeated the words to him. He commented, "By God, I have become fearful at his words, because Yaḥyā has rarely told me anything without my (ultimately) experiencing its full import."[824]

It has been related that al-Rashīd was once engaged on a journey,

---

821. Jahshiyārī, 212, mentions ʿAbd al-Malik's eloquence, gravity, and high seriousness; his asceticism in refraining from wine-drinking, contrasted with al-Rashīd's bibulousness and hedonism, emerges from the anecdote in ibid., 166–7, and from the fact of al-Rashīd's normal exclusion of ʿAbd al-Malik from the circle of his boon-companions.

822. The Cairo text, VIII, 306, has for this last phrase, "you will bring about the death of your son."

823. Ibn al-Athīr, VI, 183–4; Palmer, 135–6; Bouvat, 97.

824. Jahshiyārī, 204; Palmer, 101.

with ʿAbd al-Malik b. Ṣāliḥ in his travelling retinue, when a hidden voice [*hātif*][825] suddenly cried out to him from the unseen, at a precise moment when he was rising in ʿAbd al-Malik's company, and said, "O Commander of the Faithful, bring low his pride in his noble qualities,[826] tighten the bridle on him and make the bits firm in his mouth, for unless you do these things, he will make his region disaffected against you." Al-Rashīd turned to ʿAbd al-Malik and asked, "What do you say this is, O ʿAbd al-Malik?" The latter replied, "(It is) the speech of a person seeking to injure me and the insinuation of an envious one." Hārūn said to him, "You have spoken truly. These people are of inferior worth, and you have risen above them in eminence; they have remained behind, and you have pressed ahead of them until your outstripping them all has become apparent. Hence, these others have had to renounce the attempt to come up to your level, so that in their breasts are the burning brands of second-rateness and the feelings of uneasiness in their hearts over their own inferiority." ʿAbd al-Malik said, "May God not extinguish them (i.e., their self-torturing feelings) and may He kindle their flames against themselves until they bring them continuous and perpetual grief!"

Al-Rashīd said to ʿAbd al-Malik b. Ṣāliḥ when they had passed by Manbij, where ʿAbd al-Malik's residence and seat of power [*mustaqarr*] was, "Is this your dwelling?" ʿAbd al-Malik replied, "It is yours, O Commander of the Faithful, and then mine through your favor!" Al-Rashīd said, "What is the dwelling like?" He replied, "Not as fine as the edifice of my kinsfolk (i.e., al-Rashīd's own one), but superior to the rest of the dwellings of Manbij." Al-Rashīd said, "What are the nights like at Manbij?" ʿAbd al-Malik replied, "Like permanent dawn!"[827]

Al-Qāsim's Raid into the Byzantine Lands

In this year, al-Qāsim b. al-Rashīd entered the Byzantine lands in the month of Shaʿbān (July–August, 803). He halted before Qur-

825. On the *hātif,* see Fahd, 170–1, and idem, *EI*² s.v.

826. The Cairo text, loc. cit., has *ishrāfihi* "his eagerness, keenness" for the Leiden text's *ashrāfihi.*

827. Balādhurī, 132; Yāqūt, *Muʿjam,* V, 205–6; cf. Kennedy, 75, noting the very extensive Syrian properties acquired by Ṣāliḥ b. ʿAlī. According to Balādhurī, loc. cit., ʿAbd al-Malik b. Ṣāliḥ erected extensive buildings at Manbij when he arrived there as governor in 173 (789–90).

rah[828] and then laid siege to it, and he sent forward al-ʿAbbās b. Jaʿfar b. Muḥammad b. al-Ashʿath, who then halted before the fortress of Sinān,[829] and they made strenuous attacks. The Byzantines sent messages to him offering to hand over 320 Muslim captives if he would depart from them. He agreed to these terms, and fell back from Qurrah and the fortress of Sinān according to the terms of the peace treaty.[830] ʿAlī b. ʿĪsā b. Mūsā[831] died on this [695]
raid into the Byzantine lands whilst accompanying al-Qāsim.[832]

In this year, the Byzantine Emperor broke the peace agreement concluded between his predecessor and the Muslims and withheld the tribute which the preceding monarch had undertaken to pay the Muslims.

The Correspondence between the Byzantine Emperor Nicephorus and al-Rashīd on the Occasion of the Former's Breaking the Peace Agreement, and the Caliph's Punitive Measures against the Byzantines

The reason for the Byzantines' breaking that peace agreement was that there had been a peace agreement in operation between the Muslims and the ruler of Byzantium, their ruler being at that time Irene [*Rīnī*] (we have already mentioned previously the occasion of the peace agreement which existed between her [or, between the Byzantines, *al-Rūm*] and the Muslims). Then the Byzantines turned on Irene and deposed her, and raised to power in her place Nicephorus [*Niqfūr*].[833] The Byzantines mention that this Nice-

828. A fortress of Cappadocia, in the district of the Maṭāmīr (see Ṭabarī, III, 646, above, 165–66, and n. 603), classical Koron, possibly to be identified with the modern Turkish village Küre; see Honigmann, 45, 47.

829. Unidentified, cf. Brooks, *EHR*, XV (1900), 742. n. 139.

830. Khalīfah, *Taʾrīkh*, II, 734; Yaʿqūbī, *Taʾrīkh*, II, 512, 522.

831. Son of the excluded heir to the caliphate after al-Manṣūr, ʿIsā b. Mūsā, and at an earlier date governor of Medina.

832. Ibn al-Athīr, VI, 184; Brooks, *EHR*, XV (1900), 742.

833. *Niqfūr b. Istabrāq* "son of Stauracius," as Masʿūdī, *Murūj*, II, 337 = ed. Pellat, § 757, calls him; in fact, Stauracius was Nicephorus's son, whom Nicephorus made Co-Emperor in 803 and who was briefly his successor in 811. See Masʿūdī, *Murūj*, II, 352 = ed. Pellat, § 770; Vasiliev, I, 271; Anastos, in *Cambridge medieval history*, IV/1, 91, 95–6.

phorus was a descendant of Jafnah of the house of Ghassān[834] and that, before achieving royal power, he had been in charge of the exchequer. Then, five months after the Byzantines had deposed her, Irene died. It has been mentioned that when Nicephorus had achieved royal power and had received the obedience of all the Byzantines, he wrote to al-Rashīd thus:

From Nicephorus, ruler of the Byzantines, to Hārūn, ruler of the Arabs. As follows: The queen who was my predecessor set you up in the position of a rook (i.e., in chess), and herself as merely a pawn, and she paid over to you from her treasuries the amount whose equivalent you should by right have handed over to her; but that (arose from) the weakness and deficient sense of women. Now, when you have perused my letter, send back what you received of the money which she sent, and ransom yourself by (disgorging) what you are receiving by means of exaction; if not, then the sword will inevitably be set between us!

He related: When al-Rashīd read the letter, violent anger took hold of him, so that there was no one who dared to look at him, much less speak to him. His boon-companions dispersed, fearful lest they let slip any further words or actions. The vizier's power of judgement was too paralyzed either for him to offer the Caliph any advice or to leave him to make up his own mind unilaterally. The Caliph then sent for an inkstand and wrote on the back of the letter,

[696] In the name of God, the Merciful, the Compassionate, from Hārūn the Commander of the Faithful to Nicephorus the dog of the Byzantines: O son of an infidel woman, I have read your letter, and the reply is what you will see, without you having to hear it. Farewell![835]

Then he set off immediately and travelled on until he halted before the gates of Heraclia,[836] and then captured it; he took plunder, he selected the best items for himself, he slaughtered

834. Jafnah b. ʿAmr b. Muzayqiyā' being regarded as the founder in pre-Islamic times of the royal house of the Ghassānid Arab chiefs in southern Syria. See Ḥamzah al-Iṣfahānī, 99; Nöldeke, "Die ghassânidischen Fürsten aus dem Hause Gafna's," *AKAk. Berlin* (1887), Abt. II, 5–6.

835. Iṣfahānī, *Aghānī*, ed. Būlāq, XVII, 44 = ed. Cairo, XVIII, 239; Masʿūdī, *Murūj*, II, 337 = ed. Pellat, § 757; *K. al-ʿUyūn*, 309–10; Ibn al-Athīr, VI, 184–5; Palmer, 75–6; Brooks, *EHR*, XV (1900), 742–3.

836. Arabic Hiraqlah, a fortress on the frontier between the Arabs and the Byzan-

people, he destroyed, he burnt and he extirpated. Hence, Nicephorus sought to make peace, on the basis of an annual tribute, and al-Rashīd agreed to this. When he returned from this expedition of his, and reached al-Raqqah, Nicephorus broke the agreement and went back on the covenant. The weather was extremely cold; hence Nicephorus was confident that al-Rashīd would be unable to march back against him. The news arrived of Nicephorus's reneging on his undertaking, but no one was disposed to inform al-Rashīd about this out of solicitude for his feelings and for themselves (at the thought of) returning at a time like that. So a subterfuge was employed to let him know, through the agency of a poet from the people of Juddah[837] called Abū Muḥammad ʿAbdallāh b. Yūsuf, or, it is said, called al-Ḥajjāj b. Yūsuf al-Taymī.[838] He recited,

Nicephorus has broken the agreement which he gave to you
and the strokes of destruction are already hovering round him.
Convey glad tidings to the Commander of the Faithful, for it is indeed
an occasion for great plunder which God has brought you!
The people have announced to each other with joy that
an envoy and messenger has arrived with (the news of) the breaking of the agreement,
And they have become hopeful that your right hand will speedily launch an expedition
which will reanimate souls and whose place of battle (or, whose lofty fame) will be long remembered.
He paid over to you his stipulated tribute and lowered his cheek
(i.e., was humble and submissive)

---

tines in southwestern Anatolia, the modern Eregli. See Yāqūt, *Muʿjam,* V, 398–9; Le Strange, *Lands,* 149; *EI*² s.v. Ereğli (J. H. Mordtmann-F. Taeschner).

837. Text *J.n.dah,* but the reading of the *Addenda et emendanda,* p. DCCLXII, is followed here in the light of Iṣfahānī, *Aghānī,* ed. Būlāq, XVII, 45, 47 = ed. Cairo, XVIII, 240, 244, which has *Juddah* and the information that Abū Muḥammad was a poet of Mecca who used to live at Juddah on the Red Sea coast. Jandah indeed exists as a place in the Sawād of Iraq between al-Nīl and al-Nuʿmāniyyah; see Yāqūt, *Muʿjam,* II, 170. Ibn al-Athīr, VI, 185, has *min ahl jundihi* "from among his troops."

838. Also thus in Ibn al-Athīr, loc. cit.; but the editor of the Leiden text, n. *d,* conjectures, in the light of the section in Iṣfahānī, *Aghānī,* ed. Būlāq, XVIII, 115–25 = ed. Cairo, XX, 44–60, that the correct form should be Abū Muḥammad ʿAbdallāh b. Ayyūb al-Taymī, a poet subsequently known as the eulogist of al-Amīn and al-Maʾmūn; see Ziriklī, *Aʿlām,* IV, 199.

out of caution against the sharp-edged swords,[839] for death is a thing feared,
So you gave him protection against their onslaught, and it was as if they were in our hands firebrands of a conflagration flying upwards!
[697] And you sent back, with your power, the armies, returning homewards
from him, for the person to whom you grant protection is secure and happy.
O Nicephorus, when you act treacherously because the Imām
has become absent, you are foolish and deluded!
At the time when you played the traitor, did you imagine that you would escape?
May your mother lose you, her son! What you imagined is pure delusion.
Your destruction has hurled you into the swollen waters of its sea,
and swiftly running horses have hastened against you from the Imām.
Certainly, the Imām has the superior force to constrain you,
whether your lands be near at hand or far away.
Even though we may be heedless, the Imām is not neglectful
of what he rules over and directs with his firm management.
A ruler who has devoted himself whole-heartedly to the holy war,
hence his enemies are always destined to be overcome by him.
O you who desire God's approbation through your efforts,
the secrets of men's hearts are never hidden from God!
No counsel is ever of use from a person who gives false advice to his Imām,
but counsel from sincere advisers to him always merits thanks.
Good counsel to the Imām is an obligation on mankind,
and for those fulfilling this obligation, a means of expiation and an act of cleansing.[840]

---

839. Following the vocalization of the Cairo text, VIII, 308, *ḥadhara al-ṣawārimi.*

840. Iṣfahānī, *Aghānī,* ed. Būlāq, XVII, 45 = ed. Cairo, XVIII, 241–2, and Masʿūdī, *Murūj,* II, 338–40 = ed. Pellat, § 759, give extended texts of the poem, whilst *K. al-ʿUyūn,* 310, and Ibn al-Athīr, VI, 186, have odd verses of it.

Abū al-ʿAtāhiyah Ismāʿīl b. al-Qāsim says concerning this expedition,

O Imām of right guidance, you have become completely concerned with religion,
and you have supplied every person asking for rain with plentiful moisture (i.e., have supplied every seeker after bounty with munificence).
You have two names, derived from right direction and divine guidance,
for you are the one who is called "rightly directed" [*rashīd*] and "divinely guided" [*mahdī*].[841]
Whenever you become angered at something, it becomes an object exciting the ire of all;
but if you are pleased with something, it becomes an object of general approbation.
For our benefit, you have extended the hand of noble acts over East and West,
and you have thereby enriched both the dweller in the East and the dweller in the West.
You have embellished the face of the earth with munificence and liberality,
so that the face of the earth has become adorned through copious rain (i.e., with gifts and presents).
God has decreed that Hārūn's royal power has become clear and bright, [698]
and God's decree is something which is always accomplished among His creation.
The whole earth has flowed with compliance to Hārūn,
and Nicephorus has accordingly become bound in a relationship of submission and inferiority [*dhimmiyyā*] to Hārūn.[842]

Al-Taymī also said,

The cords of death attached themselves to Nicephorus, mockingly,

841. I.e., from his name ". . . b. al-Mahdī."

842. *Abū al-ʿAtāhiyah, ashʿāruhu wa-akhbāruhu*, 674–5, no. 296; Masʿūdī, *Murūj*, II, 337–8 = ed. Pellat, § 758; Iṣfahānī, *Aghānī*, ed. Būlāq, XVII, 45 = ed. Cairo, XVIII, 240.

when they saw that he had trifled unconcernedly with the lion's covert.
For he who visits the lion's covert will inevitably experience fear,
even if he escapes its fangs and its deep-piercing claw.
He behaved falsely over his covenants, and whoever breaks these
has split up and dissolved his own self and not his enemies.
The Imām, whose acts of munificence are hoped for,
has made him taste the fruits of the strength of purpose which he (i.e., the Imām) inherited,
And he has gone back on his state of friendliness (i.e., with Nicephorus) after his wives became bent down
and enfeebled, weeping over him with dishevelled hair.

When he had finished declaiming this, al-Rashīd exclaimed, "Has Nicephorus done this, then?" and he realized that his ministers had used a stratagem with him over that. He turned round in a state of great heaviness of heart and strong feeling of troubledness, until he halted before his (i.e., Nicephorus's) territory (literally, "his courtyard," *finā'ihi*), and did not depart until he was satisfied and had achieved his aim.[843] Abū al-ʿAtāhiyah has said,

Has not Heraclia announced publicly its own destruction,
at the hands of a monarch who is divinely favored with the correct mode of action?
Hārūn thunders with threats of approaching death,
and hurls lightning with trenchant deeds of violence.
[699] How many banners, in which victory is always inherent,
pass along (through the air) like wisps of cloud!
O Commander of the Faithful, you have gained the victory, so feel secure,
and rejoice at the booty gained and the prospect of returning home![844]

---

843. Masʿūdī, *Murūj*, II, 337–52 = ed. Pellat, §§ 757–69; Iṣfahānī, *Aghānī*, ed. Būlāq, XVII, 44–8 = ed. Cairo, XVIII, 239–46; *K. al-ʿUyūn*, 309–10; Ibn al-Athīr, VI, 185–6; Palmer, 76–8; Brooks, *EHR*, XV (1900), 743–4; Canard, in *Cambridge medieval history*, IV/1, 707.

844. *Abū al-ʿAtāhiyah, ashʿāruhu wa-akhbāruhu*, 491–3; Masʿūdī, *Murūj*, II, 350–1 = ed. Pellat, § 768, and Iṣfahānī, *Aghānī*, ed. Būlāq, XVII, 46 = ed. Cairo, XVIII, 242, both adding further poetry on this occasion of al-Rashīd's Heraclia campaign.

In this year, according to what al-Wāqidī says, Ibrāhīm b. ʿUthmān b. Nahīk was killed; but as for the other authorities, they place it in the year 188 (803–4).[845]

Al-Rashīd's Killing of Ibrāhīm b. ʿUthmān b. Nahīk

It has been mentioned from Ṣāliḥ al-Aʿmā, who lived in proximity to Ibrāhīm b. ʿUthmān, that he said: Ibrāhīm b. ʿUthmān used often to mention Jaʿfar b. Yaḥyā and the Barmakīs, and would weep profusely out of grief over them and love for them, to an extent that he passed beyond the stage of weeping for them and arrived at the stage of those who seek vengeance and who nurse inveterate hatred. When he was alone with his slave girls and drank wine, and the *nabīdh* brought him into a state of intoxication, he would say, "O slave, (bring me) my sword Dhū al-Maniyyah"—he had named his sword *Dhū al-Maniyyah* (literally, "bearer of death")—and his slave would then bring him the sword, and he would unsheathe it and then say, "Alas for Jaʿfar! Alas for my master! By God, I will certainly kill your slayer and take vengeance for your blood in the near future!" When these actions of his had been repeated several times, Ibrāhīm's son ʿUthmān went to al-Faḍl b. al-Rabīʿ and informed him about Ibrāhīm's words. Al-Faḍl went in and told al-Rashīd. The latter said, "Bring him (i.e., ʿUthmān) in!" So ʿUthmān came in, and al-Rashīd said, "What's this al-Faḍl has related from you?" So ʿUthmān informed him about what his father had said and done. Al-Rashīd said to him, "Did anyone else who was with you hear these words?" He replied, "Yes, his eunuch Nawāl." So he secretly summoned Ibrāhīm's slave and interrogated him. The latter replied, "He has said that more than once, indeed, more than twice." Al-Rashīd said, "It would not be lawful for me to kill one of my own retainers on the word of a youth and a eunuch; the two of them may have conspired together to say this because of the son's eagerness to gain his father's privileged rank and status (i.e., in the Caliph's confidence) and because of the slave's hostility engendered by lengthy contact and service (i.e., from disillusion-

845. Khalīfah, *Taʾrīkh,* II, 734, Yaʿqūbī, *Taʾrīkh,* II, 522–3, and Ibn al-Athīr, 186–7, all place this event in the year 187 (803).

ment or weariness with his master)";[846] hence, he dropped the matter for a few days.

Then he decided to put Ibrāhīm b. ʿUthmān to the trial by means of a test which would dispel the doubt from his heart and the suspicious thoughts from his mind. Hence, he summoned al-Faḍl
[700] b. al-Rabīʿ and said, "I intend to put Ibrāhīm b. ʿUthmān to the test regarding the accusation which his son has brought against him. So when the spread of food is removed, call for wine and tell him, 'Respond to the Commander of the Faithful's invitation, for he wants you as his companion because of the elevated position which you enjoy with him.' Then when he drinks wine, slip away, and leave me and him alone together." Al-Faḍl b. al-Rabīʿ did that; Ibrāhīm sat down to drink wine, and then sprang up when al-Faḍl b. al-Rabīʿ got up to go, but al-Rashīd told him, "Stay in your place, O Ibrāhīm!" so he sat down again.

Now when Ibrāhīm's mind became set at rest, al-Rashīd made a sign to his slaves, and they withdrew from his presence. Al-Rashīd then said, "O Ibrāhīm, how are you, and what are your innermost thoughts?" He replied, "O my master, I am merely like the most devoted of your slaves and the most dutiful of your servants." Al-Rashīd said, "There is a matter within my mind which I would like to entrust to your keeping; my breast has become straitened because of it and I have been kept awake by it at night." Ibrāhīm replied, "O my master, in that case, it will never go back to you again from me (i.e., I will never refer to it again), and I will conceal it from my own person lest it let it out, and from my inner self lest it divulge it abroad." Al-Rashīd said, "Good for you! I have repented violently of my killing Jaʿfar b. Yaḥyā to an extent that I cannot easily describe. I would like to abandon my royal power, and I wish he were still alive with me, for I have never experienced the savor of sleep since I parted from him nor the sweetness of life since I killed him." He related: When Ibrāhīm heard this, he shed profuse tears and wept copiously and said, "May God have mercy on Abū al-Faḍl (i.e., Jaʿfar) and forgive his offences! By God, you erred, O my master, in killing him, and you were led into a dubious affair regarding him! Where in the whole world is his like to be found? He was the nonpareil among the entire people in regard to

846. Cf. on such motives, Ayalon, "On the eunuchs in Islam," 80.

piety!" But al-Rashīd thereupon said, "Arise now, may God's curse be upon you, O son of a stinking, uncircumcised whore!" He arose, hardly conscious where he was treading.

Then he went off to his mother and said to her, "O mother, by [701] God, I have as good as lost my life!" She replied, "Surely not, if God wills; how is that, my dear son?" He said, "The reason for that is that al-Rashīd put me to a test; by God, if I had a thousand lives, I would not escape with one of them!" And indeed, only a few nights passed between this event and his son's coming to him and hacking him with his sword until he died.[847]

In this year, ʿUbaydallāh b. al-ʿAbbās b. Muḥammad b. ʿAlī led the Pilgrimage.[848]

---

847. Khalīfah, *Ta'rīkh*, II, 734; Yaʿqūbī, *Ta'rīkh*, II, 522–3; Ibn al-Athīr, VI, 186–7; Palmer, 105–6; Bouvat, 96. There is a garbled reference to this episode in Bayhaqī, *Maḥāsin*, ed. Schwally, 592 = ed. Ibrāhīm, II, 367.

848. Khalīfah, *Ta'rīkh*, loc. cit.; Yaʿqūbī, *Ta'rīkh*, II, 522; Ibn al-Athīr, VI, 189; but according to Muḥammad b. Ḥabīb, 38, al-Rashīd himself led the Pilgrimage this year.

The Events of the Year 188

(December 20, 803–December 7, 804)

Among the events taking place during this year was Ibrāhīm b. Jibrīl's leading the summer expedition and his invading the Byzantine lands by the pass [*darb*] of al-Ṣafṣāf. Nicephorus marched out to confront him, but some event took place at his rear which deflected him from encountering Ibrāhīm. Hence, he turned back, but came into contact with a Muslim force; he suffered three wounds personally and was put to flight. According to what has been mentioned, 40,700 of the Byzantine troops were killed and 4,000 riding beasts captured.[849]

In this year, al-Qāsim b. al-Rashīd stationed himself ready for frontier warfare [*rābaṭa*][850] at Dābiq.[851]

In this year, al-Rashīd led the Pilgrimage. He made his way there

---

849. Khalīfah, *Ta'rīkh*, II, 735.

850. See for this term, Balādhurī, *Glossarium*, 42.

851. Brooks, *EHR*, XV (1900), 744. According to Dīnawarī, 391, al-Qāsim was made governor of Syria in this year. On Dābiq, situated to the north of Aleppo and famed as a concentration point for *ghāzīs* and troops marching against the Greeks, see Yāqūt, *Muʿjam*, II, 416–17; Le Strange, *Palestine*, 426, 503; Canard, *H'amdânides*, 225; *EI*² s.v. (Sourdel).

(i.e., to Mecca), via Medina, and gave its inhabitants half a full pay allotment [*niṣf al-ʿaṭāʾ*]. This Pilgrimage was the last one undertaken by al-Rashīd, according to what al-Wāqidī and other authorities assert.[852]

852. Muḥammad b. Ḥabīb, 38; Khalīfah, *Taʾrīkh*, loc. cit.; Yaʿqūbī, *Taʾrīkh*, loc. cit., adding that this was the last occasion when any Caliph made the Pilgrimage; Dīnawarī, loc. cit., with details of al-Rashīd's return via Qaṣr al-Luṣūṣ to Baghdad and al-Raqqah; Masʿūdī, *Murūj*, VI, 301–2 = ed. Pellat, § 2507. Al-Faḍl b. al-Rabīʿ was in charge of the arrangements for this Pilgrimage, according to Jahshiyārī, 218.

The Events of the Year

189

(December 8, 804–November 26, 805)

Among the events taking place during this year was the Commander of the Faithful Hārūn al-Rashīd's setting off for al-Rayy.[853]

[702] ### *Al-Rashīd's Journeying to al-Rayy in Order to Investigate Complaints against the Governor of Khurāsān, ʿAlī b. ʿĪsā b. Māhān, and His Confirmation of ʿAlī in Office*

It has been mentioned that al-Rashīd had sought Yaḥyā b. Khālid's advice regarding the appointment to the governorship of Khurāsān of ʿAlī b. ʿĪsā b. Māhān, and Yaḥyā had advised him not to do it. But al-Rashīd rejected his advice over this plan of his, and appointed ʿAlī as governor over Khurāsān. When ʿAlī b. ʿĪsā went off to Khurāsān, he tyrannized over its people and treated them harshly. He gathered together an immense sum of money, and out of it sent

853. Yaʿqūbī, *Ta'rīkh,* II, 514; Dīnawarī, loc. cit.; Azdī, 307; Ibn al-Athīr, VI, 191–2.

to Hārūn presents, including horses, slaves, clothing, musk, and wealth, whose like had never been seen before.[854]

Hārūn was seated on an elevated bench [*dukkān murtafiʿ*] at al-Shammāsiyyah[855] when what ʿAlī had sent to him arrived. Those presents were brought in and were spread out before him; they appeared as a splendid sight in his eyes, and he was impressed by their great value. At that precise moment, Yaḥyā b. Khālid was at al-Rashīd's side, and the latter said to him, "O Abū ʿAlī, this is the person whom you advised us not to appoint as governor over this frontier region, but we rejected your advice concerning him and a blessing has come out of opposing your advice! (He was speaking to him, as it were, jestingly at the moment.) You may now see what has been the result of our judgment regarding him, and how little would have resulted from your opinion!"

Yaḥyā replied, "O Commander of the Faithful, may God make me your ransom! Even if I might have liked to have been correct in my judgment, and guided towards what was right in my advice, I much prefer the Commander of the Faithful's judgment to be superior, his foresight more penetrating, his learning greater than my learning, and his intuitive knowledge on a higher level than mine. How excellent this (i.e., the array of ʿAlī b. ʿĪsā's presents) is and how extensive it is, if it were not that there lay behind it what the Commander of the Faithful would abhor and what I pray God to preserve him and keep him safe from its evil consequences and unpleasant results!" Al-Rashīd said, "And what is that?" So Yaḥyā told him, saying, "That is because I believe that these presents cannot have been gathered together for ʿAlī b. ʿĪsā without his having oppressed the leading members of the community [*al-ashrāf*] and without his having taken the greater part of them by tyranny and wrongdoing; and were the Commander of the Faithful [703]
to command me, I could immediately bring to him double the

854. These presents are described in great detail in Abū al-Faḍl Bayhaqī, *Taʾrīkh-i Masʿūdī,* 417. Shaban, 37–8, regards ʿAlī b. ʿĪsā's fiscal policies in Khurāsān as a deliberate attempt to reverse the Barmakīs' advantageous financial treatment of the eastern provinces.

855. The quarter of East Baghdad lying to the northeast of al-Ruṣāfah; see Le Strange, *Baghdad,* 199–216; presumably, the Caliph was at this time in one of the palaces there which had belonged to the Barmakīs; see ibid., 200–1.

amount from a certain merchant (or, from certain merchants) of al-Karkh."[856]

Al-Rashīd said, "How is that?" Yaḥyā replied, "We recently bargained with ʿAwn[857] over a casket which he brought to us full of jewels; we offered him seven million (dirhams) but he refused to sell it. I can now send to him immediately my chamberlain, who will order him to send the casket back to us so that we might examine it afresh; then when he brings it back, we can deny ever having received it, and we will thereby gain seven million (dirhams). Then we can follow the same procedure with two others of the leading merchants. For this will be safer in regard to its consequences and a more discreet procedure than ʿAlī b. ʿĪsā's dealings over these presents with their original owners. Thus, I shall gather together for the Commander of the Faithful, in three hours, more than the value of these presents, with less effort, a simpler procedure and a more suitable way of levying taxation[858] than what ʿAlī has gathered together in three years."[859] This made a profound impression on al-Rashīd's mind; he kept it in his memory and refrained from mentioning ʿAlī b. ʿĪsā in Yaḥyā's presence.

Now when ʿAlī b. ʿĪsā had wrought damage in Khurāsān, persecuted the leading figures there, seized their wealth, and treated the menfolk there with contempt, a group of the prominent men and leaders of Khurāsān wrote to al-Rashīd, and a group from the various regions of Khurāsān wrote to their kinsfolk and friends[860] complaining about ʿAlī's evil conduct, his corrupt way of life, and the viciousness of his behavior, and asking the Commander of the Faithful to change him in the governorship of Khurāsān for any other of his competent officials, aides, supporters of the ʿAbbāsid régime, or military commanders whom he wished. So al-Rashīd summoned Yaḥyā b. Khālid and sought his advice regarding the case of ʿAlī b. ʿĪsā and the matter of his dismissal, saying, "Advise

---

856. The district of Baghdad to the south of the Round City, with an existence of its own (as its name, of Aramaic origin, "fortified town," indicates) in pre-ʿAbbāsid times. See *EI*[2] s.v. (Streck-Lassner).

857. Clearly a well-known merchant and jeweller of Baghdad.

858. Or possibly: "a way of levying taxation which gives a greater yield" (*ajmal jibāyat[in]*).

859. Cf. Ṭabarī-Balʿamī, tr. IV, 470.

860. Presumably, to members of the *Abnāʾ al-Dawlah* now settled in Baghdad who retained their Khurāsānian connections.

me in the choice of a man whom you can approve as governor of that frontier region, who will set right the corruption which this evildoer has wrought and repair the breaches which he has made." Yaḥyā accordingly recommended the appointment of Yazīd b. Mazyad; but al-Rashīd did not accept his advice.[861]

Someone had reported to al-Rashīd that ʿAlī b. ʿĪsā was contemplating rebellion against him. Because of this, al-Rashīd set out for al-Rayy as soon as he had got back from Mecca. He encamped at al-Nahrawān on the seventeenth of Jumādā I (April 21, [704]
805), having with him his two sons ʿAbdallāh al-Maʾmūn and al-Qāsim. Then he journeyed towards al-Rayy. When he reached Qarmāsīn, he had sent to him a group of judges and others, and he made them bear witness that everything belonging to him in that army encampment of his, comprising money, treasuries, weapons, horses, and so forth, was to go to ʿAbdallāh al-Maʾmūn, and he himself was to retain no share in it whatsoever, great or small. He also renewed the oath of allegiance to al-Maʾmūn by those accompanying him. He despatched the commander of his guard, Harthamah b. Aʿyan, to Baghdad, and he had Muḥammad b. Hārūn al-Rashīd and those in his court circle once again give their oath of allegiance to ʿAbdallāh and al-Qāsim; and he laid the responsibility for dealing with al-Qāsim, whether he was to be removed from the succession or confirmed in it, on ʿAbdallāh when the caliphate should pass to him.[862]

Then, when Harthamah had got back to him, al-Rashīd proceeded to al-Rayy. He stayed there about four months, until ʿAlī b. ʿĪsā came to him from Khurāsān bringing wealth, presents, and precious and rare items, comprising furnishings, musk, jewels, gold and silver vessels, weapons, and riding-beasts;[863] and after all that, he gave presents to the whole of those who had accompanied al-Rashīd, including his children, the members of his family, his secretaries, his eunuchs and his military commanders, according to their status at court and their official positions. Al-Rashīd saw,

861. Abū al-Faḍl Bayhaqī, *Taʾrīkh-i Masʿūdī,* 418–20; cf. Ṭabarī-Balʿamī, tr., loc. cit.

862. Yaʿqūbī, *Taʾrīkh,* loc. cit.; Ibn al-Athīr, VI, 191; cf. Gabrieli, "Successione," 349, 353.

863. According to Qāḍī Ibn al-Zubayr, 19, § 25, these amounted to thirty million dīnārs' worth.

from ʿAlī's actions here, the reverse of what he had suspected of him and the opposite of what had been said about him. He therefore showed his approval of ʿAlī and sent him back to Khurāsān. ʿAlī set out, with the Caliph at the same time accompanying him (i.e., on the initial stage of his journey, as a mark of respect and commendation).[864]

It has been mentioned that the oath of allegiance was taken to al-Maʾmūn and to al-Qāsim as successor to the throne after his two brothers Muḥammad and ʿAbdallāh, and al-Qāsim given the honorific of al-Muʾtaman, when Hārūn despatched Harthamah to the City of Peace for that purpose, on Saturday, the eleventh of Rajab of this year (June 13, 805).[865] Concerning this event, al-Ḥasan b. Hāniʾ[866] has written,

May the One who directs affairs through His knowledge be extolled,
and may He make Hārūn superior to all other Caliphs!
[705] We remain in a fortunate state whilst ever we retain the fear of God in our hearts,
and whilst ever the father of trusted ones[867] directs our earthly affairs.[868]

Al-Rashīd Receives the Allegiance of the Local Rulers of the Caspian Provinces and Daylam, and Appoints Various Governors in Western Persia and Eastern Arabia

In this year, when al-Rashīd went to al-Rayy, he sent the eunuch Ḥusayn[869] to Ṭabaristān. He wrote out for him three letters, comprising a letter containing a guarantee of safe-conduct for Sharwīn,[870] the father of Qārin; a second one containing a guarantee of

864. Ibn al-Athīr, loc. cit.; Palmer, 109; Kennedy, 130.
865. Actually a Friday.
866. I.e., Abū Nuwās.
867. *Abū al-umanāʾ*, with paronomasia on the names al-Maʾmūn, al-Amīn and al-Muʾtaman, all derived from the verb *amina* "to be secure, safe."
868. *Dīwān*, I, ed. Wagner, 120.
869. Again, the role of eunuchs as confidential envoys is notable; cf. also Ṭabarī, III, 716, 720–1 (below, 272, 278).
870. Ispahbadh or Prince of the Bāwandid family; see *EI*² s.v. Bāwand (R. N. Frye).

safe-conduct for Windā(d)hurmuz,[871] Māzyār's grandfather; and a third one containing a guarantee of safe-conduct for Marzubān b. Justān,[872] the ruler of Daylam. The latter came to al-Rashīd, and the Caliph gave him presents and robes of honor, and sent him back home.[873] Saʿīd al-Ḥarashī came to him with four hundred stout warriors from Ṭabaristān, who then became converts to Islam at al-Rashīd's hands. Windā(d)hurmuz came forward and accepted the Caliph's guarantee, and undertook in return to give full obedience and to pay tribute, and undertook on Sharwīn's behalf a similar obligation. Al-Rashīd accepted this from him and sent him back home. He sent Harthamah to accompany him, and Harthamah took Windā(d)hurmuz's son and Sharwīn's son as a pledge for good behavior.[874] Khuzaymah b. Khāzim, the governor of Armenia, also came to his court at al-Rayy and offered (to him) numerous presents.

In this year, Hārūn appointed ʿAbdallāh b. Mālik governor of Ṭabaristān, al-Rayy, al-Rūyān, Dunbāwand, Qūmis and Hamadhān.[875] Abū al-ʿAtāhiyah has recited concerning this expedition of Hārūn's (Hārūn had been born at al-Rayy),

Piety has deflected the faithful trustee of God over His creation
towards his own birthplace,
So that he might bring order to al-Rayy and its dependent regions,
and that he might shower down on them beneficence from his
hand.[876]

Whilst en route, Hārūn gave Muḥammad b. al-Junayd charge of the road connecting Hamadhān and al-Rayy. He also appointed [706]

871. Corruptly written in Yaʿqūbī, *Taʾrīkh*, II, 514, as Bundā (perhaps for Bundādh, the New Persian form of Windād) Hurmuz. For this ancient Iranian name, see above, n. 53, and for Windādhurmuz's family, *EI*² s.v. Ḳārinids (M. Rekaya).

872. On this Daylamī family of princes, the Justānids or Jastānids, see Aḥmad Kasrawī, *Shahriyārān-i gumnām*, 22–34; Madelung, in *Cambridge history of Iran*, IV, 208, 223.

873. Azdī, 307.

874. Yaʿqūbī, *Taʾrīkh*, loc. cit.; Ibn al-Faqīh, *Mukhtaṣar Kitāb al-Buldān*, 304; Ibn Isfandiyār, tr. 141–3; Ibn al-Athīr, VI, 191–2.

875. Azdī, 307.

876. Ibn al-Athīr, VI, 193–4. I have not been able to find these verses in the printed edition of the *Dīwān*.

ʿĪsā b. Jaʿfar b. Sulaymān[877] as governor of ʿUmān, and the latter crossed the sea in the vicinity of Jazīrat Ibn Kāwān,[878] capturing one fortress there and besieging another. Ibn Makhlad al-Azdī[879] suddenly attacked him, using deceit and trickery, but ʿĪsā captured him and brought him back to ʿUmān in Dhū al-Ḥijjah (November, 805).

Al-Rashīd's Return to Iraq

A few days after ʿAlī b. ʿĪsā's departure from Khurāsān, al-Rashīd set off from al-Rayy. The time of the Festival of Sacrifice [*al-aḍḥā*] came round when he reached Qaṣr al-Luṣūṣ,[880] so he performed the rites of the Festival there, entering the City of Peace on Monday, the twenty-seventh of Dhū al-Ḥijjah (November 24, 805). When he passed by the bridge, he ordered the corpse of Jaʿfar b. Yaḥyā to be burnt.[881] He passed through Baghdad, but did not stay there and left immediately, heading for al-Raqqah, halting for the night at al-Saylaḥūn.[882]

It has been mentioned from one of al-Rashīd's military commanders that, when he came to Baghdad, al-Rashīd said, "By God, I am passing through a city, and no city more secure or with greater ease of life than it has ever been constructed in East or West. For it is indeed my home, the home of my forefathers and the ʿAbbāsids' center of power whilst ever they endure and keep close control of it. None of my forefathers has ever experienced there any evil or ill-fortune from it, and none of them has ever been injured or wronged there. What an excellent seat of power it is! But I am

---

877. Great-grandson of ʿAlī b. ʿAbdallāh, hence, a second cousin once removed of al-Rashīd.

878. I.e., the island of Qishm adjacent to the Straits of Hurmuz (see *EI*[2] s.v. [J. B. Kelly]), this form of its name apparently being a corruption of the Iranian name Abarkāvān. See Le Strange, *Lands*, 261; Bosworth, in A. J. Cottrell et alii (eds.), *The Persian Gulf states, a general survey*, Baltimore and London 1980, p. xxiii.

879. Presumably, a descendant of the Makhlad b. al-Ḥasan al-Azdī mentioned as being in Khurāsān in 129 (746–7), see Ṭabarī, II, 1767.

880. I.e., the town of Kangawār in Jibāl. See Yāqūt, *Muʿjam*, IV, 363–4; Le Strange, *Lands*, 188–9; *EI*[2] s.v. Kinkiwar (R. M. Savory).

881. See Ṭabarī, III, 683 (above, 223).

882. Yaʿqūbī, *Taʾrīkh*, loc. cit.; Dīnawarī, 391; Ibn al-Athīr, VI, 192. Al-Saylaḥūn was a place near al-Ḥīrah and al-Qādisiyyah, mentioned in the accounts of the Arab conquests of Iran. See Balādhurī, 246, 250; Yāqūt, *Muʿjam*, III, 298–9.

going off now to install myself in a region of people of dissension and hypocrisy, who hate the Imāms of divine guidance and who love the accursed tree, the Umayyads, in addition to the religious deviants, the brigands and those who terrorize the roads there.[883] If it were not for that, I would never leave Baghdad or set foot outside it as long as I lived."[884] Al-Abbās b. Aḥnaf[885] has said concerning al-Rashīd's rapid passage through Baghdad,

We only halted in order to depart, hence were making no
clear distinction between halting and departing.
They asked us how we were when we arrived,
and we then coupled together simultaneously our saying farewell to them with the questioning.[886]

In this year, there took place an exchange of captives between the Muslims and the Byzantines. As a result, according to what has been mentioned, not a single Muslim remained unransomed [707]
in the Byzantine lands.[887] Marwān b. Abī Ḥafṣah has said concerning that,

Through you have been freed captives for whom were built
prisons wherein no kinsman or friend could visit them,
At a time when the Muslims had been unable to secure their release
and had said, "The polytheists' prisons will be their tombs!"[888]

In this year, al-Qāsim stationed himself ready for frontier warfare at Dābiq.[889]

---

883. I.e., in al-Jazīrah and Syria.

884. Al-Rashīd had already, ten years previously, stigmatized the Syrian troops as a crowd of mischief-makers, *jund sū'*; see Ibn ʿAsākir, quoted in Salibi, 37.

885. Amatory poet of Baghdad and favorite of al-Rashīd, who died towards the end of that Caliph's reign. See *GAL*, I², 73, S I, 114; *GAS*, II, 513–14; *EI²* s.v. (R. Blachère).

886. *Dīwān*, ed. ʿĀtikah al-Khazrajī, 231, no. 462 (not in the ed. of Beirut 1385 [1965]); Ibn al-Athīr, loc. cit.

887. Ibn al-Athīr, VI, 193. Al-Qāsim b. al-Rashīd's agent here was the eunuch Abū Sulaymān Faraj, and 3,700 Muslims were freed, according to Masʿūdī, *Tanbīh*, 189, tr. 255–6. On these exchanges of captives, see *EI²* s.v. Lamas-Ṣū (= the river on whose banks the exchanges were made) (Huart).

888. Masʿūdī, *Tanbīh*, 189, tr. 256; Munierah al-Rasheed, 131, no. 92; *Shiʿr Marwān b. Abī Ḥafṣah*, 61, no. 40; Harley, "Abu's-Simṭ Marwān b. Abī Ḥafṣah," 86–7.

889. Brooks, *EHR*, XV (1900), 744, XVI (1901), 87. According to Balādhurī, 171,

In this year, al-ʿAbbās b. Mūsā b. ʿĪsā b. Mūsā led the Pilgrimage.[890]

the Byzantines attacked al-Kanīsah al-Sawdā' whilst al-Qāsim was stationed here and took many captives.

890. Muḥammad b. Ḥabīb, 38–9; Khalīfah, *Ta'rīkh*, II, 736; Yaʿqūbī, *Ta'rīkh*, II, 522; Ibn al-Athīr, loc. cit.

The Events of the Year

190

(November 27, 805–November 16, 806)

Among the events taking place during this year was the appearance of Rāfiʿ b. Layth b. Naṣr b. Sayyār[891] at Samarqand, rebelling against Hārūn, throwing off his allegiance and abandoning obedience to him.

The Reason behind Rāfiʿ b. Layth's Revolt

According to what has been mentioned to us, the reason for that was that Yaḥyā b. al-Ashʿath b. Yaḥyā al-Ṭāʾī married one of the daughters, who was famed for her richness,[892] of his paternal uncle Abū al-Nuʿmān. Yaḥyā stayed in the City of Peace, and left her at

---

891. Possibly the grandson of the last Umayyad governor of Khurāsān. His father was presumably the Layth "mawlā of the Commander of the Faithful" sent in al-Manṣūr's reign as an envoy to the Turkish ruler of Farghānah. See Yaʿqūbī, *Taʾrīkh,* II, 465–6; Barthold, *Turkestan,* 201. Balādhurī, quoted in Ṭabarī-Balʿamī, tr. IV, 471, states that Rāfiʿ was a commander in the garrison of Samarqand.

892. Thus in the Cairo text, VIII, 319 and in parallel sources, *dhāt yasār*[in], which fits in well with the rest of the story. The Leiden text has here, less plausibly, *dhāt lisān*[in] "eloquent."

Samarqand. When his stay in Baghdad became protracted, and she received the news that he had taken several slave concubines and had had children by them, she sought some means of obtaining her release from him; but she did not manage to achieve this. News of her plight reached Rāfiʿ. He cast covetous eyes on her and on her money, so he sent someone secretly to her, who told her that there was no way of securing release from her husband except by renouncing belief in God's unity (i.e., renouncing Islam), for which she had to summon a body of professional witnesses [ʿ*udūl*] and uncover her hair publicly before them, and then repent of her
[708] action, so that she would then be allowable to (fresh Muslim) husbands.[893] She did that, and Rāfiʿ then married her.

The news reached Yaḥyā b. al-Ashʿath, and he raised a complaint about the matter to al-Rashīd. The latter therefore wrote to ʿAlī b. ʿĪsā ordering him to impose a separation between the two and to punish Rāfiʿ, have him flogged with the number of stripes prescribed by the *Sharīʿah* [*yajlidahu al-ḥadd*[a]], have him fettered, and have him paraded through the city of Samarqand, in irons and set on a donkey, as a warning to others. Sulaymān b. Ḥamīd al-Azdī, however, did not inflict on Rāfiʿ the *ḥadd* punishment, but merely mounted him on a donkey, in fetters, till he divorced her. Then he imprisoned him in the Samarqand jail. But Rāfiʿ escaped by night from imprisonment in the custody of Ḥamīd b. al-Masīḥ, who was at that time head of the police guard in Samarqand, and reached ʿAlī b. ʿĪsā at Balkh. He sought a guarantee of personal safety, but ʿAlī refused him this, and was about to execute him. However, ʿAlī's son ʿĪsā b. ʿAlī interceded with his father for him; Rāfiʿ repeated afresh his divorcing of the woman and was given permission to return home to Samarqand. So he went back to Samarqand, where he attacked ʿAlī b. ʿĪsā's governor there, Sulaymān b. Ḥamīd, and killed him. ʿAlī b. ʿĪsā sent his son against Rāfiʿ, but the local people gave their support to Sibāʿ b. Masʿadah and made him chief over themselves. Sibāʿ pounced on Rāfiʿ and put him in fetters, but then the local people suddenly turned on Sibāʿ,

893. I.e., her apostasy from Islam, albeit temporary and based on a technicality, thereby released her from marriage to a Muslim, since a Muslim male may marry a wife from the Protected Peoples but not an idolator or polytheist (Qur'ān, V, 7/5, II, 220; cf. *EI*[1] s.v. Nikāḥ [Schacht]).

putting him in irons, appointing Rāfiʿ as their chief, and giving him their allegiance. All the people of Transoxania combined with him. ʿĪsā b. ʿAlī went forth to encounter him; Rāfiʿ met him in battle and put him to flight. ʿAlī b. ʿĪsā then began to levy troop contingents and to prepare for war.[894]

Various Campaigns by al-Rashīd against the Byzantines and Diplomatic Exchanges with the Emperor Nicephorus

In this year, al-Rashīd led the summer expedition (against the Byzantines). He left behind his son ʿAbdallāh al-Maʾmūn as his deputy at al-Raqqah and entrusted affairs to him. He wrote letters to the (governors in the) farthermost parts of the empire ordering them to give al-Maʾmūn full obedience, and he handed over to him [709]
al-Manṣūr's seal ring so that he might benefit from its auspiciousness; this was his personal seal ring, on which was engraved the motto "God is my trusted patron, in His hands I have placed my security."[895]

In this year, al-Faḍl b. Sahl became a convert to Islam at the hands of al-Maʾmūn.[896]

In this year, the Byzantines sallied forth against ʿAyn Zarbah and Kanīsat al-Sawdāʾ.[897] They raided and took captives, hence the

---

894. Khalīfah, *Taʾrīkh,* II, 737; Yaʿqūbī, *Taʾrīkh,* II, 515 (bare mention of the fact of the revolt); Dīnawarī, 391; Ṭabarī-Balʿamī, tr., IV, 471–2; Gardīzī, 80, 132; Abū al-Faḍl Bayhaqī, *Taʾrīkh-i Masʿūdī,* 421; Narshakhī, *Taʾrīkh-i Bukhārā,* 90, tr. Frye, 76; *K. al-ʿUyūn,* 311–12; Ibn al-Athīr, VI, 195; Palmer, 110–11; Barthold, *Turkestan,* 201; Shaban, 37–8; Daniel, 172–3. Whether there is any foundation for the amusing story of the marriage with the woman of Samarqand as the reason for Rāfiʿ's original revolt is dubious; an early source like Yaʿqūbī does not mention it. Gardīzī attributes the expedition against Rāfiʿ to the latter's withholding, as governor in Samarqand, the taxes due to the central government. Dīnawarī attributes the revolt to ʿAlī b. ʿĪsā's general oppression of the people of Khurāsān, as does also, by inference, Abū al-Faḍl Bayhaqī. It seems clear that Rāfiʿ utilized a general resentment in Khurāsān and Transoxania against ʿAlī b. ʿĪsā's rule.

895. Masʿūdī, *Tanbīh,* 346, tr. 444–5; Azdī, 308; *K. al-ʿUyūn,* 312; Ibn al-Athīr, VI, 197–8; Gabrieli, "Successione," 350.

896. Jahshiyārī, 182; Azdī, loc. cit.; *K. al-ʿUyūn,* loc. cit.; Ibn al-Athīr, VI, 197; Palmer, 114.

897. ʿAyn Zarbah is the Byzantine Anabarza. Both fortresses lay in Cilicia. See Le Strange, *Lands,* 128–9; Honigmann, index, s.vv.; Canard, *H'amdânides,* 280.

people of al-Maṣṣīṣah (subsequently) sought to recover what was in the Byzantines' hands.[898]

In this year, al-Rashīd conquered Heraclia and sent out contingents of troops and detachments of cavalry to spread through the land of Byzantium. According to what has been said, he entered it with a force of 135,000 regularly paid troops [*murtaziq*], in addition to camp-followers, volunteers, and those not registered on the stipends list [*dīwān*]. ʿAbdallāh b. Mālik (al-Khuzāʿī) halted at Dhū al-Kulāʿ,[899] and sent forward Dāwūd b. ʿĪsā b. Mūsā[900] with 70,000 men to range about within the land of Byzantium. Shurāḥīl b. Maʿn b. Zāʾidah[901] captured Ḥiṣn al-Ṣaqālibah[902] and Dabasah,[903], and Yazīd b. Makhlad captured al-Ṣafṣāf and Malāqūbiyah.[904] Al-Rashīd's conquest of Heraclia took place in Shawwāl (August–September, 806). He reduced it to ruins and enslaved its people after a thirty days' siege of the town. He gave charge of the Levant coastlands of the eastern Mediterranean as far as Egypt to Ḥumayd b. Maʿyūf (al-Ḥajūrī). Ḥumayd raided as far as Cyprus, where he razed buildings, burnt property, and enslaved 16,000 of its people. He despatched them to al-Rāfiqah; the judge Abū al-Bakhtarī took charge of selling them, and the bishop of Cyprus fetched two thousand dīnārs. Al-Rashīd set out for the Byzantine lands on the twentieth of Rajab (June 11, 806).[905] He adopted a cap [*qalansuwah*] on which was written the words "Warrior for the

898. Khalīfah, *Taʾrīkh,* II, 736 (under the year 189); Balādhurī, 171; Ibn al-Athīr, VI, 198; Brooks, *EHR,* XVI (1901), 87.

899. Literally, "the stronghold, fortified place," possibly the Byzantine town of Sideropolis in Cappadocia. See Balādhurī, 150, 170; Le Strange, *Lands,* 138–9; Brooks, *EHR,* XVI (1901), 86; Honigmann, 46–7.

900. Second cousin of al-Rashīd, and subsequently, in 193 (809), governor in Mecca and Medina for al-Amīn.

901. Son of the famous general of the last Umayyads and early ʿAbbāsids; see Crone, 169.

902. "The fortress of the Slavs," which lay just north of the Cilician Gates and was possibly the modern Turkish Anasha Qalʿesi; see Canard, *H'amdânides,* 284.

903. Byzantine Thēbasa in Cappadocia. See Le Strange, *Lands,* 136; Honigmann, 47.

904. Byzantine Malakopea, modern Melegob. See Le Strange, *Lands,* and Honigmann, loc. cit.

905. Yaʿqūbī, *Taʾrīkh,* II, 519 (according to whom, al-Rashīd had previously been concerned at Manbij with negotiations for the settlement of a revolt by the people of Ḥimṣ), 523; Dīnawarī, 391; *K. al-ʿUyūn,* 312; Ibn al-Athīr, VI, 196.

faith, Pilgrim" [*ghāzī, ḥājj*], and used to wear this.[906] Abū al-Maʿālī al-Kilābī[907] said,

Whoever seeks to encounter you or wishes a meeting [710]
must do this either in the Two Holy Places [*al-Ḥaramayn*] or on the farthest frontier regions.
Hence, in the enemy's territory, on a frisky horse,
and in the land of easy and pleasant life, on a camel saddle.
Out of all creation, you are the only one who has gained control of the frontier regions,
from among all those who have acquired successively power over affairs (i.e., previous Caliphs).

After this, al-Rashīd went on to al-Ṭuwānah[908] and encamped there. Then he travelled away from there, and left behind over it ʿUqbah b. Jaʿfar (al-Khuzāʿī),[909] ordering him to build a residence there. Nicephorus sent to al-Rashīd tribute and poll-tax [*al-kharāj wa-al-jizyah*], the latter for his own head, that of his designated successor and those of his nobles [*baṭāriqah*] and the rest of the people of his realm, a total of fifty thousand dīnārs, at a rate of four dīnārs on his own head and two dīnārs on that of his son Istabrāq (i.e., Stauracius). Nicephorus also sent a letter, via two of his most prominent nobles, concerning a slave girl from among the captives from Heraclia, and its text was as follows:

To the servant of God Hārūn, Commander of the Faithful, from Nicephorus, ruler of the Byzantines, greetings! As follows: O King,

---

906. At Ṭūs, at the time of his last illness, al-Rashīd is described as wearing a tall *qalansuwah.* See Jahshiyārī, 221; Sourdel, "Questions de cérémoniale ʿabbaside," 133–4, pointing out that the *qalansuwah ṭawīlah ruṣāfiyyah* (the latter adjective indicating a material originally made in al-Ruṣāfah) became the characteristic personal headgear of the ʿAbbāsids, one possibly adopted in imitation of the Achaemenids of ancient Persia. According to Ṭabarī, III, 371, al-Manṣūr made people wear excessively high *qalansuwah*s which had to be supported by an internal framework of cane.

907. Unidentified.

908. Classical Tyana, a town lying to the north of the Taurus mountains and to the west of modern Niğde; it was subsequently captured and fortified by al-Maʾmūn. See Yāqūt, *Muʿjam,* IV, 45–6; Le Strange, *Palestine,* 547; idem, *Lands,* 139; Canard, *H'amdânides,* 285.

909. Grandson of the ʿAbbāsid deputy *naqīb* Muḥammad b. al-Ashʿath, his father being al-Rashīd's *ṣāḥib al-shurṭah*; see Crone, 185.

I have a request to make of you which will not cause any damage either to your faith or to your temporal welfare and which is a trifling and insignificant matter: that you grant to my son a slave girl, one of the maidens of Heraclia whom I had sought in marriage for my son. If you deem it expedient to fulfill for me the object of my requirement, then I would be grateful if you would do it. Peace be upon you, and God's mercy and blessing!

Nicephorus also sought from him presents of perfume and one of his (royal) tents [*surādiqātihi*].[910]

Al-Rashīd ordered the slave girl to be sought out; she was brought back, adorned with finery and installed on a seat in the tent in which he himself was lodging. The slave girl and the tent, together with its contents—vessels and fittings—were handed over to Nicephorus's envoy. He also sent to Nicephorus the perfume which he had requested, and he further sent to him dates, dishes of *khabīṣ*,[911] raisins and healing drugs (or: opium, *tiryāq*). Al-Rashīd's envoy handed over all these to Nicephorus. The latter, in return, gave al-Rashīd a load of Islamic dirhams on the back of a
[711] chestnut-colored hack [*birdhawn*], amounting to fifty thousand dirhams, one hundred satin brocade garments, two hundred garments of fine brocade [*buzyūn*],[912] twelve falcons, four hunting dogs, and three hacks. Nicephorus further contracted not to destroy Dhū al-Kulāʿ, Ṣumālū[913] or Ḥiṣn Sinān, whilst al-Rashīd guaranteed not to resettle and fortify Heraclia—this on the basis that Nicephorus would hand over three hundred thousand dīnārs [annually].[914]

910. For this loan word from Persian, probably a pre-Islamic borrowing, see Fraenkel, 29.

911. A kind of jellied dessert dish made with sesame oil or syrup; it was regarded as a typically Persian dish. See Dozy, *Supplément*, I, 349a–b; Rodinson, "Recherches sur les documents arabes relatifs à la cuisine," 103, 148, 150; Ahsan, 100.

912. The Arabic geographers (e.g., Iṣṭakhrī and Ibn Ḥawqal) mention the fame of the Byzantine and Armenian *buzyūn* brocades, and state that Trebizond was a great mart for their export; see Serjeant, 63 ff.

913. Text *ṣ.m.l.h*, which the editor takes to stand for Ṣumāluh = Ṣamālū, a place mentioned by Balādhurī, 170, and Ṭabarī, III, 497, 499, as having been already attacked by al-Rashīd in the campaign of 163 (780). Cf. Shābushtī, 341–2, Annex 4.

914. Khalīfah, *Ta'rīkh*, II, 737; Ṭabarī-Balʿamī, tr., IV, 471; Azdī, 308–9; *K. al-ʿUyūn*, 312; Ibn al-Athīr, VI, 196; Brooks, *EHR*, XV (1900), 745–6; Kennedy, 130–1;

In this year, a rebel [*khārijī*][915] from the tribe of ʿAbd al-Qays, called Sayf b. Bakr, raised a revolt. Al-Rashīd despatched against him Muḥammad b. Yazīd b. Mazyad (al-Shaybānī),[916] who killed him at ʿAyn al-Nūrah.[917]

The people of Cyprus broke their agreement, hence Maʿyūf b. Yaḥyā raided them and carried off captives from its people.[918]

In this year, ʿĪsā b. Mūsā al-Hādī led the Pilgrimage.[919]

Shaban, 38–9, who regards al-Rashīd's preoccupation with the reasonably stable Anatolian front as having been a waste of effort.

915. Here, apparently, used in a general sense, since when a rebel from the Khārijite sect is specifically intended, terms like *al-shārī* or *al-muḥakkim* or *al-ḥarūrī* are often used.

916. The son of Maʿn b. Zāʾidah's nephew Yazīd b. Mazyad; see Crone, 169.

917. Ibn al-Athīr, VI, 197. ʿAyn al-Nūrah, literally, "place where pitch bubbles up through the ground," does not seem to be mentioned by the geographers, but was possibly in Lower Iraq or Kurdistan. Azdī, 309, has "ʿAyn al-Baqarah"; ʿAyn al-Baqar was, according to Yāqūt, *Muʿjam*, IV, 176; cf. Le Strange, *Palestine*, 330–2, at Acre in Palestine; hence, Azdī's reading seems wrong, unless a different place is meant.

918. Azdī, 310; Ibn al-Athīr, loc. cit.; Brooks, *EHR*, XV (1900), 746.

919. Muḥammad b. Ḥabīb, 39; Khalīfah, *Taʾrīkh*, II, 737; Yaʿqūbī, *Taʾrīkh*, II, 522; Azdī, loc. cit.; Ibn al-Athīr, loc. cit.

The Events of the Year

191

(November 17, 806–November 5, 807)

Among the events taking place during this year was the outbreak of a rebel [*khārijī*] called Tharwān b. Sayf in the district of Ḥawlāyā,[920] who was then transferring his activities to the Sawād. Ṭawq b. Mālik was sent against him, and Ṭawq put him to flight and wounded him, killing also the greater part of his followers. Ṭawq was under the impression that he had killed Tharwān, and so wrote a letter announcing his victory; Tharwān (in fact) fled, wounded.[921]

In this year, Abū al-Nidā' rebelled in Syria, so al-Rashīd sent Yaḥyā b. Mu'ādh (b. Muslim al-Dhuhlī) in pursuit of him and appointed Yaḥyā governor of Syria.[922]

---

920. A village in the neighborhood of al-Nahrawān; see Yāqūt, *Mu'jam,* II, 322–3.

921. Azdī, 311 (with the same Marwān for Tharwān); Ibn al-Athīr, VI, 205.

922. Ibid. Yaḥyā was the son of a Khurasanian mawlā, who served al-Rashīd and al-Ma'mūn in various governorships, and brother of Ḥusayn, a foster-brother of al-Hādī (see Ṭabarī, III, 586, above, 67); he died in 206 (821–2), see Crone, 184. Previously, Mu'ādh had been al-Faḍl b. Yaḥyā's deputy in the governorship of Khurāsān; see Ḥamzah Iṣfahānī, 165.

In this year, snow fell in the City of Peace.

In this year, Ḥammād al-Barbarī seized Hayṣam al-Yamānī.[923] [712]

In this year, the affair of Rāfiʿ b. Layth at Samarqand became serious.

In this year, the people of Nasaf[924] wrote to Rāfiʿ giving him their obedience and asking him to send to them forces who would aid them in killing ʿĪsā b. ʿAlī. So Rāfiʿ despatched the local ruler of Shāsh[925] with his force of Turks and one of his own commanders. They came upon ʿĪsā b. ʿAlī, surrounded him and killed him in Dhū al-Qaʿdah (September–October, 807), but did not offer any violence to his retainers.[926]

In this year, al-Rashīd appointed Ḥammawayh al-Khādim over the postal system of Khurāsān.[927]

Various Raids into the Byzantine Lands, and Measures against the Protected Peoples

In this year, Yazīd b. Makhlad al-Hubayrī (al-Fazārī)[928] raided the Byzantine lands with a force of ten thousand men. The Byzantines

---

923. Ibn al-Athīr, loc. cit. On Ḥammād, see Ṭabarī, III, 649 (above, 173 and n. 632). According to Yaʿqūbī, *Taʾrīkh*, II, 498–9, Ḥammād had been appointed governor of Yemen in 179 (795), but his tyranny drove the local people into rebellion, led by al-Hayṣam b. ʿAbd al-Majīd al-Hamdānī. Warfare between the two sides continued for nine years (thus placing the beginning of the revolt in 182 [798]) until al-Hayṣam was captured and executed by the Caliph. Ḥammād was subsequently removed by al-Rashīd after further complaints by the oppressed people of Yemen and after a thirteen years' governorship (thus placing his dismissal in 192 [808], if we follow Yaʿqūbī's chronology; according to Ṭabarī, III, 649, Ḥammād had been appointed governor of Mecca and the Yemen in 184 [800], but this may only mean that it was in this year that he added Mecca to his existing governorship of Yemen). Khalīfah, *Taʾrīkh*, II, 743, does not give the date of Ḥammād's appointment but says that he continued till al-Rashīd's death.

924. A town of Soghdia, situated on the Khūshk Rūd, and also called Nakhshab or (in post-Mongol times) Qarshī. See Yāqūt, *Muʿjam*, V, 276; Le Strange, *Lands*, 470–1; Barthold, *Turkestan*, 136–7; *EI*¹ s.v. Nakhshab (Minorsky).

925. The region of Transoxania to the east of the Syr Darya, in which is situated the modern Tashkent. See Le Strange, *Lands*, 480–3; Barthold, *Turkestan*, 169–75.

926. Khalīfah, *Taʾrīkh*, II, 738; *K. al-ʿUyūn*, 313; Ibn al-Athīr, loc. cit.; Barthold, *Turkestan*, 200; Daniel, 173.

927. Mawlā of al-Mahdī, obviously a eunuch, and according to Yaʿqūbī, *Buldān*, 252, tr. 38, owner of a *qaṭīʿah* or land grant on the eastern bank of the Tigris at Baghdad; see Crone, 191.

928. Descendant of the family of ʿUmar b. Hubayrah and Yazīd Ibn Hubayrah who served the later Umayyads in Iraq and al-Jazīrah; see Crone, 107.

seized the defile against him, and then killed him when he was with a force of fifty men at two stages' distance from Tarsus, the remainder of the force escaping.[929]

In this year, al-Rashīd appointed Harthamah b. Aʿyan to take charge of the summer expedition (against the Byzantines) and provided him with a force of thirty thousand troops from the army of Khurāsān.[930] He was accompanied by Masrūr al-Khādim, who was responsible for the commisariat plus all other affairs except the actual military leadership. Al-Rashīd himself proceeded to Darb al-Ḥadath,[931] stationed there ʿAbdallāh b. Mālik, and stationed Saʿīd b. Salm b. Qutaybah at Marʿash. The Byzantines raided it, seized some of the Muslims as captives and then withdrew homewards, Saʿīd b. Salm meanwhile standing fast there. Al-Rashīd sent Muḥammad b. Yazīd b. Mazyad to Tarsus. Al-Rashīd remained at Darb al-Ḥadath for three days of the month of Ramaḍān (July–August, 807), and then returned to al-Raqqah.[932]

In this year, al-Rashīd ordered the churches in the frontier re-
[713] gions to be demolished, and he wrote to al-Sindī b. Shāhik ordering him to compel the Protected Peoples [*ahl al-dhimmah*] in the City of Peace to distinguish their general appearance from the Muslims in matter of their dress and their mounts.[933]

In this year, al-Rashīd dismissed ʿAlī b. ʿĪsā b. Māhān from the governorship of Khurāsān and appointed (in his stead) Harthamah.[934]

The Reason for al-Rashīd's Dismissal of ʿAlī b. ʿĪsā and His Anger against Him

Abū Jaʿfar (i.e., al-Ṭabarī) has related: We have already mentioned previously the reason for ʿAlī b. ʿĪsā's son's demise and how he was

929. Khalīfah, *Ta'rīkh*, loc. cit.; *K. al-ʿUyūn*, 312; Ibn al-Athīr, loc. cit.; Brooks, *EHR*, XV (1900), 746–7.

930. This use of Khurāsānian troops, to supplement what were normally armies of Syrian troops in these frontier campaigns, is notable; see von Sievers, "Military, merchants and nomads," 219.

931. See for this, Ṭabarī, III, 568 (above, 39, n. 156).

932. Yaʿqūbī, *Ta'rīkh*, II, 523; *K. al-ʿUyūn*, 312–13; Ibn al-Athīr, VI, 206; Brooks, *EHR*, XV (1900), 747.

933. Azdī, 311; Tritton, 117–18; A. Fattal, *Le statut légal des non-musulmans en pays d'Islam*, 100–1; *EI*[2] s.v. Ghiyār (M. Perlmann).

934. Khalīfah, *Ta'rīkh*, loc. cit.; Dīnawarī, 391; Azdī, loc. cit.; *K. al-ʿUyūn*, 313–15; Ibn al-Athīr, VI, 203–4.

killed. When his son ʿĪsā was killed, ʿAlī set off from Balkh and arrived at Marw, fearing that Rāfiʿ b. al-Layth would march against it and take control of it. Now his son ʿĪsā had buried a huge hoard of money in the garden of his house at Balkh, reportedly amounting to thirty million (dirhams) in value. ʿAlī b. ʿĪsā did not know about the money, and no one had any knowledge about that matter except one of his slave girls. When ʿAlī set out for Balkh, the slave girl revealed the matter to a certain slave (or: to certain slaves), and people talked about it. The Qurʾān readers[935] and prominent persons of Balkh gathered together and then entered the garden, plundering it and throwing it open to spoliation by the general masses of people. The news of this reached al-Rashīd and he said, "ʿAlī has left Balkh against my orders and has left behind a sum of money like this, and at the same time he alleges that he has been reduced to utilizing his womenfolk's ornaments for his expenditure on the warfare against Rāfiʿ!" He thereupon dismissed him, and appointed Harthamah as governor. He appropriated all ʿAlī b. ʿĪsā's wealth, and this amounted to eighty million dirhams.[936]

It has been mentioned from a certain mawlā that he related: We were in Jurjān with al-Rashīd at the time when he was heading towards Khurāsān. The treasuries of ʿAlī b. ʿĪsā which had been confiscated for him arrived at that point, on the backs of fifteen hundred camels. As well as all this (i.e., this wealth collected by oppressive means), ʿAlī had humiliated the most prominent of the Khurasanians and their nobles. [714]

It has been mentioned that Hishām b. Farr-Khusraw[937] and al-Ḥusayn b. Muṣʿab[938] went into ʿAlī's presence one day. They gave him the salutation of peace, but he said to al-Ḥusayn, "May God

935. Following the Leiden editor's text, *qurrāʾ ahl Balkh* (also in the Cairo text, VIII, 325), but ms. A has *ahl qurā Balkh,* thus giving possible support to the idea put forward by Shaban, 23, 50–1, and G. H. A. Juynboll, in *JESHO,* XVI (1973), 113–27, that *ahl al-qurā* is the original expression of the early Islamic sources (= "villagers," i.e., participants in the early Arab campaigns in Iraq, new converts from the desert who were settled in "villages" in the environs of towns like Medina, al-Baṣrah, and al-Kūfah) and that these were later given a religious guise and turned into *qurrāʾ* "Qurʾān readers."

936. *K. al-ʿUyūn,* 313; Ibn al-Athīr, VI, 203; Daniel, 173–4.

937. Unidentified, but from what follows, clearly a local poet and panegyrist.

938. The father of Ṭāhir Dhū al-Yamīnayn, subsequently governor of Khurāsān for al-Maʾmūn; al-Ḥusayn is described below by Ṭabarī, III, 771, as one of the leading men in Khurāsān.

not grant you peace, O heretic son of a heretic! By God, I know full well your position as an enemy of Islam and your impugning of religion! I am only awaiting the Caliph's permission for it before putting you to death, for God has made shedding your blood licit, and I only hope that God will let it be shed at my hands in the near future, and that He will speedily consign you to His punishment! Are you not the person who stirred up trouble against me in this very own house of mine after you had become intoxicated with wine, and asserted that letters had reached you from the City of Peace intimating my dismissal? Go forth, to God's wrath, may God curse you, for soon you will be one of those accursed ones!" Al-Ḥusayn replied to him, "I seek refuge in God for the Amīr, that he should accept the sayings of a slanderer or the insinuations of an evilwisher, for I am innocent of what I have been suspected!" ʿAlī said, "You have lied, may you have no mother! I have acquired ample evidence that you became intoxicated with wine and spoke words for which you have merited the most severe punishment, and it may well be that God will speedily inflict on you His violence and His retribution! Get out of my presence, unrespected and without anyone to escort you forth!" The doorkeeper then came up, gripped him by the arm, and ejected him.[939]

ʿAlī also said to Hishām b. Farr-Khusraw, "Your house has become a meeting place in which irresponsible elements [*al-sufahāʾ*] congregate around you and slander the ruling authorities [*al-wulāt*]. May God spill my own blood, if I do not shed yours!" Hishām replied, "May I be made the Amīr's ransom! By God, I am a person who has been wronged and is deserving of compassion! By God, I have exerted every possible effort and have not omitted a single eulogy of the Amīr, nor any praiseworthy description of

939. M. Kaabi, "Les origines ṭāhirides dans la *daʿwa* ʿabbāside," *Arabica,* XIX (1972), 159–62, sees ʿAlī b. ʿĪsā's violent words here to al-Ḥusayn as only explicable in the light of a long-standing rivalry and hatred between the two Khurāsānian families of Māhān and Ruzayq—though both were affiliated to the same Arab tribe of Khuzāʿah—going back to the time of the ʿAbbāsid Revolution and the respective roles of ʿĪsā b. Māhān and the sons of Ruzayq, i.e., Ṭalḥah and Muṣʿab. In support of this view, he cites ʿAlī b. ʿĪsā's alleged ill treatment, according to Shābushtī, 142–3, of Ṭāhir b. al-Ḥusayn at one point, Ṭāhir's alleged initial support for the revolt in Samarqand against ʿAlī b. ʿĪsā of Rāfiʿ b. Layth, and Ṭāhir's readiness in 194 (809–10) to combat in Khurāsān, on behalf of al-Maʾmūn, al-Amīn's representative ʿAlī b. ʿĪsā.

him, without specifically attributing it to him and reciting it about him. If, then, when I have recited words of approbation, evil slanders have been carried back to you, what recourse do I have?" He said, "You have lied, may you be deprived of your mother! I know full well from your own children and family what your heart is really concealing, so get out, for I shall be rid of you very [715]
shortly!"[940]

Hishām went away. When it was the latter part of the night, he sent for his daughter ʿĀliyah, the eldest of his children, and said to her, "O my dear daughter, I wish to tell you about a matter which, if you blazon it abroad, will bring about my death, but if you keep it to yourself, will allow me to survive safe and sound, so choose your father's preservation rather than his death!" She replied, "What is this, may I be made your ransom?" He said, "I am fearful of my life from this evildoer ʿAlī b. ʿĪsā, so I have decided to let it be known publicly that I have been struck down by a paralytic stroke. When day breaks, gather your slave girls together and go to my bed and shake me. Then when you see that my power of movement has been affected and my limbs made heavy, you and your slave girls must break out in cries of lamentation. Also, send to your brothers and give them the news about my illness. But beware strenuously of letting any single one of God's creatures, whether close to you or unconnected, learn that my body is, in reality, perfectly sound."

She accordingly did this, being an intelligent and sagacious woman. He remained laid out on his bed for a period of time, unable to move except when someone else moved his limbs. It is related that not a single person in Khurāsān knew about ʿAlī b. ʿĪsā's dismissal, by any channel of information, except for Hishām, who surmised his dismissal as likely, a surmise that turned out to be correct. It is further related that he went forth on the day when Harthamah arrived in order to meet Harthamah, and one of ʿAlī b. ʿĪsā's commanders saw him on the road. The commander said, "Your body has recovered now?" Hishām replied, "Praise be to God, it's never lost its health!" Another authority states, however, that, on the contrary, it was ʿAlī b. ʿĪsā who saw Hishām and said, "Where are you off to?" He replied, "I'm going to meet our Amīr

940. Ibn al-Athīr, loc. cit.

Abū Ḥātim (i.e., Harthamah)." ʿAlī said, "Weren't you ill?" Hishām replied, "Yes, indeed; but God has given me health." God removed the tyrant in a single night.[941]

As for al-Ḥusayn b. Muṣʿab, he set off for Mecca seeking al-Rashīd's protection against ʿAlī b. ʿĪsā, which the Caliph accorded to him.[942]

Al-Rashīd's Letter Dismissing ʿAlī b. ʿĪsā and His Charge to Harthamah

When al-Rashīd resolved on the dismissal of ʿAlī b. ʿĪsā, he sent for Harthamah b. Aʿyan—according to the reports which have reached me—and saw him privately. He said, "I have not consulted any-
[716] body about your appointment, nor have I informed anybody of my secret intentions regarding you. The frontier regions of the eastern lands have become restive against my power, and the people of Khurāsān have become discontented with ʿAlī b. ʿĪsā's rule, since he has disobeyed the charge which I gave him and has cast it behind his back. He has now written to me asking for reinforcements and additional troops, and I am writing to him and shall tell him that I am sending you to him as reinforcement and despatching to him with you supplies of money, weapons, means of strength, and equipment which will set his heart at rest and satisfy his soul's desire. I will write out a letter to accompany you, in my own hand; do not break the seal or peruse its contents until you reach the town of Naysābūr. Then when you halt there, do what it says in the letter and obey its instructions, but don't exceed them, if God wills. I intend also to despatch as your companion Rajāʾ al-Khādim with a letter to ʿAlī b. ʿĪsā which I will write out in my own hand, so that he may know what to expect at the hands of yourself and Rajāʾ. (In regard to Rajāʾ,) treat this affair concerning ʿAlī as of little importance, don't reveal it to him and don't let him know what I have decided upon. Now prepare for the journey, and give out to

941. Ibn al-Athīr, VI, 204.

942. Ibid.; cf. Kaabi, "Les origines ṭāhirides," 162–3, who conjectures that, by the time al-Ḥusayn reached al-Rashīd in Iraq, the nature of Rāfiʿ b. Layth's revolt as anti-ʿAbbāsid as well as anti-Māhānid had become apparent, so that al-Ḥusayn might well have discouraged his son Ṭāhir from giving any further support to the rebel.

your close colleagues and to people in general the ostensible information that I am despatching you as a reinforcement and as aid to ʿAlī b. ʿĪsā."[943]

He related: He then wrote out, in his own hand, a letter to ʿAlī b. ʿĪsā b. Māhān, whose text was as follows:

In the name of God, the Merciful, the Compassionate. O son of an adulteress, I have exalted your status and have raised your fame, I have caused the leaders of the Arabs to follow at your heels and have made the descendants of the kings of the Persians your slaves and followers. Yet my recompense (for this) is that you have disobeyed my charge (to you) and have cast my command to you behind your back, to the point that you have wrought mischief in the land and have ill-treated the subjects; you have aroused God's ire and that of His Caliph with your evil conduct, your vicious behavior, and your blatant treachery. I have appointed my mawlā[944] Harthamah b. Aʿyan over the frontier region Khurāsān and have ordered him to treat you harshly, together with your sons, your secretaries, and your financial officials, and have ordered him not to leave in your possession (literally, "behind your backs") a single dirham or legal claim due to any Muslim or person in covenant relationship (i.e., Dhimmī, *muʿāhad*) without securing redress from you for it, until you give it back to its rightful owner. If you, or [717]
your sons, or your financial officials refuse to do this, then he has full permission to inflict punishment on you, to rain down upon you a hail of floggings, and to visit upon you what is customarily visited upon those who break covenants, alter, change, act rebelliously, oppress, act tyrannically, and inflict wrong, as vengeance due to God, He is magnified and exalted, in the first place; to His Caliph, in the second place; and to the Muslims and the persons in covenant relationship, in the third place. Do not lay yourself open to what has no permanence, and relinquish your

---

943. Yaʿqūbī, *Taʾrīkh*, II, 515; Ṭabarī-Balʿamī, tr., IV, 472–3; *K. al-ʿUyūn*, 3131; Ibn al-Athīr, VI, 204.

944. *Mawlā* seems here to signify the close relationship of Harthamah to the Caliph, as a trusted free retainer rather than any legal or social dependence, clientage, or former slave status. Harthamah seems to have come from the Arab community of Khurāsān; see Crone, 75, 78.

duties (i.e., your office as governor) either willingly or else as one constrained![945]

He also wrote out the contract of appointment for Harthamah in his own hand:

This is what the Commander of the Faithful Hārūn al-Rashīd has written out as a contract of appointment to Harthamah b. Aʿyan when he appointed him governor over the frontier region Khurāsān, its administrative dependencies and its land tax. The Caliph commands Harthamah to keep in mind the fear of God, to obey Him and to show concern for and watch over God's interests. He should make the Book of God a guiding example in all he undertakes and, accordingly, make licit what is legally allowable according to it and prohibit what is not allowable. When he is faced with anything doubtful and uncertain, he should pause and consult those with a systematic training and acquaintanceship with God's religion and those knowledgeable about the Book of God; or alternatively, he should refer it to his Imām so that God, He is magnified and exalted, may make manifest to him His judgment in the matter and so that he may execute it according to His right guidance. The Caliph also commands Harthamah to secure a firm hold of the evildoer ʿAlī b. ʿĪsā, his sons, his financial officials, and his secretaries, and to treat them harshly, come down on them with severity and make them disgorge all the monies—the Commander of the Faithful's land tax and the income from the conquered lands meant for the Muslims' allowances [*fay*ʾ]—for which they are accountable. When he has exacted everything of these revenues which they hold and for which they are responsible, he is to look into the question of the rights of the Muslims and the people in covenant relationship [*al-muʿāhadīn*], and he is to require them to fulfill the rights of every person entitled to a right until they have fulfilled it for them. If their responsibility for any rights due to the Commander of the Faithful and for any of them due to the Muslims is validly established, but they evade them and refuse to acknowledge them, then he is to release upon them the lashings of God's punishment and the painfulness of His retribu-

945. Ṭabarī-Balʿamī, tr., IV, 473; *K. al-ʿUyūn*, 313–14.

tion, so that he brings them into the position where, if he goes beyond it with the lightest stroke of punishment, their souls will perish and their spirits cease to be without any blood-wit or retaliation being exacted. If they transgress beyond the bounds of the obedience due from every subject, he is to despatch them, if God wills, to the Commander of the Faithful's gate in exactly the same way as rebels are despatched—with harsh treatment, rough food and drink, and coarse clothing, in the custody of trusted members [718]
of his retinue.

O Abū Ḥātim, act according to the charge which I have laid upon you, for I have preferred God and my faith over my personal inclinations and will; so let your own course of action be thus and let your own conduct be on the same basis. Handle the financial officials of the districts with whom you come into contact during the course of your journeying (to Khurāsān, or, as part of your gubernatorial duties) in such a way that they do not as a result feel a need for recourse to an affair which might (consequently) disquiet them or an evil opinion which might instill fear into them.[946] Enlarge the hopes of the people of that frontier region, and increase their freedom from fear and the attainment of their desires. Then act in accordance with what will make God, His Caliph, and those over whom God has appointed you governor, pleased with you, if God wills. This is my covenant and my letter, written in my own hand, and I call to bear witness God, His angels, those who bear His throne, and the denizens of His heavens; God is sufficient as a witness! The Commander of the Faithful has written this with his own hand, with no one present but God and His angels.[947]

Then he ordered that the letter of Harthamah to ʿAlī b. ʿĪsā concerning Harthamah's giving aid to ʿAlī, reinforcing his power, and strengthening his position should be written out. This was accordingly done, and Harthamah's mission of reinforcement to ʿAlī made public. Letters from Ḥammawayh had reached Hārūn to the effect that Rāfiʿ had not abandoned his allegiance or thrown off the official ʿAbbāsid insignia of black, nor had his followers; their

946. Translation here uncertain; the florid style of this document makes absolute certainty over its translation impossible.

947. Ṭabarī-Balʿamī, tr., loc. cit.; *K. al-ʿUyūn*, 314.

sole aim was to secure the dismissal of ʿAlī b. ʿĪsā, who had imposed on them unpleasant things.[948]

[719] In this year, there took place Harthamah b. Aʿyan's departure for Khurāsān as governor there.

What Befell Harthamah in the Course of His Journey to Khurāsān, and What Happened to ʿAlī b. ʿĪsā and His Sons

It has been mentioned that Harthamah went on his way on the sixth day after the one on which al-Rashīd wrote for him his contract of appointment. Al-Rashīd accompanied him on the first part of his journey and gave him a charge concerning what he required Harthamah to do. Harthamah did not pause for any reason en route, and publicly sent on to ʿAlī b. ʿĪsā money, weapons, robes of honor, and aromatic substances, until the point when he halted at Naysābūr and then gathered together a group of his own trusty retainers and the senior and experienced persons from among these. He summoned each one of them privately and had a confidential talk with him, and then he made them accept covenants and undertakings that they would keep his plans hidden and conceal his secret. He appointed each man of them over an administrative region, roughly on the basis of the man's standing in Harthamah's estimation. Thus, he made appointments to Jurjān, Naysābūr, al-Ṭabasayn,[949] Nasā and Sarakhs, and he ordered each one of them, after he had given him his letter of appointment, to proceed to the administrative charge to which he had just nominated him, under the most covert and discreet conditions and adopting the guise of ordinary travellers in journeying to the administrative regions and then staying there until the moment which he had indicated to them. He appointed Ismāʿīl b. Ḥafṣ b. Muṣʿab[950] governor of Jurjān at al-Rashīd's express command.

He then proceeded onwards till, when he reached a point just

948. Ṭabarī-Balʿamī, tr. IV, 472; Palmer, 111–12.

949. The two oasis towns in the Great Desert of eastern Persia, Ṭabas Gīlakī, and Ṭabas Masīnān. See Yāqūt, *Muʿjam,* IV, 20; Le Strange, *Lands,* 359–63; Barthold, *An historical geography of Iran,* 134–5.

950. Possibly a grandson of the ancestor of the Ṭāhirid governors in Khurāsān, Muṣʿab b. Ruzayq.

one stage away from Marw, he summoned a group of his trusty retainers, and wrote down for them the names of ʿAlī b. ʿĪsā's sons, the members of his family, his secretaries and others, on sheets of writing material [*riqāʿ*], and handed over to each man a sheet with the name on it of the person whom Harthamah was to consign to his retainer's custody when he himself, Harthamah, entered Marw in order to dispossess ʿAlī, for fear lest they should flee when Harthamah's purpose became known. Then he sent a message to ʿAlī b. ʿĪsā, "If the Amīr—may God make him noble—would like to send his trusty retainers to take charge of the wealth which I have with me here, then let him do so; for if the money goes on [720] ahead of me, that will give the Amīr greater power and will have a more weakening effect on his enemies' strength. Moreover, I should not be confident of its safety if I were to leave it behind me, lest someone who aspires to getting hold of it should cast greedy eyes on it, to the point that he might get his hands on part of it for himself and seize the opportunity of our being distracted when we enter the city."

ʿAlī b. ʿĪsā accordingly sent his bankers [*jahābidhah*] and stewards to take charge of the money. Harthamah told his own treasurers, "Keep them distracted tonight, and adduce an excuse to them about transporting away the money, one which will accord with their own desires and dispel any doubt from their minds." They did that; the treasurers said to them (i.e., to ʿAlī b. ʿĪsā's agents), "(Leave the money here) until we consult[951] with Abū Ḥātim regarding horses and mules to convey the money." Then Harthamah travelled on towards the town of Marw. When he was two miles away from it, ʿAlī b. ʿĪsā came out to meet him with his sons, members of his family and his commanders, with a most splendid and friendly welcome. When Harthamah's eye fell on ʿAlī, he bent his leg in order to dismount from his horse, but ʿAlī cried out to him, "By God, if you dismount, then I shall dismount too." Hence, he remained in his saddle, and each one drew near to the other and then embraced each other. They travelled along together, with ʿAlī questioning Harthamah about al-Rashīd's affairs, his present state and appearance, and the state of his courtiers, his commanders and the supporters of his dynasty's power.

---

951. The Cairo text, VIII, 329, has "until you (pl.) consult."

Harthamah, meanwhile, was answering his questions, until they came to a bridge which only one horse could cross at a time. Harthamah held back his horse's reins and said to ʿAlī, "You go first, with God's blessing," but ʿAlī replied, "No, by God, I won't do that until you yourself go onwards first." Harthamah said, "By God, in that case I won't go onwards, for you are the Amīr and I am only the aide [*wazīr*]." So ʿAlī went forward and Harthamah followed him till they both entered Marw.[952]

They proceeded to ʿAlī's house. Rajāʾ al-Khādim used never to leave Harthamah's side by night or day, riding or sitting. ʿAlī called for food, and the two of them ate, with Rajāʾ al-Khādim also eating with them. ʿAlī was determined that Rajāʾ should not eat with them, but Harthamah made a sign to him (i.e., to Rajāʾ) and commented, "Eat, for you are hungry, and one cannot get sound judgment from a man who is hungry or who is suffering through having to hold his urine back!"[953] When the food was cleared away, ʿAlī told Harthamah, "I have given orders that a palace on the banks of the Māshān should be made available for you, so if
[721] you wish to go there, please do so!"[954] Harthamah said to him, "I have with me certain things, and it is no longer possible to put off a perusal of their contents," and then Rajāʾ al-Khādim handed al-Rashīd's letter to ʿAlī and delivered to him the Caliph's message.

When ʿAlī broke the letter's seal and looked at the very first word of it, he was stricken with remorse and confusion, and he realized that what he was fearing and expecting had indeed come home to him. Then Harthamah ordered him, his sons, his secretaries, and his financial agents all to be put in irons—he had made his journey (to Khurāsān) accompanied by a load of leg and neck irons. When Harthamah had made completely sure of him, he went along to the Friday mosque.[955] He made a speech and raised people's hopes (i.e.,

952. According to Ḥamzah al-Iṣfahānī, 166, Harthamah entered Marw on Monday, the twentieth of Rabīʿ II, 192 (February 22, 808), remained there for forty-five days and went on to Balkh for four days.

953. This sounds like a proverbial saying.

954. The Māshān or Mājān was one of the many canals connected with the Murghāb river and flowing through the centre of Marw; see Yāqūt, *Muʿjam*, V, 42, and Le Strange, *Lands*, 398–9. The suburb of Mājān included the great square or *maydan* of Marw, the New Friday Mosque and the *Dār al-Imārah*, all laid out by Abū Muslim.

955. Presumably, the New Mosque, of Marw's three Friday mosques, as being in the administrative area of the town; see the preceding note.

for a better and juster régime) to a high level, announcing that the Commander of the Faithful had appointed him governor over their frontier regions because of what had reached him concerning the evildoer ʿAlī b. ʿĪsā's vicious conduct, and (announcing) what al-Rashīd had commanded him to do with ʿAlī, his financial agents and his minions. (He further announced) that he was going to put this into effect, to mete out justice to the lower and upper classes alike and to set about restoring to them their rights to the utmost possible extent of those rights. He ordered the document investing him with office to be read out to them. As a result, they evinced great joy at that, their hopes became enlarged, their expectations for the future grew great, their voices were raised in *takbīrs* and *tahlīls*,[956] and numerous prayers were sent up wishing the Commander of the Faithful long life and a goodly recompense.[957]

Then Harthamah went back and sent for ʿAlī b. ʿĪsā, his sons, his financial agents, and his secretaries. He then said, "Relieve me of the burden of you, and allow me to dispense with the necessity of taking unpleasant measures against you," and he made a proclamation among those who had had entrusted to their keeping any possessions of theirs (i.e., of ʿAlī's and of his agents'), that there would be no guarantee of protection (i.e., from punishment) for anyone who had in his keeping any possession deposited by ʿAlī or by any one of his sons, secretaries, and financial agents, and who concealed it and did not reveal it. So people brought to him what had been deposited with them, with the exception of one of the natives of Marw who was a Zoroastrian [*min abnāʾ al-Majūs*]. This man employed continuous stratagems in order to procure access to ʿAlī b. ʿĪsā until he managed to get to him. He told ʿAlī secretly, "I have some wealth belonging to you in my possession, and if you have need of it, I will bring it to you in installments. I have endured on your behalf the threat of death, preferring to keep faith and seeking after handsome praise; or if you have no need of it at this moment, I will keep it stored away for you until you decide what to [722]
do with it." ʿAlī was amazed at this and said, "If only I had in my entourage a thousand men like you, neither the Sultan[958] nor Satan

956. I.e., the cries "God is most great" and "There is no god but God."

957. Yaʿqūbī, *Taʾrīkh*, II, 515; Ṭabarī-Balʿamī, tr., IV, 473–5; *K. al-ʿUyūn*, 315; Ibn al-Athīr, VI, 204–5.

958. Although in early Arabic, *sulṭān* is normally an abstract noun meaning

would ever have been avid to lay hold on me." Then ʿAlī asked the man what was the value of the wealth deposited with him, and he mentioned to him that ʿAlī had entrusted to him money, clothing, and musk, and that he did not know the value of that except that what he had entrusted to him on his (i.e., ʿAlī's) own written instructions was safely stored away with no part of it having been removed. ʿAlī told him, "Leave it where it is, and if its whereabouts become publicly known, then hand it over and save your own skin; and if I escape safe and sound with it, I will decide then what to do." ʿAlī wished him a handsome recompense, thanked him most profusely for that action of his, promised him a requital for it and showed kindness towards him. The man's fidelity became proverbial. It has been mentioned that nothing of ʿAlī's wealth remained concealed from Harthamah except for what ʿAlī had entrusted to the keeping of this man, whose name was al-ʿAlāʾ b. Māhān.[959]

Harthamah appropriated every single item which they (i.e., ʿAlī and his followers) had concealed, even to their womenfolk's personal ornaments. His agent would enter a house and then seize everything in it, to the point that, when there was nothing left in the house except a scrap of woollen cloth or piece of wood or what was valueless, the man would say to a woman, "Hand over the ornaments you're wearing," and she would then say to the man when he came up to her to snatch off her ornaments, "O fellow, if you are of good character, avert your gaze from me, for by God, I promise not to leave anything on myself of what you are seeking without handing it over to you." Then if the man did not wish to commit a sinful act by approaching her, he would agree to her plea, so that very often she would cast off to him her seal ring, her ankle ornaments, and what might be worth ten dirhams. But if the man were of the opposite character to this, he would say, "I shan't be satisfied until I examine you closely in order to make sure that you haven't concealed any item of gold, or pearls, or rubies," and he would run his hands into the folds of her body, such as the armpits

---

"governmental power," its use here in parallel with Satan seems to indicate the actual holder of such authority, the Sultan, here the Caliph.

959. Could this man have been a kinsman of ʿAlī's? But if he was, it is strange that the narrator of the tradition does not mention any relationship or that Harthamah had not already arrested him with the rest of ʿAlī's family.

and groins, in order to seek out in there what he suspected she had hidden from him.

Then, when Harthamah believed that he had done all this thoroughly, he sent ʿAlī forward on a camel, with no saddle-blanket beneath him, a chain round his neck, and heavy fetters on his legs, of such a weight that he could neither stand up nor prop himself [723] up.[960]

It has been mentioned from someone who witnessed Harthamah's mode of action that it was as follows. When Harthamah had completed the process of extracting the wealth which (rightfully) belonged to the Commander of the Faithful from ʿAlī b. ʿĪsā, his sons, his secretaries, and his financial agents, he stood them in front of the people for the latter to raise complaints of injustice and ill treatment. Whenever a man had a legal claim established as due against ʿAlī or any other one of his entourage, Harthamah would say, "Release to the man his due right, and if you don't, then I shall stretch out (my hand) against you (i.e., punish you)." ʿAlī would thereupon say, "May God grant the Amīr righteousness! Grant me a delay of a day or two." At this, Harthamah would say, "That is up to the person claiming the right; if he wishes, he may do so." Then Harthamah would go up to the man and ask him, "Are you agreeable to cease pressing him (for the moment)?" If the man assented, Harthamah said to him, "Go home, in that case, and come back to him (later)." ʿAlī would send to al-ʿAlāʾ b. Māhān and instruct him, "Settle up, on my behalf, the obligation to so-and-so for such-and-such a matter at such-and-such a rate, or on whatever basis you think fit"; al-ʿAlāʾ would then come to an agreement with the man and finally settle his claim.[961]

It has been mentioned that a man stood before Harthamah and said, "May God grant the Amīr righteousness! This miscreant took from me forcibly a precious[962] shield of hide, whose like no one else ever possessed, and bought it from me, constrainedly and

---

960. Yaʿqūbī, *Taʾrīkh*, loc. cit.; *K. al-ʿUyūn*, 314; Ibn al-Athīr, loc. cit. According to Ḥamzah al-Iṣfahānī, loc. cit., Harthamah despatched ʿAlī to Baghdad on Monday, the twenty-second of Jumādā I (March 22, 808).

961. Palmer, 112–13.

962. The variants give support for the Leiden editor's suggestion (*Addenda et emendanda*, p. DCCLXIII) that one might possibly read *yatīmah* "unique" for the text's *thamīnah*.

against my will, for three thousand dirhams. Hence, I went to his steward seeking the purchase money but he refused to give me anything. I remained for a whole year awaiting this miscreant's riding forth, and when he did in fact ride forth, I presented myself in his way and cried out to him, "O Amīr, I am the owner of the shield and to this very day I haven't received its price," but he merely said opprobrious things about my mother [*qadhafa ummī*],[963] and would not give me my due. So take for me (from him) what is legally my due, both for the money owed and also for his insulting my mother's honor." Harthamah said, "Do you have proof of this?" The man replied, "Yes, a group of people were present when he spoke those words." Harthamah therefore summoned these witnesses and made them testify to the man's claim. (After this,) Harthamah said to ʿAlī, "You have incurred the *Sharīʿah* punishment [*ḥadd*] upon yourself." ʿAlī said, "How is that?" Harthamah replied, "Because of your insulting this man's mother's honor." ʿAlī retorted, "Who gave you instruction in the religious law and taught you this point of the juridical and theological sciences?" Harthamah replied, "This is the religious law of the Muslims." ʿAlī said, "I bear witness that the Commander of the Faithful has impugned your lineage more than just once or twice, and I bear witness that you yourself have impugned the lineage of
[724] your own sons innumerable times, on occasion Ḥātim and on other occasions Aʿyan. Now who will exact from you the *Sharīʿah* penalty required for them? And who will exact it for you from your master (i.e., the Caliph)?"[964] Harthamah turned to the owner of the shield and said, "I think that the best course for you is to pursue your claim with this devil for your shield or its price, but to give up pursuing him for the insult to your mother's honor."

Harthamah's Letter to al-Rashīd Announcing the Successful Completion of His Mission

When Harthamah sent ʿAlī, mounted, on his journey to al-Rashīd, he wrote a letter to the Caliph informing him of what he had done, its text being in the following terms:

963. *Qadhf* is a technical term of Islamic law meaning "an accusation of illicit sexual relations, *zinā*," incurring a *ḥadd* penalty when falsely brought, as is implied a few lines below here; see *EI*² s.v. Ḳadhf (Y. Linant de Bellefonds).

964. I.e., ʿAlī implies that accusations of sexual misconduct made as impreca-

In the name of God, the Merciful, the Compassionate. As follows: God, He is exalted and magnified, has not ceased to shower down on the Commander of the Faithful the most extensive and most perfect of favors in regard to everything which He has entrusted to him as His Caliph, and everything involving the concerns of His servants and His lands which he has committed to his care. God has not ceased to instill into him, in everything near at hand or far of his affairs, personal and general, of minor significance or important, the most complete capability and the finest powers of governing. God has not ceased to grant him, in all that, the best of desires, nor has He ceased to bring him, in the course of this, to the farthest bounds of his aspirations, thereby according him of His favors and keeping safe what He has vouchsafed to him and what will guarantee his own exalted status and that of his retainers and the people with obligations to him and owing him obedience. We ask God to complete (for us) the highest degree of sufficiency and capability in what He has habitually given and has habitually bestowed on us in everything which He entrusts to us, and we ask Him to grant us success for our fulfilling what is incumbent upon us of His rightful due by studying His command and conforming ourselves to His way of thinking.

I myself—may God exalt the Commander of the Faithful—have not ceased, since I left the Commander of the Faithful's army camp, following closely the order which he gave me concerning the course of action which he had made me undertake; I do not go beyond that, I do not stray outside it for any other purpose, and I seek knowledge of neither prosperity nor good fortune except in fulfilling his command. (This I did) until I halted at the nearmost limits of Khurāsān, all this while guarding carefully to myself the orders which the Commander of the Faithful had enjoined me to keep safe and secret, not communicating them either to any single one of my intimates or to any single one of the people in general. I made it my policy to write to the people of Shāsh and Farghānah, to wean them from their connections with the treacherous one (i.e., Rāfiʿ b. Layth) and to put a stop to the covetous designs of Rāfiʿ and his partisans on those two groups of people. I also wrote

tions or exclamations in the course of spirited conversation, rather than as legal accusations, should not be taken into account.

to those at Balkh in the same terms as I had written and explained clearly to the Commander of the Faithful.

Then when I halted at Naysābūr, I directed my efforts to the
[725] matter of the administrative regions which I had just traversed. I issued letters of appointment as governors to those whom I had appointed over these regions before I passed through them, such as Jurjān, Naysābūr, Nasā, and Sarakhs. I was not remiss in taking careful precautions over that and in choosing capable people, reliable and sound persons from my own trusty retainers. I ordered them to keep the whole of the matter concealed and hidden, and I required them to take oaths of obedience in regard to that. I gave each man of them a letter of investiture for his governorship, and I commanded them to proceed to the regions of which they were to have charge, under the most secret and clandestine conditions and adopting the guise of ordinary travellers in their journeying to their administrative regions and their staying there, until the time which I laid down for them, this being the day when I calculated that I would arrive in Marw and would meet with ʿAlī b. ʿĪsā. I made it my policy to assign responsibility [*istikfāʾī*][965] for Jurjān to Ismāʿīl b. Ḥafṣ b. Muṣʿab in accordance with what I had previously written to the Commander of the Faithful. Those governors then put into execution my commands, and each man of them assumed responsibility for his administrative charge and extended his firm control over his particular district at the time which had been indicated to him. Thus, God relieved the Commander of the Faithful of the burden of that through His finely executed design.

When I reached just one stage before the town of Marw, I chose a number of trusty retainers, and I wrote out on sheets of writing material the names of ʿAlī b. ʿĪsā's sons, his secretaries, his family, and others, and I handed over to each man a sheet with the name of the person whom I would assign to his safe custody when I entered the town. If I had not taken these measures or delayed putting them into effect, I would not have been able to guarantee that those designated persons (i.e., those destined to be arrested) would not have disappeared into hiding or dispersed when the news became publicly known and widely disseminated. My agents put

965. For this sense, see Dozy, *Supplément*, II, 479a.

that into execution, and I myself travelled from my halting-place towards the town of Marw.

When I reached a point two miles from it, ʿAlī b. ʿĪsā came out to meet me with his sons, members of his family and his commanders, and I met him in a most splendid manner. I treated him in a friendly fashion and exerted myself in magnifying him and extolling him and seeking to dismount before him the first time I saw him to an extent which made him increase in feeling at ease [726]
and in confidence in the impression which he had previously relied upon from my letters which had been reaching him; for indeed, these had been continuously full of my extolling and magnifying him and my seeking to dispel any evil opinion away from him, lest any idea should occur to his mind which might spoil what the Commander of the Faithful had planned to have done with him and what the Commander of the Faithful had ordered me to do regarding that. But God, He is blessed and exalted, was the One who alone took charge of relieving the Commander of the Faithful of the affairs of ʿAlī, to the point that ʿAlī brought myself and himself together in his court session and I went to eat with him. When we had finished that, he set about asking me to proceed to a lodging which he had sought out for me. At that point, I told him about the things which I had with me and which could not wait any longer for a close perusal. Rajāʾ al-Khādim then handed over the Commander of the Faithful's letter and delivered to him the Caliph's message. At that, ʿAlī realized that the matter by means of which he had injured his own self and which his own two hands had procured—in that the Commander of the Faithful's ire had been aroused, the Commander of the Faithful's view of him had been changed through his going against the Commander of the Faithful's command, and his exceeding the due bounds in his conduct—had now befallen him.

Then I set about putting him into custody and proceeded to the Friday mosque. I opened wide the hopes of the people who were present, and I began by explaining how the Commander of the Faithful had charged me to journey to them, and I informed them how gravely disquieted was the Commander of the Faithful by the reports, which had reached him and which had become clear to him, about ʿAlī's evil conduct. (I further informed them) about what the Commander of the Faithful had commanded me to do with him, his financial agents, and his minions, and (told them) that I was going to put all this into effect, to mete out justice to the masses and the élite alike and to set about restoring to them their rights to the utmost possible extent. I ordered the document investing me with office to be read out to them, and I informed them that that document was my pattern and exemplar, and that I was imitating its counsels and molding my conduct on it; and if I were to abandon one single aspect of that policy, then I would have injured myself and brought down on myself that which befalls those who rebel against the Commander of the Faithful's judgment and command. The people evinced great joy and rejoicing at that, their voices were raised in *takbīr*s and *tahlīl*s, and numerous prayers were sent up by them for the Commander of the Faithful's long life and his receiving a goodly recompense.

I next turned my attention to the place of court sessions and
[727] assembly where ʿAlī b. ʿĪsā was, and set about loading him, his sons, members of his family, his secretaries, and his financial agents with irons, and securing firmly the whole lot of them. I commanded them to bring forth to me the wealth which they had appropriated for themselves, comprising the Commander of the Faithful's wealth and the revenue [*fay*ʾ] for the Muslims, and (I told them that if they did that,) I would dispense with employing harsh measures against them and beatings. I made a proclamation among those people who had had entrusted to their keeping any possessions of ʿAlī and his partisans, summoning them to disgorge what they were holding. They brought these holdings along to me until I had listed for the Commander of the Faithful a respectable portion of silver and gold coinage. I hope that God will give aid in exacting the whole of what they have in their keeping and in extracting to the last farthing what they have secretly stored away. (I hope too that) God will render easily available from that the best of what He has never ceased to accord habitually to the Commander of the Faithful, that is, in undertaking to bring about matters like this with which he is concerned, if God Most High wills.

Nor did I omit, once I arrived at Marw, to give orders for the despatch of messengers and the issuing of trenchant letters, going as far as possible in providing possible excuses, giving warning, providing clear explanation, and offering right guidance, to Rāfiʿ (b. Layth) and the people of Samarqand owing him obedience and to those at Balkh—all this because of my favorable opinion regarding the likelihood of their responding favorably and their adopting the course of obedience and uprightness. Whatever reports, about the people's either responding favorably or else adopting a hostile attitude, which my messengers bring back to me, O Commander of the Faithful, I shall follow a policy appropriate to their attitude and I shall write about that to the Commander of the Faithful, exactly according to what is right and truthful. I hope that God will communicate to the Commander of the Faithful in regard to that something of the excellence of His work and the grace of His sufficiency, which has never ceased to be His habitual procedure towards him through His munificence, power, and might. Farewell!

Al-Rashīd's Answer to Harthamah's Letter

In the name of God, the Merciful, the Compassionate. As follows: There has reached the Commander of the Faithful your letter mentioning your arrival in Marw on the day which you have specified and in the circumstances which you have described and which you have set forth in explanation; what ruses and subter- [728]
fuges you employed before you reached Marw, what measures you adopted in regard to the administrative regions which you named and in regard to the appointment of your nominees as governors over those regions before you yourself passed beyond their boundaries, and what subtle measures you used in the matter which brought about the favorable circumstances which you sought in the affair of the traitor ʿAlī b. ʿĪsā, his sons, the members of his family, and those of his financial agents and district governors who fell into your hands. (There has also reached him news of) your following exactly, in all this, what the Commander of the Faithful delineated to you as the way to proceed and what he rendered possible for you. The Commander of the Faithful has understood everything which you have written, and he has given profuse praises to God for that, for His guiding you aright and for what He helped you to accomplish through His divine aid, until you brought to pass the Commander of the Faithful's will, attained to his desire, performed well the matters about which he had been very anxious and had been dogged with worry, which he was

wanting firmly to accomplish through you and at your hands. May He reward you with beneficence for your wise counsel and your capability, and may God not deprive the Commander of the Faithful of the finest of conduct which he has experienced from you in everything which he has summoned you to undertake and for which he has relied upon you!

The Commander of the Faithful orders you to increase your efforts and determination in ferreting out the wealth of the traitor ʿAlī b. ʿĪsā, his sons, secretaries, financial agents, stewards, and bankers, just as he has commanded you, and in investigating how they have swindled the Commander of the Faithful over his wealth and how they have oppressed the subjects in regard to their wealth. (He likewise commands you to redouble your efforts) in pursuing and in bringing to light this illicit wealth from the suspected hiding places and caches which ʿAlī took under his control and from the hands of those custodians of possessions to whom they had entrusted that (ill-gotten) wealth. You are to use a mixture of softness and harshness in all that, so that you are even-
[729] tually able to extract what they have hidden. Do not spare yourself any effort over that, nor in meting out justice to the people in regard to their rights and their complaints of tyranny against ʿAlī and his followers, until no cause of complaint against them remains for any person seeking redress without your having employed all your efforts[966] on his behalf concerning that, and have set both the wrongdoer and the injured parties on the way of right and justice in regard to this grievance. When you have employed the greatest possible amount of firm measures[967] and zeal over that, send on the traitor, his sons, the members of his family, his secretaries, and his financial agents to the Commander of the Faithful in bonds and in the conditions of affliction [*taghyīr*][968] and exemplary punishment which they have merited by what

966. Thus according to the Leiden and Cairo texts, *istaqḍayta*; but the *Glossarium*, p. CDXXVII, suggests the possible reading *istaqṣayta* "(without) your having fully investigated. . . ." Again, the great floridity of the Arabic style here makes precise translation uncertain.

967. Reading, with the Cairo text, VIII, 336, *al-iḥkām* for the Leiden text's *al-aḥkām*.

968. For this sense, see Dozy, *Supplément*, II, 233b.

their hands have wrought for them. "God does not act wrongfully to his servants."[969]

Then embark upon what the Commander of the Faithful has commanded you to do, in proceeding to Samarqand and in using stratagems and blandishments with regard to the partisans of the obscure one [*khāmil*][970] and with those people of the districts of Transoxania and Ṭukhāristān[971] who have followed him in showing forth rebelliousness and defiance, by summoning them to return and revert to their allegiance and to the all-embracing offer of the Commander of the Faithful's guarantee of safe-conduct which he has charged you with offering to them. If they accept and consent to that and return to what is your own hope for them, and if they disband their forces, then this is what the Commander of the Faithful desires for them—to treat them by overlooking their misdeeds and pardoning them. For they are his subjects, and it is incumbent upon the Commander of the Faithful to treat them thus, since he answers their requests, reassures their fearful hearts, relieves them of rule by governors whose régimes they have hated, and commands that justice should be meted out to them in respect of their due rights and their complaints of oppression. But if they oppose the Commander of the Faithful's views, summon them to judgment before God, since they have rebelled and wrought evil, and have shown their aversion from the way of salvation and have rejected it. Indeed, the Commander of the Faithful has already decreed his course of action; hence, he has plunged people into affliction, inflicted exemplary punishment, dismissed people from office, substituted one person for another, overlooked the deeds of the person who has introduced an heretical innovation and pardoned the man guilty of a crime. He brings God to witness against them after that for any act of disobedience should they deliberately choose it and any act of rebelliousness should they manifest it. God is sufficient as a witness; there is no power and strength

969. Qur'ān, VIII, 53/51.

970. Contemptuous antiphrasis on the part of al-Rashīd for Rāfiʿ (literally, "the exalted one"), as is explicitly pointed out later by Ṭabarī, III, 734 (below, 298).

971. The region lying to the south of the upper Oxus, in what is now northern Afghanistan, Balkh being its mediaeval centre. See Yāqūt, *Muʿjam*, IV, 23; Le Strange, *Lands*, 426–7; Barthold, *Turkestan*, 66–8; *EI*[1] s.v. Ṭokhāristān (Barthold).

except in God, the Exalted, the Mighty; he (i.e, the Caliph) reposes his trust in Him and returns to Him in repentance. Farewell!

Ismāʿīl b. Ṣubayḥ wrote (this) in the Commander of the Faithful's presence.

[730] In this year, al-Faḍl b. al-ʿAbbās b. Muḥammad b. ʿAlī led the Pilgrimage, he being at that time governor of Mecca.[972]

After this year, the Muslims did not mount a summer expedition (against the Byzantines) until the year 215 (830–1).[973]

---

972. Muḥammad b. Ḥabīb, 39; Khalīfah, *Ta'rīkh*, II, 738; Yaʿqūbī, *Ta'rīkh*, II, 738; Azdī, 312; Ibn al-Athīr, VI, 206.

973. Brooks, *EHR*, XV (1900), 747.

The Events of the Year 192

(November 6, 807–October 24, 808)

Among the events taking place during this year was the exchange of captives between the Muslims and the Byzantines arranged by Thābit b. Naṣr b. Mālik (al-Khuzāʿī).[974]

Al-Rashīd's Preparations for His Journey to Khurāsān

In this year, al-Rashīd arrived from al-Raqqah by boat at the City of Peace, intending to set out for Khurāsān and attack Rāfiʿ. His arrival at Baghdad was on Friday, the twenty-fourth of Rabīʿ II (February 26, 808).[975] He appointed as his deputy in al-Raqqah his son al-Qāsim, giving him as support Khuzaymah b. Khāzim. Then he set out from the City of Peace on the evening of Monday (i.e., the Sunday evening), the fifth of Shaʿbān (June 4, 808), after the

---

974. Masʿūdī, *Tanbīh*, 190, tr. 256–7; Ibn al-Athīr, VI, 208; Brooks, loc. cit.; *EI*[2] s.v. Lamas-Ṣū (Huart). This exchange, the *fidā' Thābit b. Naṣr*, the second one enumerated by the sources, took place at the Budandūn river, as specified by Ṭabarī, III, 732 (below, 295).

975. Actually, a Saturday.

afternoon worship and from al-Khayzurāniyyah.[976] He passed the night in the Garden of Abū Jaʿfar,[977] and then set off the next evening for Nahrawān. He encamped there, and sent back Ḥammād al-Barbarī to his administrative charges and appointed his son Muḥammad as his deputy in the City of Peace.[978]

It has been mentioned from Dhū al-Riʾāsatayn[979] (i.e., from al-Faḍl b. Sahl) that he said: When al-Rashīd decided to set out from Khurāsān in order to attack Rāfiʿ, I said to al-Maʾmūn, "You don't know what's going to happen to al-Rashīd whilst he is en route for Khurāsān, which is your governorship; Muḥammad is your superior, and the most favorable way in which he is likely to treat you is to deprive you of the succession (after him), for he is the son of Zubaydah, his maternal uncles are the Hāshimites, and Zubaydah
[731] and all her wealth (will be an added reinforcement for him).[980] So request al-Rashīd to let you go forth with him." Al-Maʾmūn accordingly asked al-Rashīd for permission to accompany him, but the latter refused. So I said to al-Maʾmūn, "Tell him, 'You are ill, and I only wished to render you service, and I shan't be a burden upon you in any way.'" So al-Rashīd allowed him to accompany him, and he departed.[981]

Al-Rashīd's Serious Medical Condition and His Premonitions of Death

Muḥammad b. al-Ṣabbāḥ al-Ṭabarī has mentioned that his father accompanied al-Rashīd on the opening stages when he set out for Khurāsān. He went with him as far as al-Nahrawān, and al-Rashīd

---

976. The quarter of Baghdad either owned by or named after al-Rashīd's mother. See Ibn Abī Ṭāhir Ṭayfūr, 2; Abbott, 120–1.

977. I.e., of the Caliph al-Manṣūr.

978. Jahshiyārī, 214–15; Yaʿqūbī, *Taʾrīkh*, II, 520; Dīnawarī, 391; Azdī, 312; Ṭabarī-Balʿamī, tr., IV, 475; *K. al-ʿUyūn*, 315; Ibn al-Athīr, VI, 207; Abbott, 202; Sourdel, *Vizirat*, I, 188; Kennedy, 132.

979. This title, "Possessor of the two commands," i.e., military and civil, was conferred on al-Faḍl subsequent to this period, in 196 (812), by al-Maʾmūn; see Sourdel, *Vizirat*, I, 201, 203 n. 2.

980. The text here, and in the corresponding passages in the *K. al-ʿUyūn* and Ibn al-Athīr, is evidently defective; the editor of the Leiden text suggests, in n. *g*, the supplying of the phrase *ridʾ*[un] *lahu*, followed for the translation here.

981. Jahshiyārī, 215; Ṭabarī-Balʿamī, tr., IV, 475–6; *K. al-ʿUyūn*, loc. cit.; Ibn al-Athīr, loc. cit.; Palmer, 113–14; Gabrieli, "Successione," 350; Abbott, loc. cit.

began to talk with him along the road until he said to him, "O Ṣabbāḥ, I don't think you will ever see me again." He related: I replied, "Nay, God will bring you back hale and hearty; He has rendered you victorious, and has displayed to you the realization of your hopes in regard to your enemies." The Caliph said, "O Ṣabbāḥ, I don't think you know what I am suffering." I replied, "No, by God!" He said, "Come here, and let me show you." He related: He went aside from the road to a distance of a hundred cubits. He sheltered in the shade of a tree, and made signs to his personal eunuchs [*khadamihi al-khāṣṣah*],[982] and they thereupon withdrew. Then he said, "O Ṣabbāḥ, (I promise you) the protection of God if you will conceal my secret." I replied, "O my master, I am your humble servant; you are addressing me as one addresses one's child!"

He related: He bared his abdomen, and lo, he had a silken bandage round it.[983] He said, "This is a morbid condition which I conceal from everyone. Each one of my sons has an observer over me—Masrūr being al-Ma'mūn's observer, Jibrīl b. Bukhtīshūʿ being al-Amīn's one," and he named a third one whose name I have forgotten, "and every single one of them is only counting my very breaths, numbering my days and considering my life as going on too long. If you want to know this for sure, then summon a horse this very instant, and they will bring me an emaciated hack which [732]
goes with short steps, so that it makes my affliction worse." I replied, "O my master, I can't make any answer to these words, nor regarding the heirs to your succession, except that I say, May God make as a sacrifice instead of you those persons—jinn and men, close relatives and distant ones—who are showing hatred towards you, and may He consign them to that (i.e., death) before you! May God never let us see anything unpleasant happening to you! May He make Islam flourish through you, and may He, through your continued preservation, support its columns and strengthen its flanks! May God bring you back victorious and successful to the

982. It is not clear whether these were a formally constituted group within the general body of the eunuchs, but these *khadam al-khāṣṣah* are again mentioned as existing under al-Amīn, in Ṭabarī, III, 969.

983. In the editor's n. *f*, Ibn al-Jawzī's detailed description of ulcers is given; cf. Abbott, 203 n. 92. According to the Qāḍī Ibn al-Zubayr, 97, § 114, al-Rashīd had for some time suffered from hemorrhoids.

fullest extent of your hopes regarding your enemies and (grant you) what you hope from your Lord!" Al-Rashīd said, "As for you, you have shown yourself as detached from either of the two parties (i.e., the supporters of al-Amīn and al-Ma'mūn, respectively)." He related: Then al-Rashīd called for a horse, and they brought him one just as he had described. He looked at me, and then he rode off on it, saying, "Go back, without having been properly bid farewell, for you have many responsibilities and preoccupations." Accordingly, I merely said goodbye to him, and that was the last time I ever saw him.[984]

Various Items of Information

In this year, the Khurramiyyah became active in the region of Azerbaijan, so al-Rashīd sent ʿAbdallāh b. Mālik against them with a force of ten thousand cavalry; ʿAbdallāh took (male) prisoners and captured (the enemy's women and children), and met up with al-Rashīd at Qarmāsīn. Al-Rashīd then ordered the male prisoners to be killed and the captured women and children to be sold into slavery.[985]

In this year, the judge ʿAlī b. Ẓabyān died at Qaṣr al-Luṣūṣ.[986]

---

984. Ibn al-Athīr, VI, 207–8; Palmer, 120–1; Gabrieli, loc. cit.; Abbott, 203.

985. Khalīfah, *Ta'rīkh,* II, 739; Dīnawarī, 391–2; Azdī, 313; Ibn al-Athīr, VI, 208.

986. Khalīfah, *Ta'rīkh,* loc. cit.

987. Ibn al-Athīr, loc. cit.; the outbreak of his revolt was noted in Ṭabarī, III, 711 (above, 266).

988. Commander who was to be prominent under al-Ma'mūn and his successors as a military leader and provincial governor.

989. *Min abnā' al-shīʿah,* one of the designations for the Abnā'; see Ṭabarī, III, 572 (above, 46, n. 183).

990. Ibn al-Athīr, loc. cit.; Daniel, 174.

991. Apparently a local rebel in Egypt, not to be confused with the ʿAbbāsid prince of the same name later active as a supporter of the rival Caliph Ibrāhīm b. al-Mahdī and executed by al-Ma'mūn, see Ṭabarī, III, 1073, 1075–6.

992. On the Ḥawf or Aḥwāf, see Ṭabarī, III, 629 (above, 141, n. 516).

993. Ibn al-Athīr, loc. cit.; Brooks, *EHR,* XV (1900), 747. On Maṭmūrah, see Ṭabarī, III, 646 (above, 165–66, n. 603).

994. See on this exchange, Ṭabarī, III, 730 (above, 291).

995. Khalīfah, *Ta'rīkh,* II, 739, according to whom Tharwān killed Salm (?) b. Salm b. Qutaybah; Ibn al-Athīr, loc. cit. The Ṭaff ("edge, fringe, shore") was the edge of the cultivated land lying along the Euphrates in Iraq; see Yāqūt, *Muʿjam,* IV, 35–6.

996. According to Khalīfah, *Ta'rīkh,* loc. cit., Maqdisī, 114, and other geograph-

In this year, Yaḥyā b. Muʿādh brought (the Syrian rebel) Abū al-Nidā' to al-Rashīd whilst the latter was at al-Raqqah, and al-Rashīd had him killed.[987]

In this year, ʿUjayf b. ʿAnbasah[988] and al-Aḥwaṣ b. Muhājir, together with a number of members of the earlier supporters in Khurāsān of the ʿAbbāsids,[989] deserted Rāfiʿ b. Layth's side and went over to Harthamah.[990]

In this year, Ibn ʿĀ'ishah,[991] together with a number of persons from the Aḥwāf of Egypt,[992] was brought in.

In this year, he (i.e., the Caliph) appointed Thābit b. Naṣr b. Mālik governor of the frontier regions (i.e., of the Byzantine marches). He led raids and then captured Maṭmurāh.[993]

In this year, there took place the exchange of captives at al-Budandūn.[994]

In this year, Tharwān al-Ḥarūrī became active and killed the government's financial agent in the Ṭaff of al-Baṣrah.[995]

In this year, ʿAlī b. ʿĪsā was brought to Baghdad and then imprisoned in his own house.

In this year, ʿĪsā b. Jaʿfar (b. Abī Jaʿfar al-Manṣūr) died in Ṭabari- [733]
stān or, it is said alternatively, at Daskarah, whilst he was en route to join al-Rashīd.[996]

In this year, al-Rashīd had al-Hayṣam al-Yamānī killed.[997]

In this year, al-ʿAbbās b. ʿAbdallāh[998] b. Jaʿfar b. Abī Jaʿfar al-Manṣūr led the Pilgrimage.[999]

---

ical sources, ʿĪsā b. Jaʿfar died in Ṭabaristān; according to Ibn al-Athīr, loc. cit., at Daskarah (probably the Daskarat al-Malik one stage from the town of al-Nahrawān on the high road to Khurāsān; see Yāqūt, *Muʿjam,* II, 455; Le Strange, *Lands,* 62; and *EI*[2] s.v. [A. A. Duri]).

997. Yaʿqūbī, *Ta'rīkh,* II, 499; Ibn al-Athīr, VI, 209.

998. Thus, correctly for the text's ʿUbaydallāh.

999. Muḥammad b. Ḥabīb, 39; Khalīfah, *Ta'rīkh,* loc. cit.; Yaʿqūbī, *Ta'rīkh,* II, 522.

The Events of the Year 193

(October 25, 808–October 14, 809)

The Illness and Death of al-Faḍl b. Yaḥyā al-Barmakī

Among the events taking place during this year was the death of al-Faḍl b. Yaḥyā b. Khālid b. Barmak in prison at al-Raqqah in al-Muḥarram (October–November, 808). According to what has been mentioned, the onset of his illness was marked by a paralytic stroke affecting his tongue and a side of the body. He had previously been wont to say, "I don't want al-Rashīd to die (before me)," and people used to say to him in reply, "Don't you want God to grant you deliverance (i.e., release from existence in prison)?" But he would answer, "My fate is linked with his fate." He remained under medical treatment for several months and then recovered. He began to talk once again, but then became severely ill once more. His tongue and his side became paralyzed in their functions, and he moved inexorably towards death. He remained in that state on Thursday and Friday, and died during the call for the dawn prayer (on Saturday), five months before al-Rashīd's own death and at the age of forty-five. The people displayed their grief over him, and his brothers prayed over him in the palace where they were lodged before al-Faḍl's body being brought forth (from his prison). Then his corpse was brought forth, and the people performed the worship over his funeral bier.[1000]

In this year, Saʿīd al-Ṭabarī, known as al-Jawharī, died.[1001]

Al-Rashīd's Journey from Jurjān to Ṭūs

In this year, Hārūn reached Jurjān in Ṣafar (November–December, 808), and there met him in Jurjān the treasuries of ʿAlī b. ʿĪsā, conveyed on the backs of fifteen hundred camels.[1002] After this, he set out from Jurjān, according to what has been mentioned, in Ṣafar, in a sick state, to Ṭūs, where he remained till he died. He became suspicious of Harthamah, so he sent his son al-Maʾmūn twenty- [734]
three nights before he died to Marw, accompanied by ʿAbdallāh b. Mālik, Yaḥyā b. Muʿādh, Asad b. Yazīd b. Mazyad, al-ʿAbbās b. Jaʿfar b. Muḥammad b. al-Ashʿath, al-Sindī b. al-Ḥarashī,[1003] and Nuʿaym b. Ḥāzim, with Ayyūb b. Abī Sumayr[1004] to act as his secretary and vizier. Then Hārūn's suffering grew worse until he became too weak to travel.[1005]

Al-Rashīd's Vengeance on Rāfiʿ b. Layth's Brother Bashīr

In this year, there took place a battle campaign between Harthamah and Rāfiʿ's partisans, in the course of which Harthamah conquered Bukhārā and took prisoner Rāfiʿ's brother Bashīr b. al-Layth.[1006] He then sent the latter to al-Rashīd at Ṭūs. It has been mentioned from Ibn Jāmiʿ al-Marwazī, from his father, who said: I

1000. Jahshiyārī, 210–11, with the exact date of death as Saturday, the twenty-fifth of al-Muḥarram (November 18, 808); Azdī, 316; Ibn al-Athīr, VI, 210; Ibn Khallikān, IV, 436, tr. II, 467; Bouvat, 100; Abbott, 199–200.

1001. Ibn al-Athīr, loc. cit.

1002. According to Ṭabarī-Balʿamī, tr. IV, 476, these treasuries amounted to eighty million dirhams in specie plus the textiles.

1003. Maqrīzī, in *Addenda et emendanda,* p. DCCLXIII, has "al-Sindī and Yaḥyā b. Saʿīd al-Ḥarashī."

1004. Ayyūb shared with al-Faḍl b. al-Rabīʿ the duty of presenting [*ʿarḍ*] petitions and requests to the Caliph, according to Jahshiyārī, 215, and later acted as chief secretary-vizier to al-Maʾmūn. See Sourdel, *Vizirat,* I, 184, 198.

1005. Jahshiyārī, 214–15; *K. al-ʿUyūn,* 317; Ibn al-Athīr, VI, 212; Gabrieli, "Successione," 350; Kennedy, 132.

1006. Ṭabarī-Balʿamī, tr., IV, 477; Ibn al-Athīr, VI, 210; Daniel, 174.

was one of those who brought Rāfiʿ's brother to al-Rashīd. He related: Bashīr went into al-Rashīd's presence, when the Caliph was lying on a bed [*sarīr*],[1007] elevated above the ground by the length of the bone of the forearm, with a coverlet over him hanging down the same amount—or, he related, longer—and with a mirror in his hand with which he was regarding his face. He related: I heard him saying, "Indeed we belong to God and to Him we return!" and he looked at Rāfiʿ's brother and said, "By God, indeed, O son of a stinking uncircumcised whore, I certainly hope that the obscure one [*khāmil*]"—he meant Rāfiʿ—"will not escape me, just as you have not escaped me!" Rāfiʿ's brother said to him, "O Commander of the Faithful, I have been an enemy of yours, and God has rendered you victorious over me. Hence, do what God approves (i.e., show clemency), and I will be a man at peace with you; it may also be that God will soften Rāfiʿ's heart for you when he learns that you have shown benevolence towards me!" But al-Rashīd grew enraged and said, "By God, if I had no more life left to me than the ability to form a single word with my lips, I would say, 'Kill him!'" Then he summoned a butcher and told him, "Don't sharpen your knives, leave them as they are, dismember this evildoer son of an evildoer and be quick about it! I don't want death to come upon me whilst two of his limbs remain on his body!" So the butcher dismembered him until he left him a pile of chopped-up limbs. The Caliph said, "Count up the pieces of his body." I
[735] counted the pieces, and lo, they came to fourteen pieces. He raised his hands toward heaven and cried, "O God, just as you have given me power to exact vengeance for you and power over your enemy, and I have now done it to your satisfaction, grant me likewise power over his brother." Then he lost consciousness, and those present dispersed.[1008]

In this year, Hārūn al-Rashīd died.

1007. See on this piece of furniture, Sourdel, "Questions de cérémoniale ʿabbaside," 130–2; Sadan, 32–51.

1008. Masʿūdī, *Murūj*, VI, 357–8 = ed. Pellat, § 2555; Ṭabarī-Balʿamī, tr., loc. cit.; *K. al-ʿUyūn*, loc. cit.; Ibn al-Athīr, VI, 212; Palmer, 124; cf. Ibn al-Athīr, VI, 225. In Jahshiyārī, 221–2, the brother of Rāfiʿ's executed in this horrible fashion, together with others of Rafiʿ's kindred, is named as Marwān.

The Occasion of al-Rashīd's Death and the Place Where He Died

It has been mentioned from Jibrīl b. Bukhtīshūʿ that he said: I was with al-Rashīd in al-Raqqah, and I used to be the first to come in to him each morning, and I would thereby learn (or: so that I might thereby learn) how he had passed the night. If he had experienced something unpleasant, he would describe it, and then he would become more relaxed and would talk to me about what his slave girls were doing, and what he had done in his court session, the amount he had drunk and the amount of time he had spent in session, and then he would ask me for news about the activities of the common people and their conditions of life. Hence, one morning I went into his presence and greeted him, but he hardly raised his glance, and I saw that he was frowning, was sunk in thought, and was preoccupied. I stood there before him for a considerable while of the daylight, whilst he remained thus. When that continued for a long time, I stepped forward towards him and said, "O my master—may God make me your ransom!—why are you like this? Is it some illness? (If so,) tell me about it, and I may have in my possession the appropriate medicine for it. Or has something calamitous struck someone whom you love? (If this latter,) then that is something which cannot be warded off and there is nothing to be done regarding it except resignation and grieving, and there is no redress possible for it. Or has some breach occurred in the fabric of your royal power? (If so,) well, all monarchs are liable to that sort of thing. (In any case,) I am the most suitable person to whom you can pass on the news and in whom you can seek consolation through asking for advice."

He replied, "Alas, O Jibrīl, my grief and sadness are not on account of any of the things you have mentioned, but because of a dream which I had during this last night and which has terrified me, filled my breast (with foreboding), and weighed heavily on my heart." I said, "You have dispelled my fears, O Commander of the Faithful!" and I drew near him and kissed his foot, and I said, "Is all this grief because of a mere dream? Dreams only come from [736]
some fancy within the mind, or from unpleasant vapors, or some bogey arising from a fit of melancholy; they are only 'tangles of

dreams,'[1009] after all this." He replied, "Let me recount it to you. I saw, in my dream, as if I were seated on this bed of mine, when from below me, a forearm and a hand, both of which I recognized but did not know the name of the owner, appeared. In the hand was a fistful of red earth. Then someone, whose voice I could hear but not see his person, said, 'This (is) the earth in which you are going to be buried.' I said, 'Where is this earth?' The voice replied, 'At Ṭūs,' and the hand and arm disappeared from view, the voice was cut off, and I woke up." I said, "O my master, by God, this is a farfetched and confused dream! I think that you went to your bed and then started thinking about Khurāsān, the wars there and the problem of the political disintegration of part of it which has presented itself to you." He said, "It may have been that." He related: I said, "As a result of your pondering over that, these things have entered into your sleep and have given rise to this dream, so don't worry about it—may God make me your ransom!—and let this grief be followed by joy, which will dispel it from your head and not give rise to any sickness!" He related: I kept on soothing his mind with various kinds of devices until he found consolation and his spirits rose; he ordered the preparation of various things which he liked, and that day he carried his diversion and enjoyment to a high degree.[1010]

The days went by, and both he and we forgot that dream and it never came into the mind of any of us. Then al-Rashīd decided upon his journeying to Khurāsān when Rāfiʿ rebelled. When he was some way along the road, the onset of illness struck him and it got continuously worse until we reached Ṭūs. We halted at the residence of al-Junayd b. ʿAbd al-Raḥmān (al-Murrī)[1011] in an estate of his (i.e., of al-Rashīd's) called Sanābādh.[1012] Whilst he was lying ill in a garden of his in that palace, he suddenly remembered that dream. He rose up with difficulty, standing upright for a

1009. Qur'ān, XII, 44.

1010. *K. al-ʿUyūn,* 316–17; Ibn al-Athīr, VI, 211–12; Palmer, 122–3.

1011. A commander prominent under the later Umayyads, *inter alia* as governor of Sind and then in 112 (730) of Khurāsān; see Crone, 98. On the varied accounts in the sources concerning the house where al-Rashīd spent his last hours, see *EI*[1] s.v. Meshhed (Streck).

1012. Subsequently, this village was to have the graves of both al-Rashīd and the Eighth Imām of the Shīʿah, ʿAlī al-Riḍā; on this site grew up the later town of Mashhad. See Yāqūt, *Muʿjam,* III, 259; Le Strange, *Lands,* 388; Streck, op. cit.

moment and then collapsing. We gathered round him, all of us saying, "O my master, how are you feeling and what's happened to you?" He replied, "O Jibrīl, you recall my dream at al-Raqqah concerning Ṭūs?" Then he raised his head towards Masrūr and said, "Bring me some of the earth from this garden." So Masrūr went along and came back with a handful of earth, having pulled [737]
back his sleeve from his forearm. Then when al-Rashīd looked at me, he said, "By God, this is the forearm which I saw in my dream; by God, this is the very same hand; and by God, this is the red earth, you haven't omitted anything!" and he began to weep and lament volubly. Then, by God, he died in that spot three days later and was buried in that garden.[1013]

A certain authority has mentioned that Jibrīl b. Bukhtīshūʿ had made a mistake regarding al-Rashīd's illness in some treatment he prescribed for him which was, in fact, the cause of his death. Al-Rashīd had therefore decided, the night in which he died, to put Jibrīl to death and to have his limbs dismembered just as he had had Rāfiʿ's brother dismembered. He sent for Jibrīl b. Bukhtīshūʿ in order to inflict that on him, but Jibrīl said to him, "O Commander of the Faithful, grant me a respite till tomorrow morning, for you will then find yourself restored to health." Then he died that same day.[1014]

Al-Ḥasan b. ʿAlī al-Rabaʿī has mentioned that his father transmitted the information to him from his own father—who was a camel driver with a hundred camels—who related that he conveyed al-Rashīd to Ṭūs. He related: Al-Rashīd said, "Dig me a grave before I die," so they dug one for him. He related: I conveyed him in a covered litter [*qubbah*], leading him along, until he was able to see it (i.e., the grave). He related: Then he said (to himself), "O son of Adam, you are moving towards this destination!"

A certain authority has mentioned that, when his illness became

---

1013. *K. al-ʿUyūn,* 316; Ibn al-Athīr, VI, 212. Iṣfahānī, *Aghānī,* ed. Būlāq, XVII, 49–50 = ed. Cairo, XVIII, 249, has a variant of this story of al-Rashīd being shown in a dream a handful of earth from his own tomb.

1014. Ibn Abī Uṣaybiʿah, I, 128–30; Abbott, 203. In Ṭabarī-Balʿamī, tr., IV, 476–7, it is said that the Indian physician Mankah (see Ṭabarī, III, 747–8, below, 313–14) was summoned from India at this juncture to treat the Caliph and foretold that al-Rashīd would die before he could inflict vengeance on Jibrīl for his faulty treatment; but A. Müller, "Arabische Quellen zur Geschichte der indischen Medizin," 496–7, pointed out that this is most improbable.

severe, he gave orders for his grave, and it was dug in one spot of the residence where he was lodging, in a place called al-Muthaqqab in the residence of Ḥumayd b. Abī Ghānim al-Ṭā'ī.[1015] When he had completed having his grave dug, he got a group of people to descend into it, and they recited there the whole Qur'ān until they reached the end of it, al-Rashīd being meanwhile in a litter on the edge of the grave.[1016]

Muḥammad b. Ziyād b. Muḥammad b. Ḥātim b. ʿUbaydallāh b. Abī Bakrah[1017] has mentioned that Sahl b. Ṣāʿid[1018] transmitted the information to him, saying: I was with al-Rashīd in the house where he was overtaken by death and at the moment when he was near the point of death. He called for a thick coverlet, and drew up his legs to his body and wrapped it round them, and he began to
[738] suffer dreadfully. I rose up, but he said to me, "Sit down, O Sahl," so I sat down again and remained thus for a long time, without either him speaking to me or I to him, and with the coverlet meanwhile slipping down and his wrapping it round himself once more. When this had gone on for a considerable while, I got up, but he said to me, "Where are you off to, O Sahl?" I replied, "O Commander of the Faithful, my heart cannot endure watching the Commander of the Faithful suffer thus terribly from his illness; if only, O Commander of the Faithful, you would lie down, that would give you greater relief." He related: Al-Rashīd laughed as a healthy man might laugh and then said, "O Sahl, I recall, in this present state of mine, the words of the poet,

---

1015. Streck, *EI*[1] s.v. Meshhed, notes that Ḥumayd b. Abī Ghānim must in fact be the deputy *naqīb* in the ʿAbbāsid Revolution Ḥumayd b. Qaḥṭabah, governor of Khurāsān 152–9/769–76 (see Crone, 188), and the disparity between the mentions of the houses of al-Junayd and Ḥumayd as the scene of the Caliph's death is easily explicable by the latter having taken over the former's residence whilst governor, the whole estate perhaps passing into the hands of the ʿAbbāsid family after Ḥumayd's death.

1016. Ibn al-Athīr, VI, 213.

1017. Descendant of the Prophet's Companion Abū Bakrah, of mawlā origin, and of his son the Umayyad commander ʿUbaydallāh; see Crone, 140, and *EI*[2] s.v. Abū Bakra (M.Th. Houtsma and Pellat).

1018. Mentioned by Ṭabarī, III, 772–3, as being steward of al-Ma'mūn's household [*ʿalā qahramatihi*] in Marw at this time and as being one of al-Ma'mūn's two trusted envoys sent immediately after his father's death to the army of Iraq at Ṭūs to dissuade them from breaking their *bayʿah* to al-Rashīd and returning to Iraq with al-Amīn; cf. Gabrieli, "Successione," 353–4.

Indeed, I come from a noble tribe, whom adverse circumstances
only increase in refractoriness and endurance of hardship.[1019]

It has been mentioned from Masrūr al-Kabīr that he said: When the end of al-Rashīd's allotted span was nigh and he felt the onset of death, he ordered me to lay out the pieces of silk brocade and then bring to him the finest and most expensive garment I could find there. I did not in fact find all these qualities in a single garment, but I did find two garments which were the most costly ones imaginable; I found that they[1020] were similar in value, except that one was slightly more expensive than the other and that one garment was red and the other green. I brought them both to him. He looked at them, and I explained to him about their respective value. He said, "Use the finest one as my shroud, and put the other back in its place."

According to what has been mentioned, he expired in a spot called al-Muthaqqab in the residence of Ḥumayd b. Abī Ghānim in the middle of the night, on the night of Saturday (i.e., the night of Friday-Saturday), the third of Jumādā II of this year (March 24, 809). His son Ṣāliḥ prayed over him, and al-Faḍl b. al-Rabīʿ and Ismāʿīl b. Ṣubayḥ, and from among his eunuchs Masrūr, Ḥusayn, and Rashīd, were actually present at his death.[1021] His caliphate lasted for twenty-three years, two months, and eighteen days, beginning on the night of Friday (i.e., Thursday-Friday), the sixteenth of Rabīʿ I, 170 (September 15, 786) and ending on the night [739]
of Saturday (i.e., Friday-Saturday), the third of Jumādā II, 193.[1022]

Hishām b. Muḥammad (i.e., Ibn al-Kalbī) has said: Abū Jaʿfar

1019. Ibn al-Athīr, loc. cit.; Palmer, 124–5.

1020. Reading with the Cairo text, VIII, 345, *wajadtuhumā.*

1021. Yaʿqūbī, *Taʾrīkh,* II, 521; Ṭabarī-Balʿamī, tr., IV, 477–8; *K. al-ʿUyūn,* 318; Ibn al-Athīr, VI, 213–14; Abbott, 203.

1022. The sources are very much at variance here regarding the date of al-Rashīd's death. Muḥammad b. Ḥabīb, 39, has either the first or the third of Jumādā II. Jahshiyārī, 223, does not specify the actual day of Jumādā II. Khalīfah, *Taʾrīkh,* II, 740, Yaʿqūbī, *Taʾrīkh,* II, 521, Azdī, 316–17, and *K. al-ʿUyūn,* 318, have the night of Saturday-Sunday the first of Jumādā I (but this date was actually a Tuesday). Dīnawarī, 392, has Saturday, the fifth of Jumādā II (March 26, 809). Shābushtī, 227, and Masʿūdī, *Tanbīh,* 345–6, tr. 444, have Saturday, the fourth of Jumādā II (March 25, 809).

Hārūn b. Muḥammad al-Rashīd was hailed as Caliph on the night of Friday (i.e., the night of Thursday-Friday), the fourteenth of Rabīʿ I, 170 (September 13, 786),[1023] when he was twenty-two years old and he died on the night of Sunday (i.e., the night of Saturday-Sunday), the first of Jumādā I, 193 (February 20, 809),[1024] when he was forty-five years old, and he reigned for twenty-three years, one month, and sixteen days.[1025] It has also been said that, on the day he died, he was forty-seven years, five months, and five days old, his birthday being the twenty-sixth of Dhū al-Ḥijjah, 145 (March 17, 763) and the day of his death being the second of Jumādā II, 193 (March 23, 809).[1026] He was handsome, with a comely face, pale complexion and curly hair which had become white.[1027]

The Governors in the Provincial Capitals in Hārūn al-Rashīd's Reign

The governors of Medina: Isḥāq b. ʿĪsā b. ʿAlī; ʿAbd al-Malik b. Ṣāliḥ b. ʿAlī; Muḥammad b. ʿAbdallāh; Mūsā b. ʿĪsā b. Mūsā; Ibrāhīm b. Muḥammad b. Ibrāhīm; ʿAlī b. ʿĪsā b. Mūsā; Muḥammad b. Ibrāhīm; ʿAbdallāh b. Muṣʿab al-Zubayrī; Bakkār b. ʿAbdallāh b. Muṣʿab; Abū al-Bakhtarī Wahb b. Wahb.

The governors of Mecca: al-ʿAbbās b. Muḥammad b. Ibrāhīm; Sulaymān b. Jaʿfar b. Sulaymān; Mūsā b. ʿĪsā b. Mūsā; ʿAbdallāh b. Muḥammad b. Ibrāhīm; ʿAbdallāh b. Qutham b. al-ʿAbbās; Muḥammad b. Ibrāhīm; ʿUbaydallāh b. Qutham; ʿAbdallāh b. Mu-
[740] ḥammad b. ʿImrān; ʿAbdallāh b. Muḥammad b. Ibrāhīm; al-ʿAbbās b. Mūsā b. ʿĪsā; ʿAlī b. Mūsā b. ʿĪsā; Muḥammad b. ʿAbdallāh al-ʿUthmānī; Ḥammād al-Barbarī; Sulaymān b. Jaʿfar b. Sulaymān; Aḥmad b. Ismāʿīl b. ʿAlī; al-Faḍl b. al-ʿAbbās b. Muḥammad.

The governors of al-Kūfah: Mūsā b. ʿĪsā b. Mūsā; Yaʿqūb b. Abī Jaʿfar; Mūsā b. ʿĪsā b. Mūsā; al-ʿAbbās b. ʿĪsā b. Mūsā; Isḥāq b.

1023. Actually, a Wednesday.

1024. Actually, a Tuesday.

1025. Muḥammad b. Ḥabīb, loc. cit.; Shābushtī, loc. cit.; Ṭabarī-Balʿamī, IV, 478; *K. al-ʿUyūn,* loc. cit.

1026. Ibn al-Athīr, VI, 214. Yaʿqūbī, *Taʾrīkh,* loc. cit., makes him forty-six at his death.

1027. Masʿūdī, *Tanbīh,* 346, tr. 444; Ṭabarī-Balʿamī, tr., IV, loc. cit.; *K. al-ʿUyūn,* loc. cit.; Ibn al-Athīr, loc. cit.

al-Ṣabbāḥ al-Kindī; Jaʿfar b. Jaʿfar b. Abī Jaʿfar; Mūsā b. ʿĪsā b. Mūsā; al-ʿAbbās b. ʿĪsā b. Mūsā; Mūsā b. ʿĪsā b. Mūsā.

The governors of al-Baṣrah: Muḥammad b. Sulaymān b. ʿAlī; Sulaymān b. Abī Jaʿfar; ʿĪsā b. Jaʿfar b. Abī Jaʿfar; Khuzaymah b. Khāzim; ʿĪsā b. Jaʿfar; Jarīr b. Yazīd; Jaʿfar b. Sulaymān; Jaʿfar b. Abī Jaʿfar; ʿAbd al-Ṣamad b. ʿAlī; Mālik b. ʿAlī al-Khuzāʿī; Isḥaq b. Sulaymān b. ʿAlī; Sulaymān b. Abī Jaʿfar; ʿĪsā b. Jaʿfar; al-Ḥasan b. Jamīl, mawlā of the Commander of the Faithful; Isḥāq b. ʿĪsā b. ʿAlī.

The governors of Khurāsān: Abū al-ʿAbbās al-Ṭūsī; Jaʿfar b. Muḥammad b. al-Ashʿath; al-ʿAbbās b. Jaʿfar; al-Ghiṭrīf b. ʿAṭāʾ; Sulaymān b. Rāshid, over the land tax (only); Ḥamzah b. Mālik; al-Faḍl b. Yaḥyā; Manṣūr b. Yazīd b. Manṣūr; Jaʿfar b. Yaḥyā, his deputy there being ʿAlī b. al-Ḥasan b. Qaḥṭabah; ʿAlī b. ʿĪsā b. Māhān; Harthamah b. Aʿyan.[1028]

Some Aspects of al-Rashīd's Conduct and Mode of Life

Al-ʿAbbās b. Muḥammad has mentioned from his father, who had it from al-ʿAbbās, who said: Al-Rashīd used to perform one hundred (supererogatory) bowings [*rakʿahs*] per day as part of his daily sessions of worship until he departed this life, unless he happened to be ill, (in which case) he used to give as voluntary alms [*kāna yataṣaddaqu*], out of his own money, one thousand dirhams for each day, on top of what he gave as the obligatory poor- [741]
tax [*zakāt*].[1029] When he performed the Pilgrimage, there performed it with him a hundred legal scholars and their sons; and when he could not perform it personally, he sent (in his stead) three hundred men on the Pilgrimage with generous expense allowances and a splendid covering for the Kaʿbah [*kiswah*].[1030]

He used consciously to follow in the footsteps of al-Manṣūr and used to endeavor to model his own conduct on that, except in regard to the expending of money,[1031] for no Caliph before him had

1028. Khalīfah, *Taʾrīkh*, II, 741–8; Ibn al-Athīr, VI, 214–15.

1029. Cf. Ibn Khaldūn, tr. I, 33.

1030. Ibn al-Athīr, VI, 217. For the *kiswah*, see *EI*² s.v. Kaʿba (Wensinck-J. Jomier).

1031. Al-Manṣūr had put the newly established ʿAbbāsid caliphate on a firm financial footing by his careful stewardship, earning for himself the nickname of

ever been known as more lavish in distributing money, and then al-Ma'mūn after him (was likewise lavish). He would never let anyone's good action go neglected by him, nor would he put off recognition of that action as soon as it merited reward.[1032]

He used to like poets and poetry, and have a penchant for literary persons and those learned in the religious law; but he used to dislike disputes over religious matters, saying that it was a profitless exercise and that, very probably, there was no (heavenly) reward for it. He used to love panegyric poetry, especially that of an eloquent poet, and he would purchase this at a high price. Ibn Abī Ḥafṣah has mentioned that Marwān b. Abī Ḥafṣah went into al-Rashīd's presence on Sunday, the third of Ramaḍān, (1)81 (October 29, 797), and recited to him the poem of his in which he says,

Through Hārūn, the frontier gaps were closed up, and the rope strands
of the Muslims' affairs made secure through him.
His banner has not ceased to be raised in victory;
he has an army, from which other armies are shattered into splinters.
Every monarch of Byzantium has paid tribute to him
unwillingly, out of hand constrainedly, in a state of humiliation.[1033]
Hārūn has left al-Ṣafṣāf ("the Willow Fortress") a plain razed level [*ṣafṣaf*],[1034]
as if no person had ever left there traces of his own presence and his animals.
[742] He halted before al-Ṣafṣāf until he sacked and threw it open for plundering,
and then a most tenacious one, one vying for superiority,

Abū al-Fulūs "Father of farthings." See Thaʿālibī, *Laṭā'if*, 22, tr. 50, and on these accusations and denials of his stinginess, Sadan, "The division of the day and programme of work of the Caliph al-Manṣūr," *Studia orientalia memoriae D. H. Baneth dedicata*, 256 n. 3.

1032. Ibn al-Athīr, loc. cit.

1033. Echoing Qur'ān, IX, 29, in which it is said that the People of the Book (which would here, by extension, include the Byzantines) are to be combatted till they pay the poll-tax, in a state of humiliation [*wa-hum ṣāghirūn*].

1034. Cf. Ṭabarī, III, 646 (above, 165) for a *rajaz*-verse using the paronomasia (here, technically, *jinās al-ishtiqāq*).

contended with him (i.e., the Byzantine Emperor) for possession of it among the frontier fortresses.

All eyes are raised to his face, whereas all other eyes
gazing on people have never been raised to the like of Hārūn.

You see all around him the rich masters of the house of Hāshim,
just as the shining stars surround the full moon.

The noble ones of Quraysh urge along his hands,
and both of these hands are a swollen sea (i.e., of bounty) to the people.

When the people lack clouds (i.e., of largesse), there come down successively
on them, through the agency of your two hands, thick clouds bearing rain.

Quraysh entrusted their affairs (i.e., in the matter of the caliphate) to you with full confidence,
just as the traveller throws down his staff (i.e., he arrives and halts at his final destination, and hence can dispense with his staff),

Affairs handed down as the inheritance of the Prophet, of which you have taken control,
and which you, with your firm resolution, keep concealed or divulge.

They have finally reached you, and have then come to rest (in you); and it is only
to those who are worthy of it (i.e., of the Prophet's inheritance) that the end of affairs finally reaches.

You have left us as your successor one who is divinely guided in justice and liberality,
and the virtue of kindness is not one to be belittled nor is the decision an unjust one.

The sons of ʿAbbās are light-giving stars;
when one star disappears from view, another shining one comes into sight.

O progeny of the one who provided water for the pilgrims (i.e., Hāshim),[1035] [743]
the first installments and the latter ones of your generosity have come upon me successively,

1035. See on Hāshim's right of *siqāyah*, Ṭabarī, III, 631 (above, 144, and n. 532).

So that I have become quite certain that I cannot give
adequate thanks for your beneficence, although I am truly thankful.
The people are just like a man who goes down to your cisterns to drink,
and who goes away from them with thirst quenched with water.
The arms of the children of ʿAbbās, in every straitened place of fighting,
(are) the foremost parts of spear shafts and sharp-edged swords.
Hence, on one occasion they brandish trenchant swords and spears[1036]
while on another, the sceptres and staffs of royal authority are waved in their hands.
In the hands of those who are powerful in conferring benefits and wreaking harm, which never become tired
for them in conferring gifts, even when death is pressing hard.
May the royal power, whose throne and pulpits
have become through you proudly exalted, bring joy to you!
Your forefather (i.e., al-ʿAbbās) was the helper of the Chosen One, and not Hāshim,[1037]
even though the haughty noses (i.e., the pride) of those who envy you may be brought low![1038]

Al-Rashīd then gave him five thousand dīnārs, and Marwān took possession of it on the spot; he gave him his own robe as a token of honor, ordering him to be given ten Greek slaves, and he provided him with a horse from his choicest mounts.[1039]

It has been mentioned that Ibn Abī Maryam al-Madanī was one of al-Rashīd's companions, and he was full of fun with the Caliph, full of stimulating conversation, and cheerful company. Al-Rashīd could not bear to be without him and never got tired of talking

1036. Following the emendation suggested by Von Kremer, in *Addenda et emendanda*, p. DCCLXIII, and the Cairo text, VIII, 348, *makhāṣir*, instead of the text's *maḥāḍir* "judicial decrees."

1037. Thus, implicitly excluding the family of ʿAlī, descendents of al-ʿAbbās's brother Abū Ṭālib.

1038. Munierah al-Rasheed, 122–3, no. 68; *Shiʿr Marwān b. Abī Ḥafṣah*, 53–4, no. 34; Harley, "Abu's-Simṭ Marwān b. Abī Ḥafṣah," 84.

1039. Ibn al-Athīr, loc. cit.

with him. He was one of the persons who combined these last [744] qualities with knowledge of stories about the Ḥijāzīs, the nicknames of the noble Arabs, and the ruses of the dissolute persons and scoffers [*mujjān*]. Ibn Abī Maryam's intimacy with al-Rashīd grew so close that the latter established him in a lodging in his own palace, and let him mingle with his womenfolk, his intimates, his mawlās and his slaves. Al-Rashīd went along one night, when Ibn Abī Maryam was asleep, although the dawn had started to gleam and he himself had got up to perform the worship, and found Ibn Abī Maryam asleep. So he pulled the coverlet off from his back and then said to him, "How are you this morning?" Ibn Abī Maryam replied, "O you there, I don't yet know how I feel this morning, go away, and get on with your work." Al-Rashīd said, "Shame on you! Get up for the worship!" He replied, "This is the time for the morning worship according to Abū al-Jārūd,[1040] whereas I am a follower of the judge Abū Yūsuf."[1041] So al-Rashīd went on his way and left him sleeping. Al-Rashīd got ready for the worship. Then Ibn Abī Maryam's slave came to him and said, "The Commander of the Faithful has gone along for the preliminary stages of the worship."[1042] So Ibn Abī Maryam got up, threw over himself his robes, and proceeded towards him, and lo, there was al-Rashīd reciting the Qur'ān in the dawn worship. He came up to him when he was reciting the words, "And why should I not worship the One who created me?"[1043] and Ibn Abī Maryam said, "By God, I don't know!" Al-Rashīd could not prevent himself from bursting into laughter in the midst of the worship. Then he turned to Ibn Abī Maryam, as if he were angry, and said, "O Ibn Abī Maryam, you even jest in the middle of the worship?" Ibn Abī Maryam replied, "O you there, and what have I done?" Al-Rashīd said, "You've interrupted the thread of my act of worship." He replied, "By God, I haven't done that. I merely heard some words

---

1040. Abū al-Jārūd Ziyād b. al-Mundhir was a legal scholar and commentator who supported the Fifth Imām of the Shīʿah Muḥammad al-Bāqir's son Zayd and consequently founded the Jārūdiyyah subsect of the Zaydīs. See Van Arendonck, 78–80; Madelung, *Der Imām al-Qāsim*, 44 ff.; *GAS*, I, 528, 552.

1041. See Ṭabarī, III, 609 (above, 109 and n. 417).

1042. I.e., for the *iqāmah*, the second call to worship which begins the *ṣalāt* proper; see *EI*² s.v. Iḳāma (T. W. Juynboll).

1043. Qur'ān, XXXVI, 21/22.

from you which disturbed me when you said, 'And why should I not worship the One who created me?' so I said, 'By God, I don't know!'" Then he went back. Al-Rashīd laughed, but he added, "Take care not to joke about the Qur'ān and religion; but apart from those two topics, you can say what you like."[1044]

A certain one of al-Rashīd's eunuchs has mentioned that al-ʿAbbās b. Muḥammad[1045] presented al-Rashīd with a valuable compound of perfumes [*ghāliyah*].[1046] He went into his presence, having brought it with him, and said, "O Commander of the Faithful, may God make me your ransom! I have brought you some *ghāliyah* whose like no one else possesses; its musk is from the navels of choice Tibetan musk-oxen [*al-kilāb al-tubbatiyyah*];[1047] its amber is from the amber of the Sea of Aden; its olibanum comes from so-and-so al-Madanī, famed for the excellent way he pre-
[745] pares it; and the man who compounds it is a man in al-Baṣrah who is knowledgeable about blending it together and expert at compounding it. If the Commander of the Faithful thinks fit to be gracious to me by accepting it, then I hope he will do so." Al-Rashīd said to Khāqān al-Khādim, who was standing by his head, "Khāqān, bring in the *ghāliyah*." So Khāqān brought it in, and lo, it was in a large silver jar [*burniyyah*] with a spoon in it. He uncovered the top. Ibn Abī Maryam happened to be present and said, "O Commander of the Faithful, give me this!" The Caliph said, "Take it for yourself." At this, al-ʿAbbās grew irate and flamed up with anger, saying, "Shame upon you! You have tried to get your hands on something which I denied myself and chose to present to my lord, and now you have taken it!" Ibn Abī Maryam replied, "May my mother be a whore, if I smear any part of my body with it except my anus!"

He related: Al-Rashīd laughed. Then Ibn Abī Maryam sprang up; he threw the fringe of his tunic over his head, put his hand in the jar

---

1044. Ibn al-Athīr, VI, 217–18; Ibn Khaldūn, tr. I, 33–4; Palmer, 171–2.

1045. Unidentified; clearly not, on chronological grounds alone, the senior ʿAbbāsid prince al-ʿAbbās b. Muḥammad b. ʿAlī, see Ṭabarī, III, 547 (above, 7, and n. 19).

1046. Although highly valued, not every ruler liked the use of *ghāliyah*; cf. the anecdote concerning al-Muʿtaṣim's detestation of it, in Hilāl al-Ṣābi', 32–3, tr. Salem, 30–1.

1047. Tibet was famed as the producer of the finest musk; see Thaʿālibī, *Laṭā'if*, 224, 238, tr. 142, 146.

and began to extract from it as much as his hand could hold, and began to smear it on his anus in the first place, and in the second place on his groins and armpits. Then he smeared it on his face, head, and extremities, until he had covered all his limbs. He said to Khāqān, "Bring in my slave to me!" Al-Rashīd said, hardly able to think straight for laughing, "Summon the slave!" so he summoned him. Ibn Abī Maryam said to the slave, "Go and take the remainder of this to so-and-so," meaning his wife, "and tell her, 'Smear this on your vulva, until I come home and copulate with you.' " The slave took it and went off, while al-Rashīd was in uncontrollable transports of laughter. Then Ibn Abī Maryam went up to al-ʿAbbās and said, "By God, you are a stupid old man. You come to God's Caliph and you praise *ghāliyah* in his presence. Do you not realize that everything which the heavens shower down and everything which the earth brings forth is his? Likewise, everything which is in this present world is the possession of his hand, beneath his seal ring and in his grasp! Even more remarkable than this is the fact that the Angel of Death has been instructed, 'Look at everything which this person (i.e., the Caliph) asks you to do, and do it,' and then a fellow like this has popped up in his presence, praising the *ghāliyah* and orating at great length in describing it, as if he were a grocer, or druggist, or date-merchant!"[1048] He related: At this, al- [746]
Rashīd laughed till he almost choked to death, and he gave Ibn Abī Maryam on that day one hundred thousand dirhams.

It has been mentioned from Zayd b. ʿAlī b. Ḥusayn b. Zayd b. ʿAlī b. al-Ḥusayn b. ʿAlī b. Abī Ṭālib,[1049] who said: One day, al-Rashīd intended to drink some medicine, so Ibn Abī Maryam said to him, "What about making me your doorkeeper tomorrow, when you take the medicine, and everything which I get we'll share between us." He said, "I agree!" So he sent a message to the (permanent) doorkeeper, "Stay at home tomorrow, for I have appointed Ibn Abī Maryam to the office of doorkeeper (temporarily)." Ibn Abī Maryam went along the next morning, and the (doorkeeper's) seat was put in place for him. Al-Rashīd took the medi-

---

1048. The thinking seems here to be that al-Rashīd's power is so mighty that even the Angel of Death hastens, on God's express instructions, to carry out his desires; so why should he have to suffer being harangued about a mere pot of *ghāliyah*?

1049. See on him Ṭabarī, III, 673 (above, 210, and n. 718).

cine. The news reached the circle of his intimates. Hence, there came along Umm Jaʿfar's messenger, enquiring how the Commander of the Faithful was and about the medicine he had taken. Ibn Abī Maryam had him introduced into his own presence; he learned about the Caliph's condition and returned home with the answer. Ibn Abī Maryam said to the messenger, "Inform the noble lady how I managed to get you in before all the other people." So the messenger informed Umm Jaʿfar, and she sent him (i.e., Ibn Abī Maryam) a large sum of money. Then Yaḥyā b. Khālid's messenger came along, and he did the same with him. Then the messenger of Jaʿfar and al-Faḍl came along, and he did likewise. Each one of the Barmakīs sent him a handsome present. Then al-Faḍl b. al-Rabīʿ's messenger came along, but he sent him away and would not allow him to enter. The messengers of the military commanders and the great men came along, but he would not facilitate the admission of any of them unless he sent him a handsome present. Before the time of the afternoon worship, sixty thousand dīnārs had already rolled in to him. When al-Rashīd recovered from his indisposition and his system was purged of the medicine, he sent for Ibn Abī Maryam and said to him, "What have you been doing today?" He replied, "O my master, I have earned sixty thousand dīnārs." Al-Rashīd was astonished at the size of the sum and said, "And now, where is my share?" He replied, "Set aside (for you)." Al-Rashīd said, "We have granted our own share to you, but present us with ten thousand apples (instead)!" Ibn Abī Maryam did that; he was the most financially successful person with whom al-Rashīd ever did business.

It has been mentioned from Ismāʿīl b. Ṣubayḥ, who said: I went
[747] into al-Rashīd's presence, and lo, there was a slave girl by his head with a bowl in one of her hands and a spoon in the other, and she was feeding him with it in successive spoonfuls. He related: I saw a thin, white substance and had no idea what it was. He related: He realized that I was eager to know what it was, so he said, "O Ismāʿīl b. Ṣubayḥ!" and I answered, "Here I am, O my lord!" He said, "Do you know what this is?" I replied in the negative. He said, "It's a kind of gruel [*jashīsh*] made from rice, wheat, and the water in which the bran in white flour has been steeped.[1050] It's beneficial

1050. *Jashīsh* or *dashīsh* was a porridge-like dish; see Dozy, *Supplément*, I, 442b.

for contorted limbs and contraction of the tendons, it makes the skin clear, dispels red blotches on the face, puts fat on the body, and clears away impurities." He related: When I returned homewards, the sole thought in my mind was to summon the cook. I said to him, "Set before me each morning a dish of *jashīsh*." He replied, "What's that?" So I described to him the recipe I had heard. He said, "You'll be fed up with it on the third day." However, he made it on the first day, and I found it good; he made it on the second day, and it became less appetizing; he brought it on the third day and I told him, "Don't offer it (to me) any more!"

It has been mentioned that al-Rashīd once fell ill. The physicians gave him treatment, but he did not recover at all from his sickness. So Abū ʿUmar al-Aʿjamī said to him, "There is a physician in India called Mankah, to whom they accord preeminence, as I have observed, over all others in India. He is one of their devout ascetics and philosophers. If therefore the Commander of the Faithful were to send for him, it might well be that God would vouchsafe for him a cure at his hands." He related: Hence, al-Rashīd sent someone who would provide him with a mount, and he sent him a sum of money for his travel expenses. He related: Mankah arrived; he prescribed for al-Rashīd and the latter was cured of his illness through Mankah's treatment. So al-Rashīd allotted to him a substantial allowance and a comfortable amount of wealth.

One day, Mankah was passing by al-Khuld when he found himself in the presence of a man from the Manichaean sect [*min al-Māniyyīn*[1051]], who had spread out his cloak and displayed on it numerous drugs and simples. He stood there describing a remedy
which he had in the form of an electuary [*maʿjūn*], and in his [748]
description stated that "This is a remedy effectual for continuous fever, fever occurring on alternate days, quartern and tertian fever; for curing aches in the back and knees, hemorrhoids and flatulence; for pain in the joints and in the eyes; for pain in the abdomen, headache and neuralgia; for incontinence of urine, hemiplegia and trembling in the limbs and body,"[1052] and he did not

1051. Thus in both the Leiden and Cairo texts (VIII, 352); but the editor of the Leiden text suggests, n. *e*, following A. Müller, the possibility of the reading *min al-māʾinīn* "one of the quacks, charlatans."

1052. *Irtiʿāsh*, perhaps something like Parkinson's disease.

omit a single illness of the human body without mentioning that remedy as a cure for it. Mankah said to his interpreter, "What is this man saying?" The interpreter conveyed to him what he had heard. At this, Mankah smiled and said, "On all counts, the ruler of the Arabs is a fool [*jāhil*]. For if the state of affairs is as this quack alleges, why did he transport me from my land, cut me off from my family, and incur heavy expenses on my behalf, when he could find this fellow in front of his eyes and right before his face? And if the state of affairs is not as this quack says, why doesn't the ruler have him killed? For the *Sharīʿah* has declared the shedding of his blood licit, and the blood of those like him, because if he is killed, it is a case of many people being preserved alive through the killing of a single soul. Whereas if the ruler leaves this ignoramus untouched, he will bring about someone's death every day, and indeed, it is very likely that he will be the death of two or three or four each day. This indicates poor control over affairs and is a weakness in the state."[1053]

It has been mentioned that Yaḥyā b. Khālid b. Barmak appointed a man to one of the posts involving collection of the land tax in the Sawād. He went into al-Rashīd's presence to say farewell to him, and the Caliph happened to have with him Yaḥyā and Jaʿfar b. Yaḥyā. Al-Rashīd said to Yaḥyā and Jaʿfar, "Give him some suitable advice!" Yaḥyā told the man, "Make economies in expenditure,[1054] and render the land prosperous and populous"; Jaʿfar said to him, "Mete out justice for others and be just with yourself"; and al-Rashīd said to him, "Act with equity and kindness!"[1055]

It has been mentioned concerning al-Rashīd that he once became angry with Yazīd b. Mazyad al-Shaybānī, but then once more showed him his favor, and gave him permission to come to his court session. Yazīd accordingly came into his presence and said, "O Commander of the Faithful, praise be to God who has made

---

1053. Ibn Abī Uṣaybiʿah, II, 33–4; Müller, "Arabische Quellen zur Geschichte der indischen Medizin," 480–3, 496–7.

1054. This meaning of the imperative *waffir* seems to fit best here, as is likewise advocated in the *Glossarium*, pp. DLXI–DLXII, instead of the other, apparently opposing sense of "expand, stimulate growth." As with so many of the *aḍdād* or words with contrary meanings in Arabic (see on them *EI*² s.v. [G. Weil]), the contradiction in meaning is more apparent than real; the basic meaning is "to take care lest something diminish, to maintain something integrally."

1055. Echoing Qurʾān, XVI, 92/90; Ibn al-Athīr, VI, 218.

easy for us the way of liberality, who has brought down to us beneficence through proximity to you and who has removed from us the tendency towards anxiety through your heaping munificence upon us! So may God recompense you, in your condition of anger, with the favor accorded to those who repent and turn to God, and in your condition of approval, with the reward of those who confer beneficence, accord their favor and distribute munificence! For God—and to Him be praise—has placed you in a position so that you relent, thus avoiding sin, when you are carried away by anger, so that you bestow lavishly benevolence, and so that you overlook wrongdoing, granting as a favor your forgiveness!" [749]

Muṣʿab b. ʿAbdallāh al-Zubayrī[1056] has mentioned that his father ʿAbdallāh b. Muṣʿab related to him that al-Rashīd once said to him, "What's your view about those who have impugned ʿUthmān?" I replied, "O Commander of the Faithful, one group of people have impugned him, whilst another group have defended him. Now as for those who have impugned him and who then have diverged from him, they comprise various sects of the Shīʿah, heretical innovators and various sects of the Khārijites; whereas in regard to those who have defended him, these are the mainstream Sunnī community [*ahl al-jamāʿah*] up to this present day." Al-Rashīd told me, "I shan't need ever to ask about this again after today."[1057] Muṣʿab related: My father said: He further asked me about the status [*manzilah*] which Abū Bakr and ʿUmar enjoyed in regard to the Messenger of God. I told him, "Their status in regard to him during his life was exactly the same as at the time of his death." Al-Rashīd replied, "You have provided me with a completely satisfactory answer for what I wanted to know."

He related: Sallām (al-Abrash) or else Rashīd al-Khādim—one of the eunuchs of the Caliph's close entourage—was appointed administrator of al-Rashīd's estates in the Byzantine frontier region and the districts of Syria. Letters arrived continuously bringing news of his excellent conduct, of his economical administra-

1056. See Ṭabarī, III, 591 (above, 75, and n. 292).

1057. See, for discussions on these attitudes to the first caliphs, Watt, *The formative period of Islamic thought*, 9–12, 163, 166 ff., and on one aspect of the Shīʿī attacks on them, Goldziher, "Spottnamen der ersten Chalifen bei den Schîʿiten," *WZKM*, XV (1901), 321–34 = *Gesammelte Schriften*, IV, 295–308.

tion,[1058] and of the people's praise for him. Hence, al-Rashīd ordered him to be summoned to the court and to be handsomely rewarded, and he added, as seemed good to him, the estates in al-Jazīrah and Egypt to his responsibilities. He related: So the man in question arrived and came into the Caliph's presence whilst the latter was eating a quince which had been brought from Balkh, peeling it and eating sections of it. Al-Rashīd said to him, "O so-and-so, what excellent reports have been reaching your master about you! You can have from him whatever you wish! I have already ordered you to be given such-and-such an amount, and have given you charge of such-and-such, so now ask whatever personal request you have!" He related: So the man spoke, and
[750] mentioned his own excellent conduct, and said, "By God, O Commander of the Faithful, I have caused them to forget the conduct of the two ʿUmars!" He related: Al-Rashīd grew angry and flared up, and took his quince and threw it at him, saying, "O son of a stinking uncircumcised whore! (You keep on saying) the two ʿUmars, the two ʿUmars, the two ʿUmars! Granted that we have conceded it for ʿUmar b. ʿAbd al-ʿAzīz, are we then to concede it for ʿUmar b. al-Khaṭṭāb?"[1059]

ʿAbdallāh b. Muḥammad b. ʿAbdallāh b. ʿAbd al-ʿAzīz b. ʿAbdallāh b. ʿAbdallāh b. ʿUmar b. al-Khaṭṭāb has mentioned that Abū Bakr b. ʿAbd al-Raḥmān b. ʿUbaydallāh b. ʿAbdallāh b. ʿUmar b. ʿAbd al-ʿAzīz transmitted the information to him from al-Ḍaḥḥāk b. ʿAbdallāh and spoke well of him, saying: One of the sons of ʿAbdallāh b. ʿAbd al-ʿAzīz related to me, saying: Al-Rashīd said, "By God, I don't know what I should do about this al-ʿUmarī (i.e., ʿAbdallāh b. ʿAbd al-ʿAzīz)![1060] I don't want to approach him personally, since he has progeny whom I detest. I would very much like to hear something about his mode of life and his way of thinking, but I haven't got anyone trustworthy whom I might send

---

1058. Following the reading of the *Addenda et emendanda,* p. DCCLXIII, and of the Cairo text, VIII, 353, *tawfīrihi;* see also n. 1054 above.

1059. Clearly expecting the answer, No! Al-Rashīd's exasperation at continually having to listen to the praises of his predecessors recalls the exasperation of the Athenians leading to the exiling of Aristides the Just.

1060. This al-ʿUmarī was a noted ascetic and descendant of the Caliph ʿUmar I, who lived in the desert outside Medina and died there in 182 (798) or 184 (800). See Ibn Qutaybah, 186; Masʿūdī, *Murūj,* III, 138 = ed. Pellat, § 990, idem, *Index,* VII, 474.

to him." ʿUmar b. Bazīʿ and al-Faḍl b. al-Rabīʿ said, "Then send us, O Commander of the Faithful!" He replied, "All right, you two then." Hence, they set out from al-ʿArj[1061] to a spot in the desert called Khalṣ,[1062] taking with them guides from the people of al-ʿArj, until when they reached ʿAbdallāh in his dwelling, they came upon him in the early morning and lo, ʿAbdallāh was in his oratory. They, and those of their escort who were accompanying them, made their camels halt and kneel to allow them to descend. Then they came to ʿAbdallāh in the guise of monarchs, having pleasant perfume, fine clothes, and fragrant substances, and the two of them sat down before him, he being in an oratory of his.

They said to him, "O Abū ʿAbd al-Raḥmān, we are envoys from the people of the East whom we have left behind and who say to you, 'Fear God, your Lord, and if you are so disposed, rise up (in rebellion)!' " He came up close to them and said, "Woe upon you both! Regarding whom have you come, and for whom are you seeking?" They replied, "You!" He said, "By God, I wouldn't like to meet God even with just a cupping-glass full of the blood of a man from the Muslims, and as for myself, I have at my disposal whatever the sun rises upon." When they despaired of getting him implicated, they said, "We have with us something which you [751]
would find useful for all your life." He replied, "I have no need of it, I am perfectly well off without it." They told him, "It's twenty thousand dīnārs." He retorted, "I have no need of it." They said, "Give it then to whomsoever you like." He replied, "You two, you give it to whomsoever you consider fit; I'm not your servant or minion." He related: When they had given up all hope of interesting him (in these worldly gains and ambitions), they rode off on their camels until they reached the Caliph in the morning at al-Suqyā[1063] at the second stage (i.e., from Mecca) and found him awaiting them. When they went into his presence, they related

1061. A settlement in the Ḥijāz, in the territory of Hudhayl, on the road from Mecca to Medina. See Bakrī, III, 930–1; Yāqūt, *Muʿjam*, IV, 98–9; Al-Wohaibi, 52–7.

1062. A wadi also lying between Mecca and Medina, known as Khalṣ of Ārah. See Bakrī, I, 91, II, 507; Yāqūt, *Muʿjam*, II, 382–3; Al-Wohaibi, 122–3.

1063. A stage on the road northward from Mecca and al-Juḥfah to Medina. See Bakrī, III, 742–3; Yāqūt, *Muʿjam*, III, 228; al-Wohaibi, index, s.v.

to him what had taken place between them and ʿAbdallāh. The Caliph thereupon said, "After this, I don't care what I do!"[1064]

Then ʿAbdallāh made the Pilgrimage in that same year. Whilst he was standing by one of those traders there, buying something for his children, behold, Hārūn appeared, making the *saʿy* between al-Ṣafā' and al-Marwah on a horse. At that point, ʿAbdallāh interposed himself before Hārūn, leaving off what he was about to do, and he went up to the Caliph till he gripped his horse's bridle. The troops and guards pounced on him immediately, but Hārūn brushed them away from ʿAbdallāh, and then the latter spoke with him. He related: I saw Hārūn's tears, and they were running down on to his horse at the place where the mane grows; then he turned away.

Muḥammad b. Aḥmad, the mawlā of the Banū Sulaym, has mentioned, saying: Al-Layth b. ʿAbd al-ʿAzīz al-Jūzjānī, who was one who had come into Mecca from outside[1065] and had been settled there [*kāna mujāwir*[an]] for forty years, transmitted the information to me that a certain doorkeeper (of the Kaʿbah) transmitted the information to him that, when al-Rashīd made the Pilgrimage, he entered the Kaʿbah and he stood on his tiptoes (i.e., in order to reach as high as possible) and said, "O You who are master of the requests of those making petition and who know the hearts of those who remain silent, You have a ready rejoinder and an answer at hand for every petition made to You, and for everyone who remains silent before You, You have an all-encompassing knowledge which gives expression to Your sincere promises, Your outstanding favors and Your all-extending mercy. Grant blessings to Muḥammad and his house, forgive us our sins and pardon our misdeeds! O You whom sins do not harm, from whom no faults are hidden and whose power the forgiveness of offences does not diminish! O You who have spread out the earth over the waters, have filled up the air with the heavens, and have chosen the (Most Beautiful) Names for Yourself, grant blessings to Muḥammad and

---

1064. I.e., the Caliph now feels secure and relieved that no danger is to be expected from ʿAbdallāh.

1065. Presumably, from the region of Jūzjān or Gūzgān in what is now northern Afghanistan. See Le Strange, *Lands*, 423; Barthold, *An historical geography of Iran*, 32–5; *EI*[2] s.v. Djūzdjān (R. Hartmann).

choose for me the best course in all my affairs. O You before whom [752]
voices speak with submissiveness and with all kinds of utterances laying before You their petitions, one of my petitions to You is that You may grant me forgiveness when You bring my term of life to an end and when I am laid in my sepulchral niche and my family and children have all gone away from me. O God, praise be to You, a praise which is superior to all other praise just as You Yourself are superior to all creation! O God, grant blessings to Muḥammad in a way which will indicate approval for him, and grant blessings to Muḥammad in a way which will be a source of protection for him, and reward him with the finest and most complete reward of the afterlife for what he has done for us. O God, grant us life as fortunate ones, fulfill our term of life as martyrs, and make us fortunate ones provided with sustenance, and not wretched and deprived ones!"[1066]

ʿAlī b. Muḥammad (al-Madāʾinī) has mentioned from ʿAbdallāh, saying, al-Qāsim b. Yaḥyā related to me, saying: Al-Rashīd sent a message to Ibn Abī Dāwūd and those who look after the tomb of al-Ḥusayn b. ʿAlī at al-Ḥayr.[1067] He related: They were brought along. Al-Ḥasan b. Rashīd looked at Ibn Abī Dāwūd and said, "What's happened to you?" He replied, "This man"—he meant al-Rashīd—"has sent a message to me and summoned me to his presence, and I don't trust him with my personal safety." Al-Ḥasan b. Rāshid told him, "Now, when you enter his presence and he questions you, tell him, 'Al-Ḥasan b. Rāshid has appointed me to that position.'" So when he entered the Caliph's presence, he repeated these words. Al-Rashīd said, "That this confusion has been caused by al-Ḥasan's meddling is just what I would have expected! Summon him here!" He related: When al-Ḥasan was present, al-Rashīd said, "What impelled you to appoint his man in al-Ḥayr?" He replied, "May God have mercy on the one who appointed him in al-Ḥayr! Umm Mūsā ordered me to appoint him there and to assign to him thirty dirhams a month." He said, "Send him back to al-Ḥayr and assign to him the same as Umm Mūsā

1066. Ibn al-Athīr, VI, 218–19.

1067. I.e., al-Ḥāʾir (literally, "the enclosure"). See Yāqūt, *Muʿjam,* II, 208; Le Strange, *Lands,* 79; *EI*² s.v. Karbalāʾ (Honigmann).

did." (Umm Mūsā[1068] was the mother of al-Mahdī and the daughter of Yazīd b. Manṣūr.)

ʿAlī b. Muḥammad has mentioned that his father transmitted the information to him, saying: I went into al-Rashīd's presence in the house of ʿAwn al-ʿIbādī,[1069] and there he was with summer
[753] arrangements in an open pavilion, with no carpet or covering in the place at all, on a low seat by a door in the right-hand side of the pavilion. He was wearing a thin shift [*ghilālah*][1070] and a Rashīdī[1071] loincloth, with ornamented borders and dyed a deep red color.[1072] He did not use to have the pavilion where he sat cooled down by artificial means for bringing in fresh air [*lā yukhayyishu al-bayta*] because it used to discommode him, but the cool air created by the *khaysh* arrangements[1073] used to reach him, even though he was not actually sitting in it. He was the first person to cause to be made a second, internal roof [*saqf dūna saqf*][1074] for the pavilion where he took his siesta in summer. This arose from the fact that, when he heard the information that the former Persian emperors used to have the outer surfaces of their pavilions plastered with mud each day, from the outside, in order to keep the

---

1068. I.e., Arwā, wife of al-Manṣūr, whose father Yazīd b. Manṣūr (also in the sources, simply Manṣūr) al-Ḥimyarī was governor for the Caliph of al-Baṣrah and the Yemen and who claimed descent from the ancient kings of South Arabia. See Ibn Qutaybah, 379; Abbott, 15–16.

1069. See on this, Ṭabarī, III, 678 (above, 216, and n. 733).

1070. Here, clearly a very thin, cool garment, like an undershirt, rather than the "cloak" rendered thus by Serjeant, 62 n. 11. *Ghilālah* was also used for a thin, often transparent women's undergarment; see Ahsan, 41, and *EI*² s.v. Libās. 1. In the central and eastern Arab lands (Yedida K. Stillman), at V, 737.

1071. Obviously some kind of thin linen material, conceivably from the town in the Nile delta al-Rashīd (Rosetta), since Egypt was famous for its linens, as suggested in the *Glossarium*, pp. CCLXIII–CCLXIV. Serjeant, 62 n. 11 (cf. Ahsan, 35), suggests that the Caliph al-Rashīd may himself have popularized the material or that it may have had *tirāz* or embroidered borders with his name.

1072. *Shadīd al-tadrīj*, thus interpreted by the editor of the Cairo text, VIII, 356; but the phrase could also bear the meaning "laid wide open" in reference to the slit down the front of the shift.

1073. *Khaysh*, literally "coarse linen or canvas (sheet)," i.e., one which could be hung up and moistened in order to create a supply of cooled air in the intense heat of the Iraqi summer, and thence any kind of arrangement, such as a fan or punkah, to achieve this effect; see Agius, 229–33, and *EI*² s.v. (Pellat). The use of a moistened sheet is said to have been introduced under al-Manṣūr; see Ṭabarī, III, 418, and Thaʿālibī, *Laṭāʾif*, 19–20, tr. 48–9.

1074. Presumably, some kind of false ceiling, the space between the roof and this ceiling acting as an insulation layer.

heat of the sun away from themselves,[1075] he himself adopted the use of a (second, internal) roof next to the main roof of the pavilion where he used to take his siesta.

ʿAlī (further) related from his father: I was informed that, on every day of scorching summer heat, al-Rashīd used to have a silver urn [*tighār*][1076] in which a perfume merchant used to make up a mixture of fragrant perfume, saffron, aromatic substances, and rose water. He would then go into the pavilion where he took his siesta and there would be brought in with him seven Rashīdī shifts of fine linen material [*qaṣab*],[1077] of feminine cut, and these last would then be dipped into that aromatic mixture. Each day, seven slave girls would be brought in; each girl would have her dress taken off and then a shift would be given to her, and she would sit down on a seat which was pierced with holes and the shift would be unloosed and draped over the seat so that the shift covered it over. Then it was fumigated with perfumed vapor from beneath the seat, with aloes wood conjoined with amber, for a certain period of time, until the garment should dry on her. He used to follow that practice with the slave girls, and this procedure would take place in the pavilion where he took his siesta; as a result, the pavilion would become permeated with the fragrant incense and the perfume.

ʿAlī b. Ḥamzah has mentioned that ʿAbdallāh b. ʿAbbās b. al-Ḥasan b. ʿUbaydallāh b. al-ʿAbbās b. ʿAlī b. Abī Ṭālib said: Al-ʿAbbās b. al-Ḥasan told me: Al-Rashīd said to me, "I notice that you talk a great deal about Yanbuʿ[1078] and its characteristic features, so describe it to me in a concise fashion." I said, "In ordinary speech, or in verse?" He replied, "In both." He related: I said, "Its [754]
special quality lies basically in its luscious date clusters, and its luscious date clusters make up its easeful nature."[1079] He related: Al-Rashīd thereupon smiled, and I then recited to him,

---

1075. The wet mud acting by evaporation as a cooling agent.

1076. See Dozy, *Supplément*, I, 147b, and Fraenkel, 69, for its previous Aramaic form (also found in Arabic as *ṭinjīr*).

1077. This plain linen (and possibly also silk) material was often woven or decorated with gold or silver thread. See Serjeant, 37; Agius, 264–5.

1078. The port on the Red Sea coast of the Ḥijāz. See Bakrī, IV, 1402; Al-Wohaibi, 53 ff.; *EI*[1] s.v. (A. Grohmann).

1079. I.e., its fine dates provide an easy life for those residing there and resorting to there.

O watercourse of the palace, what a fine palace and watercourse,
with the features of a residence in the settled lands, if you prefer it, or those of the desert!
You see its long ships, with the whitish-fawn camels halted there,
and the lizard, the fish, the boatman, and the camel driver![1080]

Muḥammad b. Hārūn has mentioned from his father, who said: I was once in al-Rashīd's presence, and al-Faḍl b. al-Rabīʿ said to him, "O Commander of the Faithful, I have summoned Ibn al-Sammāk[1081] just as you commanded me to do."[1082] He said, "Bring him in!" So Ibn al-Sammāk entered and al-Rashīd said to him, "Deliver to me a piece of spiritually edifying advice [*ʿiẓnī*]!" He replied, "O Commander of the Faithful, fear God, the Unique One who has no partner, and know that on the morrow you will be standing before God your Lord, and then consigned to one of the two future states—there is no third one—either paradise or hell-fire." He related: Hārūn wept until his beard became damp with tears. Al-Faḍl went up to Ibn al-Sammāk and said, "God forbid, does anyone have any possible doubt that the Commander of the Faithful will be consigned to paradise, if God wills, through his efforts to uphold God's rights, his justice among his subjects and his benevolence?" He related: Ibn al-Sammāk took no notice of al-Faḍl's words and did not turn towards him; instead, he went up to the Commander of the Faithful and said, "O Commander of the Faithful, this fellow"—he meant al-Faḍl b. al-Rabīʿ—"will not, by God, be with you or at your side, on that day, so fear God and look to yourself!" He related: At this, Hārūn wept until we were afraid for his well-being. Al-Faḍl b. al-Rabīʿ was rendered speechless, and did not say a word until we all went out.

1080. These verses are stated in other sources to refer to a palace constructed by the ʿAbbāsid prince Muḥammad b. Sulaymān at al-Baṣrah (see Ṭabarī, III, 607–8, above, 105–7), e.g., by Masʿūdī, *Murūj*, VI, 291–2 = ed. Pellat, § 2497, attributing the verses to the poet Ibn Abī ʿUyaynah al-Muhallabī; by Yāqūt, *Muʿjam*, IV, 361–2, referring to a palace of ʿĪsā b. Jaʿfar b. Sulaymān at al-Ḥarbiyyah of Baghdad, attributed to the same poet; and in Bakrī, II, 659, merely recited, as in Ṭabarī, in reference to Yanbuʿ.

1081. I.e., Muḥammad b. Ṣubayḥ or Ṣubḥ, Kūfan traditionist and frequent preacher [*wāʿiẓ*] at al-Rashīd's court, who died in 183 (799). See al-Khaṭīb al-Baghdādī, V, 368–73, no. 2895, and further references in Masʿūdī-Pellat, Index, VII, 648.

1082. Cf. Ibn Khaldūn, tr. I, 33.

He related: Ibn al-Sammāk went into al-Rashīd's presence one day. Whilst he was there with him, the Caliph called for a drink of water. So an earthenware pitcher of water was brought in. But when he tipped it up to his mouth in order to drink from it, Ibn al-Sammāk said to him, "Gently now, O Commander of the Faithful, by your relationship to the Messenger of God! If this drink of water were to be withheld from you, how much would you purchase it for?" He replied, "For half my kingdom." He said, "Drink, may God render it wholesome for you!" When the Caliph had drunk it, Ibn al-Sammāk said to him, "I ask you, by your relationship to the Messenger of God, if you were prevented from passing that drink of water from out of your body, how much would you purchase that for?" He replied, "For the whole of my kingdom." Ibn al-Sammāk said, "A kingdom whose value is only a drink of water isn't, indeed, worth aspiring to (or: contending over, *allā yunāfasa fīhi*)!" At this, Hārūn wept. Al-Faḍl b. al-Rabīʿ then made a sign to Ibn al-Sammāk to depart, so the latter left.[1083] [755]

He related: ʿAbdallāh b. ʿAbd al-ʿAzīz al-ʿUmarī[1084] addressed a spiritually edifying discourse to al-Rashīd. The latter received his words with "Yes indeed, O my uncle!" and when ʿAbdallāh turned away to depart, al-Rashīd sent after him two thousand dīnārs, in a purse, with al-Amīn and al-Maʾmūn. The two of them confronted al-ʿUmarī with the money and said, "O uncle, the Commander of the Faithful says to you, 'Take this and use it for your own benefit, or else distribute it (among the deserving).'" He replied, "The Caliph knows best to whom he should distribute it," but then he took just one dīnār from the purse and said, "I don't want to add an unpleasant action to an unpleasant word." After that incident (i.e., on a subsequent occasion), al-ʿUmarī set off towards the Caliph at Baghdad, but al-Rashīd was apprehensive about his coming to the capital, and he gathered together the members of the ʿUmarī family. He then told them, "What's happened to the relationship between myself and the son of your uncle? I could endure him in the Ḥijāz, but he has now made his way to the seat of my power and is seeking to subvert my followers! Make him go back from my court!" But they replied, "He won't accept that from us!" Hence,

1083. Ibn al-Athīr, VI, 219–20.
1084. Cf. Ibn Khaldūn, tr. I, 33, n. 87, on this ascetic.

al-Rashīd wrote to Mūsā b. ʿĪsā,[1085] (asking him) to approach al-ʿUmarī in a circumspect and diplomatic manner in order to make him go back. So ʿĪsā summoned for approaching al-ʿUmarī a young lad of only ten years' age who knew by heart sermons and pious homilies. The boy spoke to al-ʿUmarī at great length and addressed to him pious exhortations, the like of which al-ʿUmarī had never before heard, and he warned off al-ʿUmarī from approaching and troubling the Commander of the Faithful. Al-ʿUmarī took off his sandal and stood there, repeating, "So they shall confess their sin; hence cursed be the companions of hell-fire!"[1086]

[756] A certain person has mentioned that he was with al-Rashīd at al-Raqqah after he had set out from Baghdad. He went out hunting with al-Rashīd one day, when an ascetic appeared before him and addressed him, "O Hārūn, fear God!" The Caliph said to Ibrāhīm b. ʿUthmān b. Nahīk, "Take this man with you, until I get back." When he returned, he called for his midday meal. Then he gave orders for the man to be fed with the choicest of his food. When he had eaten and drunk, he summoned him and said, "O fellow, treat me fairly when you deliver your sermons and make your intercessions!" The man replied, "That is the least which is due to you." The Caliph said, "Tell me now, am I an evil and most wicked person, or a Pharaoh (i.e., a tyrant)?" The ascetic replied, "Nay, a Pharaoh." The Caliph quoted, "I am your Lord, the Most High,"[1087] and the man responded, "I know no god for you except myself."[1088] The Caliph said, "You have spoken truly; now tell me, who is better, you yourself or Moses, son of ʿImrān?" He replied, "Moses is the one who spoke with God and was His chosen one, whom He took as his protégé and upon whom He relied for delivering His inspired revelations, and He singled him out to speak with Him out of all His creation." The Caliph said, "You have spoken truly; are you not aware that when He sent Moses and his brother to Pharaoh, He said to them, 'Speak to him gently, perhaps he will take heed or show fear.'[1089] The Qurʾānic commentators have

---

1085. At this time (ca. 192 [808]) governor of Mecca, see Ṭabarī, III, 739 (above, 304).

1086. Qurʾān, LXVII, 11.

1087. Ibid., LXXIX, 24.

1088. Ibid., XXVIII, 38.

1089. Ibid., XX, 46/44. This and the two preceding quotations all allude to the

mentioned that He ordered the two of them to call Pharaoh by his patronymic, this (daring move[1090]) being done when Pharaoh was in his status of arrogance and overweening pride, as you have well known. Yet you have come to me at a moment when I am in this position of which you are aware! I fulfill the greater part of the prescriptions which God has imposed upon me as obligatory, and I worship none but Him. I obey the most important of the limits against transgression laid down by God, His commands and His prohibitions. But you have harangued me with the most violent and unseemly words, and the roughest and foulest of speech; you have not been schooled in the practice of God's praiseworthy discipline nor have you adopted the good qualities of the righteous ones! So what has been making you feel confident that I shall not come down heavily upon you? If this last is in fact the case, you will have laid yourself open to what was a quite unnecessary risk!" The ascetic replied, "I have made a mistake, O Commander of the Faithful, and I ask your pardon." He replied, "God has already pardoned you," and ordered him to be given twenty thousand dirhams. However, the ascetic refused to accept it and said, "I don't need the money at all, I am an ascetic who wanders round [*rajul sā'iḥ*[1091]]." Harthamah spoke to him and looked at him askance, [757]
"You boorish fellow, are you hurling back the Commander of the Faithful's present in his face?" But al-Rashīd said, "Leave him alone," and then told the ascetic, "We didn't offer you the money because you are in need of it, but simply because it is our custom that no one who is neither one of the Caliph's entourage nor one of his enemies ever addresses him without the Caliph giving him a present and rewarding him. So accept what proportion you like of our gift, and spend it how you please!" The man took two thousand dirhams from the sum of money and divided it out among the doorkeepers and those present at the court.

---

stories of Pharaoh (the archetypal tyrant in the Qur'ān, see *EI*² s.v. Firʿawn [Wensinck and G. Vajda]) and Moses.

1090. Because the use of the *kunyah,* a designation of respect, implies equality of status and familiarity; see *EI*² s.v. (Wensinck). Schwally, in Bayhaqī, *Maḥāsin,* 190 n. 1, notes that the Caliph never addressed his ministers by their *kunyah* but only by their *ism* or given name.

1091. *Sā'iḥ* or *sayyāḥ* was a frequent designation for wandering dervishes.

*Al-Rashīd's (Free) Wives Who Were Endowed with Substantial Dowries [*al-mahā'ir*]*

It is said that he married Zubaydah, that is, Umm Ja'far bt. Ja'far b. al-Manṣūr, and consummated the marriage with her (*a'rasa bihā*, literally "he had her conducted to him in marriage") in the year 165 (781–2) during al-Mahdī's caliphate, at Baghdad and in the residence of Muḥammad b. Sulaymān. She subsequently (i.e., after al-Rashīd's death) went to live with al-'Abbāsah and then with al-Mu'taṣim billāh. She gave birth for al-Rashīd to Muḥammad al-Amīn, and died at Baghdad in Jumādā I, 216 (June–July, 831).[1092]

He also married Umm Muḥammad, the daughter of Ṣāliḥ al-Miskīn, and consummated his marriage with her at al-Raqqah in Dhū al-Ḥijjah, 187 (November–December, 803). Her mother was Umm 'Abdallāh the daughter of 'Īsā b. 'Alī and mistress of (or: owner of, *ṣāḥibah*) the residence of Umm 'Abdallāh in al-Karkh, at which were the date-juice makers [*aṣḥāb al-dibs*]. She had been married to Ibrāhīm b. al-Mahdī, but then she was repudiated by him and al-Rashīd married her.[1093]

He also married al-'Abbāsah, the daughter of Sulaymān b. Abī Ja'far and consummated his marriage with her in Dhū al-Ḥijjah, 187 (November–December, 803); both she and Umm Muḥammad, the daughter of Ṣāliḥ, were brought to him (in that same year).[1094]

He also married 'Azīzah, the daughter of al-Ghiṭrīf (b. 'Aṭā').[1095] She had previously been married to Sulaymān b. Abī Ja'far, but he divorced her, and al-Rashīd then married her in the second instance. She was the daughter of al-Khayzurān's brother.

[758] He also married al-Jurashiyyah al-'Uthmāniyyah, the daughter of 'Abdallāh b. Muḥammad b. 'Abdallāh b. 'Amr b. 'Uthmān b. 'Affān, called al-Jurashiyyah because she was born at Jurash in the Yemen.[1096] Her father's grandmother was Fāṭimah bt. al-Ḥusayn b. 'Alī b. Abī Ṭālib, and her father's paternal uncle was 'Abdallāh b.

1092. See *EI*[1] s.v. Zubaida (K. V. Zettersteen) and Abbott, 137 ff., Part II. Zubaidah.

1093. Cf. Abbott, 137.

1094. Ibid.

1095. Hence, niece of al-Khayzurān; see Abbott, 29, 68, 137.

1096. Abbott, 137. For the town of Jurash, see Hamdānī, 255–8; Yāqūt, *Mu'jam*, II, 126–7.

Ḥasan b. Ḥasan b. ʿAlī b. Abī Ṭālib, may God be pleased with them.

Al-Rashīd died leaving behind four of these noble, highly dowried wives: Umm Jaʿfar; Umm Muḥammad, the daughter of Ṣāliḥ; ʿAbbāsah, the daughter of Sulaymān; and al-ʿUthmāniyyah.[1097]

Al-Rashīd's Children

Of male children, al-Rashīd had Muḥammad the Elder (i.e., al-Amīn), by Zubaydah; ʿAbdallāh al-Maʾmūn, by a slave concubine mother [*umm walad*] called Marājil;[1098] al-Qāsim al-Muʾtaman, by a slave concubine mother called Qaṣif; Abū Isḥāq Muḥammad al-Muʿtaṣim, by a slave concubine mother called Māridah; ʿAlī, by Amat al-ʿAzīz; Ṣāliḥ, by a slave concubine mother called Riʾm;[1099] Abū ʿĪsā Muḥammad, by a slave concubine mother called ʿIrābah;[1100] Abū Yaʿqūb Muḥammad, by a slave concubine mother called Shadhrah; Abū al-ʿAbbās Muḥammad, by a slave concubine mother called Khubth;[1101] Abū Sulaymān Muḥammad, by a slave concubine mother called Rawāḥ; Abū ʿAlī Muḥammad, by a slave concubine mother called Duwāj; and Abū Aḥmad Muḥammad, by a slave concubine mother called Kitmān.[1102]

Of female children, al-Rashīd had Sukaynah, by Qaṣif, and hence the sister of al-Qāsim; Umm Ḥabīb, by Māridah, and hence the sister of Abū Isḥāq al-Muʿtaṣim; Arwā, by Ḥalūb; Umm al-Ḥasan,

---

1097. Ibn al-Athīr, VI, 216.

1098. A gloss from Maqrīzī's *Kitāb al-Muqaffā,* in *Addenda et emendanda,* p. DCCCLXIII, adds the explanation, "a slavegirl who was called Marājil, thus nicknamed by her fellow-concubines because she had beautiful hair, and was always busy combing it (*tarjīlihi*) and looking after it."

1099. The Cairo text, VIII, 360, has *R.th.m,* possibly *Rathim,* literally, "having a white mark on the nose or upper lip (of a horse)"; but the Leiden text's *Riʾm* "white gazelle" is more appropriate and is, moreover, well-attested as a woman's name till the present day.

1100. Literally, "foul, obscene talk," and hence applied by antiphrasis.

1101. Literally, "foulness, wickedness," again by antiphrasis; in various places of Iṣfahānī, *Aghānī,* we have *Khinth,* literally "fold of cloth, interior of the cheek," more feasibly to be vocalized as *Khanith, Khunuth* "delicate, languid (of a woman)."

1102. Ṭabarī-Balʿamī, tr., IV, 478. Yaʿqūbī, *Taʾrīkh,* II, 521, and *K. al-ʿUyūn,* 319, list twelve sons, the extra one being Abū Ayyūb; Ibn al-Athīr, loc. cit., also lists twelve sons, the extra one being Abū Muḥammad. Ibn Qutaybah, 383, merely names a selection of eight children.

by ʿIrābah; Umm Muḥammad, that is, Ḥamdūnah; Fāṭimah, by Ghuṣaṣ,[1103] whose (other) name was Muṣaffā; Umm Abīhā, by Sukkar; Umm Salamah, by Rahīq; Khadījah, by Shajar, and hence
[759] the sister of Karīb;[1104] Umm al-Qāsim, by Kh.z.q; Umm Jaʿfar Ramlah, by Ḥaly; Umm ʿAlī, by Anīq; Umm al-Ghāliyah, by Samandal; and Rayṭah, by Zīnah.[1105]

More Aspects of al-Rashīd's Conduct and Mode of Life

Yaʿqūb b. Isḥāq al-Iṣfahānī has mentioned, saying: al-Mufaḍḍal b. Muḥammad al-Ḍabbī[1106] said: Al-Rashīd sent for me, and I had no idea what it was about except that the messengers came to me at night and said, "Respond to the Commander of the Faithful's summons!" So I went out until I came to him, this being on a Thursday, and behold, the Caliph was reclining, propped on his elbow, with Muḥammad b. Zubaydah on his left and al-Maʾmūn on his right. I greeted him and he motioned to me, so I sat down. Then he said to me, "O Mufaḍḍal!" I replied, "Here I am at your service, O Commander of the Faithful." He said, "How many names of persons are indicated in the word *fa-sa-yakfīkahumu* ("and He [i.e., God] will suffice you regarding them")?[1107] I replied, "Three names of persons, O Commander of the Faithful." He said, "What are they, then?" I replied, "The letter *kāf* (i.e., the pronoun suffix *-ka*) refers to the Messenger of God, the *hāʾ* and *mīm* (i.e., the pronoun suffix *-humu*) refer to the unbelievers, and the *yāʾ* (i.e., the verbal prefix *ya-*) refers to God, He is magnified and exalted." The Caliph commented, "You have spoken correctly;

1103. Literally, "death rattles," and hence by antiphrasis; but according to Ibn al-Sāʿī, *Nisāʾ al-khulafāʾ*, 53, Ḥamdūnah's mother had the (orthographically very similar) name of Ghaḍīḍ. Now in the light of the mention in al-Khaṭīb al-Baghdādī, III, 392, no. 1513, of Muḥammad b. Yūsuf b. al-Ṣabbāḥ al-Ghaḍīḍī "who used to have charge of the affairs of Ḥamdūnah bt. Ghaḍīḍ, the *umm walad* of Hārūn al-Rashīd, and thus acquired this *nisbah*," it would seem that Ghaḍīḍ rather than Ghuṣaṣ is in fact correct.

1104. Thus in the Cairo text, loc. cit., for the apparently barely legible reading of the Leiden editor's manuscript.

1105. Ibn al-Athīr, VI, 216–17. All these daughters were by slave mothers.

1106. Celebrated Kūfan philologist, author *inter alia* of a collection of proverbs and of a poetical anthology, the *Mufaḍḍaliyyāt*; he died ca. 170 (786–7). See *GAL*, I², 118–19, S I, 36–7, 179; *GAS*, II, 32, VIII, 115–16; *EI*¹ s.v. (Ilse Lichtenstaedter).

1107. Qurʾān, II, 131/137.

this shaykh"—he meant al-Kisā'ī[1108]—"has given us the same interpretation." Then he turned to Muḥammad and asked him, "Did you comprehend, O Muḥammad?" He replied, "Yes." The Caliph said, "Repeat the problem to me just as al-Mufaḍḍal interpreted it," and he repeated it. Then he turned to me and said, "O Mufaḍḍal, do you have any knotty problem which you would like to ask us about in the presence of this shaykh (i.e., al-Kisā'ī)?" I replied, "Yes, O Commander of the Faithful." He asked, "What is it?" I said, "The words of al-Farazdaq,

We have seized the far horizons of the heavens against you,
their two moons and their rising stars are ours.[1109]

He said, "An unnecessary question; this shaykh provided us with the interpretation of this on a previous occasion before you came. By 'their two moons are ours' he means the sun and moon, just as one says 'the *Sunnah* of the two 'Umars,' (meaning) 'the *Sunnah* of Abū Bakr and 'Umar.'" He related: I said, "May I now proceed further with my query?" He said, "Carry on!" I said, "Why do people consider this a neat expression?" He said, "Because when two nouns of the same kind come together, and one of them is lighter on the tongues of those uttering it, they make that lighter one of the two names prevail over the other and refer to the other
by it.[1110] Now when 'Umar's reign proved longer than Abū Bakr's [760]
one, and 'Umar's conquests became more numerous and his name was lighter on the tongue, they made his name the dominant one, and referred to Abū Bakr by his (i.e., 'Umar's) name. God, He is magnified and exalted, has said, 'the distance between the two Orients,'[1111] and this means the Orient and the Occident." I said, "There has remained a further point in the question." He (al-

---

1108. Philologist and authority on the "readings" of the Qur'ān. He had been tutor to the young al-Rashīd, and the Caliph in turn made him tutor to his sons al-Amīn and al-Ma'mūn and took him as one of his own boon-companions; he died in 189 (805). See *GAL*, I², 117–18, S I, 177–8; *GAS*, VIII, 117, IX, 127–31; *EI²* s.v. al-Kisā'ī, Abu 'l-Hasan 'Alī (R. Sellheim).

1109. *Naqā'iḍ Jarīr wa-al-Farazdaq*, ed. Bevan, II, 700; *Sharḥ Dīwān al-Farazdaq*, ed. al-Ṣāwī, II, 519.

1110. This is the phenomenon which the Arabic grammarians called *taghlīb*, giving one term in a pair "predominance"; see Wright, *Arabic grammar*, I, 189–90.

1111. Qur'ān, XLIII, 37/38.

Rashīd?) then said (to al-Kisā'ī?),[1112] "Is there anything more regarding this question than what we have already said?" He replied, "This is the fullest extent of what they say, and the whole of the explanation according to the Arabs." He related: Then he turned to me and he said, "What else remains?" I said, "There remains the topic of the aim towards which the vaunting poet was tending in the poem of his." He said, "What's that?" I replied, "By 'the sun' he meant Ibrāhīm (i.e., Abraham)[1113] and by 'the moon' he meant Muḥammad, and by 'the stars' the Rightly Guided Caliphs from your own pious forefathers."

He related: The Commander of the Faithful lifted up his head and said, "O Faḍl b. al-Rabī', convey one hundred thousand dirhams to him in order to satisfy his debts; see what poets there are at the gate, and then let them be allowed in." And behold, (there turned out to be at the gate) al-'Umānī[1114] and Manṣūr al-Namarī, so he allowed them both to enter. The Caliph said, "Bring the shaykh (i.e., al-'Umānī) to me," and he approached the Caliph, at the same time reciting,

Say to the Imām, whose rightful course is to be followed,[1115]
"Qāsim is not inferior to the son of his mother (i.e., al-Rashīd's mother, meaning al-Rashīd himself) in extent of qualities."
We have become content with him, so arise and nominate him (as successor to the caliphate)!

Al-Rashīd said, "You're not content to call for the oath of allegiance as successor to be made to him whilst I am still sitting down, but you want me to arise and proclaim it standing (i.e., to give it greater forcefulness)!" He said, "An act of standing indicat-

1112. The Cairo text, VIII, 361, has here explicitly "Then he turned to al-Kisā'ī and said . . . ," whereas the Leiden text is ambiguous; cf. n. *b*.

1113. Echoing the leading role accorded in Islamic lore to Abraham as the first *ḥanīf* or worshipper of the One God and as the founder of the *millat Ibrāhīm* which Muḥammad claimed to have rediscovered and to have restored; see *EI*[2] s.v. Ibrāhīm (R. Paret).

1114. I.e., Muḥammad b. Dhu'ayb al-Ḥanẓalī, *rajaz* poet of al-Baṣrah and eulogist of the 'Abbāsids; he died in the reign of al-Rashīd. See Iṣfahānī, *Aghānī*, ed. Būlāq, XVII, 78–82 = ed. Cairo, XVIII, 311–21; Pellat, *Le milieu baṣrien*, 160; *GAL*, S I, 91–2; *GAS*, II, 464.

1115. Following in *Addenda et emendanda*, p. DCCLXIII (as also in Iṣfahānī, *Aghānī*, ed. Cairo, XVIII, 315, and *Lisān al-'Arab*[1], XV, 398), *al-muqtadā biammihi*.

ing intention, O Commander of the Faithful, not one for promulgating a fully decided decree!" The Caliph said, "Let al-Qāsim be brought in," so he was brought in. Al-ʿUmānī recited his *rajaz* poem in a low murmur. Al-Rashīd then said to al-Qāsim, "This shaykh has called for allegiance to be given to you (as my successor), so bestow a generous gift on him." He replied, "As the Commander of the Faithful ordains!" Al-Rashīd said, "I've had enough of this![1116] Bring forward al-Namarī!" so al-Namarī came up to him and recited to him,

No grief of ours, nor agitation of soul, dies away . . .

until he reached the words, [761]

How excellent were the days of youth, and how
 enduring is the sweetness of remembrance of it which remains!
I was not able to fulfill for my youth the highest point of its choicest part,
 before it vanished away, and lo, the present world is a mere sequel (i.e., an anticlimax)![1117]

Al-Rashīd said, "There is nothing good in the present world; the garment of youth is not called to mind in it."[1118]

It has been mentioned that Saʿīd b. Salm al-Bāhilī came into al-Rashīd's presence. He greeted the Caliph; al-Rashīd motioned to him and he sat down. Then Saʿīd said, "O Commander of the Faithful, there is a Bedouin from the tribe of Bāhilah standing at the Commander of the Faithful's gate, and I've never seen anyone more poetically eloquent than he!" He said, "Indeed, have you not made these two poets"—he meant al-ʿUmānī and Manṣūr al-Namarī, who were both present in his court at that moment—"lawful plunder, aiming your stones at them?" (i.e., not taking them into consideration).[1119] Saʿīd replied, "O Commander of the Faithful,

---

1116. This anecdote continues from here briefly and with a divergent ending in Iṣfahānī, *Aghānī*, ed. Būlāq, XVII, 80 = ed. Cairo, XVIII, 315.

1117. *Shiʿr Manṣūr al-Namarī*, 95–6, no. 24; Bayhaqī, *Maḥāsin*, ed. Schwally, 376 = ed. Ibrāhīm, II, 43.

1118. Iṣfahānī, *Aghānī*, ed. Būlāq, XII, 19 = ed. Cairo, XIII, 145.

1119. The text here, and especially the words *istabaḥta . . . nuhbā*, is conjectural and the translation accordingly uncertain.

they are making me a gift to you (i.e., committing him to the Caliph's protection, so that the two of them will not attack him); so may the Bedouin now be permitted to enter?" Permission was accordingly given to him, and lo, there appeared a Bedouin in a silken gown and a Yemeni cloak, who had tucked it up round his waist and then folded it over his shoulder, and a turban which he had tied round his two cheeks and had let one end hang loose.

He appeared in front of the Commander of the Faithful, and seats were laid out. Al-Kisā'ī, al-Mufaḍḍal, Ibn Salm and al-Faḍl b. al-Rabī' all then sat down, and Ibn Salm said to the Bedouin, "Start eulogizing the Commander of the Faithful's ancestral nobility." So the Bedouin embarked on his poetry. The Commander of the Faithful said to him, "I hear you, as one who finds the poetry good, but I have a guarded view of you, being suspicious about you (i.e., suspicious that he was not the true author of the poetry which he had just declaimed). If this poetry really is your own and you have indeed recited it from your own poetic inventiveness, then recite to us a couple of verses on these two"—he meant Muḥammad and al-Ma'mūn, who were standing on each side of him. The Bedouin
[762] replied, "O Commander of the Faithful, you have imposed on me as an ineluctable decree (or: on the spur of the moment, *'alā al-qadar*) and without any warning, the awesomeness of the caliphate, the splendor of poetic inspiration, and the intractableness of the rhymes from adequate consideration. If the Commander of the Faithful will grant me a pause for thought, the refractory rhymes will all fall into place for me and my agitation of mind will be quietened down." The Caliph said, "I have granted you a period for reflection, O Bedouin, and have substituted your being allowed to put forward your excuses in place of putting you to the test." He replied, "O Commander of the Faithful, you have removed the cord which was strangling me and have made easy the forum for hypocrisy! (i.e., for poetic exaggeration). Then he began to recite,

The two of them—may God grant them blessing!—are its two
supporting ropes (i.e., of the caliphate, likened here to a tent), and you, O Commander of the Faithful, are its supporting pole.

You have constructed, with 'Abdallāh, after Muḥammad,
the protective shelter of the cupola of Islam, and its trunk has thereby grown upwards healthily!

The Caliph said, "As for you, O Bedouin, may God grant you blessing! Now ask us (for a gift), and don't let what you ask be below the value of your excellent achievement!" He replied, "A herd of one hundred camels, O Commander of the Faithful!" He related: The Commander of the Faithful smiled, and ordered him to be given one hundred thousand dirhams and seven robes of honor.

It has been mentioned that al-Rashīd said to his son al-Qāsim, on an occasion when al-Qāsim had come into his presence and at a time before al-Rashīd had proclaimed his succession rights, "You are connected with al-Ma'mūn through part of this flesh[1120] of yours." Al-Qāsim added, "(And also) through part of his good fortune!"[1121]

One day, before the succession oath was made to al-Qāsim, al-Rashīd said to him, "I have entrusted your interests to al-Amīn and al-Ma'mūn." Al-Qāsim replied, "For your part, O Commander of the Faithful, you have assumed personal responsibility for the two of them, yet you have entrusted my interests to someone else!"

Muṣʿab b. ʿAbdallāh al-Zubayrī related: Al-Rashīd came to the city of the Messenger of God (i.e., Medina), accompanied by his two sons Muḥammad al-Amīn and ʿAbdallāh al-Ma'mūn. There, he gave out numerous gifts and in that year distributed among the men and women of the city three rounds of gifts, these three rounds of gifts which he distributed to them amounting to one million and fifty thousand dīnārs. During that year, he also made payments to five hundred of the leading mawlās of Medina, and to some of them he gave payments at the highest rate [*fī al-* [763]
sharaf[1122]], including Yaḥyā b. Miskīn, Ibn ʿUthmān and Mikhrāq the mawlā of the Banū Tamīm, who used to act as Qur'ān reciter in Medina.

Isḥāq the mawlā has related: When al-Rashīd had homage made to his sons as successors in the caliphate, among those who gave

---

1120. Following the Cairo text, VIII, 363, here, *laḥmika.*

1121. Following ibid., here, *ḥaẓẓihi.*

1122. I.e., they received payment at the highest level, that of *sharaf al-ʿaṭā'*, the level of the stipends paid to the aristocracy of early Islam; see Balādhurī, *Glossarium,* 57.

homage was ʿAbdallāh b. Muṣʿab b. Thābit b. ʿAbdallāh b. al-Zubayr.[1123] When he came forward to offer homage, he recited,

May the two of them not fall short in it (i.e., in the task of upholding the caliphate), but may it not reach them both (yet),
so that your own period of power in it may be protracted!

Al-Rashīd found the quotation which ʿAbdallāh had adduced neat and apposite, and gave him an appropriately rich reward. He related: The actual verse is by Ṭurayḥ b. Ismāʿīl,[1124] who recited it in regard to (the Caliph) al-Walīd b. Yazīd and his two sons.

Abū al-Shīṣ recited,[1125] elegizing Hārūn al-Rashīd,

A sun has sunk in the East,
and because of this, two eyes flow with tears.
We have never seen a sun
which has set in the same place as it rises.[1126]

Abū Nuwās al-Ḥasan b. Hāniʾ has recited,

Maidens have hurried in bringing reports of both good fortune and ill luck,
and we are in states of mourning at a funeral and of a wedding celebration.
The heart is weeping whilst the teeth gleam in laughter,
and we are in states of both sadness and conviviality.
The one who has assumed control of the state, al-Amīn, moves us to joyous mirthfulness, whilst
the death of the Imām just recently makes us weep.
Two full moons: one moon has appeared clearly in Baghdad, at al-Khuld, whilst the other moon is at Ṭūs in a grave.[1127]

1123. Probably governor of al-Madīnah (see Ṭabarī, III, 739, above, 304) at this time of the promulgation of the "Meccan documents," i.e., in 186 (802).

1124. A poet of Thaqīf, eulogist of the last Umayyads and then of al-Manṣūr, who died in 165 (782). See Iṣfahānī, *Aghānī*, ed. Būlāq, IV, 74–86 = ed. Cairo, IV, 302–29; *GAS*, II, 452.

1125. Muḥammad b. ʿAbdallāh b. Razīn al-Khuzāʿī, eulogist of al-Rashīd and al-Amīn, who died in 196 (812) or shortly afterwards. See *GAL*, I², 83, S I, 133; *GAS*, II, 532–3; *EI*² s.v. Abu 'l-Shīṣ (A. Schaade-Pellat).

1126. *Ashʿār Abī al-Shīṣ wa-akhbāruhu*, ed. ʿAbdallāh al-Jubūrī, 78, no. 36; Azdī, 317. In Iṣfahānī, *Aghānī*, ed. Būlāq, XVII, 50 = ed. Cairo, XVIII, 249, these two verses are attributed in Ashjaʿ al-Sulamī. The allusion to the sun rising and setting in the same place is, of course, to the Caliph's birth and now death at Ṭūs.

1127. *K. al-ʿUyūn*, 318–19. These verses are translated by Wagner in his *Abū*

It has been said that when Hārūn al-Rashīd died, there were nine [764]
hundred million odd (dirhams) in the state treasury.[1128]

Nuwās, 352–3, from a text, with variants, in Ibn ʿAbd Rabbihi's *al-ʿIqd al-farīd* but attributed by him to Abū al-Shīṣ. The verses are not included in the part of the *Dīwān* of Abū Nuwās so far published by Wagner and G. Schoeler. Uncertainty about the correct authorship of these verses is shown by the fact that the literary critic Ibn Abī ʿAwn attributes them—implausibly, from their light tone—to Abū al-ʿAtāhiyah.

1128. Azdī, 317; Qāḍī Ibn al-Zubayr, 213, 299.

Bibliography of Cited Works

I. Primary Sources: Texts and Translations

al-ʿAbbās b. al-Aḥnaf, Abū al-Faḍl. *Dīwān*. Edited by ʿĀtikah al-Khazrajī. Cairo, 1373 (1954). Also edited Beirut, 1385 (1965).

Abū al-ʿAtāhiyah, Abū Isḥāq Ismāʿīl b. al-Qāsim, *Abū al-ʿAtāhiyah, ashʿāruhu wa-akhbāruhu*. Edited by Shukrī Fayṣal. Damascus, 1384 (1975).

Abū Nuwās, al-Ḥasan b. Hāniʾ al-Ḥakamī. *Dīwān*. 3 vols. Vols. I–II edited by E. Wagner. Bibliotheca Islamica 20 a–b. Cairo-Wiesbaden, 1958–72. Vol. IV edited by G. Schoeler. Bibliotheca Islamica 20 d. Wiesbaden, 1982.

Abū al-Shīṣ, Abū Jaʿfar Muḥammad b. ʿAbdallāh al-Khuzāʿī. *Ashʿār Abī al-Shīṣ wa-akhbāruhu*. Edited by ʿAbdallāh al-Jubūrī. Baghdad, 1387 (1967).

Anon. *Ḥudūd al-ʿālam*. Translated and explained by V. Minorsky under the title *The regions of the world. A Persian geography 372 A.H.–982 A.D.* GMS N.S. XI. London, 1937.

Anon. *Taʾrīkh-i Sīstān*. Edited by Malik al-Shuʿarāʾ Bahār. Tehran, 1314 A.S.H. (1935). Translated by Milton Gold under the title *The Tārikh-e Sistān*. Literary and historical texts from Iran 2. Rome, 1976.

Anon. *Kitāb al-ʿUyūn wa-al-ḥadāʾiq fī akhbār al-ḥaqāʾiq*. Edited by M. J. De Goeje. Fragmenta historicorum arabicorum, pars tertia. Leiden, 1871.

al-Azdī, Abū Zakariyyāʾ Yazīd b. Muḥammad. *Taʾrīkh al-Mawṣil*. Edited by ʿAlī Ḥabībah. Cairo, 1387 (1967).

al-Azraqī, Abū al-Walīd Muḥammad b. ʿAbdallāh. *Akhbār Makkah*. 2 vols. Edited by Rushdī al-Ṣāliḥ Malḥas. Riyadh, 1385 (1965–6). Also edited by F. Wüstenfeld in *Die Chroniken der Stadt Mekka*. Vol. I. *Geschichte und Beschreibung der Stadt Mekka von . . . el-Azrakí*. Leipzig, 1858.

al-Baghdādī, Abū Jaʿfar Muḥammad b. Ḥabīb. *Kitāb al-Muḥabbar*. Edited by Ilse Lichtenstaedter. Hyderabad, Dn., 1361 (1942).

al-Bakrī, Abū ʿUbayd ʿAbdallāh b. ʿAbd al-ʿAzīz. *Muʿjam mā ʾstaʾjam min asmāʾ al-bilād wa-al-mawāḍiʿ*. 4 vols. Edited by Muṣṭafā al-Saqqā. Cairo, 1364–71 (1945–51).

al-Baladhūrī, Abū al-Ḥasan Aḥmad b. Yaḥyā. *Futūh al-buldān*. Edited by M. J. De Goeje under the title *Liber expugnationis regionum*. Leiden, 1866.

Bayhaqī, Abū al-Faḍl Muḥammad b. Ḥusayn, *Taʾrīkh-i Masʿūdī*. Edited by Qāsim Ghanī and ʿAlī Akbar Fayyāḍ. Tehran, 1324 A.S.H. (1945).

al-Bayhaqī, Ibrāhīm b. Muḥammad. *Kitāb al-Maḥāsin wa-al-masāwī*. Edited by F. Schwally. Giessen, 1900–2. Index in O. Rescher. *Index und Stellennachweise zu Fr. Schwally's Baihaqî-Ausgabe*. Stuttgart, 1923. Edited by Muḥammad Abū al-Faḍl Ibrāhīm. 2 vols. Cairo, 1380 (1961).

al-Dīnawarī, Abū Ḥanīfah Aḥmad b. Dāwūd. *Kitāb al-Akhbār al-ṭiwāl*. Edited by ʿAbd al-Munʿim ʿĀmir and Jamāl al-Dīn al-Shayyāl. Cairo, 1960.

al-Farazdaq, Abū Firās Tammām b. Ghālib. *Sharḥ Dīwān al-Farazdaq*. 3 vols. Edited by ʿAbdallāh Ismāʿīl al-Ṣāwī. Cairo, 1354 (1936). Edited by A. A. Bevan. *The Naḳāʾiḍ of Jarīr and al-Farazdaḳ*. 3 vols. Leiden, 1905–12.

al-Fāsī, Taqī al-Dīn Abū al-Ṭayyib Muḥammad b. Aḥmad. *Shifāʾ al-gharām bi-akhbār al-balad al-ḥarām*. Extracts in Wüstenfeld, *Die Chroniken der Stadt Mekka*. Vol. II. *Auszüge aus den Geschichtsbüchern der Stadt Mekka von . . . el-Fâkihí, . . . el-Fâsí und Muhammed Ibn Dhuheira*.

Gardīzī, Abū Saʿīd ʿAbd al-Ḥayy b. al-Ḍaḥḥāk. *Kitāb Zayn al-akhbār*. Edited by ʿAbd al-Ḥayy Ḥabībī. Tehran, 1347 A.S.H. (1968).

al-Hamdānī, Abū Muḥammad al-Ḥasan b. Aḥmad. *Ṣifat Jazīrat al-ʿArab*. Edited by Muḥammad b. ʿAlī al-Akwaʿ and Ḥamad al-Jāsir. Riyadh, 1394 (1974).

Ibn al-Abbār, Abū ʿAbdallāh Muḥammad b. ʿAbdallāh. *Iʿtāb al-kuttāb*. Edited by Ṣāliḥ al-Ashtar. Damascus, 1380 (1961).

Ibn Abī Ṭāhir, Abū al-Faḍl Aḥmad Ṭayfūr. *Kitāb Baghdād*. 2 vols. Edited and translated by H. Keller under the title *Sechster Band des Kitâb Bagdâd*. Leipzig, 1908.

Ibn Abī Uṣaybiʿah, Abū al-ʿAbbās Aḥmad b. al-Qāsim. *ʿUyūn al-anbāʾ fī ṭabaqāt al-aṭibbāʾ*. Edited by A. Müller. Vols. I–II. Cairo, 1290 (1882). Vol. III. Königsberg, 1884.

Ibn al-Athīr, ʿIzz al-Dīn Abū al-Ḥasan ʿAlī b. Muḥammad. *al-Kāmil fī al-taʾrīkh*. 13 vols. Beirut, 1385–7 (1965–7).

Ibn al-Athīr, Majd al-Dīn Abū al-Saʿādāt al-Mubārak b. Muḥammad. *al-Nihāyah fī gharib al-ḥadīth wa-al-athar.* Edited by Ṭāhir Aḥmad al-Zāwī and Maḥmūd Muḥammad al-Ṭannāḥī. 5 vols. Cairo, 1383 (1963).

Ibn Durayd, Abū Bakr Muḥammad b. Ḥasan. *Kitāb al-Ishtiqāq*. Edited by ʿAbd al-Salām Muḥammad Hārūn. Cairo, 1378 (1958).

Ibn al-Faqīh, Abū Bakr Aḥmad b. Ibrāhīm al-Hamadhānī. *Mukhtaṣar Kitāb al-buldān*. Edited by M. J. De Goeje. BGA V. Leiden, 1885.

Ibn Hishām, Abū Muḥammad ʿAbd al-Malik al-Ḥimyarī. *Sīrat al-Nabī*. Edited by Muṣṭafā al-Saqqā, Ibrāhīm al-Abyārī and ʿAbd al-Ḥafīẓ Shalabī. 4 vols. Beirut, n.d. Translated by A. Guillaume under the title *The life of Muhammad, a translation of Isḥāq's* (*sic*) Sīrat Rasūl Allāh. London, 1955.

Ibn Isfandiyār, Muḥammad b. al-Ḥasan. *Taʾrīkh-i Ṭabaristān*. Abridged translation by E. G. Browne under the title *History of Ṭabaristán*. GMS II. Leiden-London, 1905.

Ibn Khaldūn, Walī al-Dīn Abū Zayd ʿAbd al-Raḥmān b. Muḥammad. *al-Muqaddimah.* Translated by F. Rosenthal under the title *The Muqaddimah, an introduction to history.* 3 vols. New York, 1958. Translated by V. Monteil under the title *Discours sur l'histoire universelle* (*al-Muqaddima*). 3 vols. Beirut, 1967–8.

Ibn Khallikān, Abū al-ʿAbbās Aḥmad b. Muḥammad al-Irbilī. *Wafayāt al-aʿyān wa-anbāʾ abnāʾ al-zamān.* 8 vols. Edited by Iḥsān ʿAbbās. Beirut, 1968–72. Translated by Baron McGuckin de Slane under the title *Ibn Khallikan's biographical dictionary.* 4 vols. Paris, 1842–71.

Ibn Manẓūr, Jamāl al-Dīn Abū al-Faḍl Muḥammad b. Mukarram al-Anṣārī. *Lisān al-ʿArab.* 20 vols. Būlāq, 1300–8 (1883–91).

Ibn al-Nadīm, Abū al-Faraj Muḥammad b. Isḥāq al-Warrāq. *Kitab al-Fihrist.* Translated by B. Dodge under the title *The Fihrist of al-Nadīm, a tenth century survey of Muslim culture.* 2 vols. New York and London, 1970.

Ibn Qutaybah, Abū Muḥammad ʿAbdallāh b. Muslim. *Kitāb al-Maʿārif*. Edited by Tharwat ʿUkkāshah. Cairo, 1960.

Ibn al-Sāʿī, Abū Ṭālib ʿAlī b. Anjab. *Nisāʾ al-khulafāʾ, jihāt al-aʾimmah al-khulafāʾ min al-ḥarāʾir wa al-imāʾ*. Edited by Muṣṭafā Jawād. Cairo, n.d.

Ibn Taghrībirdī, Jamāl al-Dīn Abū al-Maḥāsin Yūsuf. *al-Nujūm al-zāhirah fī mulūk Miṣr wa-al-Qāhirah.* 16 vols. Edited by Jamāl Muḥarriz *et alii.* Cairo, 1383–92 (1963–72).

Ibn al-Ṭiqṭaqā, Ṣafī al-Dīn Muḥammad b. ʿAlī b. Ṭabāṭabā. *Kitāb al-Fakhrī fī al-ādāb al-sulṭāniyyah wa-al-duwal al-islāmiyyah.* Cairo, 1317 (1899). Translated by C. E. J. Whitting under the title *Al Fakhri: on the systems of government and the Moslem dynasties.* London, 1947.

Ibn al-Zubayr, Qāḍī Abū al-Ḥusayn Aḥmad b. al-Rashīd. *Kitāb al-Dhakhā'ir wa-al-tuḥaf.* Edited by Muḥammad Ḥamīd Allāh and Ṣalāḥ al-Dīn al-Munajjid. Kuwait, 1959.

al-Iṣfahānī, Abū ʿAbdallāh Ḥamzah b. al-Ḥasan. *Ta'rīkh Sinī mulūk al-arḍ wa-al-anbiyā'.* Beirut, n.d. (ca. 1961).

al-Iṣfahānī, Abū al-Faraj ʿAlī b. al-Ḥusayn. *Kitāb al-Aghānī.* 20 vols. Būlāq, 1285–6 (1868–70). Edited at the Dār al-Kutub al-Miṣriyyah and by Muḥammad Abū al-Faḍl Ibrāhīm *et alii.* 24 vols. Cairo-Beirut, 1927–74.

———. *Maqātil al-Ṭālibiyyīn.* Edited by Kāẓim al-Muẓaffar. Najaf, 1385 (1965).

al-Jāḥiẓ, Abū ʿUthmān ʿAmr b. Baḥr. *al-Bayān wa-al-tabyīn.* Edited by ʿAbd al-Salām Muḥammad Hārūn. 4 vols. Cairo, 1380–1 (1960–1).

———. *Kitāb al-Bukhalā'.* Edited by Ṭāhā al-Ḥājirī. Cairo, 1971. Translated by Ch. Pellat under the title *Le livre des avares de Ǧāḥiẓ.* Paris, 1951.

———. *Kitāb al-Ḥayawān.* Edited by ʿAbd al-Salām Muḥammad Hārūn. 7 vols. Cairo, 1357–64 (1938–45).

———. *Risālah fī Manāqib al-Atrāk wa-ʿāmmat jund al-khilāfah.* In *Majmūʿat rasā'il,* no. 2. Cairo, 1323 (1905–6). Translated by C. T. Harley-Walker under the title "Jāḥiẓ of Basra to al-Fatḥ b. Khaqan on the 'Exploits of the Turks and the army of the Khalifate in general.'" In *JRAS* (1915): 631–97.

al-Jahshiyārī, Abū ʿAbdallāh Muḥammad b. Abdūs. *Kitāb al-Wuzarā' wa-al-kuttāb.* Edited by ʿAbdallāh Ismāʿīl Ṣāwī. Baghdad, 1357 (1938).

al-Khalīfah, Abū ʿAmr b. Khayyāṭ. *Taʿrīkh.* 2 vols. Edited by Suhayl Zakkār. Damascus, (1967–8).

al-Khaṭīb al-Baghdādī, Abū Bakr Aḥmad b. ʿAlī. *Ta'rīkh Baghdād aw Madīnat al-Salām.* 14 vols. Cairo, 1349 (1931).

al-Khuraymī, Abū Yaʿqūb Isḥāq b. Ḥassān. *Dīwān.* Edited by ʿAlī Jawād al-Ṭāhir and Muḥammad Jabbār al-Muʿaybid. Beirut, 1971.

al-Kindī, Abū ʿUmar Muḥammad b. Yūsuf. *Kitāb al-Wulāt wa-Kitāb al-Quḍāt.* Edited by R. Guest under the title *The governors and judges of Egypt.* GMS XIX. Leiden and London, 1912.

Labīd b. Rabīʿah, Abū ʿAqil al-Kilābī. *Dīwān.* Edited and translated by

C. Brockelmann under the title *Die Gedichte des Lebîd, aus dem Nachlasse des Dr. A. Huber.* Leiden, 1892.

Manṣūr al-Namarī, Abū al-Faḍl Manṣūr b. Zibriqān. *Dīwān.* Edited by al-Ṭayyib al-ʿAshshāsh under the title *Shiʿr Manṣūr al-Namarī.* Damascus, 1401 (1981).

al-Maqdisī, Abū ʿAbdallāh Muḥammad b. Aḥmad. *Aḥsan al-taqāsīm fī maʿrifat al-aqalim.* Edited by M. J. De Goeje. BGA III. Leiden, 1906.

al-Maqdisī, Abū Naṣr al-Muṭahhar b. Ṭāhir. *Kitāb al-Badʾ wa-al-taʾrīkh.* Edited and translated by Cl. Huart under the title *Le livre de la Création et de l'Histoire.* 6 vols. Paris, 1899–1919.

al-Marāghī, Abū al-Fakhr Abū Bakr b. al-Ḥusayn. *Taḥqīq al-nuṣrah bi-talkhīṣ maʿālim dār al-hijrah.* Edited by Muḥammad ʿAbd al-Jawād al-Aṣmaʿī. Medina, 1374 (1955).

Marwān b. Abī Ḥafṣah, Abū al-Simṭ Marwān b. Sulaymān. *Dīwān.* Edited by Ḥusayn ʿAṭawān under the title *Shʿr Marwān b. Abī Ḥafṣah.* Cairo, 1973. Edited in Munierah Muḥammad al-Yūsuf al-Rasheed, *The Abū Ḥafṣah family of poets, together with a critical edition of the poetry of the principal members of the family.* Manchester University Ph.D. thesis, 1980, unpublished.

al-Marzubānī, Abū ʿUbaydallāh Muḥammad b. ʿImrān. *Muʿjam al-shuʿarāʾ.* Edited by ʿAbd al-Sattār Aḥmad Farāj. Cairo, 1379 (1960).

al-Masʿūdī, Abū al-Ḥasan ʿAlī b. al-Ḥusayn. *Murūj al-dhahab wa-maʿādin al-jawhar.* Edited and translated by C. Barbier de Meynard and Pavet de Courteille under the title *Les prairies d'or.* 9 vols. Paris, 1861–77. Edited and partially translated by Ch. Pellat under the title *Les prairies d'or.* 7 vols., including two of Indices. Paris and Beirut, 1962–79.

———. *Kitāb al-Tanbīh wa-al-ishrāf.* Edited by M. J. de Goeje. BGA VIII. Leiden, 1894. Translated by Baron Carra de Vaux under the title *Le livre de l'avertissement et de la revision.* Paris, 1897.

al-Maydānī, Abū al-Faḍl Aḥmad b. Muḥammad. *Majmaʿ amthāl al-ʿArab.* Translated by G. W. Freytag under the title *Arabum proverba.* 3 vols. Bonn, 1838–43.

al-Mubarrad, Abū al-ʿAbbās Muḥammad b. Yazīd. *al-Kāmil.* Edited by Muḥammad Abū al-Faḍl Ibrāhīm and al-Sayyid Shaḥḥātah. 4 vols. Cairo, 1376 (1956).

Muḥammad b. Ḥabīb. See al-Baghdādī.

al-Nahrawālī, Quṭb al-Dīn Muḥammad b. ʿAlī. *al-Iʿlām bi-aʿlām balad Allāh al-ḥarām.* Edited by Wüstenfeld, *Die Chroniken der Stadt Mekka.* Vol. III. *Geschichte der Stadt Mekka und ihres Tempels von Cuṭb ed-Dîn . . . el-Nahrawâli.*

Naqāʾiḍ Jarīr wa-al-Farazdaq. See al-Farazdaq.

Narshakhī, Abū Bakr Muḥammad b. Jaʿfar. *Taʾrīkh-i Bukhārā.* Edited by

Mudarris Riḍawī. Tehran, n.d. (ca. 1939). Translated by R. N. Frye under the title *The history of Bukhara.* Cambridge, Mass., 1954.

al-Ṣābi', Abū al-Ḥusayn Hilāl b. al-Muḥassin. *Rusūm dār al-khilāfah.* Edited by Mīkhā'īl ʿAwwād. Baghdad, 1383 (1964). Translated by Elie A. Salem under the title *The rules and regulations of the ʿAbbāsid court.* Beirut, 1977.

Salm al-Khāsir, Salm b. ʿAmr. *Dīwān.* Edited by G. E. von Grunebaum in "Three Arabic poets of the early Abbasid age (the collected fragments of Muṭīʿ b. Iyâs, Salm al-Ḫâsir and Abû 'š-Šamaqmaq). V. Salm al-Ḫâsir." *Orientalia* XIX (1950): 53–80. Also in *Themes in medieval Arabic literature.* London, 1981. Also as *Shuʿarā' ʿAbbāsiyyūn: Muṭīʿ b. Iyās, Salm al-Khāsir, Abū al-Shamaqmaq.* Edited by von Grunebaum and reviewed by Muḥammad Yūsuf al-Najm and Iḥsān ʿAbbās. Beirut and New York, 1959.

al-Samʿānī, Abū Saʿd ʿAbd al-Karīm b. Muḥammad. *Kitāb al-Ansāb.* 13 vols. Edited by M. ʿAbd al-Muʿīd Khān *et alii.* Hyderabad, 1382–1402 (1962–82).

al-Samhūdī, Nūr al-Dīn Abū al-Ḥasan ʿAlī b. Aḥmad. *Wafā' al-wafā' bi-akhbār dār al-Muṣṭafā.* Edited by Muḥyī al-Dīn ʿAbd al-Ḥamīd. 4 vols. Beirut, 1393 (1973).

al-Shābushtī, Abū al-Ḥasan ʿAlī b. Muḥammad. *Kitāb al-Diyārāt.* Edited by Gurgis ʿAwwād. Baghdad, 1370 (1951).

al-Ṭabarī, Abū Jaʿfar Muḥammad b. Jarīr. *Taʾrīkh al-rusul wa-al-mulūk.* Edited by M. J. De Goeje *et alii* under the title *Annales quos scripsit Abu Djafar . . . at-Tabari.* 13 vols. and 2 vols. *Indices* and *Introductio, glossarium, addenda et emendanda.* Edited by Muḥammad Abū al-Faḍl Ibrāhīm. 10 vols. Cairo, 1960–9. Partially translated by Th. Nöldeke under the title *Geschichte der Perser und Araber zur Zeit der Sassaniden.* Leiden, 1879. Partially translated by E. Marin under the title *The reign of al-Muʿtaṣim (833–842).* New Haven, 1951.

———. Persian version by Abū ʿAlī Muḥammad Balʿamī. Translated by H. Zotenberg under the title *Chronique de . . . Tabarî, traduite sur la version persane d'Abou-ʿAlî Moʿhammed Belʿamî.* 4 vols. Paris, 1867–74.

al-Thaʿālibī, Abū Manṣūr ʿAbd al-Malik b. Muḥammad. *Laṭā'if al-maʿārif.* Edited by Ibrāhīm al-Abyārī and Ḥasan Kāmil al-Ṣayrafī. Cairo, 1960. Translated by C. E. Bosworth under the title *The book of curious and entertaining information.* Edinburgh, 1968.

———. *Thimār al-qulūb fī al-muḍāf wa-al-manṣūb.* Cairo, 1326 (1908).

ʿUmar b. Shabbah, Abū Zayd al-Numayrī. *Taʾrīkh al-Madīnah al-munawwarah.* Edited by Ḥabīb Muḥammad Aḥmad. 4 vols. Jeddah, 1393 (1973).

al-Ya'qūbī, Abū al-'Abbās Aḥmad b. Isḥāq, called Ibn Wāḍiḥ. *Kitāb al-Buldān.* Edited by de Goeje. BGA VII. Leiden, 1892. Translated by G. Wiet under the title *Les pays.* Cairo, 1937.

———. *Ta'rīkh.* Edited by M. Th. Houtsma under the title *Historiae.* 2 vols. Leiden, 1883.

Yāqūt, Abū 'Abdallāh Ya'qūb b. 'Abdallāh al-Ḥamawī al-Rūmī. *Mu'jam al-buldān.* 5 vols. Beirut, 1374–6 (1955–7).

al-Zubayrī, Abū 'Abdallāh al-Muṣ'ab b. 'Abdallāh. *Kitāb Nasab Quraysh.* Edited by E. Lévi-Provençal. Cairo, 1953.

II. Secondary Sources and Reference Works

Abbott, Nabia. *Two queens of Baghdad: mother and wife of Hārūn al-Rashīd.* Chicago, 1946.

Agius, D. A. *Arabic literary works as a source of documentation for technical terms of the material culture.* Islamkundliche Untersuchungen 98. Berlin, 1984.

Ahsan, M. M. *Social life under the Abbasids 170–289 AH, 786–902 AD.* London and New York, 1979.

Amedroz, H. R. "The Mazālim jurisdiction in the Ahkam Sultaniyya of Mawardi," *JRAS* (1911): 635–74.

Anastos, M. V. "Iconoclasm and imperial rule 717–842." In *The Cambridge medieval history.* Vol. IV, *The Byzantine empire.* Part I, *Byzantium and its neighbours,* edited by J. M. Hussey, 61–104. Cambridge, 1966.

Ashtor, E. *A social and economic history of the Near East in the Middle Ages.* London, 1976.

Ayalon, D. *The military reforms of Caliph al-Mu'taṣim: their background and consequences.* Unpublished communication to the International Congress of Orientalists, New Delhi 1964. Printed in offset, Jerusalem, 1963.

———. "Preliminary remarks on the *Mamlūk* military institution in Islam." In *War, technology and society in the Middle East.* Edited by V. J. Parry and M. E. Yapp, 44–58. London, 1975.

———. "On the eunuchs in Islam." *JSAI* I (1979): 67–124.

Barthold, W. *Turkestan down to the Mongol invasion.* GMS, n.s. V. London, 1968.

———. *An historical geography of Iran.* Translated by S. Soucek. Edited by C. E. Bosworth. Princeton, 1984.

Becker, C. H. *Beiträge zur Geschichte Ägyptens unter dem Islam.* Vol. II. Strassburg, 1903.

Bencheikh, J. "Les sécretaires poètes et animateurs de cénacles aux IIe et

IIIe siècles de l'Hégire. Contribution à l'analyse d'une production poetique." *JA* CCLXIII (1975): 264–315.

Bosworth, C. E. *Sīstān under the Arabs, from the Islamic conquest to the rise of the Ṣaffārids (30–250/651–864).* Rome, 1968.

———. "Abū ʿAbdallāh al-Khwārazmī on the technical terms of the secretary's art: a contribution to the administrative history of mediaeval Islam." *JESHO* XII (1969): 113–64. Also in *Medieval Arabic culture and administration.* [London, 1982].

Bouvat, L. *Les Barmécides d'après les historiens arabes et persans.* Paris, 1912.

Brockelmann, C. *Geschichte der arabischen Literatur.* 5 vols. Leiden, 1937–49.

Brooks, E. W. "Byzantines and Arabs in the time of the early Abbasids." *EHR* XV (1900): 728–47. XVI (1901): 84–92.

Canard, M. *Histoire de la dynastie des H'amdânides de Jazîra et de Syrie* I. Algiers, 1951.

———. "Byzantium and the Muslim world to the middle of the eleventh century." In *The Cambridge medieval history.* Vol. IV, *The Byzantine empire.* Part I, *Byzantium and its neighbours,* 696–735.

Chejne, A. J. "Al-Faḍl b. al-Rabīʿ—a politician of the early ʿAbbāsid period." *IC* XXXVI (1962): 167–81.

Clauson, Sir Gerard. *An etymological dictionary of pre-thirteenth century Turkish.* Oxford, 1972.

Cottrell, A. J. *et alii,* editors. *The Persian Gulf states, a general survey.* Baltimore and London, 1980.

Crone, Patricia. *Slaves on horses. The evolution of the Islamic polity.* Cambridge, 1980.

Daniel, E. *The political and social history of Khurasan under Abbasid rule 747–820.* Minneapolis and Chicago, 1979.

Donaldson, Bess A. *The wild rue, a study of Muhammadan magic and folklore in Iran.* London, 1938.

Dozy, R. P. A. *Dictionnaire detaillé des noms de vêtements chez les arabes.* Amsterdam, 1845.

———. *Supplément aux dictionnaires arabes.* 2 vols. Leiden, 1881.

Dunlop, D. M. *The history of the Jewish Khazars.* Princeton, 1954.

Encyclopaedia of Islām. First edition. 4 vols. and Supplement. Leiden, 1913–42.

Encyclopaedia of Islam. New edition. 5 vols. and Supplement. Leiden and London, 1960–.

Fahd, T. *La divination arabe. Etudes religieuses, sociologiques et folkloriques sur le milieu natif de l'Islam.* Leiden, 1966.

Farmer, H. G. *A history of Arabian music to the XIIIth century.* London, 1929.

Fattal, A. *Le statut légal des non-musulmans en pays d'Islam.* Beirut, 1958.

Forand, P. G. "The relation of the slave and the client to the master or patron in medieval Islam." *IJMES* II (1971): 59–66.

Fraenkel, S. *Die aramäischen Fremdwörter im Arabischen.* Leiden, 1886.

Frye, R. N. *The golden age of Persia, the Arabs in the East.* London, 1975.

Gabrieli, F. "La successione di Hārūn ar-Rašīd e la guerra fra al-Amīn e al-Ma'mūn (Studio storico su un periodo del Califfato ʿAbbāside)." *RSO* XI (1926–8): 341–97.

———. "Documenti relativi al Califfato di al-Amīn in aṭ-Ṭabarī." *RCAL,* Serie sesta III (1927): 191–220.

———. "La «zandaqa» au Ier siècle abbasside." In *L'élaboration de l'Islam. Colloque de Strasbourg 12–13–14 juin 1959,* 23–29. Paris, 1961.

Gaudefroy-Demombynes, M. *Le pèlerinage à la Mekke.* Paris, 1923.

———. *Mahomet.* Second edition. Paris, 1969.

Goldziher, I. "Ueber Dualtitel." *WZKM* XIII (1899): 321–9. Also in *Gesammelte Schriften,* vol. IV edited by J. Desomogyi, 195–203. Hildesheim, 1969–73.

———. "Spottnamen der ersten Chalifen bei den Schīʿiten." *WZKM* XV (1901): 321–34. Also in *Gesammelte Schriften,* vol. IV, 295–308.

———. "Der Seelenvogel im islamischen Volksglauben." *Globus* LXXXIII (1902): 301–4. Also in *Gesammelte Schriften,* vol. IV, 403–6.

———. "Zwei Schwerter." *Isl.* XII (1922): 198–201. Also in *Gesammelte Schriften,* vol. V, 469–72.

von Grunebaum, G. E. See under Salm al-Khāsir.

Harley, A. H. "Abu's-Simṭ Marwān b. Abī Ḥafṣah—a post-classical Arab poet." *JRASB,* Letters III (1937). Article no. 8: 71–90.

Hebbo, Ahmed. *Die Fremdwörter in der arabischen Prophetenbiographie des Ibn Hischam (gest. 218/834).* Heidelberger Orientalische Studien 7. Frankfurt a. M., 1984.

Homerin, Th. E. "Echoes of a thirsty owl: death and afterlife in pre-Islamic Arabic poetry." *JNES* XLIV (1985): 165–84.

Honigmann, E. *Die Ostgrenze des Byzantinischen Reiches von 363 bis 1071 nach griechischen, arabischen, syrischen und armenischen Quellen.* In *Byzance et les Arabes.* Vol. III, edited by A. A. Vasiliev. Brussels, 1935.

Justi, F. *Iranisches Namenbuch.* Marburg, 1895.

Kaabi, M. "Les origines ṭāhirides dans la *daʿwa* ʿabbāside." *Arabica* XIX (1972): 145–64.

Kaḥḥālah, ʿUmar Riḍā. *Aʿlām al-nisāʾ*. 5 vols. Damascus, 1379 (1959).

Kasrawī, Aḥmad. *Shahriyārān-i gumnām*. 3 parts. Tehran, 1307–8 A.S.H. (1929–30).

Kennedy, H. *The early Abbasid Caliphate, a political history.* London and Totowa, N.J., 1981.

Kimber, R. A. "Hārūn al-Rashīd's Meccan settlement of AH 186/AD 802." *University of St. Andrews, School of Abbasid Studies, Occasional Papers* 1, 55–79. Edinburgh, 1986 [1987].

Kindermann, H. *"Schiff" im Arabischen. Untersuchung über Vorkommen und Bedeutung der Termini.* Zwickau-im-Sa., 1934.

Köcher, Erika. "Yaʿqūb b. Dāʾūd, Wezir al-Mahdīs." *Mitteilungen des Instituts für Orientforschung* III (1955): 378–420.

Kraemer, J., H. Gätje, M. Ullmann, *et alii. Wörterbuch der klassischen arabischen Sprache, auf Grund der Sammlungen von A. Fischer, T. Nöldeke, H. Reckendorf und anderer Quellen herausgegeben.* Letters K, L. Wiesbaden, 1957–.

Lane, E. W. *An Arabic-English lexicon, derived from the best and most copious Eastern sources.* 8 vols. London, 1863–93.

Lassner, J. *The topography of Baghdad in the early Middle Ages. Text and studies.* Detroit, 1970.

———. *The shaping of ʿAbbāsid rule.* Princeton, 1980.

Le Strange, G. *Palestine under the Moslems, a description of Syria and the Holy Land from A. D. 650 to 1500.* London, 1890.

———. *Baghdad under the Abbasid Caliphate from contemporary Arabic and Persian sources.* Oxford, 1900.

———. *The lands of the Eastern Caliphate, Mesopotamia, Persia, and Central Asia from the Moslem conquest to the time of Timur.* Cambridge, 1905.

Levy, R. *The social structure of Islam.* Cambridge, 1957.

Lewis, B. "The regnal titles of the first Abbasid caliphs." In *Dr. Zakir Husain presentation volume,* 13–22. New Delhi, 1968.

Lieu, S. N. C. *Manichaeism in the later Roman empire and medieval China. A historical survey.* Manchester, 1985.

Løkkegaard, F. *Islamic taxation in the classic period, with special reference to circumstances in Iraq.* Copenhagen, 1950.

Lyall, Sir Charles J. *Translations of ancient Arabian poetry, chiefly pre-Islamic.* London, 1930.

Madelung, W. *Der Imam al-Qāsim ibn Ibrāhīm und die Glaubenslehre der Zaiditen.* Studien zur Sprache, Geschichte und Kultur des islamischen Orients, Beihefte zur Zeitschrift "Der Islam," Neue Folge, Band 1. Berlin, 1965.

———. "The origins of the controversy concerning the creation of the Koran." In *Orientalia hispanica sive studia F. M. Pareja octogenario dicata.* Volumen 1, Arabica-Islamica. Pars prior, 504–25. Leiden, 1974.

———. "The minor dynasties of northern Iran." In *The Cambridge history of Iran.* Vol. IV. *The period from the Arab invasion to the Saljuqs,* edited by R. N. Frye. 198–249. Cambridge, 1975.

Marçais, G. "La Berbérie au IXe siècle d'après El-Yaʿqoûbî." *R.Afr.* LXXXV (1941): 40–61.

———. *La Berbérie musulmane et l'Orient au moyen âge.* Paris, 1946.

Marquet, Y. "Le Šīʿisme au IXe siècle à travers l'histoire de Yaʿqūbī." *Arabica* XIX (1972): 1–45, 101–38.

Mez, A. *The renaissance of Islam.* Translated by S. Khuda Bakhsh and D. S. Margoliouth. Patna, 1937.

Minorsky, V. *A history of Sharvān and Darband in the 10th–11th centuries.* Cambridge, 1958.

Morony, M. G. *Iraq after the Muslim conquest.* Princeton, 1984.

Moscati, S. "Studi storici sul califfato di al-Mahdī." *Orientalia,* N.S. XIV (1945): 300–54.

———. "Nuovi studi sul califatto di al-Mahdī." *Orientalia,* N.S. (1946): 155–79.

———. *Le califat d'al-Hādī.* Studia orientalia . . . societas orientalis fennica XIII/4. Helsinki, 1946.

Müller, A. "Arabische Quellen zur Geschichte der indischen Medizin." *ZDMG* XXXIV (1880): 465–556.

al-Munajjid, Ṣalāḥ al-Dīn. *al-Ḥayāt al-jinsiyyah ʿind al-ʿArab min al-Jāhiliyyah ilā awākhir al-qarn al-rābiʿ al-hijrī.* Second enlarged edition. Beirut, 1975.

Musil, A. *The middle Euphrates.* American Geographical Society. Oriental explorations and studies 2. New York, 1927.

Muth, F.-C. *Die Annalen von aṭ-Ṭabarī im Spiegel der europäischen Bearbeitungen.* Heidelberger orientalische Studien 5. Frankfurt a. M., 1983.

Nöldeke, Th. "Die ghassânidischen Fürsten aus dem Hause Gafna's." *AKAk. Berlin* (1887), Abt. II: 1–63.

al-Nukhaylī, Darwīsh. *al-Sufun al-islāmiyyah ʿalā ḥurūf al-muʿjam.* N.p. [Alexandria], 1974.

Öhrnberg, K. *The offspring of Fatima: dispersal and ramification.* Studia orientalia . . . societas orientalis fennica LIV. Helsinki, 1983.

Omar, F. *ʿAbbāsiyyāt, studies in the history of the early ʿAbbāsids.* Baghdad, 1976.

———. *EI*² s.v. Hārūn al-Rashīd.

Palmer, E. H. *Haroun Alraschid, Caliph of Baghdad.* The New Plutarch, lives of men and women of action. London and Belfast, 1881.

Pedersen, J. *Der Eid bei den Semiten in seinem Verhältnis zu verwandten Erscheinungen sowie die Stellung des Eides im Islam.* Strassburg, 1914.

Pellat, Ch. *Le milieu baṣrien et la formation de Ǧāḥiẓ.* Paris, 1953.

Pipes, D. *Slave soldiers and Islam, the genesis of a military system.* New Haven and London, 1981.

al-Rasheed, Munierah Muḥammad al-Yūsuf. See under Marwān b. Abī Ḥafṣah.

al-Rashid, Saad. A. *Darb Zubaydah, the Pilgrim Road from Kufa to Mecca.* Riyadh, 1980.

Rodinson, M. "Recherches sur les documents arabes relatifs à la cuisine." *REI* (1949): 95–165.

Sadan, J. *Le mobilier au Proche Orient médiéval.* Leiden, 1976.

———. "The division of the day and programme of work of the Caliph al-Manṣūr." *Studia orientalia D. H. Baneth dedicata.* 255–73. Jerusalem, 1979.

———. *"Kings and craftsmen—a pattern of contrasts. On the history of a medieval Arabic humoristic form."* *SI* LVI (1982): 5–49.

Salibi, K. S. *Syria under Islam: empire on trial, 634–1097.* Delmar, N.Y., 1977.

Scarcia Amoretti, B. "Sects and heresies." In *The Cambridge history of Iran.* Vol. IV. *From the Arab invasion to the Saljuqs,* 481–519.

Schwarz, P. *Iran im Mittelalter nach den arabischen Geographen.* 9 parts. Leipzig, Stuttgart and Berlin, 1896–1936.

Serjeant, R. B. *Islamic textiles. Material for a history up to the Mongol conquest.* Beirut, 1972.

Sezgin, F. *Geschichte des arabischen Schrifttums.* 9 vols. Leiden, 1975–.

Shaban, M. A. *Islamic history. A new interpretation. 2. A.D. 750–1055 (A.H. 132–448).* Cambridge, 1976.

Sievers, P. von. "Military, merchants and nomads: the social evolution of the Syrian cities and countryside during the classical period, 780–969/164–358." *Isl.* LVI (1979): 212–44.

Sourdel, D. "La valeur littéraire et documentaire du 'Livre des Vizirs' d'al-Ǧahšiyārī d'après le chapitre consacré au califat de Hārūn al-Rašid." *Arabica* II (1955): 193–210.

———. *Le vizirat ʿabbāside de 749 à 936 (132 à 324 de l'Hégire).* 2 vols. Damascus, 1959–60.

———. "Questions de cérémonial ʿabbaside." *REI* XXVIII (1960): 121–48.

———. "La politique religieuse du calife ʿabbāside al-Maʾmūn," *REI* XXX (1962): 27–48.

———. *EI*² s.v. al-Hādī ila ʾl-Ḥaḳḳ.

Storey, C. A. *Persian literature, a bio-bibliographical survey.* 2 vols. London, 1927–77.

Terrasse, H. *Histoire du Maroc des origines à l'établissement du Protectorat français.* 2 vols. Casablanca, 1949–50.

Togan, A. Z. V. *Ibn Faḍlan̄s Reisebericht.* Abh. für die Kunde des Morgenlandes XXIV/3. Leipzig, 1939.

Tyan, E. *Institutions du droit public musulman.* Vol. I. *Le califat.* Paris, 1954.

Vajda, G. "Les zindîqs au pays d'Islam au début de la période abbaside." *RSO* XVII (1938): 173–229.

Van Arendonck, C. *Les débuts de l'Imāmat Zaidite au Yemen.* Leiden, 1960.

Vasiliev, A. A. *Byzance et les Arabes.* Vol. I. *La dynastie d'Amorium (820–867).* Brussels, 1935.

———. *History of the Byzantine empire 324–1453.* Madison and Milwaukee, 1952.

Veccia Vaglieri, L. "Divagazioni su due rivolte Alidi." In *A Francesco Gabrieli, studi orientalistici offerti nel sessantesimo compleanno dai suoi colleghi e discepoli.* Università di Roma. Studi orientali pubblicati a cura della Scuola orientale V, 315–50. Rome, 1964.

Wagner, E. *Abū Nuwās, eine Studie zur arabischen Literatur der frühen ʿAbbāsidenzeit.* Wiesbaden, 1965.

Watt, W. M. *Muhammad at Mecca.* Oxford, 1953.

———. *The formative period of Islamic thought.* Edinburgh, 1973.

Wellhausen, J. *Reste arabischen Heidentums.* Second edition. Berlin, 1897.

Al-Wohaibi, Abdullah. *The Northern Hijaz in the writings of the Arab geographers.* Beirut, 1973.

Wörterbuch der klassischen arabischen Sprache. See under Kraemer, J.

Wüstenfeld, F. *Die Chroniken der Stadt Mekka.* See under al-Azraqī.

al-Ziriklī, Khayr al-Dīn. *al-Aʿlām, qāmūs tarājim li-ashhar al-rijāl wa-al-nisāʾ min al-ʿArab wa-al-mustaʿribīn wa-al-mustashriqīn.* 10 vols. Damascus, 1373–8 (1954–9).

Index

The index contains all proper names of persons, places, tribal, and other groups, as well as topographical data, occurring in the introduction and the text (but not normally in the footnotes), together with technical terms; where the latter are explained in the footnotes, they are also noted.

The definite article, the abbreviations b. (for ibn "son") and bt. (for bint "daughter"), and everything in parentheses are disregarded for purposes of alphabetization.

B

T

U

W

Y

Z